Rethinking Urban Risk and Resettlement in the Global South

Rethinking Urban Risk and Resettlement in the Global South

Edited by
Cassidy Johnson, Garima Jain and Allan Lavell

UCL PRESS

First published in 2021 by
UCL Press
University College London
Gower Street
London WC1E 6BT

Available to download free: www.uclpress.co.uk

A CIP catalogue record for this book is available from The British Library.

ISBN: 978-1-78735-830-0 (Hbk.)
ISBN: 978-1-78735-829-4 (Pbk.)
ISBN: 978-1-78735-828-7 (PDF)
ISBN: 978-1-78735-831-7 (epub)
ISBN: 978-1-78735-832-4 (mobi)
DOI: https://doi.org/10.14324/111.9781787358287

Contents

List of figures and tables

Figures

Tables

List of contributors

Editors

Cassidy Johnson is Professor of Urbanism and Disaster Risk Reduction at the Bartlett Development Planning Unit, UCL. She was principal investigator on the 'Reducing Relocation Risk in Urban Areas' project that this book is based on. Her academic interests are linked by a commitment to improving the quality of life and livelihoods of low-income groups living in urban areas in the global South. Her research contributes to the area of disaster risk reduction and disaster recovery and to the role of local governments and civil society in this – and to integrating an understanding of disaster risk into development. This encompasses issues of urban planning, housing quality, building code regulations, informal settlements (and upgrading) and evictions. Her work engages internationally with policymakers as well as with local communities and she has worked in countries across Asia and Africa, including Turkey, Thailand, Bangladesh, India, Tanzania, Uganda and Malawi.

Garima Jain leads the urban risk and resilience team at the Indian Institute for Human Settlements. She was the co-principal investigator for the 'Reducing Relocation Risk in Urban Areas' project that this book is based on. Her research and practice lie at the interface of development and climate and disaster risks, and her most recent work delves into the issues of disaster recovery with a focus on housing, land and infrastructure development policies and narratives. She teaches courses on integrated urban disaster risk reduction, urban sustainability and mixed research methods. She has a master's degree in public policy and urban planning from Harvard Kennedy School of Government and Harvard Graduate School of Design and has been an Urban Knowledge Network Asia Fellow at the Development Planning Unit, UCL. She provides strategic advisory to the National Disaster Management Authority in India, and has also been part of the Secretariat for the Sustainable Development Goals Agenda for Cities (SDG 11) for the United Nations Sustainable Development Solutions Network (UNSDSN).

Allan Lavell was the co-principal investigator for the 'Reducing Relocation Risk in Urban Areas' project that this book is based on. He has a BSc from UCL and

MSc and PhD in geography from the London School of Economics and Political Science. He is a founding member of the Latin American Network for the Social Study of Disaster Prevention (LA RED). He has spoken at more than 150 international conferences in 47 countries, written and published over 95 specialised items on disaster risk management and undertaken more than 90 consultancy missions in 32 different countries, for more than 20 international agencies. He was awarded the 2015 UN Sasakawa Award for contributions to disaster risk management under the theme 'Forging the Future'. His present work involves technical support for the UNDRR regional assessment report on disaster risk in Latin America and the Caribbean, and work on systemic risk governance for the future and methodologies for evaluating COVID-19 response in Uruguay. He is now retired but was formerly employed between 1992 and 2020 for the Latin American Social Science Faculty.

Contributors

Giovanna Astolfo is an urban researcher with a background in architectural theory and practice. As a lecturer at the Bartlett Development Planning Unit at UCL, she combines research-based teaching and action learning from several contested and ungovernable urban geographies in South-East Asia, the Amazon region and southern Europe with a focus on non-conventional urbanisms, continuous displacement and migration, spatial violence and housing justice. She is principal investigator of the three-year project 'European Platform for Integrating Cities' funded by the Asylum, Migration and Integration Fund. The project aims to reframe migration and integration away from current dominant, colonial and top-down paradigms, and instead conceptualise them as relational practices. She is also principal co-investigator of the two-year research project 'Framing Living Heritage as Tool to Prevent Spatial Violence in Yangon', funded by the British Academy. The project aims to frame the potential of a living heritage approach to informal settlements and to challenge existing spatial violence dynamics in Yangon, Myanmar.

Amir Bazaz is a senior consultant for the Indian Institute of Human Settlements, where he works on issues at the intersection of economics, climate change mitigation and sustainable development. He has substantial experience of working with various top-down and bottom-up economy–energy–environment modelling frameworks. His current research interests are low-carbon societies and infrastructure, climate change adaptation and urban–climate change linkages. He started his career in the manufacturing industry, working across functional responsibilities of projects, production planning/control and engineering. He has been the expert consultant to India's Ministry of Environment and Forests and for the National Communication to the UNFCCC project, and has taught courses in development and environmental economics.

Yves Cabannes is an urban planner and Emeritus Professor of Development Planning and Chair of Development Planning (2006–15) at the Bartlett Development Planning Unit, UCL. He was previously a lecturer in urban planning at Harvard University Graduate School of Design and the regional coordinator of the UN-Habitat/United Nations Development Programme (UNDP) urban management programme for Latin America and the Caribbean. He worked for many years with local governments, NGOs and social movements in various countries and has long experience of supporting, researching, teaching on and advocating for participatory budgeting, housing rights, food sovereignty in cities and alternatives to forced and market-driven evictions in different regions of the world, and has published widely on these topics.

José Delfín Cáceres-Martínez is a specialist in spatial planning and disaster risk management, and currently works as the country technical analyst for the International Fund for Agricultural Development, a UN agency specialising in rural development. He has a background in spatial planning and urban studies, with a bachelor's degree in geography and environment from the Pontificia Universidad Católica in Peru, and an MSc in urban development planning from UCL. He has worked in disaster risk management in the Superintendencia Nacional de Servicios de Saneamiento, the Peruvian regulation agency for water and sanitation, and in Practical Action, an international NGO that promotes development among poor communities worldwide.

Anne-Catherine Chardon was a researcher and teacher at the School of Architecture and Urbanism at the National University of Colombia, Manizales for almost two decades and is now a researcher-teacher at the ESPI (Higher School of Real Estate Professions) in Paris. She has a doctorate in geography with emphasis on vulnerability and risk management and has been involved in several research projects and written many papers on this topic, analysing the case of Manizales and other Latin American urban contexts, by relating the vulnerability, planning and sustainability nexus with the concept of human habitat.

Angel Wilson Chávez Eslava earned his undergraduate degree in sociology from the National University of San Marcos before studying for a master's degree in disaster risk management at the National University of Engineering in Peru. He has participated in various projects looking at prevention, preparedness and disaster relief and reconstruction in Peru and the Andean region. He has specialised in social, economic and environmental studies related to disaster risk management and climate change. He is currently an international consultant for the UN and other international agencies as a researcher at the Latin American Social Science Faculty (FLACSO) in San José, Costa Rica. He is director of GRACC Consultants.

Bill Flinn works as a senior humanitarian shelter advisor at CARE International UK. He is a qualified architect and has worked in development and humanitarian relief in four continents, as well as in domestic construction in the UK. For nine years he worked in Central America and Mexico on appropriate technology and human rights, before returning to the UK to specialise in shelter after disaster. In recent years he has been a leading proponent of self-recovery as an appropriate and powerful force for post-disaster recovery, collaborating on research projects with the Overseas Development Institute, UCL and the British Geological Survey. He also teaches Shelter after Disaster at the Centre for Development and Emergency Practice, Oxford Brookes University.

Teddy Kisembo is a researcher at the Urban Action Lab (UAL) in the Geography Department of Makerere University, Kampala, Uganda. She has an urban planning background with a master's degree in land use and regional development. Her main interests are in cities, environment, land and housing, urban governance and sustainable development. She has engaged in projects that have focused on flood risk relocation, land markets and their impacts on urban development, urban resilience and community capacity building and energy transitions (turning waste into energy). She is currently working on the UCL project 'Knowledge in Action for Urban Equality'.

Shuaib Lwasa's interests are in urban geography, spatial planning, landscape ecology, climate change, urban health, the adaptation of cities to climate change and disaster risk reduction, and urban sustainability, with links to livelihood systems and resilience to climate change. He researches cities and climate change adaptation, the health impacts of climate change, land use and landscape ecology, resource efficiency and spatial planning for sustainability. He is a coordinating lead author for the Intergovernmental Panel on Climate Change Sixth Assessment Report.

Teja Malladi heads the Geospatial Lab and is part of the practice team at the Indian Institute of Human Settlements in the domain of urban risk and resilience. He has an MSc in geo-information sciences and earth observation, with specialisation in natural hazards and disaster risk management, from the University of Twente and a B.Arch from Jawaharlal Nehru Architecture and Fine Arts University. Teja's research interests and practice areas are focused on assessing risks and vulnerabilities to natural hazards, examining links between urban morphology, urban disaster and climate risks using geospatial technologies.

Elizabeth Mansilla is an economist who graduated from the National Autonomous University of Mexico (UNAM) with a master's degree and PhD in urban and regional planning. She has taught in the post-graduate programme in earth sciences at the Institute of Geophysics, UNAM, and worked as an independent consultant in development projects and risk management. She has more than 30 years' academic experience in teaching and research and has published in several books and journals. She is also a founding member of the Network for the Social Studies on Disaster Prevention in Latin America (LA RED).

Colin Marx is a town planner, adult educator and geographer by training and has extensive experience in community-driven struggles against inequalities in African cities. He works on different aspects of urban land dynamics in African cities and has published in relation to land markets, property rights and land conflict. He is the co-editor (with Charlotte Lemanski) of *The City in Urban Poverty* (Palgrave Macmillan). He previously directed a large urban advocacy NGO in South Africa in the post-apartheid period. He currently lectures on the MSc in Urban Development Planning and directs the PhD programme at the Bartlett Development Planning Unit, UCL.

Vineetha Nalla is an associate at the Indian Institute for Human Settlements, Bangalore, where she researches disaster risk, recovery, climate justice, migration and affordable housing. She has a bachelor's degree in architecture from the School of Planning and Architecture, Bhopal, and an MSc in building and urban design in development, from the Bartlett Development Planning Unit, UCL. At IIHS, Vineetha works on projects related to disaster risk reduction such as the 'Recovery with Dignity' project, focusing on experiences of post-disaster recovery, and the 'Disaster Resilience Leadership' project. She worked on migration and climate justice in the 'CapaCITIES' project in Coimbatore and Siliguri and also on the 'Urban Resilience Baseline' study in India to implement the MHA-USAID-UNDP partnership project on 'Developing Resilient Cities'. She is principal investigator on a study to understand low-income rental housing in Coimbatore city funded by the Tacit Urban Research Network. At IIHS, she has taught courses on urban risk and resilience and affordable housing.

Anthony Oliver-Smith is Professor Emeritus of Anthropology at the University of Florida. He has also taught at the Universidad Complutense de Madrid and held the Greenleaf Chair of Latin American Studies at the Stone Center for Latin American Studies at Tulane University in New Orleans. He held the Munich Re Foundation Chair on Social Vulnerability at the United Nations University Institute on Environment and Human Security in Bonn (2005–9). He was awarded the Bronislaw Malinowski Award of the Society for Applied Anthropology for 2013 for his lifetime achievement and work in disaster studies and resettlement research. He has done research and consultation on issues relating to disasters and involuntary resettlement in Peru, Honduras, India, Brazil, Jamaica, Mexico, Panama, Colombia, Japan and the United States. He is a member of the Network for the Social Studies on Disaster Prevention in Latin America (LA RED). He also served on the scientific committee on integrated research on disaster risk of the International Council for Science (2009–15) and the Climate Change Task Force of the American Anthropological Association (2009–13).

Holly Schofield works as a housing and migration specialist for the land, housing and shelter section of the United Nations Human Settlements Programme (UN-Habitat). She holds a PhD and master's degree in humanitarian and conflict response from the University of Manchester. Prior to joining UN-Habitat she worked in the field of emergency shelter and settlements for the United Nations High Commissioner for Refugees (UNHCR) and CARE International, where she led the organisation's contribution to several collaborative research projects exploring self-recovery after disasters and worked in emergency and recovery contexts in Philippines, Nepal, Mozambique and Colombia.

Chandni Singh is a researcher and faculty member at the Indian Institute for Human Settlements, Bangalore. Her research examines the human dimensions of global environmental change, focusing on drivers of vulnerability to climate change and natural hazards, links between climate change adaptation and development, and behavioural aspects of climate adaptation. She is a lead author on the Intergovernmental Panel on Climate Change (IPCC) Sixth Assessment Report, contributing author on the IPCC Special Report on 1.5 degrees, and serves on the editorial boards of *Regional Environmental Change, Climate and Development* and *Progress in Development Studies*.

Emily Wilkinson is a senior research fellow in the Overseas Development Institute's Risk and Resilience Programme and knowledge exchange fellow of the Global Risks and Resilience Programme. She currently holds two additional positions in the Caribbean: as chief scientific adviser to the Climate Resilience Execution Agency for Dominica and co-director of the Caribbean Resilience and Recovery Knowledge Network. Emily is an expert in disaster and climate risk management, with interests in public policy, governance frameworks and innovative financing solutions for resilient development in small-island developing states. She has a PhD in human geography from UCL and has published more than 50 articles, reports and book chapters on disasters, climate change and resilience.

Acknowledgements

We would like to thank the team at UCL Press, in particular Chris Penfold for his support and help in the commissioning and production of the book and Robert Davies for his assistance in preparations for production.

This book is part of a collaborative research project led by the editors of the book, called 'Reducing Relocation Risk in Urban Areas', with team members from the Secretariat General's Office of the Latin American Social Science Faculty (FLACSO), the Indian Institute for Human Settlements, Makerere University, Uganda, and the Bartlett Development Planning Unit at UCL. There are many from the project team who we would like to thank, including Aromar Revi, Amir Bazaz, Rohit Jigyasu, Teja Malladi, Sushmita Ramoji, Sunil Kraleti, Aishwarya Balasubramanian, Mohan Raju JS, Devi Kalyani, Greeshma Hegde, Zohrab Reys Gamat, Pallavi Sharma, Rekha Raghunathan, Archita Suryanarayanan, Gautam Bhan, Amlan Goswami, Shuaib Lwasa, Teddy Kisembo, Peter Kasaija, Gloria Nakigaba Nsangi, Hakimu Sseviiri, Disan Byarugaba, Colin Marx, Charlotte Barrow, Giovanna Astolfo, David McEwen, Elizabeth Mansilla, Angel Wilson Chavez Eslava, Omar-Dario Cardona, Maria-Pilar Perez and Belen Desmaison.

In addition to the project team, we are pleased to also have contributions in this book from advisors to the project, Emily Wilkinson and Professors Anthony Oliver-Smith and Yves Cabannes, and from our colleagues Professor Anne-Catherine Chardon, Bill Flinn and Holly Schofield.

Many thanks to Monica Bernal Llanos for her support in preparing the chapters for submission to UCL Press and communicating with the chapter contributors.

We would like to acknowledge the financial support of the Climate and Development Knowledge Network for the project funding, and Amy Kirbyshire who administered the grant.

Introduction

Allan Lavell, Cassidy Johnson and Garima Jain

The problem

In cities of the global South, low-income populations suffer disproportionately the impacts of climatic and other hazard events, as well as being exposed to everyday risks to health, life, livelihood and human security. Within these populations, women, the elderly, disabled people and those belonging to particular ethnic or social groups may be especially vulnerable. The COVID-19 pandemic is reconfirming the nature of who is most exposed and vulnerable to the different hazards society faces on a recurrent or long-term basis. The growing inequality faced by society and its repercussions on many livelihoods and lifestyle conditions are of major concern in terms of understanding this relationship.

As one way of reducing existing disaster risk, national and local governments, often supported by international funding agencies, engage in resettlement and relocation processes. While this may reduce people's exposure to hazard, it can lead to numerous other problems, which can leave people more vulnerable or worse off than they were before. This volume seeks to understand better the challenges and associated outcomes of such interventions on people and cities, and to examine ways forward for avoiding the need for resettlement or undertaking this endeavour in more holistic and integrated ways.

There are many examples and studies of the resettlement of populations, its causes and motivations, and the search to reconstitute their livelihoods and their infrastructural, economic, social, cultural and psychological foundations (Ferris 2012; de Sherbinin, Castro and Gemenne 2010; Mathur 1995; Mathur and Marsden 1998; Satiroglu and Choi 2015). These include the demand for land for the development of large-scale infrastructure projects or for urban renovation, or the need to settle persons expelled from their places of origin due to conflict. Relocation and resettlement due to the incidence or potential incidence of damaging climatic and other natural hazards are becoming increasingly common, especially in urban areas (Correa 2011). Climate change and its impact on hydro-meteorological hazards will probably increase this need in the future.

These movements and processes (unless completely spontaneous) require legal or normative frameworks in which to operate, institutional and organisational set-ups for achieving set goals, mechanisms for financing and systems for monitoring (Ferris 2014). Experience has shown that many such processes incite social conflict, competing demands and dissatisfaction with (or suspicion of) government and its ability to provide solutions. Many have not been carried out in planned, participatory, sustainable and sustained manners (Menon-Sen and Bhan 2008; Cabannes, Guimarães Yafai and Johnson 2010; Cernea and Mathur 2007).

When relocation or resettlement are related to the presence or potential presence and impact of damaging physical events of climatic and meteorological, geological, geomorphological or oceanographic origin, such practice is often conceived as part of what is now commonly known as disaster risk management (DRM). It then constitutes one of the many methods available for 'reducing' (corrective management) or 'anticipating or preventing' (prospective management) disaster risk. The latter may increasingly be related to climate change hazards (de Sherbinin et al. 2011).

Disaster risk-related relocation and resettlement may take one of many forms and be inspired and implemented according to many institutional and organisational, legal and normative, planning and participatory schemes. When decision and implementation are led by different organisations and institutions, varying rationales and processes may prevail. Thus, for example, resettlement and relocation are often related to land use planning processes as well as to disaster risk reduction goals. In fact, independent of the disaster risk link, resettlement may be seen as a concern that essentially derives from land use planning needs. In this case, the criteria for decision-making could differ substantially from those where disaster risk management concerns and practices are prevalent and the starting point for the process.

In general, similar conditions and processes play out in different time periods and help explain the permanently growing populations in areas exposed to hazards, and to hydro-meteorological hazards in particular. Little has been studied or written based on empirical evidence about the future impacts of climate change on the insecurity of such settlements, but the general notion is that climate change will increase hazards and eventually the risk conditions that are a prelude to disasters (Revi et al. 2014). A consideration of the data and the facts presented allows us to identify a number of challenges and defining factors for risk reduction among urban populations and how resettlement interventions address regional-level systemic issues and the impact of large-scale investments in resettlement programmes on climate change.

Firstly, the number of persons living in highly hazard-prone areas is large and is growing. Here it should be noted that the notion of 'unmitigable' risk is specific to a particular population group. What is unmitigable for the urban poor is not necessarily unmitigable for the urban rich and economic and commercial interests as a whole. Beyond the prevailing economic processes and the concentration of income in cities, the continued migration of poorer populations is the main cause of location in unsafe areas, and climate change is expected to impact rural populations in such ways that rural-to-urban migration continues. The sum of these processes and their accumulative results means that countries face an almost impossible task in promoting pre-impact resettlement of even the most 'at-risk' populations. The numbers are simply too great and the resources too scarce. Also, the administrative process leading to state-incentivised resettlement is still nascent. This suggests that resettlement can most appropriately be seen as a means of last resort, once all other options for risk reduction have been considered and discarded (Ferris 2012). This is relevant not only when we consider the social and economic disruption resettlement can and has caused, but also because it is impossible to think of resettlement for all those in such need, even less so if one thinks of future population growth in unsafe areas.

A second question and challenge relate to the ability to offer alternatives to continued location in highly risk-prone areas, thus avoiding, from the outset, the need for future resettlement. Resettlement is mostly a palliative for disaster risk: a needed option due to prior failure to control location in already hazard-prone areas. Only in cases where the physical hazard has developed in post-location periods, as can be the case with changed conditions due to environmental degradation and climate change, for example, can we think of resettlement as a needed solution for changed conditions. It is, however, a need principally dictated by humanitarian, social and political considerations in post-impact situations. The search for greater prospective control over settlement in hazard-prone areas is present but still latent. This means that now, and in the future, resettlement will probably only be a real option in most cases for post-impact populations, those that have suffered disaster and where decision-making as to need and priority is dictated by the pressure of circumstances, political considerations and short-term needs. This of course does not exonerate us or government from searching for mechanisms for the prospective control of location in insecure sites.

On population movement and resettlement

A consideration of the extensive literature on voluntary and involuntary population movements, relocation and resettlement reveals that we are dealing with a complex topic with common roots but also clear differences in context and circumstance (Ferris 2012, 2014; Oliver-Smith 2012). Thus, understanding what is what and recognising the diversity of different circumstances and conditions is essential. This diversity also indicates that we are perhaps not dealing with a single integrated, easily identified problem, but rather with a series of different circumstances which, if examined jointly, show common features but also a sum of significant differences. When this diversity of circumstances is applied to the problem of classifying, constructing typologies or systematising the different conditions under which movement takes place or is induced, this must be accompanied by a heterogeneous understanding of the proposed or possible solutions to the problems identified.

Here we will provide a view from the inside that derives from a consideration of prior terminologies and ideas, but which is coloured by the experience of the research project this book is predicated on (Ferris 2012, 2014; Correa 2011; Oliver-Smith and de Sherbinin 2014). Neither here nor later are we postulating a conceptual frame for the research as such (although this is implicit in what is said and analysed), but rather we are offering an advance on conclusions derived from the research itself. It is not our intention to review existing terminologies and notions, but instead to derive a conclusion about the most appropriate terms to be used in understanding and constructing typologies that lead to an understanding of causal factors, conditions for and solutions to the problem of hazard-prone urban populations.

The starting point for any discussion on terminology is the notion of the spatial movement, mobility or displacement of population. Such movement may be voluntary – planned as a collective response, or spontaneously undertaken at an individual family level, normally stimulated by the search for betterment or security. Or it may be involuntary or obligatory – dictated by a hierarchically more pervasive social institution or force, normally some level of government, which applies the law according to established norms or imposes its will through some form of repression. Repression and force may and have been used by private-sector interests in the search to increase land rent for economic gain. This is a form of usurpation which constitutes theft unless undertaken with the complicity of the state, which may give it some appearance or status of legality. For example, land grabbing is now a major problem in the developing world, and can be couched in terms related to risk and natural hazards.

Voluntary or involuntary movements in response to climate-related hazards may occur under a series of different circumstances or contexts: firstly, and most dominantly, as a response to a disaster event which seriously impacts the existing population or community, leading to wide-scale loss of housing and site security. Secondly, in response to a series of smaller sequenced events that accumulatively have led to damage and loss, insecurity and fear of the future and which stimulate preventive thought and maybe action by population or authorities. Thirdly, as a preventive measure where it can be shown through scientific analysis or it is perceived that a serious event could and will occur in the near to medium-term future. Fourthly, where processes of environmental degradation have led to a changed physical environment for a community with the possibility of hazard event occurrence in the future (socio-natural events such as land sliding and flooding due to deforestation on site and upstream). And lastly, where the average climate conditions have changed to such a degree that livelihoods as practised are no longer viable at the present location (this situation can be increasingly expected in areas severely affected by climate change and where there is dependency on agricultural or natural resource-based initiatives).

Under any of these conditions the voluntary or obligatory movement and relocation of persons may be justified in terms of reduced disaster risk. At the same time, obligatory movement may also at times be explained by ulterior motives such as the potential revalorisation of the abandoned site, development needs and redevelopment of city centres by private-sector and government actors. Nothing undermines the credibility of government or the private sector more than the development of abandoned land for private or public gain where this was not explicit when the resettlement was proposed. In the case of preventative (as opposed to post-disaster) movements, the onus of responsibility for justifying the move, the complexity this involves and the technical arguments favouring it are seriously increased due to uncertainty and the fact that resettlement will seriously interrupt accepted ongoing livelihood processes and patterns and service provision on-site.

Considering the population that moves under conditions of climate and hydrological stress, we may identify two different contexts. Firstly, entire communities or zones of a city (including at times multi-community zones, contiguous in geographical terms). These may be of varied sizes from small – let us say 15–30 families – to very large, up to or above a population size of fifteen thousand. At times whole towns have been relocated or the functions of cities reassigned to new locations, even though the original city persists with changed or modified functions (for example the resiting of the capital of Belize from Belize City to Belmopan due to hurricane threats to the functioning of government and society).

Secondly, individual families or small groups of families from diverse hazard-prone communities in the same urban centre who are selected at the same time or in the frame of the same relocation/resettlement process or political decision. Such a process normally follows the occurrence of hazard events that seriously affect various parts of a town or city contemporaneously and which have affected some but not all of the community. The impacts of such 'splitting' of communities or families can be considerable, reducing access to social networks and livelihood options. Resettlement, particularly of this sort, can also occasion considerable emotional stress and sentiments of loss and alienation that can affect the adaptive process to the new environment (Quinn et al. 2018).

On options and solutions to voluntary and involuntary movement and the idea of typologies

In any attempt to provide a conceptual basis for understanding the processes of planned human movement under hazard stress it is necessary to also consider the range of options that exist as regards a solution to the problem of hazardous location. Here, evidence (including that from the present research) suggests various generic types of solution. Firstly, the movement all together of a community, small or large, to a single alternative location, where access to an adequate site is critical in the decision (adequate in the multiple sense of cost efficient, security of tenure, safe from hazard, well located as regards employment opportunities, services and communications, non-invasive of protected ecological zones, etc.).

Secondly, the movement all together of more than one community from different or the same parts of a town or city to a single new site and where access to adequate land and considerations of intercommunity cooperation and social networks will be outstanding factors to consider.

Thirdly, the creation of new communities in safer locations made up of individual families from different hazard-prone locations from the same or different cities or towns.

Fourthly, the movement of families or individuals from an existing community to diverse and different parts of a town or city according to their own choices and options for purchase or renting of alternative accommodation. This may include such schemes as those where persons offered relocation to a common site may reject this but are given the option of finding a family from a non-hazard-prone area that does want to occupy the new location and where the original beneficiary occupies their house. This demands that the house is certified as being in a safe and adequate location. This implies that people will be integrated into existing communities, which in itself may occasion a series of problems and challenges with respect to competition with the host community for resources as well as a potential for conflict on ethnic or class bases.

Clearly, in terms of populations in movement and the creation of new living habitats and spaces, if we consider the different conditions that stimulate movement and the characteristics of the moving populations, any typology (or double typology) would be very large. If we assume that defined types of population situations or contexts determine the need for specific and identifiable optimums in terms of types of solution, such a crossing of typologies could be a basis for the evaluation of real cases and the factors governing their success or not. Refer to Appendix A for a summary of typology of resettlement and relocation interventions from the research project.

On terminology

The case studies in this volume, together with past experience, lead us to a reflection on terminology in the search to differentiate between contexts or situations which are of importance when considering process and success and failure vis-à-vis the social and economic impacts of change.

A basic difference in types of movement, and their spatial and social aspects, requires a consideration of the relationship between livelihoods and the social structure of the original and the new location. Although the physical distance between these is important in any distinction, the notion of social and functional distance is more important. Thus, population that is moved or moves but can, without additional cost or major effort, maintain its current livelihood schemes, its access to services and determined levels of social relation and cohesion can be considered under one category of movement. This category we can refer to as 'relocation'.[1] This category may include whole communities, large and small, single or composite, or individual families and persons from different or the same locations that are dispersed in the city or located together in a new habitat.

On the other hand, where movement clearly interrupts or seriously modifies the existing livelihood options and the types of access to existing services, and involves a need for consideration of past, or the development of new social relations and patterns of coexistence, we will refer to this as 'resettlement'.[2] This derives from a consideration of the term 'settlement' itself, which constitutes a condition characterised and defined by the creation of habitat and the generation and consolidation of livelihood options and social relations between members of a new community, made up of extended families, friends and others.

An alternative to this form of definition, and more in line with ongoing developments in international work on the topic, would be to consider all movements as planned (or administered or supervised) relocation and then distinguish between the two contexts discussed above using some other terminology. However, from our perspective the key distinction between relocation and resettlement derives from the fact that the notion of settlement implies a complex development of multiple dimensions of human existence, whereas relocation does not necessarily mean this, as structures, relations, behaviour patterns and goals may stay the same despite a change of location (relocation). A distinction should be made between forms of resettlement that bring a resource bundle with it, however meagre or inadequate, and outright displacement with no assistance of any sort.

The relevance of the details we provide in the examination of the multiple factors that change and condition the population movement scenario can be found in its relevance for an understanding of decision-making and implementation. Clearly, given the array of different circumstances under which movement takes place and for which solutions are sought, there can be no single theory or materialisation of decision-making and implementation procedures. Certain key factors and circumstances can be seen to come into play in general, but beyond these generic aspects, many cases show *sui generis* and idiosyncratic characteristics, and the notion of standard processes and procedures or set policy briefs and recommendations becomes difficult to achieve (there is now a plethora of guidelines developed internationally regarding relocation, forced movement and resettlement related to climate, often based on knowledge derived from prior development-induced movement and the guidelines developed for this (for example see Leckie 2013). Relocation and resettlement are dynamic, context-related processes that show an enormous range of options, decisions and implementation challenges. This does not of course mean that lessons cannot be learned from a comparative study of different cases, nor that such a study cannot serve to identify a series of key elements which, if not taken into consideration, will lead to severe implementation and outcome problems. In pointing out the idiosyncratic character of many schemes, we are merely indicating the need for caution when decisions are taken and implementation is made effective.

Scope of the book

This book draws on the empirical findings of the 'Reducing Relocation Risk in Urban Areas' project, with contributions from the project team, as well as contributions from authors not directly part of the project but in line with its areas of enquiry. The book aims to reflect widely on the problem of resettlement and relocation from areas exposed to climate and non-climatic risks. It sees this problem firmly within the context of several strands of literature, including that on preventative resettlement and development displacement, on disaster risk management, and on planning, development and resilience in urban areas of the global South.

About the research project 'Reducing Relocation Risk in Urban Areas'

The project 'Reducing Relocation Risk in Urban Areas' ran from 2015 to 2017. Funded by the Climate and Development Knowledge Network, it was conducted by the researchers at four partner organisations from the global South and North, including the Bartlett Development Planning Unit at UCL, the Indian Institute for Human Settlements, the Secretariat General's Office of the Latin American Social Science Faculty (Facultad Latinoamericana de Ciencias Sociales – FLACSO) and Makerere University, Uganda.

Through empirical analysis, the project looked across several case studies[3] from India, Colombia, Peru, Mexico and Uganda to understand 1) the political, economic and institutional contexts in which relocation and resettlement from disaster risk areas takes place; 2) the costs and benefits of relocation and resettlement from both governments' and individuals' perspectives; and 3) how relocation and resettlement impacts people's wellbeing and resilience over different timeframes. The aim was not to be comparative, but to understand the realities in each of the country contexts in order to build an empirical and theoretical basis for understanding the problem.

The research took place in four phases. For the first, diagnostic, phase of the research, each of the country studies began in 2015 with a documentary review to look for experiences of resettlement in the country and to create an inventory of case studies, as is evidenced in Appendix A, which outlines the typologies of interventions. The second phase of the research was fieldwork in each country, focused on the selected case studies. The selection of case studies was dependent on addressing the relevant typologies in the country, and the scale of the research endeavour was dependent on the resources available to teams, which differed by country. The objective of the fieldwork was to find out the experiences of resettlement from the perspectives of individuals, communities, governments and other stakeholders. These took the form of interviews, focus groups and surveys with households and stakeholders, conducted in local languages. The third phase of the research was to draw upon the fieldwork in each country to develop a method for cost–benefit analysis for each country, trying to understand from the government, individuals' and collective perspectives how relocation and resettlement impacts people's wellbeing and resilience over different timeframes. The fourth phase of the research was a cross-regional analysis, of which this book forms an element, in addition to the policy brief in Appendix B. All of these reports can be found on the project website.[4]

In India, the field study included nine sites in the state of Odisha and seven in the state of Andhra Pradesh. The study also included five rural sites to present a counterpoint to urban resettlement practices, highlighting the distinct issues and challenges faced in the urban area. These sites represented a mix of resettlement, relocation, in situ housing and infrastructure upgrading interventions (see Table 3.1 for more detail). Decision-making and implementation processes were understood through 26 interviews with key officials and policymakers and two consultations each with 45 policymakers. Community-level information, for example on infrastructure conditions and cultural norms, was gathered through 10 group discussions. To understand more household-level risks, 158 primary household-level surveys were conducted to assess changes in various indicators before and after the intervention. Some individuals, especially those with special needs such as the disabled, elderly, minorities and women, were identified and 15 were interviewed to get a better sense of the risks faced by them during such rehabilitation interventions. The methods and sample design used in the India study are discussed in more detail in Chapter 3 of the book, and references to the original reports are included there.

In Colombia, the fieldwork was not specifically done for the project, but rather was based on fieldwork and research carried out by the Colombian team in Manizales over some years, using interviews and documentary sources.

In Mexico, the research was carried out in the municipality of Celestún, and the fieldwork methodology consisted of visits to selected projects in the municipality of Celestún: Las Charcas and Colonia FONDEN, and included meetings with focus groups in both resettlements and free-form interviews with residents and government authorities of federal, state (Yucatán) and municipality (Celestún) levels. The case study is elaborated in Chapter 13.

In Peru, the research focused on the Amazonian city of Belén, and was based on interviews and focus groups in high-risk zones and in the area of the resettlement, interviews with government authorities and employees at a national, regional and local level, and interviews with the Lower Belén population that had moved spontaneously to other resettlement sites. The case study, and more details about the sample sizes, are presented in Chapter 8.

In Uganda, the fieldwork was focused in Kampala, and particularly on two settlements in the central part of the city (Bwaise III and Natete) that are located in low-lying, often flooded neighbourhoods and have been subject to relocation from a drainage channel expansion. The fieldwork consisted of interviews with residents living in both settlements, as well as families that had relocated out of the settlements; in total 70 interviews were conducted. This was complemented by interviews with nine stakeholders including municipal officials. The case study is detailed in Chapters 4, 9 and 15.

The key findings from across the countries are generalised and have been published as a policy brief, which is included in Appendix B. However, it is worthwhile to indicate, in a succinct way, the key findings here in the introduction. They set up a framework or a starting point for our analysis in this book.

1. Resettlement and relocation may reduce people's exposure to hazards – but experience shows that in most cases, it leaves people worse off overall in social and economic terms than they were before.
2. In some cases, hazard exposure also continues despite the resettlement, owing to uninformed planning. Planning needs to guarantee

safer locations for new green-site settlements, in order to avoid future needs for resettlement due to poor location in hazard-prone areas.

3. Resettlement should always be considered a last resort after all options for on-site mitigation or upgrading have been exhausted. Decision-making authorities may, and often do, understand risks differently from the communities living in environments that they know and understand, and alternative actions to resettlement may be possible.
4. Policies and procedures must ensure people's rights are protected; legal frameworks may need to be strengthened; and international covenants on resettlement must be honoured.

Organisation of the book

The book is organised into five parts in addition to this introduction and a concluding chapter. Each part addresses a particular issue of disaster risk-related resettlement and relocation. It should be mentioned that most chapters touch on more than one issue and thus many of the themes explored cross the boundaries of the parts described below.

Part 1 provides a critical framing of the related concepts, placing resettlement and relocation in context within the development and planning discourses in urban areas of the global South. Contributors discuss the meanings we place on important terms in the discourse, such as 'settlement' and 'habitat': notions that influence how we see the problem of resettlement and relocation. The chapters frame resettlement as a last-resort approach for disaster risk management, and as an unfortunate outcome of development failures. The contributions point to current deficiencies in the implementation of resettlement schemes and provide a critical examination of the elements that need to go into decision-making.

Part 2 scrutinises the understanding and interpretation of the subjective concept of 'risk': how risk is understood, calculated and employed to decide who is at risk and to what extent it is possible to mitigate these risks. The interpretation of risk is a crucial element in whether resettlement is an appropriate course of action. The contributions shed light on how residents and communities tolerate disaster risks as a trade-off for other benefits and aspects they value about a particular location. This is juxtaposed against how institutional decision-makers in resettlement see disaster risk as a more classic calculation of possible losses associated with calculations of hazard, vulnerability and exposure.

Following that, Part 3 looks particularly at how urban communities are resisting and protesting against being resettled. The contributions in this section examine how power and politics often undermine confidence that communities have in a proposed resettlement. Resistance takes many forms, and the chapters look at how resistance activities have impacted on decision-making for resettlement.

How land is held and transacted is an important puzzle piece in understanding patterns of disaster risk-related resettlement and relocation. This theme is examined in Part 4. The contributions look at how land rights and land tenure patterns influence decisions about resettlement and on-site upgrading. Evictions and dispossession are key themes across the chapters, highlighting that what is termed disaster risk-related 'resettlement' is often akin to eviction, as people may be displaced without adequate compensation that allows them to resettle, and may have little voice in the process.

Part 5 contains contributions that examine the issues of resettlement or relocation to or from ecologically sensitive areas of the city. They explore the contradiction between desired development and required conservation, which leads to a clear paradox in natural protected areas. Occupation of wetland or riverside areas means people are more exposed (so they may want to relocate if given the option), but these occupations can also impact on the functioning of the wider city, if, for example, water resources are affected for the population as a whole. The contributions explore how enhanced management of these resources may be better than resettlement.

Part 1: framing the issues

In Chapter 1, Allan Lavell seeks to deconstruct the hypothesis that resettlement is beset by decision-making and implementation procedures that lack understanding of the structural and contextual reasons for risk existing in the first place. The chapter therefore delves into visions, concepts, mindsets and notions that are used in the practice of resettlement. It also critically analyses the failures in disaster risk management policy in general, recognising that resettlement is most likely to be used as a last-resort mechanism for disaster risk reduction.

Anne-Catherine Chardon, in Chapter 2, critiques the current approaches of resettlement for their focus on physical or natural spaces in place of understanding the fundamental factors of 'habitat' and 'inhabitation' that relate to social, cultural, economic or financial vulnerability. She bases her arguments on an examination of resettlement projects in Manizales, Colombia. She argues that while in theory there is reason to focus on 'inhabiting' and all that entails, in praxis there is an incomplete institutional vision that does not allow for these qualitative factors.

Chapter 3 by Garima Jain uses case studies from both rural and urban contexts in India to understand to what extent disaster and everyday risks are really reduced by a resettlement and relocation intervention. Through detailed empirical data collected as part of the 'Reducing Relocation Risk' project, this chapter examines the decision-making processes and implementation procedures that went into the resettlement and relocation, and links this to the outcomes of the projects. This yields several important observations about urban resettlement projects, including that post-disaster housing developments focus narrowly on reducing hazard exposure, and in the process create other socio-economic risks.

Part 2: understanding and interpreting risk

In Chapter 4, Cassidy Johnson, Garima Jain, Vineetha Nalla and José Delfín Cáceres-Martínez look at how policy actors measure and interpret risks, and how this affects decisions that are made about resettlement. The authors consider national policies, including those related to 'non-mitigable risk' in Peru and 'non-tenable slums' in India. Also drawing on Uganda as a case study, they consider how risk, as understood in those policies, is quite different from residents' risk tolerance and their tipping points for relocation.

How to weigh up the costs and benefits of resettlement is the topic of Chapter 5 by Shuaib Lwasa, Amir Bazaz and Garima Jain. This chapter draws on empirical data from research undertaken in India and Uganda, as part of the 'Reducing Relocation Risk' project, to illustrate how the narrow economic valuation of risk can be enhanced with an extended value list to inform decisions at various levels of actors.

Emily Wilkinson, in Chapter 6, draws on research in Montserrat after the 1995–9 volcanic eruption, which destroyed the capital Plymouth and led to the resettlement in the north of all those remaining on the island. Looking at aligning attitudes to risk tolerance, she argues that the resettlement policy 'worked' when local and central levels of risk tolerance were closely aligned, but this is beginning to unravel. This chapter analyses why attitudes towards risk tolerance have changed and what are the impacts of these changes.

Part 3: protest and power: resistance to resettlement

Focusing specifically on the urban question of disaster- and climate change-induced resettlements, in Chapter 7 Anthony Oliver-Smith explores the reasons why residents in urban areas resist resettlement. He argues that rights, governance regimes and policies can be drivers of resistance. He pinpoints the aspects of a community that make resistance to resettlement possible and offers a typology of tactics for resistance.

Chapter 8, by Angel Wilson Chávez Eslava, looks in depth at the resistances to the New City of Belén resettlement project in Iquitos, Peru. Drawing on research conducted during the 'Reducing Relocation Risk' project, he presents an analysis of the conflicts and power relations among the different actors and reflects on what this means for resilience and local culture.

Part 4: land issues in resettlement

Based on the study of Kampala, Uganda, in Chapter 9 Colin Marx looks at how property rights influence who is accountable for risk, and for resettlement and compensation. The tangle of property rights in Kampala means that local authorities have little prospect in enforcing people to stay away from settling in flood-prone areas, and it also means that when residents were evicted due to risk-reducing infrastructure investments, complex land tenure arrangements isolated residents from receiving assistance for their losses.

Chapter 10, by Yves Cabannes, looks at forced evictions in order to place risk-induced resettlement and relocation within the context of drivers of forced evictions in urban areas. He uses David Harvey's model of 'accumulation through dispossession' to explain the breadth, depth and variety of evictions taking place worldwide, primarily those that are climate change or disaster induced. The end of the chapter offers some glimpses of innovative programmes of emerging anti-hegemonic practices.

Giovanna Astolfo navigates the history and current urban transformation trajectory of Phnom Penh, Cambodia in Chapter 11. Using a comparative analysis of four relocation sites in the city, she traces the unprecedented scale of dispossession that made relocation and resettlement a lawful exercise of violence. She reflects that the production and sharing of knowledge is a central issue to be addressed in risk-related resettlement.

Chapter 12, by Bill Flinn and Holly Schofield, focuses on the concept of self-recovery, which has been adopted by humanitarian practitioners as a method of supporting people's agency and choices about how and where to rebuild after a disaster. This chapter examines recovery in an urban and a rural area after the 2013 Typhoon Haiyan, which devastated the Visayas region of the Philippines and illustrates how land tenure security influences people's choices to rebuild on-site or relocate.

Part 5: natural resource and human occupation issues

Chapter 13 draws on research Elizabeth Mansilla undertook as part of the 'Reducing Relocation Risk' project about resettlement in the Ría Celestún Biosphere Reserve in Yucatán, Mexico. She questions the logic that a conventional approach to wholesale resettlement of the population is the answer, and instead proposes that a more imaginative idea of development, based on a comprehensive management of the environmental, social and urban challenges prevailing in the area, could be a better alternative.

In Chapter 14 Garima Jain, Chandni Singh and Teja Malladi offer a case study of Chennai, India to exemplify how post-disaster resettlement can further aggravate risks for the settlers and for the city if the resettlement locations are also exposed to hazards. They show how the direct socio-economic implications of first the disaster, and then the process of resettlement and the degraded conditions of living in risk-exposed resettlements, further exacerbate vulnerabilities. In effect, new socio-economic and ecological risks are created for the people as well as the city at large as a consequence of poorly planned interventions.

In the final chapter of the book (Chapter 15), Teddy Kisembo looks at household-level decision-making about relocation in Kampala. Based on empirical data from two neighbourhoods in environmentally sensitive wetland areas, she analyses the reasons why people tolerate risks and stay in the neighbourhood, and what are the tipping points that promote people to move. Although some people are drawn to staying in the neighbourhoods due to social and business ties, the lack of financial ability to move generally inhibits people from relocating to safer locations – as most would prefer to do, if they could.

Conclusion

The concluding chapter of the book synthesises and integrates the issues raised in the preceding chapters. The lessons learned about relocation and resettlement from multiple perspectives and geographical contexts are discussed, outlining the way forward through a series of recommendations. These suggestions are aimed at helping practitioners to develop better processes for implementation and decision-making for disaster risk reduction and resettlement.

Notes

1. Equivalent to *relocalización* or *reubicación* in Spanish.
2. *Reasentamiento* in Spanish.
3. See Appendix A for a mapping of the case studies across the relocation and resettlement typology described earlier.
4. https://www.ucl.ac.uk/bartlett/development/reducing-relocation-risk-urban-areas.

References

Cabannes, Yves, Silvia Guimarães Yafai and Cassidy Johnson, eds. 2010. *How People Face Evictions*. London: Development Planning Unit/University College London. https://world-habitat.org/wp-content/uploads/2016/03/How-people-face-evictions.pdf.

Cernea, Michael M., and Hari Mohan Mathur, eds. 2007. *Can Compensation Prevent Impoverishment? Reforming resettlement through investments and benefit-sharing*. New Delhi and Oxford: Oxford University Press.

Correa, Elena. 2011. *Populations at Risk of Disaster: A resettlement guide*. With Fernando Ramírez and Haris Sanahuja. Washington, DC: World Bank and GFDRR. https://www.gfdrr.org/sites/gfdrr/files/publication/resettlement_guide_150.pdf.

de Sherbinin, Alex, Marcia Castro and François Gemenne. 2010. *Preparing for Population Displacement and Resettlement Associated with Large Climate Change Adaptation and Mitigation Projects. Background paper for the Bellagio workshop, 2–6 November*. https://doi.org/10.1007/3-540-55215-4_2.

de Sherbinin, A., M. Castro, F. Gemenne, M.M. Cernea, S. Adamo, P.M. Fearnside, G. Krieger et al. 2011. 'Preparing for resettlement associated with climate change'. *Science* 334 (6055): 456–7. https://doi.org/10.1126/science.1208821.

Ferris, Elizabeth. 2012. *Protection and Planned Relocations in the Context of Climate Change*. UNHCR Geneva. https://www.unhcr.org/protection/globalconsult/5024d5169/27-protection-planned-relocations-context-climate-change-elizabeth-ferris.html.

Ferris, Elizabeth. 2014. *Planned Relocations, Disasters and Climate Change: Consolidating good practices and preparing for the future. Background document. Sanremo consultation, 12–14*

March, 2014. UNHCR, Brookings-LSE and Georgetown University. https://www.unhcr.org/53c4d6f99.pdf.

Leckie, Scott. 2013. *The Peninsula Principles on Climate Displacement within States*. Geneva: Displacement Solutions. http://displacementsolutions.org/wp-content/uploads/2014/12/Peninsula-Principles.pdf.

Mathur, Hari Mohan. 1995. *Development, Displacement, and Resettlement: Focus on Asian experiences*. New Delhi: Vikas.

Mathur, Hari Mohan, and David Marsden, eds. 1998. *Development Projects and Impoverishment Risks: Resettling project-affected people in India*. Oxford: Oxford University Press.

Menon-Sen, Kalyani, and Gautam Bhan. 2008. *Swept off the Map: Surviving eviction and resettlement in Delhi*. New Delhi: Yoda Press.

Oliver-Smith, Anthony. 2012. 'Debating environmental migration: Society, nature and population displacement in climate change'. *Journal of International Development* 24 (8): 1058–70. https://doi.org/10.1002/jid.2887.

Oliver-Smith, Anthony, and Alex de Sherbinin. 2014. 'Resettlement in the twenty-first century'. *Forced Migration Review* 45: 23–5.

Quinn, Tara, François Bousquet, Chloe Guerbois, Elias Sougrati and Matthieu Tabutaud. 2018. 'The dynamic relationship between sense of place and risk perception in landscapes of mobility'. *Ecology and Society* 23 (2). https://doi.org/10.5751/ES-10004-230239.

Revi, A., D. Satterthwaite, F. Aragón-Durand, J. Corfee-Morlot, R.B.R. Kiunsi, M. Pelling, D.C. Roberts and W. Solecki. 2014. 'Urban areas'. In *Climate Change 2014: Impacts, adaptation, and vulnerability. Part A: Global and sectoral aspects. Contribution of Working Group II to the Fifth Assessment Report of the Intergovernmental Panel on Climate Change*, 535–612. Cambridge and New York: Cambridge University Press.

Satiroglu, Irge, and Narae Choi. 2015. *Development-Induced Displacement and Resettlement: New perspectives on persisting problems*. London: Routledge. https://doi.org/10.4324/9781315760520.

Part 1
Framing the issues

The overall problem and definition of relocation, resettlement and rehabilitation, notions guiding such processes and possible alternatives, success and failure defined according to outcomes and the challenges of decision-making and implementation are common in different balances in the following three chapters. Allan Lavell's contribution is generic and general, seeking to highlight the major dilemmas and contexts that have led to mostly unsuccessful resettlement and the combination of structurally determined circumstances and conjunctural, context-based causes. Anne-Catherine Chardon, following an initial definition of habitat and habitat development as the basis for successful resettlement, examines the outcome of three interventions in Manizales City, Colombia over a 25-year period; and Garima Jain, drawing from the Indian cases of resettlement and relocation, analyses the combination of decision-making and implementation processes that led either to failure or at times to successes in resettlement. All three recognise that resettlement or relocation is far more likely post-hazard impact and that pre-emptive, prospective schemes are rarely undertaken.

The greater complexity and need for integrated, holistic approaches with resettlement as opposed to relocation is highlighted in all three contributions. Resettlement, seen as human habitat development by Chardon, as is implicit in the contributions of Lavell and Jain, emphasises the frequent lack of achievement of processes that go beyond merely building a house in a location that is safer from physical hazards.

Failures are analysed by Chardon, who examines the outcome side and the dissatisfaction or satisfaction of beneficiaries as expressed through interviews and on-site observation, including the size and design of housing and options and needs for modification and redesign, the integration of built and natural environments, the options for movement to and from employment options, difficulties in payment of rent or loans, conflicts between neighbours due to proximity and incompatible lifestyles. The 'why' of these contradictions is implicit but not the subject of explicit reasoning, except in the case of the one successful scheme of Yarumales.

Jain concentrates on the decision-making and implementation processes and the ways these lead to different positive and negative outcomes across the cases under study. These include the lack of consideration of on-site upgrading as opposed to resettlement, discrimination against the marginalised in selection processes for beneficiaries, transit housing provision, resettlement distances from original locations, indebtedness of persons prohibiting lack of access to new credit, housing style, lack of concern for caste and disability and grievance redressal, social support networks and financial security measures and trade-offs between different risk contexts – chronic and disaster related.

The overall institutional set-ups for resettlement are examined and referred to particularly by Lavell and Jain, and the lack of integrality in these is highlighted. Two dominant themes arise. First, disaster risk management as a basis for resettlement often lacks a development basis and is more likely to concentrate on straightforward hazard reduction as opposed to integrated human development in a habitat mode. And second, while development projects as such rarely consider hazard risk, resettlement projects rarely consider development needs and parameters. Only when multi-institutional, multi-criteria schemes are developed can there be hope for more consistently successful resettlement, but this is limited by the mindsets, visions and objectives of different institutions in a mode of working not sufficiently informed by contextual analysis and the needs and wishes of the so-called beneficiary population.

Questions raised by Jain in her conclusions are backed by the debate and findings in the other two chapters: the need for more consideration of on-site upgrading; how to avoid the exclusion of the already marginal from beneficiary processes; greater sensitivity to context; and how to promote more prospective and pre-emptive resettlement under existing hazard and changing climate conditions.

1
Resettlement and relocation: an approach to understanding failure and guiding success

Allan Lavell

Characterising and evaluating past climate-related resettlement at the urban or other territorial scales tends to lead to a number of pervasive overriding conclusions. One is the generally low level of success achieved with resettlement, when this is judged in terms of the satisfaction of the overall livelihood, economic, social and physical security needs of the resettled population (de Sherbinin et al. 2011; Oliver-Smith 1991, 2013). Empirical analysis in many different places, at many times, on schemes of different size and complexity, enacted in different time periods, has revealed many of the common and *sui generis* reasons for failure or inadequate implementation of schemes. Shortfalls on finance, sector-based decisions and processes that fail to consider the satisfaction of livelihood needs, failure to consider social integration and employment creation, lack of access to transport, and poor house and urban planning are among the failings that appear with surprising regularity (Cernea 2000; Jha and Duyne 2010). Thus, understanding failure in an immediate causal sense is not difficult, as the same factors or reasons come up repeatedly, although with different weights, balances and formats.

When the same problems appear repeatedly and are rarely dealt with adequately, despite ample knowledge of their importance and impact, we must assume that the type and content of questioning required to understand failure probably needs modifying. Repetition of the same or similar problems time after time in the same or in different countries and the occasional appearance of a successful case, the exception that proves the rule, undoubtedly indicates a mistaken mindset, vision, concept or structural interpretation of ends and means by decision-makers and implementers. That is to say, the processes and decisions are flawed due to an inadequate framing and contextualising of the problem.

The cross-continental, comparative research project whose results are presented in the present collection of essays sought to understand the decision-making, implementation and cost–benefit processes involved in urban hazard-induced 'resettlement' or 'relocation'. This was achieved through discussion and thought on conceptual and theoretical matters, backed up with the use of selected case studies in six countries of Asia, Africa and Latin America (India, Uganda, Tanzania, Colombia, Mexico and Peru).

A basic starting hypothesis for research was that the results, benefits or negative aspects of resettlement were defined by the nature and content of decision-making and implementation procedures and that this was structurally and contextually determined (see Figure 1.1 for a synthesis of the causal chain hypothesised). Implicit in this hypothesis, and increasingly explicit as the project proceeded, was the fact that decision and implementation are based on stakeholder visions, concepts, mindsets, ideas and notions on the why and what of the process referred to as 'resettlement'. Framed as a research question, this means examining what factors in the structural, contextual or stakeholder visions and

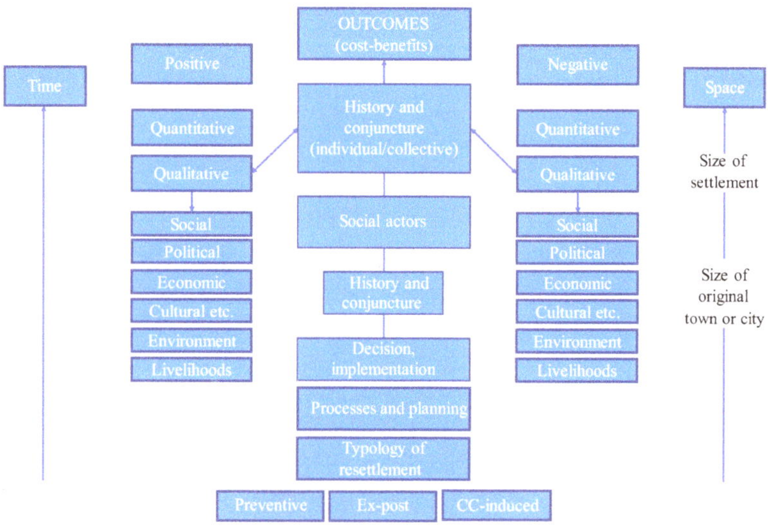

Figure 1.1 From need to outcome: process and context. An illustration of the structurally and contextually determined causal chain for the process of resettlement. © Allan Lavell.

concepts best explain outcomes (see Chapter 3 by Jain in this book). This can be typified in terms of segregated or partial knowledge and interest domains. The contrasting views and needs of stakeholders come much into play in conditioning the result of such processes. Of course, this does not discount the influence of such aspects as bureaucracy, inefficiency and inefficacy of government structures and organisations, the lack of collaboration and harmony among beneficiaries and other such contextual aspects. However, the critical analytical framework for understanding success and failure, gains and losses, has, from our perspective, to be found in the goals, visions and mindsets present as resettlement is considered and planned.

While the aspect of mindsets and visions and sector-defined goals and procedures may be used to analyse the process of resettlement, a second analytical strand must, we postulate, be taken up in deliberating on successful or failed resettlement. This relates to the social context and origins of the settlement, for which resettlement is seen to be a solution. Here it is clear that the resettlement of poorer, more disadvantaged and excluded persons and families is vastly different to that of more well-off populations, even where the prime stimulus for resettlement is similar – in our case, security from physical hazard. Whereas in the second case, government intervention is limited and the population can account for the livelihood security that needs to accompany the decision on a safer location, this is not the case with poorer populations (Jain et al. 2017). In this latter case, a safe location will always be seen in the light of and will often conflict with a location that offers sufficient livelihood opportunities and adequate income, employment and social relationships.

The objective of the present chapter is to deconstruct the former hypotheses or frames of reference and examine the factors that explain a mindset and social context interpretation of failure or inadequacy, as well as considering the minimum requirements for good resettlement policy and practice. At the same time, the arguments put forward examine evolving critical thought on the failures in disaster risk management (DRM) policy in general, recognising that resettlement is most likely to be seen and used as a mechanism for disaster risk reduction.

This chapter is structured as follows. A first substantive section considers the notions of settlement and resettlement, location and relocation. A second considers the ways settlement is induced among predominantly poor populations and the limitations and satisfiers of this, as well as the type of demands that lead to the need for resettlement. A third section considers the ways DRM is practised and the disassociation that often exists between place and livelihood security. A last section highlights needed changes in mindsets and attention to context in order to make resettlement correspond far more truly to social needs and demands.

Resettlement and relocation as notions

'Resettlement' derives, as a term and concept, from the notion of 'settlement', as 'relocation' derives from 'location'. The derivative should thus reflect the original in sense and purpose.

Settlement, when used in the context of persons, families, groups or communities laying down roots in any particular place, can be defined intuitively and in experiential terms. In its simplest sense, it is the act of settling which in itself is the act of establishing oneself (individually or collectively) in a place. Experientially, it signifies creating the basis for a secure work and livelihood scheme (security includes life opportunities and security of place – from outside attack or from floods, from eviction or landslides, etc.). Historically, it has signified, in different places and at different times, a process of occupation and conquest of territory, the expansion of population and production frontiers and the creation of hamlets, towns and cities. It has also signified the creation of new modes of life, the challenge of newness, the development of community and common ties and values, a sense of being and the developing of cultural and emotional ties to land and place. The notions of settlement and community, settlement and commonality in goals, settlement and collaboration, tend to go hand in hand. Most early settlement was typified by a movement of persons bonded by familial, ethnic, racial, religious or other ties. To settle (successfully), whether physically or emotionally, involves a process and product defined by an integrated and holistic relationship between the social unit that settles (be it an individual, family or community) and the local environment that provides the resources or opportunities for livelihood and welfare (Ferris 2012). It also involves the construction of habitat, a built environment that provides shelter, services and options for communication and movement (see Chapter 2 by Chardon in this book). It signifies the construction of social meaning and relationships in a place. To successfully settle means the establishment of the bases for a productive, fruitful and successful human existence on an individual and social level. It inevitably signifies a relative level of harmony and collaboration with neighbours in what may be defined variously as a community or neighbourhood.

Location is a far easier and less committed or compromised term. Settlement involves location, but location does not require settlement in order to be defined. To locate signifies simply to place (permanently or in transitory fashion) something or someone (or identify their positioning in a particular place), in order to satisfy a permanent or transitory function – production, consumption, communication, residence, etc. It assumes that by locating, a function is achieved, but this is not a defining part of the notion or concept as such. Any value judgement about objectives or function would be achieved by qualifying the idea of location as such – location searching for proximity to work or resources; an ideal location for climate; etc. To settle, settling or settlement encapsulates, we would suggest, a wider definition of welfare and wellbeing than do the ideas of location or locating (see Chapter 5 by Lwasa, Bazaz and Jain in this book).

Resettlement and relocation are of course derivatives of settlement and location, and their significance can be recognised by referring to the original definition, concept or state of settlement and location. To be resettled or relocated, one has to have been located or settled in the first place. This in itself, although obvious, leads to a consideration of how new settlement as opposed to resettlement of population is processed at a government and social level. For example, when new housing areas or estates are constructed, following urban planning regulations, this is done considering factors such as the need for proximity to work, play and schools, service provision and recreational facilities of potential buyers. This original context and its structure are, or should be, critical factors in considering and understanding the pros and cons, gains and losses achieved through movement and relocation. But many times, this is not the case.

Translating these arguments into definitions of use in urban resettlement studies, relocation may be used to depict a movement in space, a placing of a social unit, whether family or community, where the wider concerns associated with resettlement do not necessarily have to be taken up – new livelihood sustenance, new service provision, new social relations, etc. This is due to the fact that where movement is induced by government in a planned fashion, and relates to poorer disadvantaged groups, the distance of relocation is relatively short and allows prior relations to be maintained, while providing a safer place with new housing and internal community links but not a whole new social and economic, physical and environmental infrastructure, as is the case with resettlement. Alternatively, relocation takes place over a greater distance where knowledge of opportunity and the wish to relocate exists and motives are explicit (Ferris 2012).

Resettlement and existing social conditions and demands

In order for hazard exposure-inspired resettlement to be successful, it must at least reduce disaster risk and maintain the overall balance of social or economic goods or advantages of the original location. This is particularly true where poorer populations are concerned, and the government is the promoter of movement. The only other alternative is that reduction of disaster risk sufficiently compensates for loss of livelihood and lifestyle benefits accumulated over time at the original location due to the imperative of impeding future loss (particularly of life) and a high perception of the opportunities for reconstruction of livelihoods over the short and medium terms at the new site (Cernea 2008). This exists for example in the Peruvian case recorded in this volume (see Chapter 8 by Chávez Eslava), where mothers took the decision to resettle to the new area offered by government in order to avoid the threat of death by drowning of their children every rainy season, despite opposition from their husbands, who felt they would lose their livelihood base.

The basis for any effective approach which considers needs and wants and satisfaction of livelihood demands must be rooted in an integrated understanding of the root causes of the disaster risk suffered by the at-risk population. This is normally a direct result of the vulnerability and exposure which result from the very condition of poverty, lack of resources and ability to determine and gain access to an adequate site for home and house, community and relations suffered by the population (Gaillard 2008). That is to say, disaster risk is a result, an outcome, of the precarious life conditions of the population and the basis of their original location decision. This is an obvious but easily forgotten or ignored fact in our sector-based, specialised world.

Any approach to resettlement of the poor or destitute that ignores this basic premise and considers disaster risk due to hazard exposure in isolation of other contextual and historical factors is likely to fail. The bases or drivers of disaster risk and the conditions that the population need to overcome are to be found in livelihood, lifestyle, existential and everyday risk concerns, and not directly in exposure to hazards and disaster risk. If disaster risk reduction propounded as a goal does not account for and integrate a search to resolve the principal problem for the population, which is poverty and livelihood security, service access and educational and health opportunity for children, difficulties will inevitably be encountered. This is even more the case where disaster risk is not associated with large-scale death and destruction and where affected populations have traditionally received government support during crisis in the form of food, roofing and building materials, blankets etc. The opportunity for good resettlement rests on the satisfaction of everyday, chronic risk reduction needs, and only secondarily on reduction of disaster risk as such. This points to the fact that only development-based, holistic approaches to resettlement can hope to be successful.

A second attendant consideration is that society and communities are often dynamic, creative and resilient, especially where social capital is strong and functional in bonding, linking and integrational modes. Society creates and recreates itself and turns adversity into accepted reality. This in itself becomes a permanent feature of a social environment which is not easily torn apart or replaced. The reading of what change means by a resettlement decision-maker or implementer is many times vastly different to that of the population itself (see Chapter 4 by Johnson et al. in this book). The objective/subjective dimensions play out differently. What is unacceptable or untenable or non-mitigable from one angle or institutional perspective is not so from the perspective of population. Personal and family life histories are forged, created and recreated in the process of satisfying basic needs. These needs and their satisfaction, even though meagre, become the basis for constancy and permanence. Disaster risk becomes a technocratic concern under many circumstances, whereas everyday risk mitigation, where basic needs and the means of achieving them are satisfied, is a central and permanent concern of affected people. Disaster risk and the conditions that explain it in any one location become a dimension of opportunity, not disadvantage. This is expressed through location-based access to diverse resources that are an integral part of 'livelihood security' – these may be physical-locational, integrational, relational, systemic or occupational.

Disaster risk management: current sector as opposed to integral mindsets

Structural conditions link to the ways the resettlement problem is constructed socially and politically, and this in itself reflects how hazard proneness and disaster risk are conceived and built into mindsets on development and human security in general. This is determined by the type of resettlement identifiable from a typology of approaches and causes. This includes post-disaster impact movements that are often more part of recovery and reconstruction in their logic and governance than preventative resettlement; pre-impact preventative schemes seeking to anticipate and avoid future impacts; and on-site improvements and risk reduction. Each of these when enacted may derive from a different mindset and vision, from a different process of social and political construction. Thus, although they seem to be types of something, which is essentially generically the same, they are in fact at times very different things with very different origins, arguments in favour, decision-making and implementation limitations and processes.

It is our contention that much resettlement planning (if that is what much experience can be called) when faced with hydro-meteorological hazards has been unilateral, partial, sectoral and exclusive. It has been determined by immediate pressures of disaster and humanitarian support or simply underestimated in its complexity due to partial views originating in different implementing sectors or thematic areas – disaster risk, territorial organisation and land use planning, housing, environment, social integration, health, etc. Here we recognise from the outset that resettlement can be an instrument for dealing with hydro-meteorological hazards that is of unilateral or combined concern for all these sectors or areas of concern and can be used to help advance each of their different aims (see Chapter 13 by Mansilla in this book). However, the dominant concern that directs action is that of getting people out of harm's way (reducing or eliminating disaster risk as such; see Chapter 14 by Jain, Singh and Malladi in this book). Little due consideration is given to the 'how' and content of this action when seen from the angle of livelihood security and social welfare in a wider sense. Rarely has social development or development as a whole been the guiding light and central stated objective for action.

Much of the partiality and lack of integrated approaches with livelihood sustainability as the centre of concerns may be explained by a series of contexts that require change if an advance is to be made.

Firstly, disaster risk, the primary motivation and justification for resettlement intervention (that is to say, the action would not be promoted unless a decision had been taken that the existing location is untenable due to the level of hazard suffered by the population), is considered as a standalone context. It is seen as a sector of concern independent of other considerations and where cause and context are essentially governed or delimited by exposure to hazard, as opposed to a consideration of more integral underlying causes, drivers and contexts of risk. In many ways, the resettlement scene has been typified by a dependence on physicalist interpretations of risk with little real consideration of complex social causation and the origins of such contexts in social practice and position. Rather than being seen as a dependent variable, disaster risk is seen as a situation in itself, self-generated or exogenously caused. The hazard is the primary problem and getting people out of harm's way at whatever cost is the prime objective. This does not of course mean that hazard is not, at times, used as an excuse for achieving other implicit goals, such as redevelopment of the recovered areas for the urban rent gains it will signify. Where this is present, the chances of good resettlement being enacted are even less likely.

Secondly, and related to the prior context, the roots of disaster risk and the contradictions or trade-offs that come into play are not adequately taken into consideration in an understanding of the situation and context of affected populations (see Chapter 4 by Johnson et al. in this book). Due to this, solutions are based on single-factor approaches that deny or ignore the underlying causes of risk and the conditions and demands this creates for the affected populations. A livelihood approach based on an understanding of want and lack, struggle and resilience, and competing risk demands, among other things, would lead to more integrated and realistic approaches that could even include the rejection of resettlement as an option or effective solution.

From a pragmatic and programmatic perspective, the resettlement problem may most easily be seen from the partial but basic perspective of access to alternative safe land and to adequate housing and service provision. Although apparently simple, dealing with these three aspects can be extremely complicated. From a conceptual and process level it involves an understanding of i) land use and land rent patterns and problems, including the role of speculation and excess speculative urban earnings (see Chapter 9 by Marx in this book); ii) the problem of community and housing design and the use of vernacular, culturally acceptable versus standardised, industrial approaches to construction en masse; and iii) density of service provision according to location with the cost considerations involved. Resolving the sum of these three interacting contexts and needs adequately can be daunting in itself, without even starting to consider the other imperious needs present in a holistic, integrated, development-based view of resettlement.

It is in this second set of requirements for good resettlement that problems are often found which are rarely taken up in comprehensive fashion. As we have pointed out in our definition of resettlement as opposed to relocation, this process is far more than physical and infrastructural and relates to the reconstruction or construction of integrated livelihood and lifestyle options that replace or reconstitute those previously existing. Such a process requires careful consideration and resolution of demands associated with employment and income, including functional access and distance considerations. It requires respect for the environment and its resources and maintenance of ecosystem values and services. Due consideration for existing populations in resettled areas is needed. The maintenance and strengthening of social relations and networks and the consolidation of social capital in bonded, linked and integrative forms must be achieved. In addition, relationships to the wider urban environment and structure and a role of urban planning and structuring in the location of resettlement schemes should be considered.

As can be appreciated, satisfying the sum of the demands that arise with regard to each of these different elements requires a comprehensive, interrelated conceptual scheme and the participation of multiple organisations and institutions from local and regional/national government, along with private-sector and NGO participation. But this is often required in environments where governance is weak, decentralisation almost non-existent, severe problems in inter-sector coordination exist, competing interests and approaches are found, lack of permanence of government officials and lack of training in implementation and conception are prevalent, and budgetary allocations and timeframes are inadequate.

Resettlement can be seen to be the prerogative of many different institutions that have different central goals (safety from hazard, reordering the city, saving ecological resources, reducing poverty and increasing social integration, increasing employment and income opportunities). However, few or none is really in a position, resource- or knowledge-wise, to adequately comply. And DRM has had as yet little success in bringing multiple development-based organisations and institutions together in an endeavour that must promote social advance at the same time as reducing or controlling disaster risk.

The way forward

A reading of the literature and a consideration of the bases of many hazard resettlement initiatives allows us to reach the conclusion that this is in fact a severely under-conceptualised and under-theorised topic, dominated by empirical approaches, dictated by circumstances, that are more descriptive and prescriptive than prospective. One possible reply to the overall question of why little is done to change this and improve implementation may well lie not only in the sporadic and passing nature of concern for the problem once need arises, but also in the severe lack of an adequate reading and conceptualisation of the problem. The mindsets with which resettlement is approached and the institutions that dominate in its execution are deficient.

Given this, what are the major factors that should be brought together in constructing an adequate conceptual frame for thinking about resettlement, which can adequately guide decision-making and implementation processes and that are the result of our collective research effort and prior conceptual debates and search for precision?

A primary factor or starting point is the mindset with which resettlement is approached and the role it is designated in terms of human and societal advancement and security. The options vary from restricted sector and thematic concerns, with the inevitable dominance of those related to disaster risk reduction, through to holistic concerns whereby integrated human development is central and particular objectives such as disaster risk reduction are collateral and supportive, if important.

From our perspective, the starting point for conceptual development is the affirmation that disaster risk is essentially a social construction (IPCC 2012), closely related to the workings of economic growth and proposed development processes, the result of a series of risk drivers or dynamic processes and an indicator of failed development processes, marked by exclusion and marginalisation. This is in tune with increasingly mainstream thought on the disaster risk problem. Thus, the extent to which it may be reduced or controlled should be seen as a derivative of collateral development processes, and any attempt to reduce or control its growth must be formulated in a development framework where the integration between different drivers and processes is considered at a sector and territorial level and confronted in an integrated manner.

When considered from a resettlement policy and practice angle, this means that although a central and necessary objective is the elimination, reduction or prospective control of disaster risk for a set group of population or community, this must be achieved in ways that tackle and confront the major drivers of the original disaster risk.

This conclusion is confirmed by a second context. Disaster risk as suffered by exposed hazard populations is the result in great part of poverty, lack of choice and exclusion, as we have affirmed previously. Therefore, such disaster risk is only one of many contexts of adversity that communities face. However, all these contexts are in one way or another related. Chronic risk contexts such as poverty, unemployment, bad health, drug addiction, and social and family violence increase vulnerability to physical hazards or their effects and after-effects and reduce resilience. At the same time disaster, whether recurrent small-scale or singular large-scale, adds to the chronic risk context. In times of non-manifest disaster risk and disaster itself, populations survive and exist by eking a living out of the local resources available and the opportunities that exist. Social capital is built up among and between groups and in relation to external agents from government and civil society. Life goes on, even under conditions not considered acceptable for many external agents. Everyday life is certain and its challenges sure. Disaster risk is ephemeral, sporadic and uncertain in its consequences, time- and space-wise. Therefore, at-risk populations constantly play off one set of risks against another and search for the maximum overall livelihood security possible. In view of this, the planning for the reduction of disaster risk can only effectively be achieved where due and serious consideration is paid to reducing and controlling everyday chronic risk. Negation of the satisfaction of everyday needs and demands in lieu of increased disaster risk security is a non-viable option. A total, integrated livelihood approach must be followed, whereby creation and consolidation of economic and social assets, livelihood satisfiers and balanced overall security are considered.

The prior considerations relate to the position of the individual, family and community affected by disaster risk and the concatenated processes of everyday and disaster risk, poverty, exclusion and confrontation that demand integrated, holistic concepts and processes.

However, the resettlement process and the need for it can also be seen from a wider societal angle and the role it can and should play in achieving greater social, economic and environmental efficiency and efficacy, justice and equity. Resettlement, beyond being a mechanism for increases in social welfare and security of affected populations, is also a mechanism for resolving created problems of ecological downgrading, spatial inefficiency, territorial organisation, social integration and transport planning.

Each of these aims has its own conceptual framework, and the search to integrate ideas and aims will always be difficult not only pragmatically, but also institutionally. This then pushes us to consider what is the most appropriate institutional and organisational set-up to promote and implement resettlement and which can guarantee consistency, integration, multiple objectives, social efficacy and societal gains, planning and livelihood goals, among others. This includes the vertical integration of different spatial scales from community to nation and beyond. The answer will depend on the country dealt with, but we can be sure that only an institution or organisational mode that provides for integrated thought and action, and strategic planning that brings multiple goals and ends together at a local level, will be successful.

References

Cernea, Michael M. 2000. 'Risks, safeguards and reconstruction: A model for population displacement and resettlement'. *Economic and Political Weekly* 35 (41): 3659–78.

Cernea, Michael M. 2008. 'Compensation and benefit sharing: Why resettlement policies and practices must be reformed'. *Water Science and Engineering* 1 (1): 89–120. https://doi.org/10.1016/S1674-2370(15)30021-1.

de Sherbinin, A., M. Castro, F. Gemenne, M.M. Cernea, S. Adamo, P.M. Fearnside, G. Krieger et al. 2011. 'Preparing for resettlement associated with climate change'. *Science* 334 (6055): 456–7. https://doi.org/10.1126/science.1208821.

Ferris, Elizabeth. 2012. *Protection and Planned Relocations in the Context of Climate Change*. UNHCR Geneva. https://www.unhcr.org/protection/globalconsult/5024d5169/27-protection-planned-relocations-context-climate-change-elizabeth-ferris.html.

Gaillard, Jean-Christophe. 2008. 'Alternative paradigms of volcanic risk perception: The case of Mt. Pinatubo in the Philippines'. *Journal of Volcanology and Geothermal Research* 172 (3–4): 315–28. https://doi.org/10.1016/j.jvolgeores.2007.12.036.

IPCC. 2012. *Managing the Risks of Extreme Events and Disasters to Advance Climate Change Adaptation: A special report of Working Groups I and II of the Intergovernmental Panel on Climate Change*. Edited by Christopher B. Field, Vicente Barros, Thomas F. Stocker, Qin Dahe, David J. Dokken, Kristie L. Ebi, Michael D. Mastrandrea et al. Cambridge and New York: Cambridge University Press.

Jain, Garima, Chandni Singh, Karen Coelho and Teja Malladi. 2017. *Long-Term Implications of Humanitarian Responses: The case of Chennai*. London: International Institute for Development (IIED).

Jha, Abhas Kumar and Jennifer E. Duyne. 2010. *Safer Homes, Stronger Communities: A handbook for reconstructing after natural disasters*. Washington, DC: International Bank for Reconstruction and Development/World Bank.

Oliver-Smith, Anthony. 1991. 'Successes and failures in post-disaster resettlement'. *Disasters* 15 (1): 12–23. https://doi.org/10.1111/j.1467-7717.1991.tb00423.x.

Oliver-Smith, Anthony. 2013. 'Disaster risk reduction and climate change adaptation: The view from applied anthropology'. *Human Organization* 72 (4): 275–82. DOI:10.17730/humo.72.4.j7u8054266386822.

2
Resettling, re-enabling: the challenge of reconstructing a human habitat

Anne-Catherine Chardon

During the last few decades Latin America has been one of the most affected and most studied regions as regards urban vulnerability to natural phenomena. Studies have been produced to better analyse, understand and intervene in not only the physical threats but also the vulnerability that generates fragility and instability in urban settlements. The aim has been to mitigate risks and build resilient human habitats. Indeed, the vulnerable city is primarily a habitat, when this is considered in its broader meaning, and needs to be dealt with using holistic and cross-cutting approaches. This is required in order to deal with the problem as a whole and to intervene in all its shortcomings and weaknesses, taking advantage of the strengths that characterise a community and its environment.

In the Colombian Andes region, urban areas are subject to high seismicity, mudslides and mass movements. The latter are the more frequent and significant, leading to the greatest amount of accumulated losses. These are in good part borne by the inhabitants of such settlements themselves. In today's context where things may get worse, as an effect of climate change, one of the measures to reduce risk in a preventive way or to respond to the situation of affected households is population resettlement. This is enacted in different ways. Many attempts are unsuccessful. In the present chapter, following some conceptual reflections, various cases of resettlement in Manizales, Colombia, developed since the mid-1980s, will be discussed.

Vulnerable habitats: a needed reflection

When analysing mitigation policies for natural hazards in Latin American urban areas, significant orientation and intervention failings can be found. Policies have been directed almost exclusively towards the physical-natural or physical-spatial fields, leaving aside fundamental factors relating to social, cultural, economic and financial vulnerability.

Vulnerability, a complex concept

In a resettlement context, it is important to consider the vulnerable object as a habitat. Habitat is proposed as an 'articulating' concept used to address the proposed theme of resettlement. Indeed, when we talk about the vulnerability of a community and resettlement as a possible solution, what is really at stake is the multidimensional habitat built by this community. Therefore, the resettlement process cannot be limited only to the group of persons involved. It needs to contemplate the resettlement of the habitat in its totality.

Inhabit, habitat, habits

Logically, the habitat should allow for the notion of 'inhabitation', the complex expression of being and remaining on the land. This is the central topic covered in the present chapter.

The act of inhabiting goes far beyond using and occupying a space, since the dynamic process of inhabiting derives from the confluence of different worlds: the natural, social, economic, cultural, emotional and physical-spatial. In 'dwelling', the human being materialises the building of place, territory and a life system, in order not only to relate to and own something but also to belong to, develop roots and grow. Inhabiting is multidimensional, because the settler establishes connections with all the elements of their environment, by using and transforming them. Buchot (2012) also indicates that to inhabit means to be mobile: that is to say, to be able to move physically and mentally in time, space and towards others. Such an understanding means that to inhabit is, in fact, a process marked by an evolution and individual or community transformations in different directions.

This singularity in the ways of living, coexisting and relating to the environment leads to the concept of human habitat, that is to say, the object or space that is inhabited. Different to the use of the term in the environmental field, the concept of human habitat has increasingly evolved considering the leading role of the settlers themselves. This allows us to speak of human territory and territoriality, which refers to the dynamic acts of appropriation, transformation, 'culturisation' and 'anthropomorphisation' of space. This signifies a territory, a space with actors, owners, defenders and mourners with a sense of belonging and where they are recognised because they participate in its construction and development.

These reflections and definitions are fundamental since in the process of resettlement, actions of territorialisation, the expression of culture and identity, must be allowed in order to prevent traumas. This must also be applied to the habitat which is left behind, the original habitat.

For the reasons argued above, habitat does not exist on its own, but rather, is built around the life space of human beings, around their possessions, and is characterised by an exclusively anthropomorphic dimension (González-Escobar 2002). Of course, when we introduce the concept of belonging, one approximates the notion of housing. This tends to be seen as a container for material goods and intangibles, without completely implying that habitat is limited to the living space of a house. However, the house is a principal component of habitat. It is important here to recognise that it is not limited to the space between the walls (the house), but also includes the space from the walls outward, the proximate environment, generally of public use, and necessary for acceptable daily life (Hurtado Isaza and Chardon 2012).

In praxis, it can be asserted that the institutional vision of habitat cannot be limited to the house, the form. It is important to be able to inhabit, that is, to choose to live in the place and out of the place, beyond its structure. Policies should allow for the design of productive housing models and habitats should provide acceptable living conditions, achieving, among other things, economic sustainability.

Elsewhere (Chardon 2010, 30) I have considered the urban habitat to be 'a bio-physical-eco-space-system. A system whose components are the urban space itself, its inhabitants (characterised by a context, social, economic and cultural processes, routes and means of communication), the natural, physical-spatial environment, the political and institutional context and the relationships that link these elements.' Also, habitat is the expression of the dynamics, nexus and networks human beings establish with their environment (Ramírez Hernández 2014). This means occupying a meaningful territory where, beyond the notion of being in a physical sense, one can 'be'. This recognises that habitat is loaded with a strong dose of subjectivity, the product of affection, perception, dreams, yearnings and symbols. It is an intimate social way of representing territory, of appropriating it. This multidimensional view of habitat allows us to understand that at the moment resettlement processes are promoted, the focus of the action needs to be comprehensive.

Resettlement: a challenge

In practice, as we will demonstrate with case study analysis, the concept of resettlement, seen first as a mitigation of hazard exposure, is often developed and implemented with little consideration of aspects that go beyond such mitigation. This has implications that require careful analysis. As Lavell explains in Chapter 1, the term resettlement is often confused in common institutional languages with concepts such as relocation, which, if considered closely, refers to a different situation, even if both terms are motivated by changes in the life of the inhabitants, especially in spatial terms (see Lavell's chapter in this book for arguments that support the critical notions developed here and below).

In order to consider human resettlement, it is important to reflect on the meaning of the verb 'to settle'. This refers to the act of establishment at a site, but with a particular connotation of security, decisiveness, permanence and durability over time. This permanence means settling is not sudden but rather the result of a process, spatial or physical, as well as social, cultural, political and economic. Settling derives from identity. It corresponds to the establishment of a place, of a community and finally of a habitat with a sense of roots. The term 'locate', and its derived term, relocation, is not associated with durability and a sense of belonging. Rather, it supposes the act of putting in a place, but not in an intentional or definitive way. As to the concept of resettlement, there are approaches guided by the 'simple' search for security of life and property (Duque-Botero 2006). This is a view many local authorities hold.

Resettlement programmes should signify habitat recreation. This cannot, of course, be achieved without some unpleasant experiences. If it is not carried out with a multisector approach, there is a risk that one type of marginality is transformed into another type at the new site, due to poor management by the authorities.

A conceptualisation of resettlement inspired by my earlier article (Chardon 2010) is proposed for the analysis in this chapter. This concept suggests that resettlement is the construction of a new territory or real habitat, framed within a policy for city reorganisation. This is seen to be the only valid option since it demonstrates a systemic view of the situation. Effectively, the resettlement process is primarily human and, through changes and transformations in multiple aspects, the process should lead to optimal individual and collective habitat conditions, sustained over time. Its purpose is at least to restore and at best to achieve a general improvement in the daily lives, the environment and the quality of life of the targeted population. Initially, one has to think about the physical context, looking for safe spatial conditions. But implementation also has to be carried out in structural and non-structural areas, internal or external to the community, i.e. in social, cultural, economic, financial and physical-spatial aspects. Here, community participation in sustainable development is fundamental.

Resettling populations signifies building for them and with them (through community participation and reflection, planning, design and execution) a new living space in order that they feel they have a *life territory* – that is to say, a comfortable, friendly space, where this is recognised and felt, where the inhabitant has appropriated place, is rooted in it and has become a recognised, legitimate actor.

Resettlement projects have to respond in a holistic and definitive way to complex individual and collective situations, and therefore have to go far beyond the simple search for a safe roof. The processes involve a high social, economic, cultural and political cost as well as important physical-territorial impacts both in the home habitat and in the destination area. Due to this it is important to operate in such a way that the result is the observance of a continuous development of the resettled community.

Resettlement: reality may be far from the theory

In Colombia, resettlement is a risk mitigation option used in situations where it is deemed impossible to provide in situ vulnerability reduction due to the high hazard-proneness of place. Because of this the settler can opt for a social housing programme providing housing in safe sectors or choose to buy a used home. The Colombian state does not currently have specific regulations to formulate and implement resettlement plans. Such plans are considered to be similar to simple projects for housing of social or priority interest ('VIS' and 'VIP', in Spanish).

Through a comparative analysis of three resettlement processes developed in Manizales in the last 20 years, we will observe the distance between theory and imposed practice.

Resettlement praxis in Manizales: from one habitat to another

Manizales is an intermediate-sized Andean city (400,000 inhabitants). It is located in an area of very rugged topography, with lowly compacted volcanic soils and high levels of seismicity. The area is characterised by a bimodal equatorial mountain climate (between 2,500 and 3,000 mm of rain per year, of torrential characteristics and with strong erosive power). This situation partially explains the frequent occurrence of erosive processes in the city and constant mass movements of large destructive power. In this context, the municipality proposes solutions for the mitigation of vulnerability through resettlement processes. These consist in the acquisition of new or 'used' housing by the vulnerable community members, in a supposedly safe place when seen from the physical-natural angle. The primary objective is to effectively protect the population's life and goods. The projects are mostly designed as VIP projects (maximum value of 70 monthly minimum wages, equalling US$17,300 as of March 2017) or less frequently as VIS (maximum value of 135 monthly minimum wages). According to income levels, the beneficiaries can receive a subsidy from the state of up to 22 monthly minimum wages and 14 monthly minimum wages from the municipality. The remaining amount is financed through the banking system.

Before commenting on different modalities of resettlement, it is important to briefly present the initial living conditions of the settlers in order to apprehend the situation.

The habitat of origin

In Manizales, the population subject to resettlement processes lived previously on very steep slopes near the city centre (see Figure 2.1). The families, generally numerous (more than six members), with low and irregular incomes, lived in precarious dwellings, seen in terms of materials and construction systems, and suffered very low hygiene and health conditions. The built area often did not meet optimum needs. However, the space people occupied was much larger than that later given to them as a supposed solution to their vulnerability. The residents occupied the site as owners, as de facto owners or by paying a moderate rent. The physical and

Figure 2.1 San José district, on the northern hillside of the city. Self-built bamboo housing forms organic neighbourhoods where a united urban community with a partly rural way of life has developed. © A.C. Chardon.

spatial environment was characterised by an organic morphology where, despite the evident overcrowding, there were green areas, generally cultivated, and people walked to and from their homes. There was access to all required urban services and piracy of public services was very common. Extended nuclear families lived in the same neighbourhood or the same house, thus increasing family interrelationships. Neighbourhood relations encouraged solidarity in the human environment.

The prior living conditions of settlers help us understand why becoming a homeowner in a safe place is a very attractive proposal, without settlers really worrying about the multidimensional conditions of the process. Three resettlement projects are discussed below. The programmes were developed in different modalities and at various times. By considering three cases, we may analyse benefits and reprehensible aspects, from an integrated vision of habitat.

Destination habitats

The three projects respond to local and national conditions and policies: Yarumales (1995), Altos de Santa Ana (2005) and Bosques de Bengala (2013).

Yarumales (see Figure 2.2) was holistically designed and could be described as a visionary, integrated model to follow. In 1993 and over a two-year period, the local government's Popular Housing Fund along with El Minuto de Dios, a local organisation, carried out a resettlement project for 36 families that previously lived in very different vulnerable parts of the city. The project consisted not only in relocating the settlers but also in constructing a sustainable socio-eco-cultural community, aspects that were developed in workshops organised with the mandatory participation of all family members. Also, it was important to build *community* with future neighbours, given that each actor was seen as someone committed to and responsible for the project. Among other activities, training in the fields of dressmaking, shoemaking and baking were offered, so that families could earn the necessary income for their support and to pay for the new house. A building was equipped in the neighbourhood with the necessary machinery for the development of these trades so that the newly qualified people could work there. Families had to be able to sustain themselves and their new life project in the short, medium and long terms. In addition, households, as a way of

Figure 2.2 Yarumales, an integrated resettlement programme built according to the modality of the individual house, in a consolidated neighbourhood with all services and equipment. © A.C. Chardon.

participating in the project and reducing costs of acquiring housing, had to contribute 700 hours of work on the site.

In effect, the project was not subsidised. Families had to fully finance the acquisition of their new homes, including the initial deposit and a credit in the bank. This was essential. Full participation, especially financial, was deemed essential if the project was to work. This generates a sense of belonging and respect for the project, and allows it to be appreciated in all its dimensions. In resettlement programmes (as with housing programmes), paternalism and clientelism distort the objectives of programmes. That is to say, it is an opportunity for participatory development and not a gift or a bargaining block between different interest groups.

As regards the physical-natural and physical-spatial dimensions, the project also sought to improve the quality of life of the settlers and it considered them worthy of a dignified and pleasant life. The lot was located near a main road in an already consolidated traditional sector of the city that had access to all needed urban services and equipment. From the urbanistic point of view, the public areas were composed of front yards, walkways, a small playground, a sports court and parking, all of which are currently in excellent condition. This is proof of the sense of belonging in the community.

Finally, the architectural design of the project was undertaken by a group of students and professors from the School of Architecture and Urbanism at the National University of Colombia in Manizales. Design provided for areas of around 55 m^2 distributed on two levels and with a back yard. In 1995, the families moved to Yarumales and after more than 20 years, we can observe that only 30 per cent of the buildings have undergone remodelling or enlargement, which shows that the dwellers have felt at ease with the initial project.

Overall, the project was conceived of in integrated terms. Vulnerability was not only seen to be due to physical factors but also to the negative social, cultural and economic context at a family and community level. Intervention using a correct vision of habitat was needed in order to favour development among the families. The project has been sustainable ever since, in all its dimensions. To date, in Manizales, the Yarumales project is unique (in part, possibly because of the limited number of resettled households). During the twenty-first century, processes have unfortunately been promoted that have a very limited and erroneous vision and approach to the concept of human habitat.

The Santa Ana resettlement project (finished in 2005) was developed by the municipality for the benefit of families affected by the night of 18 March 2003, when in three hours 144 mm of rain fell, causing 82 large landslides in several unstable sectors of the city. Deciding on and executing the project took a little more than two years. This is a short period when compared to the range of tasks that had to be undertaken, including financing, finding and purchasing adequate land (given the low income levels of the recipient population), tendering and building. No social dimension was considered and the project was run like any social housing project, with the right to a 50 per cent financial subsidy from the state and municipality. This obliged the families to obtain a loan to pay the other 50 per cent of building costs. Although it is important that the recipient population assume some financial responsibility for their homes, the lack of employment and income-generating training options led to immense difficulties as regards paying for bank loans and public utility services. This led on many occasions to owners selling or renting their homes against the rules of the game, and returning to less costly areas, which are often unstable, insecure and dangerous in general. Homes have also been sold off by the bank to recover unpaid loans. Such results completely eliminate the objectives of a resettlement programme.

The Santa Ana housing development is located on peripheral forest lands and consists of 11 blocks that group 392 houses, each with an area of 29 m^2, on 35 m^2 lots. Families moved to live there in October 2005. Urban development is oriented in the direction of the slope, with roads and laddered buildings and difficult access to public spaces, which also lack services (see Figure 2.3).

Architecturally, each house of 29 m^2 is distributed between a social space, a bedroom, a patio and a bathroom, which a family group, always numerous, 'enjoys'. Critical overcrowding does not allow the separation of social, private and intimate areas. Curtains are used to separate spaces. Social or service space is private, and decks or terraces become a place where children play, clothes are dried, vegetables are grown or domestic animals are kept, thus revealing the rural customs of the settlers. The lack of space, as in many similar situations, forces the occupation of public spaces. This is the case of the use given to front yards.

In this type of settlement, it is very common to observe that the living space is also a source of income. Lack of training and of formal employment opportunities means that people create their own employment opportunities that allow, among other things, them to cover the financial responsibilities entailed in purchasing the house (payment of loans, public services, transport etc.).

As Torres-Tovar and Robles-Joya (2014) underline, in the processes of resettlement, the economic aspects are rarely considered. They are assumed to be already solved. This is how, in the same 29 m^2, in addition

Figure 2.3 The basic deliverable unit in Altos de Santa Ana. The terrace allows for a doubling of the available area. © A.C. Chardon.

to the confusion and overlap of domestic uses, small-scale commercial activities such as a shop, a stall or a hairdresser are developed. Limited habitability is not restricted to the built area as such, but also applies as regards light (a single span), acoustics (a thin wall is shared with the neighbouring house), ventilation and humidity (the deck-terrace generates water filtration). Because they were not taken into account during the design process, families had to expand or transform their home to take economic advantage of it, demonstrating that the desire is to have a home as opposed to a house. And soon after occupation, second and third storeys, windows, balconies and personalised colours appear, and the patio gets covered. These modifications are not always undertaken using adequate building standards, thus endangering the structure and its habitants.

The peripheral location of the project requires public transport in order to be able to connect to the rest of the city, mainly the centre. This situation generates an additional expense for families who used to live previously in very central areas. Moreover, the absence of social actors, the high unemployment rate among young people and the reduced living spaces and service provision lead to conditions that foment delinquency. Since the keys to houses were handed over in 2005, local authorities have had no further contact with settlers and no official process of follow-up has occurred.

The Bosques de Bengala urban development project is one of the housing schemes totalling one hundred thousand houses to be built as part of the free-of-charge home policy the Colombian government launched in 2012, mainly for families displaced by armed conflict and by disasters. In Manizales, a total of 1,420 housing units will be built, all using the multifamily mode. This programme is an unfortunate example of where by receiving a new house a family has its immediate physical needs satisfied but little consciousness exists as to the fact that the what, the where and the how of things are highly significant social variables.

By the end of 2013, 240 families had 'benefited' from the project. It consists of six blocks of five storeys with eight fully subsidised apartments each. Additionally, the housing complex is provided with a court, green areas, playgrounds and parking (see Figure 2.4). Families came from rural areas, fleeing armed conflict. They were employed mostly in agricultural pursuits. A move to the city created a complete change in work environments, with no support given in this context of forced urban adaptation and acculturation.

While the new living conditions allow some degree of stability and access to basic services which the inhabitants did not have as displaced or affected persons, the smallness of apartments (scarcely 42 m^2, with three rooms but no opportunity for enlargement as in the case of Santa Ana), the non-resolution of their economic situation and the new rules of coexistence considerably affect their daily lives. The hallways become an extension of the apartments, to dry clothes and store bicycles. People also linger on the outside railings as if it was their balcony because inside, not everything fits. In the same way, the apartment becomes an economic unit and the windows of the apartment that border with the outside corridor are turned into windows to serve the customers of the businesses that many families set up. Some of these use hazardous equipment such as industrial bakery ovens! Thus, as in Santa Ana, shops, bakeries, manicure salons and hairdressing salons are opened, with their own advertisements on the facades. In the parking lot, *arepas* (a typical Colombian food) are also made and sold at certain times of the day.

Even though the houses were given away by the state (a policy that also generated employment in the construction sector), families find it difficult to pay public services, or costs of the administration of the complex, and other essential daily obligations. Due to this, housing has to become productive, even if it was not designed for this, and the situation

Figure 2.4 Bosques de Bengala, 40 apartments per block. Appropriation of the exterior corridors. © A.C. Chardon.

often leads to conflicts. What seems to be inexpensive as a solution turns out to be expensive. Owners can neither rent nor sell for 10 years according to the rules. But the lack of economic solvency has led to many selling their apartment or renting them out. Severe economic difficulties are recurrent in these projects, as they almost inevitably generate an increase in household expenses.

The first stage of the San Sebastián de Betania project (close to Bosques de Bengala and where the construction of almost all the free housing of the city is carried out) was in part subsidised. More than 80 per cent of households have not been able to keep up with their debts or pay for public services. This has led to a crisis that has required much negotiation, a search for sponsors to pay off the debts, the suspension of services (with illegal connection then being made to neighbours' services), and even auction of goods (Toro 2014; Arango-Arango 2015). Resettlement, when legally constituted, has a cost and generates new expenses, which not all families can assume. It requires the development of educational policies, training opportunities and the creation of employment to enable income generation at the household level. But such policies are not put into action.

Numerous problems of coexistence exist in the housing projects, even leading to homicide. These are caused by the lack of respect and tolerance of some residents towards their neighbours. They are also possibly, in part, the responsibility of the architectural and urban design (Sánchez 2014). The narrowness of place leads to forced existence under high-density conditions. Guayacundo-Chaves (2015) points out that the problem is recurrent in this modality of multifamily units. It is obvious that a process of resettlement, as well as urban renewal, cannot be successful and contribute to the quality of life of the settlers, without taking into account socio-economic and cultural conditions and their implications for the development and management of projects at the financial, socio-cultural, architectural and urbanistic level. A project must be, to some degree, personalised with regard to the community to be resettled and, of course, designed to offer an integrated, comfortable life context, i.e. as a habitat.

Conclusion

In light of the examples analysed above, evidence exists that resettlement praxis is still far from the theory that the author considers valid. This situation is largely due to an incomplete institutional vision of the conditions required for the acceptable development of a vulnerable population. This view seems to assume that quality of life is merely having a safe roof over one's head and few qualitative factors are taken into account. The 'house' as an object also appears in the foreground of the families' imaginary. But they later become aware that other social, economic, cultural and urban requirements must be satisfied. In effect, it is important to mention the large-scale, very detailed survey I developed (Chardon 2010) among families resettled in Manizales, which showed how families accept the housing programmes because they allow them to abandon a risk zone and become low-cost owners. At first, they consider that their new situation offers new opportunities. But then their vision usually changes, and they feel nostalgic about their original habitat. This occurs when they realise that at both the housing level and with regard to the quality of life in general, the project does not satisfy their needs and expectations. Over time, they become resigned to their situation and accommodate to it. So, in most respects, people exist more in line with the habits and needs that existed before the transfer. This scenario generally leads to them adapting to their new place of 'life' and gradually trying to build a sustainable, manageable habitat.

The Yarumales project demonstrated that comprehensive and transdisciplinary management – including participation (financial as well), training and integration into the labour market and the dynamics of the city – propitiates a process of successful resettlement. This has allowed people to 're-inhabit', while facing all aspects of vulnerability, articulating the interests of the various actors and allowing a real dialectic between the different levels of intervention (housing unit, neighbourhood, city), thus achieving the construction of a habitable city, from the perspective of the city and the polis.

References

Arango-Arango, Mónica. 2015. 'Deudores por viviendas, con padrinos para pagar'. *El Tiempo*, 28 January 2015. https://www.eltiempo.com/archivo/documento/CMS-15160659.

Buchot, Nathalie. 2012. 'La mobilité contextuelle comme lien entre la mobilité quotidienne et la mobilité résidentielle: Du concept à la pratique'. *VertigO: La revue électronique en sciences de l'environnement*, no. hors-série 11. https://doi.org/10.4000/vertigo.11727.

Chardon, Anne Catherine. 2010. 'Reasentar un hábitat vulnerable: Teoría versus praxis'. *Revista INVI* 25 (70): 17–75. https://doi.org/10.4067/invi.v25i70.506.

Duque-Botero, Juan David. 2006. 'El reasentamiento poblacional: Fenómeno social, político y de progreso'. *Estudios Socio-Jurídicos* 8 (1): 145–65. http://dx.doi.org/10.12804/esj.

González-Escobar, Luis Fernando. 2002. 'La concepción tecnológica del hábitat'. *Ensayos FORUM* 19: 18–29. http://www.bdigital.unal.edu.co/2230/1/lfg02-For19.PDF.

Guayacundo-Chaves, Luis Fernando. 2015. 'Vivienda social y conflicto vecinal: Lo físico espacial como componente en la mitigación de conflictos en copropiedad', master's thesis, Universidad Nacional de Colombia. http://bdigital.unal.edu.co/51210/1/Vivienda%20Social%20y%20Conflicto%20Vecinal.pdf.

Hurtado Isaza, Juan Gabriel and Anne-Catherine Chardon. 2012. *Vivienda social y reasentamiento, una visión crítica desde el hábitat*. Bogotá: Editorial Universidad Nacional de Colombia.

Ramírez Hernández, Leidy Tatiana. 2014. 'Habitar humano: Interacciones entre formas de habitar y condiciones de habitabilidad', master's thesis, Universidad Nacional de Colombia, Sede Medellín. http://bdigital.unal.edu.co/41942/1/43989579.2014.pdf.

Sánchez, Margaret. 2014. 'Viviendas gratis forman comunidad'. *La Patria*, 23 February 2014. https://www.lapatria.com/en-domingo/viviendas-gratis-forman-comunidad-55693.

Toro, Kevin. 2014. 'Sin plata para pagar la cuota de vivienda, en el barrio San Sebastián de Manizales'. *La Patria*, 8 May 2014. https://www.lapatria.com/manizales/sin-plata-para-pagar-la-cuota-de-vivienda-en-el-barrio-san-sebastian-de-manizales-80711.

Torres-Tovar, Carlos Alberto and Solanyi Robles-Joya. 2014. 'Estrategias de inclusión-exclusión de la ciudad colombiana autoproducida mediante políticas de reasentamiento barrial'. *Bulletin de l'Institut Français d'études Andines* 43 (3): 587–609. https://doi.org/10.4000/bifea.5975.

3

How do relocation decisions and implementation impact risk outcomes? Raising questions after learning from India

Garima Jain

India has experienced many disasters, both climatic and non-climatic, but it was only after the 1999 super cyclone, 2001 Latur earthquake and 2004 Indian Ocean tsunami that the National Disaster Management Act was passed in 2005 and institutional action began to be taken for long-term disaster risk reduction.[1] Before the 1990s, efforts were limited to relief and response, with some exceptions involving investments in early warning systems, but once the State Disaster Management Authorities were set up (first in Odisha in 1999 and then Gujarat in 2001), systematic action was initiated for mitigation and preparedness in certain states. Large investments began to be made to improve early warning systems for hydro-meteorological hazards. Many international development lenders such as the World Bank and Asian Development Bank also increased investments in India, with a view to strengthening disaster risk management and building resilience (Jain 2016b, 37). Affected states learned from their past experiences of disasters that providing early warning and investing in evacuation response systems greatly reduced the numbers of lives lost. However, what remained a challenge was when people returned to their broken homes and disrupted livelihoods. Thus, many states – such as Gujarat, Tamil Nadu, Bihar, Uttarakhand, Odisha and Andhra Pradesh – began investing in rehabilitation[2] projects by helping people rebuild their houses post-disaster, with the objective that future events would have the least possible impact on their lives.

Some of these housing rehabilitation projects also involved moving people (post-disasters or pre-emptively) by relocating or resettling them in new locations. It is well known within development literature that housing has far-reaching social, environmental, economic and political implications, well beyond its function as a shelter (Bhan, Anand and Harish 2014; Mathur 2006, UN-Habitat 2014). Despite this, delivery of housing for 'risk reduction'[3] continues to fail to address many of these needs (see Chapter 14 by Jain, Singh and Malladi in this book). Undoubtedly, there has been a great deal of learning in the last decade for post-disaster rehabilitation, but the long-term monitoring and impact evaluation is still in its nascent stages and the timeframe of such evaluations is short. Further, the knowledge from these experiences is still limited to certain states and regions, and all long-term implications for people's lives are not understood well (Jain et al. 2017).

In this chapter, I use cases of rehabilitation undertaken in the context of risk reduction in the city of Visakhapatnam in Andhra Pradesh and Ganjam district in Odisha in order to understand the differential outcomes from varying interventions made by different actors, within the context of their decision-making and implementation processes. In the cases discussed, where people were resettled in Jawaharlal Nehru Urban Renewal Mission (JnNURM), Rajiv Awas Yojna (RAY) and Indira Awas Yojna (IAY) housing schemes, the housing was built under development schemes prior to the occurrence of the disaster and affected people were moved there later, whereas the Odisha Disaster Recovery Project (ODRP) sites were designed and implemented after the cyclonic event in 2013. Some cases referred to in this chapter are discussed in more detail in Chapters 4 and 5 of this book.

I use a governance framework of decision-making and implementation processes in each of these intervention options and argue that in both post-impact and pre-emptive action scenarios, the specific pathways taken are leading to differential outcomes, and creating further risks for the communities and the cities at large. With this review of cases, I attempt to lay out a variety of options for processes to consider that could improve the rehabilitation processes undertaken by various state and non-state actors. The options presented here are by no means comprehensive, but are a means to question the current practices and offer alternative ways to think.

Structure

The key question of enquiry was set out as, 'How, whose, what and to what extent are the risks reduced (or intended to be reduced) through forms of rehabilitation?' This was understood by conceptualising a rehabilitation intervention in three phases: decision-making processes, an implementation phase, and their effect on the outcomes of these interventions. See Figure 3.1 for the structure of the analysis.

The project team and I set out to understand the various decision-making processes that lead to rehabilitation interventions in the context of disaster risk reduction (DRR). We aimed to understand the various triggers that instigate these processes and what alternatives for achieving DRR are proposed before arriving at the decision to rehabilitate and the form of rehabilitation. These triggers could be corrective, pre-emptive or compensatory (UN Secretary-General 2016) in nature and the various alternatives of rehabilitation could be relocation, resettlement, in situ housing or infrastructure upgrading. These decisions further lead to beneficiary identification where some are included and others are not. Another important aspect of rehabilitation is related to land in terms of location decisions and alternate uses of the vacated land and how they may affect the outcomes for the people. The institutional design of these interventions is envisioned in multiple ways, particularly differentiating between urban and rural contexts. In this process, we asked how and when participation is enabled and imagined, and how various incentives and disincentives are built into the intervention design.

To study the implementation phase better, we set out to understand the various operational challenges faced during the implementation of rehabilitation, in urban versus rural areas. These may be standard procedures, but might also involve context-specific flexibilities. There could be innovative ways to scale these methods up. Reflecting on the relationship between various decision-making aspects, such as timing and sequencing, that may have an effect on implementation, is a further aim of the chapter.

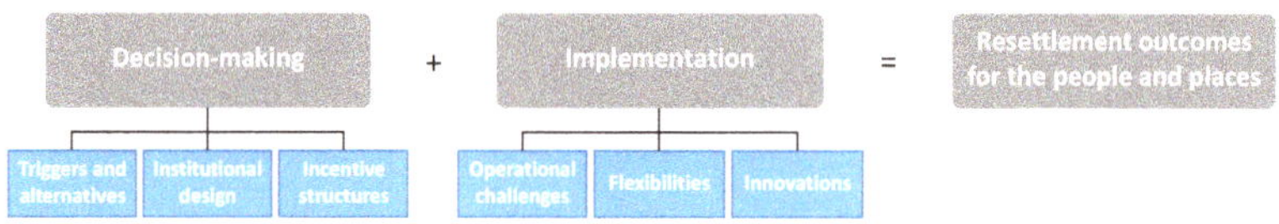

Figure 3.1 Research framework. The study focused on decision-making and implementation processes in these resettlements to understand their impact on outcomes for the people. © Garima Jain.

Various combinations of decisions and the processes of implementation affect the trajectory and experiences of rehabilitation outcomes. This chapter aims at outlining some of the emerging connections between the phases of decision-making and implementation, and how they could be reimagined for better risk reduction and development outcomes for households and the city.

Methods and sample design

Based on a preliminary secondary review and initial interviews with housing and DRR experts in the region, 16 rehabilitation sites were identified across urban and rural areas of Odisha and Andhra Pradesh covering a variety of resettlement, relocation, in situ housing and infrastructure upgrading interventions (see Table 3.1) to find patterns in decision-making and implementation processes leading to long-term outcomes. Unlike developmental projects, detailed socio-economic surveys or environmental assessments are not available for post-disaster projects. Therefore, the team relied more on rapid needs assessments and other secondary studies, apart from using site observations and surveys as instruments of research and analysis (Government of Odisha, Asian Development Bank and World Bank 2013).

Decision-making and implementation processes were understood through interviews with key officials and policymakers (n=26), and consultations (n=2 with 45 stakeholders) (Jain 2016a; Malladi et al. 2016). Community-level information on experiences, e.g. on infrastructure conditions and cultural norms, was gathered through 10 group discussions. To understand more household-level risks, primary household-level surveys (n=158) were conducted to assess changes in various indicators before and after the intervention. Some individuals, especially those with special needs such as the disabled, elderly, minorities and women, were identified and interviewed to get a better sense of the risks faced by them during such rehabilitation interventions (n=15).

Six different kinds of respondents were identified and interviewed: (1) Non-beneficiaries who were cyclone-affected but excluded from the housing intervention (n=31); (2) In situ housing upgrading beneficiaries (n=8); (3) Beneficiaries in the process of rehabilitation (n=20); (4) Relocated or resettled (R&R) beneficiaries (n=44); (5) Beneficiaries identified for infrastructure upgrading (n=20); and (6) Beneficiaries identified for R&R in the future (n=35).

Table 3.1 Selected sites in urban and rural Odisha and Andhra Pradesh, sample description and type of resettlements studied through the project. © Garima Jain based on data sources BeMC (2014a), BeMC (2014b), Census of India 2011, GVMC (2015a), GVMC (2015b), Sarma 2015, and key stakeholder interviews.

Site	Population	Study sample size (households)	Respondent type	Rehabilitation type
Odisha (Urban)				
Khaja Sahi	922	5	Type 6	Proposed resettlement
Pichipicha Nagar	807	5	Type 1, 6	Proposed resettlement
Ramnagar Odiya Sahi	387	15	Type 4	Resettlement site
Bada Harijan Sahi	686	10	Type 4	Resettlement site
Canal Street		20	Type 5	Infrastructure upgrading
Odisha (Rural)				
Ramayapalli	190	22	Type 1, 2, 3, 4	Partial relocation in progress and in situ housing upgrading
Lakhshmipur	690		Type 1, 2, 3, 4	Partial resettlement in progress and in situ housing upgrading
Devi Nagar			Type 4	Relocation site
Markandi	3,210	18	Type 1, 2, 3, 4	Partial relocation in progress and in situ housing upgrading
Andhra Pradesh (Urban)				
ASR Nagar	1,112	8	Type 1, 6	Proposed relocation

(continued)

Table 3.1 *(continued)*

Site	Population	Study sample size (households)	Respondent type	Rehabilitation type
Jalaripeta	26,262	10	Type 1, 2, 5, 6	Proposed partial resettlement and infrastructure upgrading
Paradesipallyam	3,708	12	Type 4	Resettlement site
Sevanagar	3,832	16	Type 4	Resettlement site
Sonia Gandhi Nagar	2,200	4	Type 2	In situ housing upgrading
Vambay Housing	14,400	8	Type 4	Resettlement site
Andhra Pradesh (Rural)				
Pudimadaka	9,912	5	Type 1, 3, 6	Resettlement in progress
Total households interviewed		158		

Findings

Decision-making processes

Triggers and rehabilitation alternatives

Disaster risk reduction projects are undertaken with a high sense of urgency. Following disaster incidences, states feel the need to respond quickly and 'visibly' to showcase their effectiveness and action (Scott 1998). Housing, being one of the most visible types of damage, attracts their attention (Few et al. 2021). Similar to post-disaster compensation amounts that are seen as the state's moral responsibility or *ex gratia*, the state also provides post-disaster housing from a moral high ground and sees people as 'beneficiaries' irrespective of whether the provision is in fact beneficial to them (Jain et al. 2017).

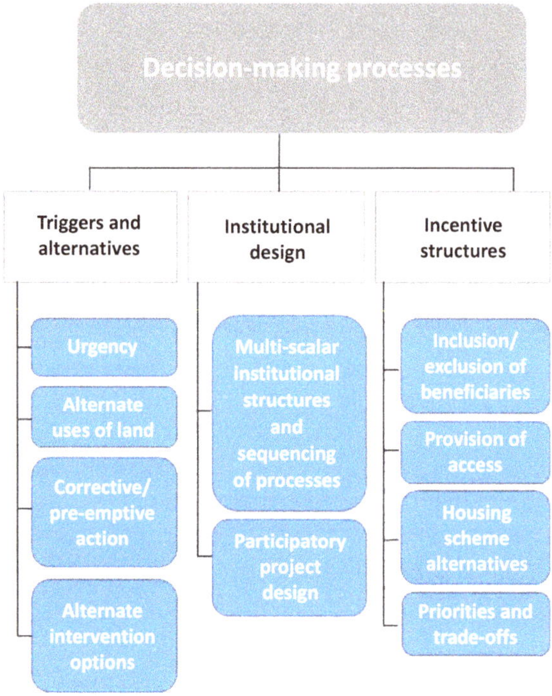

Figure 3.2 Elements of decision-making processes. Triggers and alternatives considered, institutional design, and incentive structures were identified as key decision-making elements that had implications for resettlement outcomes. © Garima Jain.

Funding and actions taken in the context of disasters are often response-centric one-time efforts, lacking a long-term view. In development programmes, systems for assessments, implementation design, beneficiary identification, pre-defined compensatory mechanisms and long-term monitoring and impact evaluation are standard, whereas, in a disaster context, action is required to be taken soon after an extreme event, when affected families require immediate support, and there is little time to conduct any detailed socio-economic, risk or environmental assessments. Effectively, post-disaster recovery remains considerably divergent from other development objectives (Chandrasekhar, Zhang and Xiao 2014; Olshansky and Chang 2009); at best it is seen as urban development activities compressed in time and space (Olshansky and Johnson 2017).

Normatively, the objectives of both DRR and development interventions must be to improve the overall sustainable outcomes for the people. However, owing to the fundamental differences between the two contexts in which they operate, the approaches may be different. Post-disaster interventions focus on reducing long-term vulnerabilities to recurring events, but there is a need for them to adopt processes from development projects such that the overall outcomes are more sustainable, while development projects need to become more risk-informed.

Alternatives to R&R are not assessed fully. Particularly in urban areas, where inner-city land is priced very highly, alternatives to R&R are not considered as such, especially when the land is occupied by people living in slums or those who do not have land rights. In many cases, 'untenability' is used as a pretext for moving people to peripheral areas (e.g. Sevanagar in Visakhapatnam, where people were evicted from a 'hazardous' inner-city location to several miles away from the city), without sufficient assessments of social, economic and environmental costs and benefits to the households in question or the city at large (see Chapter 5 in this volume on risk tolerance). Alternatives to moving people far, such as not moving them at all, and instead investing in in-situ upgrading, are not considered at the time of decision-making. The 'value' of land in providing in situ housing needs to be reconsidered in the larger development frame (see Chapter 5 by Lwasa, Bazaz and Jain in this book), alongside the discussion on the alternative use of land argument discussed later in the chapter.

When the vacated land is put to alternate uses other than environmental recovery, the costs of resettlement and upgrading the site for this new use seem unjustifiable vis-à-vis in situ upgrading. While people are being relocated to new sites replacing the existing environmental or other functions, the original settlement sites often also undergo land use changes. In New Golabanda in Odisha and Sevanagar in Visakhapatnam, the entire neighbourhoods were resettled and the land was traded in the first case with a military base and in the second case used by the railways as a stadium.

In the case of the ODRP in Ganjam district of Odisha, people were allowed to keep their original lands and houses which they owned, and in many cases family members continued living there to retain a connection. While the relocated residents were required to live in the new sites for a minimum of seven years to get *patta* (legal tenure), they could not rent out their lands and houses in either location. In cases such as Lakshmipur, the distance between the old and new sites was so large that many continued to live in the old sites, with one of the family members going to the new site only to sleep. This approach may be acceptable to residents as it likely supports their accumulation strategy (Bazaz et al. 2016), but it is yet to be seen if these older sites continue to remain exposed to hazard risk. Thus, the risk reduction outcome in these cases may not be completely achieved despite the provision of new and safe houses.

Institutional design

Multi-scalar institutional delivery designs and sequencing of processes significantly affect the levels of participation and thereby the outcomes of the intervention. ODRP pursued a unique institutional design. Odisha State Government asked the World Bank to fund the recovery project, and Odisha State Disaster Management Authority (OSDMA) anchored the delivery of housing. OSDMA is part of the Department of Revenue, which in turn controls rural land for the state, making the otherwise contested task of land allocation easier for the R&R programme. In addition, Gram Vikas, a local NGO, was brought in as a key socio-technical partner. Well-documented experiences from the World Bank's past DRR and development projects (Jain 2016b, 37) as well as ground experiences of Gram Vikas and OSDMA, were effectively employed in the programme design. District authorities first identified the affected people and villages, following which suitable land was found in agreement with the village development committees through the Department of Revenue. The resulting R&R was largely acceptable to the rehabilitated communities.

In contrast, in Visakhapatnam, the development agencies took the lead on delivering 'disaster-resilient' housing. The State Housing Board raised public and private humanitarian funds to build housing on the land that was allotted by the State Department of Revenue. Housing was constructed well before the district authorities started their beneficiary identification. This resulted in a situation where the beneficiaries could not participate in the decision-making process, and eventually resisted moving (Sarma 2015). Institutional design, sequencing of processes that involve participation, and learning from past experiences are critical for more sustainable outcomes.

Participation can enable a sense of ownership that can have longer-term benefits for the development. One clear distinction observed between the cases of Paradesipallyam and Sevanagar in Visakhapatnam, which were both resettled at Madhurvada at a distance of 20-plus km from their original locations in the city, was the willingness of people to move. Both were moved to housing sites that were built under the centrally sponsored JnNURM housing programme, and therefore the provisions of social and physical infrastructure, distance from the original site, timing, etc. were equally deficient. While Paradesipallyam was inhabited mostly by people who were renters in the city who 'chose' these sites from among three location choices through an application process, Sevanagar inhabitants were evicted from railway lands on the grounds of 'untenability' and were left with no choice but to move.

Eventually, people in Paradesipallyam formed a management committee to take care of open drains and waste management and made a collective effort to get bus access improved, whereas the people of Sevanagar took no ownership over maintaining the place, and, with time, increasing health hazards, accidental deaths, the crime rate, education dropouts and other issues became rampant. While there may be other reasons for these differential outcomes, the level and sense of ownership evidently had direct implications which need to be considered in such resettlement scenarios.

Incentive structures

'Inclusion' criteria exclude many and can exacerbate inequalities within the existing social structures. Most housing schemes are selective in their 'beneficiary identification'. Usually, the criteria are set during programme design, based on which the assessments are conducted by different teams comprising various government officials with differing skills and expertise. To avoid discrepancies across assessment teams and to keep the assessments 'objective', the criteria are based on tangible indicators, such as:

- Level of house damage (e.g. fully, severely or partially). It is taken as a proxy for all damages and does not include other losses, such as damaged productive or non-productive assets or loss to working days, thereby excluding many affected people.
- Proof of residence in the state and land title/ownership. Not everyone has these documents to prove residence, or they may have lost them during the disaster itself. Furthermore, renters may have been living in a place for a long time without having any proof of residence, and may not have an alternative place to stay.
- Proof of identity (including a below poverty line card). People, especially those in rural areas, migrants or those with limited education, do not have sufficient proof of identity, and therefore risk being excluded.
- Non-participation in other housing schemes.

One proof of identity that is often made mandatory is the below poverty line (BPL) card. While the poverty line itself is a contentious statistic across the country, there are several other challenges in getting a card even for those who are BPL. This played out in Markandi village in Odisha. Predominantly consisting of thatched roof houses, the village caught fire in 1997. Many people took loans at that time to rebuild their houses using asbestos sheets, but again lost what they had rebuilt in the 1999 super cyclone, and were thus burdened by more loans. Those who had not taken out loans earlier took them this time, to rebuild parts of their houses (usually one room) using concrete slabs to avoid such shocks in the future. Since then, however, their names have been taken off the BPL list, because roof quality is a criterion in BPL selection. Thus, when the 2013 cyclone struck, even though they were still repaying high-interest 10-year-old loans and were affected by the cyclone, they were not entitled to get new houses since they were not BPL any more. There are many such cases where self-investment becomes a disincentive for building resilience.

These 'objective' criteria often lead to the exclusion of others despite them being equally or even more affected. Consider the simplified illustration (Figure 3.3) of how this might manifest. Assume that before the intervention takes place, there are four kinds of people in a neighbourhood: the poorest of the poor, with no residence proof, no land and no identity proof; the poor, with inadequate housing; long-term renters to informal landowners, with no proof of residence; and the affluent. But since the beneficiary identification criteria are such that only the poor with damaged housing and proof of residence are allotted new housing, the poorest of the poor and the renters are left out. Despite large investments made in housing provision, opportunity costs of not improving the lives of the poorest of the poor through the process still exist.

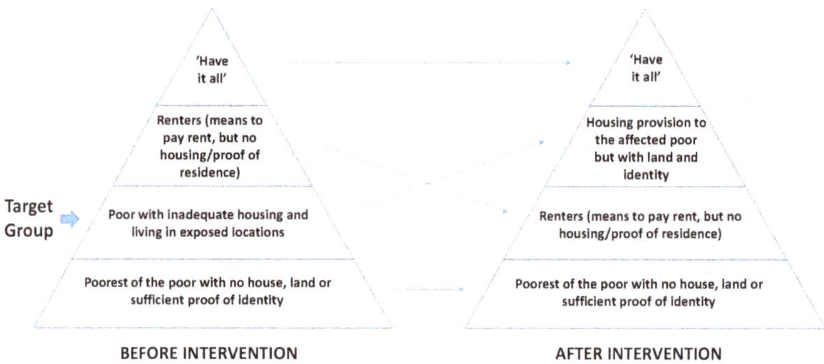

Figure 3.3 Beneficiary inclusion and exclusion criteria can have a pervasive impact on social inequities. © Garima Jain.

Universal housing allocation is neither a solution nor implementable. It is worthwhile examining if a rights-based universal provision could be considered as an approach for such programmes, as opposed to targeting. This has been a matter of debate in the public distribution system of food in India, where universal access is seen to reduce the errors of excluding the ones in need (type 1 error) and the costs of targeting are found to be more than the costs of including ones not in need (type 2 error). This approach also worked during the Odisha relief distribution after Cyclone Phailin, when 500 rupees and 50 kg of rice were given to everyone, irrespective of whether they were affected or not. Every household we spoke to received this one-time relief, although in many cases people opted out, based on their needs, and the value of their time and convenience.

But the provision of rice or compensation is very different from housing. With limited funds and other resources (such as land), it is impossible to make such commitments. Even notionally, if all the people in one neighbourhood were to be resettled together, it might have a positive impact vis-à-vis the social continuity of these settlements, but this is easier said than done. Even in one neighbourhood not everyone is equally able – economically, politically and socially – and not everyone would want these provisions. Five of the 35 type 1 respondents (non-beneficiaries) in our surveys who owned houses but suffered little damages did not want the housing provision. They may still be at risk in the future due to the increasing intensity and frequency of climatic hazards, but they do not perceive those risks. This is a form of residual risk post-intervention. Some upgrading interventions may be considered so that even the non-beneficiaries could get some risk reduction benefits for safeguarding their future as a preventive approach to risk reduction.

Meanwhile, states have largely focused on dealing with type 2 leakages within such housing schemes, to ensure that people who do not need such allocations are unable to get them through unfair means or by using incorrect identities. A Collector from Andhra Pradesh described a new system under development for a holistic application process for housing schemes. This would involve linking the *Adhaar* card (national identity card), ration cards, property tax information and BPL status of people, making it easy to monitor anyone who is not eligible for a house (i.e. if they have received a house before, if they already own a house, or if their family member owns a house, etc.). While this system may reduce type 2 error, type 1 error continues to plague the process and to create inequality.

Proximity or provision of public transport is not the same as access. The outcomes of R&R varied greatly based on the distance of the original settlement from the new sites: beyond 2 km in rural areas and 5 km in urban areas. Further investigation shows that outcomes are based on the connections people have with the original location – for their workplaces, schools, health facilities, temples, etc. – and as long as they were able to reproduce these connections, R&R was more acceptable to them. The literature calls it the 'place attachment' (Lewicka 2011) (see Chapter 4 by Johnson et al. in this book). In rural areas, people are dependent on walking, and some men use bicycles. They would pay for a bus commute for long distances, but are not used to paying for their everyday local commute. Even if such transport options were provided, it would still be an additional burden that they may be unable or unwilling to take on. People in rural areas indicated that relocation within walking distance of 1–2 km would be acceptable.

In urban areas, however, people were used to travelling on buses and public transport over short distances. When asked how far they would be willing to go, most people said they would be fine with relocating within 3–5 km. But it is also in the urban areas that resettlement sites (in Visakhapatnam particularly) were located 20+ km from original sites, largely owing to price-based land allocations made for affordable housing. So even if a bus service were provided, which is not often the case, it may be too expensive for the poor, or not accessible due to their age, physical abilities, gender or cultural or safety concerns. The question then is whether the provision of transportation services is enough to address the problem of access. In many cases, despite having schools across the main highway from the resettlement, it was still difficult for families and children to cross over and access the school. Safety is a big concern, and proximity does not confirm access.

Different per-unit investments for ongoing housing schemes are seen as disincentives in participating in one over the other. There have been many housing schemes in the last few years, often running simultaneously within the same geographies, but the spend per house on each varies widely. While IAY provides 75,000 rupees, JnNURM offers 125,000–175,000 rupees per house. ODRP offered houses worth 300,000 rupees, in order to provide 'dignified housing' to everyone, and in Visakhapatnam cyclone-resilient housing was worth 225,000 rupees per unit. The stated reason for the last two being higher than those built under development programmes is the inclusion of disaster-resilient construction technologies and specifications that increased costs. People are often excluded from one scheme because of their participation in another scheme earlier, even though the support received in the past might not have been sufficient to build a house. In ODRP in Odisha, people agreed to return the money they had received previously (under IAY) in order to become part of the new housing scheme (they could not use the plinths built earlier as they did not align with the new programme's house designs). Does the lower cost of regular affordable housing indicate that it is not disaster resilient? In one case (see Chapter 5 by Lwasa, Bazaz and Jain in this book for more details on the case), using relief aid money, more expensive 'disaster-resilient' housing was built adjacent to regular framed structures for JnNURM housing in Madhurvada in Visakhapatnam. Both were far from the city and remained vacant for a long time after construction, indicating that the construction techniques or quality were not sufficient to attract residents (GVMC 2015a).

One size does not fit all. Even within one programme, the budget needs may not be same for all. In ODRP, 300,000 rupees have been disbursed in six tranches based on the signing of the agreement, completion of plinth, lintel, roof, removal of centring, and full completion. Another 12,500 rupees are disbursed before roof casting for the toilet construction, as part of the National Clean India Mission. While people at the completed sites said that this sum was sufficient, most of the houses were contractor-built, where the sum to be paid was fixed and built houses were delivered en masse. In many such instances, quality was seen to have been compromised. Also, while the sum was considered adequate at the beginning, costs of labour, material and transport inflated over the year, so many owners of sites under construction found this sum insufficient, but lacked recourse to further funds. Besides, residents were to receive 20,000 rupees to build up to the plinth level. In cases where the location was close to the coast and people were advised to build higher plinths to avoid storm surge, this amount quickly ran out. In many cases, people ended up taking loans at an interest rate of 3 per cent per month for constructing these plinths, and hoped to repay those with the next tranche of money. Many remained indebted long after completion. While households with bigger families were being encouraged to build additional rooms, or access to the roof, most people did not have the resources to do so. Many mentioned that some additional low-interest loans would have been useful.

People prioritise risks and make trade-offs differently than the state, and both act based on their understanding of these risks as well as their abilities to respond to them. Different people prioritise risks differently depending on who they are, what they have, whom they can approach, etc. This informs each of their actions towards risk reduction and trade-offs. Those who stay close to the coastal areas have learned to deal with onsets of cyclones and flooding, but for them to not have a secure livelihood and access to other services is a much greater risk. The state is seen as inactive if it does not take actions to safeguard people from extreme events, and often takes actions to avoid this image, but ends up creating more everyday challenges for the people (see Chapter 4 by Johnson et al. in this book).

Implementation and its challenges

Operational challenges

Provision of temporary transit housing needs to be integral to housing schemes, including those that involve in situ housing, for greater success of the intervention. Although people who lost their houses in the disaster

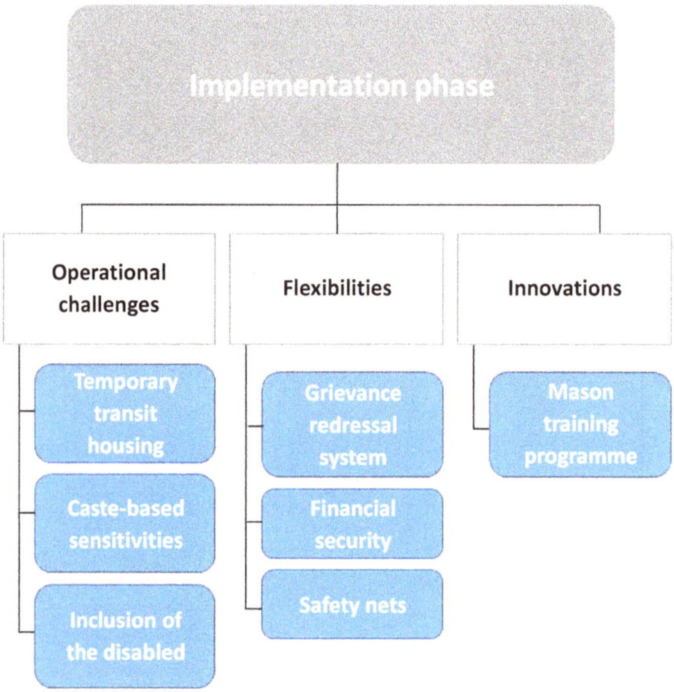

Figure 3.4 Operational conditions, programme flexibilities and innovations were key levers identified in the implementation processes that affected resettlement outcomes for people. © Garima Jain.

have been identified, and they have been offered newly constructed housing, provision of temporary housing is still a big challenge. In cases where in situ development is planned, e.g. in Sonia Gandhi Nagar in Visakhapatnam, people still need to find alternative locations to stay in until their promised homes are completed. But the insecurity of being excluded and other locational dependencies compel them to stay close to the construction sites, leaving them exposed to physical hazards and safety issues. These self-build 'temporary' shelters often propagate more informal settlements (Bornstein et al. 2013). Such a situation could be avoided if transit housing were made a formal part of the project.

In many cases people also choose to rent neighbouring houses so that they can continue with their original livelihoods, but not all are able to take the additional financial burden of a rent. In ODRP, some steps are taken to support people with rents and shifting allowances up to 12,000 rupees. But in other national and state scheme-related rehabilitations, temporary housing needs to become an important consideration.

There is still a lack of caste sensitivity at the time of beneficiary identification, and this is leading to high risks for some resettled households. Social clustering, particularly by caste, is deeply ingrained in India – both urban and rural – and has implications for the outcomes of R&R interventions. In rural Odisha, for instance, people of many castes cohabit these villages, but they have their own sub-communities which act as social binders and economic networks. We encountered a situation in Devinagar in Odisha, where a single lower-caste family was resettled along with other higher-caste families, and had to face serious challenges when a woman in the family had to deliver a child but there was no one willing to help or touch her. Higher-caste families are also wary of housing schemes such as RAY and JnNURM where they have to share common spaces with people from lower castes. While there is some consideration for caste-based allocations within the RAY, for instance, not being aware of this, beneficiaries remain wary of outcomes.

While one may be tempted to assume that caste-based vagaries of society could be reduced through such interventions by remaining 'caste-blind' and treating everyone 'equally', these practices are so deep-rooted that any forceful changes can only create more challenges, especially for the marginalised section. The participation of the community during planning, decision-making and allocation of housing units is one way of managing this. For example, in Markandi in Odisha, house allocations were carried out as per the community's suggestions on matters of caste and professional segregation. Three sites were identified for this one village, according to the needs of its three sub-communities.

Standard housing provisions are not accessible for the disabled. The Persons with Disabilities Act 1995 marked a shift in India when disability started being addressed from a rights-based instead of a largesse-based (generous gift) perspective. Steps have since been taken by governments to give preference to disabled people by providing housing to them on a priority basis. Yet the steps taken are currently not sufficient and the design of these projects further impairs access. For instance, some state governments offer wheelchairs to those who cannot walk after disasters. But design factors in these rehabilitation sites such as quality of internal roads and habitations being located on the seashore make these entitlements impractical and unusable. The act of accessing systems and services (common toilets, public water pipes, public transport to local markets, etc.) makes disabled people dependent on others for their daily needs. Even during emergency evacuations, the process was found to be extremely harsh for them.

Mental illness is another challenge and cannot be conflated with physical disability. This is understood even less, despite the fact that there are a large number of people living with such challenges, or those who experience mental trauma due to the disaster. In R&R interventions, it has been observed that priority is accorded to those who are physically disabled, but not to those who are mentally ill. Cases of mental illness are also much more difficult to identify as there are often no objective and universal characteristics to 'tick off' on a form. The verification process needs to be sensitised to enable people's inclusion and protect their rights.

Flexibilities

A multi-stage grievance redressal system needs to be in place, especially in urban areas. Some type 1 responders felt that they were left out for reasons other than not meeting the selection criteria. There are undertones of class and caste politics that may give some people more voice to gain access or raise concerns than others have. Although a four-stage grievance redressal system was set up for the ODRP's rural components in Ganjam with a ground verification system that seemed to work for people in having their needs addressed, no such system was planned for the project's urban component. Due to their heterogeneity, urban dwellers are unable to unite to demand their rights, and they are often left worse off than their rural counterparts. This problem was faced by those who were evicted, but had no recourse other than approaching the judiciary. This would take several years to come to any conclusion, disincentivising this course of action by most people. Elected council members, to whom people had access, were also seen to be politically biased and did not address issues equally for all.

Shelter is not the only need people have after a disaster, but they have no savings to fulfil those needs. All households we spoke with (158), in urban as well as rural areas, claimed to have bank accounts, which goes against popular belief. Many opened these accounts to receive disbursements from the government, including for house construction. At the same time, most people stated that they would either not use them due to lack of trust, or because they did not save enough to put in a bank; whatever little they did save, they kept at home for any emergency needs. Thus, having access to a bank account itself may not mean better financial security.

Many women we spoke to were part of more informal self-help groups (SHGs) or social kitty systems, where 20–25 women got together and put 10,000–20,000 rupees per person into one account. They used these funds based on their needs and returned the amount with interest over a fixed period of time. The system works primarily on the basis of the social trust that people have in each other. Many people who have asset-based livelihoods, such as grocery stores, were also seen investing in buying more assets for their shops, instead of retaining liquidity.

In disaster scenarios, where people have limited liquid assets or financial security, they are left with no other option but taking loans at very high rates. There is a need to improve people's awareness and their access to non-life and multi-hazard insurance products for housing and assets to help themselves recover in case of an extreme event. There could also be provisions made to provide low-interest loans as part of the rehabilitation schemes, to help people supplement for other needs not covered under the programme.

Formal and informal safety nets can be strengthened to improve people's resilience and ability to cope with losses due to hazard event impacts, thereby reducing the burden on the state for providing for housing losses. People trust their social knowledge more than formal knowledge, particularly when it comes to asking for help. Many women we spoke to who worked as domestic help in urban areas mentioned taking financial help from their employers at zero interest rates, as well as other health-related support. They got paid leave while rebuilding, which is uncommon even in many formal jobs. Many received regular subsidies on food supplies and other needs, while others took help from their neighbours, friends and relatives during and after the cyclone, but these cases were rarer in the urban context than the rural, potentially because of the large distances or the lack of adequate resources available to share.

There are also other institutionally supported yet informal safety nets. In the case of the informal settlement of Khaja Sahi in urban Odisha, after the cyclone flattened the entire neighbourhood, the local Muslim Trust helped the residents rebuild again. The Tata Group of Industries, as part of its 'corporate social responsibility', sent medical vans to the areas where their factories are located in Ganjam, and many people mentioned how their health costs have gone down dramatically since the vans started visiting. There is a need to understand and enhance these safety nets and people's access to them, even if they are informal.

Anganwadis (childcare and maternal support centres) and registered SHGs are formal institutions put in place by the government to provide support to people in different ways. While in a few situations, the anganwadis seemed to work well, in many others, particularly in urban areas, people raised concerns about trust, access and quality of services provided by their anganwadis. At the same time, anganwadi members also face many challenges in delivering their services. For instance, even if they were able to train people in generating livelihoods such as making candles, agarbattis (incense sticks), papads (crisp breads) or pickles, they did not have the capacity to market all the goods made by the residents, and so were unable to pay the latter as promised. This creates an atmosphere of mistrust towards the anganwadis, and they are even accused of corruption. Improved trust in anganwadis could in turn improve local resilience, as they could offer much-needed services during and after disasters in helping people recover, mentally and economically.

SHGs are meant to provide more financial support by using a saving pooling system. But in most instances, people are still involved in unregistered social kitty systems and are therefore not able to access other benefits, such as the National Development for Agriculture and Rural Development scheme of loans that is open for formal SHGs. If these informal SHGs could be brought under the formal system, they may also substantially help building peoples capabilities to self-recover.

Innovations

Innovative interventions such as the mason training programme described below could reduce the challenges of labour scarcity during large-scale interventions, but their impacts on long-term economic diversification and other social outcomes are still unknown. Large reconstruction projects right after a disaster lead to a shortage of material and labour. These are managed by bringing resources from neighbouring regions, but price escalation cannot always be avoided. This was envisioned at the outset in the ODRP project in Ganjam, where sixteen thousand houses were planned to be constructed. A local NGO, Gram Vikas, had been conducting mason training in these areas for a few years. They started training the beneficiaries to build their own and their neighbours' houses. It was observed in many cases that people, including women, who were earlier employed as unskilled labour were now able to earn a lot more after being trained. But a number of challenges were also noted.

According to the project community mobilisers, the training attracted people more for the stipend it paid than for the training itself, so attrition rates were high. Even for those who attended, people did not think that 30 days of training was enough for anyone to become a master mason, and many beneficiaries from the same village were not comfortable getting these newly trained masons to build their houses. This was mitigated by sending trainees to other villages instead, where people would not know the masons personally. It was observed that many men and women who were 60 years of age and above, and hence not eligible for the training, were using incorrect age proofs to get into the programme; they were advised by the mobilisers not to join the training as it could be a health hazard for them.

Many people who received training under this programme were observed to be migrating for work. They were earning 700 rupees per day in bigger cities versus 500 rupees per day in the rehabilitation sites. However, temporary reverse migration cases were also encountered, where unskilled labour migrants returned to the villages to get trained. Some women, who had been unskilled labourers and earned only 100 rupees, stated that they were earning considerably more, although they did not migrate for work.

The questions that remain unanswered are whether the vision of using the mason training programme to diversify people's incomes has been accomplished in the long term. While many women have attended the programme, it is yet to be determined if post-training earning has improved their status and empowered them more than before.

Some emerging questions

- Once the land is known to be exposed to hazards and is being vacated, could it still be considered for alternative uses? If yes, then with what justification and for what uses? If infrastructure upgrading is considered for using these sites for commercial purposes, then why are they not considered for rehousing people in situ? What are the costs and benefits of moving people and using these lands, versus keeping them there and upgrading the physical and social infrastructure, and who bears the burden of these costs and who gets the benefits?

- Does the 'objective' beneficiary identification process widen the inequality in society by excluding the already marginalised? Do these selection processes for interventions disincentivise self-investment in building resilience? In such scenarios, how can verification be made more subjective for beneficiary identification such that those in need do not lose out on entitlements?
- How can the state be made more aware of context-specific dependencies, caste sensitivities and everyday risks, and people made more aware of the hazard risks they are exposed to, so that a mutually agreeable and sustainable outcome can be achieved? Can a bridge between these differential understandings be built, and if yes, can that help incentivise better inclusion practice and better perceptions of hazard risk for the people?

Conclusion

The various processes and the contexts in which these decisions on resettlement and relocation are made have far-reaching impacts on implementation as well as outcomes. Resettlement almost always disturbs the balance of the existing neighbourhood, particularly if people have resided there for a long period of time, and the distances between the old and new locations are such that they disturb the existing locational dependencies. If the new locations do not address everyday socio-economic needs, people continue staying in existing locations. In situ housing, infrastructure upgrading or relocating nearby are preferred by most households, largely in that order, but the conditions for risk reduction without reducing exposure need to be assessed. Also, the problem of transit housing persists after the loss of shelter after disasters, lack of which could lead to extensions of informal settlements.

In many cases, people's experiences post-resettlement suggested that 'once resettled, long forgotten'. Many people in the post-cyclone resettled colonies in urban areas could not access public or private aid any longer owing to their distance from the city centre. While earlier they would manage to get back to normalcy quite quickly using their regular earnings, but with reduced income, this was also now difficult. Overall, when people's needs are not addressed in the long term, they are left more vulnerable than they were before getting resettled.

Pre-emptive relocation is difficult to undertake and faces the most resistance from the people. Other pre-emptive actions for reducing risk, using planning instruments and building capacity to adapt using risk-sharing mechanisms such as insurance, could be considered.

Housing undertaken in a purely developmental context often ignores hazard risk reduction, whereas post-disaster housing developments focus narrowly on reducing hazard exposure, and in the process create other socio-economic risks. Long-term and emerging climate risks are understood even less, and relocation interventions which may seem 'successful' now may still be exposed to hazards in the future.

Top-down decisions of relocating people as a means to reduce their hazard risk, often without enabling their participation in the process, have led to resistance and cases of forced eviction. This has further led to a lack of a sense of ownership from the people, and long-term functioning of these settlements suffers a great deal. Time taken between decisions, implementation and completion also affects the outcomes significantly; when it is too quick, participation could become difficult.

There is a clear relationship between land ownership and the decision to relocate or not, and this needs to be studied in greater detail.

The above findings merely provide some insights from the primary work in terms of new questions, but this chapter does not attempt to and is not able to provide all answers. While the insights might be from specific sites, they lead to questions which are relevant to the larger context of R&R after extreme events. These may not be an exhaustive set of concerns and questions but help frame the relationship between decision-making processes, implementation design and eventual outcomes on people and places. Although there was limited scope within this research to address all these emerging questions, the author invites greater discussion with a larger community to challenge existing norms and try to find practical solutions such that the outcomes of R&R interventions could be made more inclusive, thus making it possible to accomplish the intended objective of reducing risks and improving people's lives.

Acknowledgements

The author would like to acknowledge all the effort on and off the field that the Indian Institute for Human Settlements team (Teja Malladi, Amir Bazaz, Sushmita Ramoji, Aishwarya Balasubramanian and Sunil Kraloti) provided during the research project. The author would also like to thank Kaavya Kumar for copy-editing this piece.

Notes

1. The chapter is adapted from Jain, G. (2016) *Risk-Related Resettlement and Relocation in Urban Areas: Research framework and summary of findings. Site report I*. London: UCL.
2. In this chapter, I use the terms 'resettlement' and 'relocation' as defined in the framing of this book. Resettlement is a major integrated, comprehensive movement of people and families which normally involves significant distance between the original and new location. Resettlement involves not only new housing and services but also new social and economic relations, and new challenges such as access to work and social cohesion (Ferris 2014). Relocation, meanwhile, refers to non-systematic movements of families or individuals from hazard-prone locations to nearby areas. Relocation therefore would involve less upheaval in terms of access to work and social networks (Ferris 2012). In situ redevelopment is another approach used to improve living conditions at the same site, by housing upgrading, infrastructure improvements or both. This ensures minimal changes to all other connections people may have owing to their location. I use the term 'rehabilitation' as an overarching term that encompasses different forms of housing provisions, including relocation, resettlement or in situ redevelopment (Jain et al. 2017, 11).
3. For the purposes of this chapter, I define 'risk' as a composite of everyday socio-economic vulnerabilities, exposure to intensive or extensive natural hazards, and lack of capabilities to cope or adapt (UNISDR 2015). Effectively, I see 'risk reduction' in the context of overall developmental gains.

References

Bazaz, Amir, Sushmita Ramoji, Garima Jain and Teja Malladi. 2016. *Exploring Relocation Risk Assessment Methodologies and Findings*. Bangalore: Indian Institute for Human Settlements. https://doi.org/10.24943/cirf5.2016.

Behrampur Municipal Corporation [BeMC]. 2014a. *Detailed Project Report on Slum Redevelopment Project under Rajiv Awas Yojana – Phase VI*. Behrampur: Behrampur Municipal Corporation.

Behrampur Municipal Corporation [BeMC]. 2014b. *Detailed Project Report on Slum Redevelopment Project under Rajiv Awas Yojana – Phase VIII*. Behrampur: Behrampur Municipal Corporation.

Bhan, Gautam, Geetika Anand and Swastik Harish. 2014. *Policy Approaches to Affordable Housing in Urban India: Problems and possibilities*. Bangalore: Indian Institute for Human Settlements. https://smartnet.niua.org/content/09f2e91c-4bd5-4666-bb60-28ca6d891831.

Bornstein, Lisa, Gonzalo Lizarralde, Kevin A. Gould and Colin Davidson. 2013. 'Framing responses to post-earthquake Haiti: How representations of disasters, reconstruction and human settlements shape resilience'. *International Journal of Disaster Resilience in the Built Environment* 4 (1): 43–57.

Chandrasekhar, Divya, Yang Zhang and Yu Xiao. 2014. 'Nontraditional participation in disaster recovery planning: Cases from China, India, and the United States'. *Journal of the American Planning Association* 80 (4): 373–84. https://doi.org. /10.1080/01944363.2014.989399.

Ferris, Elizabeth. 2012. *Protection and Planned Relocations in the Context of Climate Change*. UNHCR Geneva. https://www.unhcr.org/protection/globalconsult/5024d5169/27-protection-planned-relocations-context-climate-change-elizabeth-ferris.html.

Ferris, Elizabeth. 2014. *Planned Relocations, Disasters and Climate Change: Consolidating good practices and preparing for the future. Background document. Sanremo consultation, 12–14 March, 2014*. UNHCR, Brookings-LSE and Georgetown University. https://www.unhcr.org/53c4d6f99.pdf.

Few, Roger, Hazel Marsh, Garima Jain, Chandni Singh and Mark Tebboth. 2021. 'Representing recovery: How the construction and contestation of needs and priorities can shape long-term outcomes for disaster-affected people'. *Progress in Development Studies*, forthcoming.

Government of Odisha, Asian Development Bank and World Bank. 2013. *India, Cyclone Phailin in Odisha, October 2013: Rapid damage and needs assessment report*. https://openknowledge.worldbank.org/bitstream/handle/10986/17608/838860WP0P14880Box0382116B00PUBLIC0.pdf?sequence=1.

Greater Visakhapatnam Municipal Corporation [GVMC]. 2015a. *JnNURM Housing: Occupation status of completed housing*. Visakhapatnam: Greater Visakhapatnam Municipal Corporation.

Greater Visakhapatnam Municipal Corporation [GVMC]. 2015b. *Layout and Area Wise Report under JnNURM Housing Scheme*. Visakhapatnam: Greater Visakhapatnam Municipal Corporation.

Jain, Garima. 2016a. *Risk-Related Resettlement and Relocation in Urban Areas: Research framework and summary of findings*. Bangalore: Indian Institute for Human Settlements. https://doi.org/10.24943/cirf1.2016.

Jain, Garima. 2016b. *Risk-Related Resettlement and Relocation in Urban Areas: Data from primary work (site report III)*. Bangalore: Indian Institute for Human Settlements. http://iihs.co.in/knowledge-gateway/wp-content/uploads/2017/09/Site-Report-for-Urban-Risks-and-Resettlements-III.pdf.

Jain, Garima, Chandni Singh, Karen Coelho and Teja Malladi. 2017. *Long-Term Implications of Humanitarian Responses: The case of Chennai*. London: International Institute for Development (IIED). http://pubs.iied.org/10840IIED.

Lewicka, Maria. 2011. 'Place attachment: How far have we come in the last 40 years?' *Journal of Environmental Psychology* 31 (3): 207–30. https://doi.org/10.1016/j.jenvp.2010.10.001.

Malladi, Teja, Garima Jain, Sushmita Ramoji, Sunil Kraleti, Aishwarya Balasubramanian and Mohan Raju JS. 2016. *Site Report for Urban Risks and Resettlements: Transcripts and appendices*. Bangalore: Indian Institute for Human Settlements. https://doi.org/10.24943/cirf4.2016.

Mathur, Hari Mohan. 2006. *Managing Resettlement in India: Approaches, issues, experiences*. New Delhi: Oxford University Press.

Olshansky, Robert and Stephanie Chang. 2009. 'Planning for disaster recovery: Emerging research needs and challenges'. *Progress in Planning* 72 (4): 200–9. https://doi.org/10.1016/j.progress.2009.09.001.

Olshansky, Robert B. and Laurie A. Johnson. 2017. *Clear as Mud. Planning for the Rebuilding of New Orleans*. Abingdon: Routledge.

Sarma, G.V. Prasada. 2015. 'Housing plan for hudhud-hit fishermen faces hurdles'. *The Hindu*, 24 June 2015. https://www.thehindu.com/news/cities/Visakhapatnam/housing-plan-for-hudhudhit-fishermen-faces-hurdles/article7349182.ece.

Scott, James C. 1998. *Seeing like a State: How certain schemes to improve the human condition have failed*. New Haven, CT: Yale University Press.

UN-Habitat. 2014. *The Right to Adequate Housing*. https://www.ohchr.org/documents/publications/fs21_rev_1_housing_en.pdf.

UNISDR. 2015. *Proposed Updated Terminology on Disaster Risk Reduction: A technical review*. https://www.preventionweb.net/files/45462_backgoundpaperonterminologyaugust20.pdf.

UN Secretary-General. 2016. *Report of the Open-Ended Intergovernmental Expert Working Group on Indicators and Terminology Relating to Disaster Risk Reduction*. https://www.preventionweb.net/files/50683_oiewgreportenglish.pdf.

Part 2
Understanding and interpreting risk

The three chapters in this part deal with the questions that arise when prompted with the need to reduce risk, either pre-emptively or post-disaster: how are 'risks' defined, by whom and at what scale, and how do these definitions of risks inform risk reduction approaches? They further enquire about what role 'at-risk' people have at various stages of decision-making, and what bearing these decision-making processes have on resettlement outcomes for the people and places at large.

Cassidy Johnson, Garima Jain and co-authors (Chapter 4), and Emily Wilkinson (Chapter 6), contrast institutional perspectives of risks with those prioritised by households and individuals. They point to many factors – including potential for livelihoods, dangers of poverty, existence of social networks, cultural identities and place attachment – that often outweigh the hazard risk for the people. Johnson et al. suggest looking at risk as a spectrum, where people's risk perception varies from acceptable through tolerable to unacceptable risks, informing their trade-offs as a means to maximise benefits in the context of their everyday risks. Johnson et al. as well as Shuaib Lwasa et al. (Chapter 5) highlight that people's position within this spectrum is not a static one, and that it changes over time with experiences and choices available for adaptation. They also bring to fore that for poor communities, especially those in the global South, abilities (or lack thereof) to take actions are a significant limiting factor affecting their choices for risk reduction measures.

Johnson et al. and Wilkinson note that, in contrast with communities, institutions tend to rely on specialised technical information to justify their understanding of risk. These framings are devoid of everyday risks that are integral to people's everyday developmental needs and wellbeing. Using cases from India, Peru and Montserrat, they illustrate how these understandings and definitions of risk find their way into legal, policy or investment frameworks, and how they play a consequential role in the conceptualisation and delivery of risk reduction interventions at scale. Such interventions, while made with an attempt of reducing risk, are often detrimental for overall developmental objectives.

Lwasa et al. present another perspective on risk in terms of geographical and temporal scales. They offer an approach to 'valuing' risk from the perspectives of households and policymaking processes but within the larger systemic regional conditions including changing climate, in the absence of which interventions taken could introduce new, unknown risks in the future. They suggest the use of the asset accumulation strategy to understand households' decision-making behaviours, but they also stress the role of institutions in asset building and in enabling or limiting households' accumulation of assets. Founding their argument on the principles of the social construction of risk, they stress the need to address endemic deficits in social, economic and environmental assets driven by inequitable processes of development, as a means to enable households to accumulate assets and reduce their own risks over time.

Wilkinson presents the Montserrat case as a unique condition counter to those presented through case studies of India, Uganda and Peru elsewhere in this book, where an infrequent but high-intensity long-lasting event such as a volcanic eruption widely changes perceptions of risks. This case also demonstrates that a longer-term view of risk (as was adopted by UK and local authorities, scientists and local communities) could result in substantial investments in safer locations. It offers lessons, especially for the Small Island Developing States (SIDS) and other cities in the global South where few options for resettlement exist, in terms of how to anticipate and plan for deliberative dialogues in the event of a major disaster.

Altogether, the three chapters do not suggest the need to calculate precisely how much risk is acceptable by who, or to create a no-risk condition; rather, they point towards building platforms that promote a shared understanding of risks between multiple actors, developing capacities to identify and mitigate processes which impose unacceptable threats on a part of the society, and promoting integration of these multi-stakeholder deliberative processes within larger developmental agendas. Drawing from all the cases presented – from Uganda, Peru, India and Montserrat – it becomes evident that achieving an agreement on the most appropriate risk management responses requires dialogue and well-integrated risk governance systems.

4
Risk as a subjective concept and its influence on decision-making

Cassidy Johnson, Garima Jain, Vineetha Nalla and José Delfín Cáceres-Martínez

There is ample evidence that points out that resettlement is not advisable, unless it is indeed the last resort (Jain et al. 2017), and can be achieved through a thorough, holistic, participatory and inclusive social process. Faced with this conclusion, then, why is it still undertaken, increasingly frequently, and who initiates it? When resettlement is promoted with the objective of reducing risks, either pre-emptively or post-disaster, how are 'risks' defined and by whom? How much power do 'at-risk' people have in these decisions and at what stages? Ultimately, what bearing do these decision-making processes have on the resettlement outcomes?

This chapter examines how different stakeholders interpret 'risk' and how this influences decisions about resettlement and relocation. Residents make habitation decisions based on their values and sets of available choices to cope with threats and take advantage of opportunities. The understanding of risk by the planning authorities is often divergent from that of residents. Policies that seek to reduce the collective burden of exposure to hazard for a given population tend not to factor in individual perspectives on why residents might choose to tolerate or accept certain risks. This divergence in views is important in the issue of resettlement, because how a person perceives their own risks and their ability to mitigate them, or how risk is calculated or understood by decision-makers, has a bearing on actions for risk reduction, including the decision as to whether to participate in/undertake resettlement and relocation or not.

The chapter opens with three case studies, from Peru, India and Uganda, researched during the 'Reducing Relocation Risk in Urban Areas' project. The cases are all different in the scale of resettlements undertaken and as regards who has the power to make decisions. The Peru and India cases exemplify institutional perspectives, while the Uganda case offers household-level approaches. Each of these cases examines: 1) how risk was 'calculated' and defined, 2) what were the legal frameworks and responsible institutions, 3) what alternatives were considered, apart from resettlement and relocation, 4) whether the affected had the power and agency to act and see risk differently than the institutions, and 5) the outcomes of relocation and resettlement. The case studies are followed by a discussion which seeks to engage with current understanding of risk perception and its influence on decision-making.

We find that legal and policy frameworks are increasingly important elements of how institutional actors perceive and act on risks. The concepts of 'unmitigable' in Peru and 'untenable' in India present visions of risk that are acted on by institutional actors, resulting in resettlement or relocation of communities that are determined to be 'at risk'. However, those conceptions of 'unmitigable' or 'untenable' derived through the application of policy seem to be very different from how communities or individuals see their own everyday risks. We argue that the concept of 'tolerable risks', what residents are willing to live with because of other trade-offs and opportunities, and 'tipping points', the point at which they decide that relocation or resettlement is necessary, must be examined and thus understood from the differing vantage points of communities, governments and other stakeholders (see also Chapter 15 by Kisembo in this volume on tipping points). We argue for the need for a common platform to engage with all stakeholders, build consensus on a shared understanding of risk, enhance their knowledge about hazard exposure, learn from them about the everyday needs and priorities, and arrive at a common consensus for subsequent actions towards risk reduction and longer-term sustainable and resilient development outcomes.

Case 1: Peru

In Peru, a special law exists on preventive and post-impact resettlement (see also Chapter 8 in this volume by Chávez Eslava). This was established in 2011 along with new laws on disaster risk management, as a reaction to various serious seismic and hydrological disaster events that occurred towards the end of the 1990s (the Arequipa earthquake and El Niño episode). The resettlement law enables the regional governments and the Ministry of Housing to declare 'non-mitigable risk areas', the founding argument for a resettlement to take place (Congreso de la Republica 2017a, 2017b). A non-mitigable risk area is defined as 'a zone where the probability exists that the population and its livelihoods will suffer damage and loss because of the impact of events and where the implementation of mitigation measures leads to greater costs and complexity than relocating housing and urban infrastructure' (Congreso de la Republica 2012).

In Peru, the expansion of urban areas over the last decades has been typified by increasing numbers of informal settlements, self-constructed, often in ecologically fragile areas, and with the 'legalisation' of unsafe lots and construction of risk reduction infrastructure in return for votes. According to official figures more than 21 million people live in conditions of extensive risk and 1 per cent of these are in areas of non-mitigable risk, subject to the need for resettlement (Lavell et al. 2015).

A national institution, the Centre for Estimation of Risk and Disaster Risk Prevention (CENEPRED), developed a risk evaluation tool, which aids in the identification of non-mitigable risk and is used as a basis for decisions on resettlement. The risk evaluation is essentially quantitative and uses a scientific approach based on numerical data and very limited qualitative information (Cáceres-Martínez 2017). The calculation of the probability of natural hazard incidence in a specific area is based on frequency and magnitude. The CENEPRED manual for risk assessment has detailed information on how to measure the possible hazard and requires multiple specialists to achieve this (CENEPRED 2014). For any such study, all relevant technical entities are required to participate, which can amount up to 15 institutions (Presidencia del Consejo de Ministros 2013). For measuring vulnerability, the current resettlement law establishes that the socio-economic baseline should be generated by the National Institute for Statistics and Informatics. The vulnerability of people and structures, defined by exposure, fragility and resilience, are assigned weighted averages. Once the level of hazard and the level of vulnerability are defined, the levels of risk are established following the criteria shown in Table 4.1. The thresholds for each vulnerability level are defined solely by the assessing entity or staff, based on their prior experience and knowledge, without participation or definition through consultation with affected communities. This leads to the conclusion that the decision is also political.

The resettlement law stipulates that a working group made up of persons from local, provincial and regional governments, as well as CENEPRED, decide on the resettlement process (Presidencia del Consejo de Ministros 2013). There have been numerous difficulties in applying

Table 4.1 The current resettlement law establishes the need for generating a baseline for vulnerability of people and structures, defined by exposure, fragility, and resilience based on assigned weighted averages. Level of risk are established based on level of vulnerability and hazard exposure. © Adapted by authors from CENEPRED (2014, 156).

Very high hazard	High risk	High risk	Very high risk	Very high risk
High hazard	Medium risk	Medium risk	High risk	Very high risk
Medium hazard	Low risk	Medium risk	Medium risk	High risk
Low hazard	Low risk	Low risk	Medium risk	High risk
	Low vulnerability	Medium vulnerability	High vulnerability	Very high vulnerability

the law, due to technical aspects being counterposed with political considerations, and a long list of legal requirements that need to be fulfilled (Lavell et al. 2015). Once approved, some resettlement projects have had to be suspended or remain unfinished. Others have been undertaken through special laws passed to promote them (which is contradictory or duplicative of the more general resettlement law). For example, the flood-prone area of lower Belén in Iquitos, Amazonia, following a 2014 presidential promise of relocation.

But what happens when someone does not want to take part in the process? Residents' views on the resettlement are secondary and not binding for the decisions on resettlement. In practice, the affected communities have undertaken strategies to resist resettlement outright, to delay it as much as possible or to negotiate the terms in which this resettlement takes place. Examples of this can be seen in the cases of Belén (see Chapter 8 by Chávez Eslava in this book) as well as several other cases across Peru, such as Polvorines, the Lomo de Corvina and Carosio. In all of these situations, many people consider that risk could be mitigated, that they have already built their lives and livelihoods around the place, and that the frequency of extreme events has previously stimulated them develop preparedness and mitigation measures on their own (Modesto n.d.).

Under the law, participation is intended only to provide information and feedback for the implementation of the resettlement process, rather than to influence the decision on proceeding with resettlement in the first place (Presidencia del Consejo de Ministros 2013). Although there are spaces for dialogue and community representatives on a resettlement committee, these are not binding or with voting rights.

Case 2: India

A quarter of the urban population of India lives in slums.[1] To address this challenge, the central and state governments often introduce affordable housing schemes with the objective to provide 'appropriate' housing for the poor. One such centrally sponsored scheme was introduced in 2011 called the Rajiv Awas Yojna or RAY (later, in 2014, renamed Pradhan Mantri Awas Yojna/PMAY) by the Ministry of Housing and Urban Poverty Alleviation (MoHUPA). According to the RAY guidelines, slums were categorised as tenable, semi-tenable and untenable – and intervention strategies were guided by these categories. Tenable slums were defined simply as those that were 'not untenable' and 'considered fit for in-situ redevelopment/improvement' (MoHUPA 2011, 32). 'Semi-tenable' slums were defined as those which were located on sites earmarked for non-residential uses, including government lands, and after further review would be categorised as tenable or untenable.

These definitions make the definition of untenable slums key. These have been defined as slums which were a 'safety' or 'health hazard' even if redeveloped. These would include slums located on major stormwater or other drains, railway lines, major transport alignment, banks of rivers or water bodies, or other hazardous or objectionable areas, including those proximate to high-tension electric lines. Such untenable sites were earmarked for resettlement, preferably within the same zone or ward. But owing to the 'unavailability' of land, in practice, they have been moved to more distant locations. In a sense, this definition of 'untenability' assumes that the conditions of hazard exposure could not be addressed by any other intervention (such as infrastructure upgrading).

Meanwhile, it is argued that a robust methodology for measuring such tenability is not universally applied, and many resettlement programmes are pursued on the grounds of 'untenability' (*Counterview* 2015). In situ upgrading is often rejected by public authorities arguing that the community is 'untenable' not because of the presence of a hazard but, rather, because they do not adhere to the minimum development control norms or service level benchmarks (Bhan, Anand and Harish 2014). Our research, which looked at decision-making processes and outcomes of such resettlement interventions, showed that low-income households build dwellings and settlements over time, and those who have lived in these locations for several years tend to develop adaptation/coping strategies to deal with the hazard risks (Malladi et al. 2016). We found that the allowable intervention strategies for such slums could be widened, to include in situ redevelopment or slum upgrading, for instance, and resettlement should be avoided since it tends to increase the socio-economic burden on the people, apart from a financial, political and environmental burden on the city at large.

For illustration, consider the case of Sevanagar, a slum settled for decades on railway authority-owned land in Visakhapatnam (Andhra Pradesh, India) which was identified as 'untenable' by the local authorities under the RAY programme. The railway company received the help of the Greater Visakhapatnam Municipal Corporation (GVMC) to evict the residents on the pretext of hazard reduction and their 'untenable' status. According to anecdotal sources, in return the railways gave GVMC a larger piece of land on the periphery of the city. Despite a court case between the evicted residents and the railways and GVMC, the vacated area was developed as a railway stadium, nullifying the definition of 'untenability' on account of un-addressable exposure. Meanwhile, the residents were resettled as part of the RAY programme more than 25 km northward in Madhurvada, with limited access to livelihood options or social services. The poor social, psychological and economic outcomes following the eviction were felt deeply by the residents in their day-to-day lives. In addition, they were also left worse off during Cyclone Hudhud in 2014, when they did not receive any aid or government help owing to their distance from the centre (Malladi et al. 2016).

This is one of the many instances where resettlement has been undertaken pre-emptively on the grounds of false risk reduction arguments (Jain et al. 2017; Menon-Sen and Bhan 2008). It illustrates the unidimensional understanding of risk and risk reduction approaches, the skewed power dynamics in these decision-making processes devoid of any participation, and poor developmental outcomes disproportionately experienced by already poor people.

India also has a weak national policy, legal framework or safety net mechanisms to protect or compensate such internally displaced populations, especially those affected by disasters or resettled on account of risk. The 2004 National Policy on Rehabilitation and Resettlement did not accommodate the government's own experience of resettlement and relocation in the past 50 years of dealing with development, disaster and ethnicity-induced displacement. The policy gave no guidelines for calculating the cost or damage to a family but rather allocates an arbitrarily fixed amount of 10,000 rupees per family, which ultimately harms the interests of the affected family (Kumar, Das and Banerjee 2004).[2] It does not specify the timeframe for the rehabilitation, or the right to say 'no' to being displaced. Moreover, these measures cover only 'project affected people', i.e. development-induced resettlements, and not those affected by disasters or pre-emptive action, such as those described above. These concerns continue in the 'updated' 2007 Policy (Ministry of Rural Development 2007).

The 2013 Land Acquisition Rehabilitation and Resettlement Act aimed to provide fair rehabilitation of landowners and those directly affected by the loss of livelihoods due to resettlement with fair compensation of land. It included persons residing in areas affected by natural hazard-based calamities, as a provision under the 'Urgency Clause'. But the abuse of this clause has raised questions about land acquisitions in such scenarios, or their pretext, and what goes beneath, in the guise of development (Goswami 2011).

Case 3: Uganda

In Uganda's capital city, Kampala, it is estimated that 85 per cent of the 1.8 million residents live in informal settlements (see also Chapter 15 by Kisembo in this book). Rapid urbanisation has exacerbated a land shortage, leading to intense formal and informal encroachment on wetland areas, which are more prone to flooding. Despite an awareness of the problems and clear understanding of the importance of wetland management for the sustainability of Kampala's infrastructure and quality of life, the Kampala Capital City Authority (KCCA) has a very low capacity to stop encroachment. This is partly because of the value of the wetlands as a site for industrial development, enabled through the Industrial Location Policy (Lwasa et al. 2009). Moreover, complex and overlapping land tenure patterns seemingly limit the powers of the local government to enforce compliance with environmental regulatory measures meant to protect the wetlands, leading to informal settlements in wetland areas.

Unlike Peru and India, Uganda has no specific policy on resettling or relocating people from exposed or high-risk areas.[3] However, from our study, we found that disaster risk-induced relocation and resettlement does occur in Kampala in two distinct situations (Barrow et al. 2016a, 2016b). Firstly, when people make their own decisions to relocate autonomously from highly flood-prone areas if they have the means to (see Chapter 15 by Kisembo in this book). Secondly, in the case of urban infrastructure projects to address disaster risks where resettlement has been enacted to make way for drainage improvements. The resettlement within these projects, for example Kampala Institutional and Infrastructure Development Project and its successor, are subject to the regulatory controls of the Resettlement Policy Framework, and attendant World Bank resettlement guidelines (see Chapter 9 by Marx in this book). Our case study in this chapter focuses on autonomous relocation processes, because this is where decisions about relocation are more directly affected by perceptions of risk.

The research focused on two case studies of informal settlements in Kampala, Bwaise III and Natete. These neighbourhoods were chosen because they are both affected by flooding on a regular basis and they both have a large-scale drainage infrastructure project planned or implemented. The two settlements are centrally located within the city, but have different economic contexts; one is a grain and agricultural processing area (Natete), whereas the other has a stronger service economy (Bwaise). Interviews with households, businesses and other stakeholders looked at the drivers, the tipping points and limits of acceptable risks that push or enable people to move out of flooding areas.

The research revealed that households' autonomous decision-making about whether to move or stay in a particular location is a trade-off between the opportunities or benefits that the location provides and the risks or costs of living with frequent flooding events. Thus, the way that residents view risk is related to, or in tension with, other factors that they value in their lives.

There are several reasons that people tolerate the flood risks in Bwaise and Natete. One of the reasons for settling in these neighbourhoods is the cost of land and the ease of access to land through informal means. For example, access to land is predominantly through family or other social connections within Bwaise, and land in the two settlements is affordable compared to other locations. Secondly, many households interviewed indicated that they have lived in the area for more than 20 years; their life revolves and evolves around these neighbourhoods with livelihoods and investments (largely in housing). For example, in Natete the attractiveness emerges from these social relationships, the affordability of living in the area, proximity to jobs and opportunities, and good transport links, which reduce living costs. Connected to livelihoods are the issues of relocation costs that include costs for land, building houses and travel to working locations if such relocation is to places distant from the city. Some of the relocated households that were interviewed indicated that the cost of living becomes higher, because they have been moved away from easy access to their jobs.

Despite the arguably high degree of tolerance of flood risk in the settlements, there are some households that moved from the settlements due to flood risk. For example, in Natete for the households that relocated, the tipping point is when floodwaters inundate the houses consistently for long periods during the rainy seasons. Health risks, such as reported outbreaks of cholera, have also played a role in making households consider relocating in both settlements. Some have relocated temporarily, perhaps seasonally (only to return during the dry season), or moved back after temporary settlement in other locations. However, those moving out permanently could be relatively well-off (by the standards of these neighbourhoods) households that had the capacity to relocate, taking into account the costs of relocation. Others have been able to sell off their land rights to buffer the relocation costs. Relocation is a luxury and generally only those with the means to relocate can do so.

Discussion

That risk is socially constructed and is not limited to hazard exposure is now a widely accepted perspective (IPCC 2012). But who decides the threshold beyond which risk is too great to bear? What methodology do authorities use in their calculations in situations of potential resettlement? There are two specific elements at play here: one is around power, and who has the power to make decisions or take actions; the other is how those in power measure or perceive the risk. Risk is essentially a subjective concept and the threshold of tolerable risk varies by circumstance. Despite this, as can be seen in the Peru and India cases, authorities attempt and need to establish supposedly objective calculations of risk.

Institutional perspectives on risk

Formal institutions, such as the Ministry of Housing in Peru or MoHUPA in India in the case studies described above, are tasked with addressing development issues at scale, and they rely on specialised technical information to justify their understanding of risk. This specialised information is largely based on historical data, which has traditionally been biased towards documenting intensive catastrophic events, instead of the more frequent but smaller everyday losses, even though it is the latter that may form the bulk of the total losses experienced (UNISDR 2009). This produces a large 'primary bias' among institutions of over-estimating the rare causes of losses, and under-estimating the more frequent but less intense risks (Lichtenstein et al. 1978). This explains why intensive risks attract more political, administrative and media attention, and therefore more resource allocations.

Risks to poorer communities remain unaccounted for, as their assets are neither perceived to be 'significant' at a larger scale nor are they insured. Current valuation processes look at insured losses and do not effectively capture the losses experienced by the poor, even in extreme events. There are limited tools accessed for measuring everyday risks, that are largely driven by inequality, poverty and other more invisible/intangible socio-economic conditions. While everyday risks and vulnerabilities accumulate over time (Bull-Kamanga et al. 2003), there is an evident disconnect in official practices and parlance between these developmental deficits and disaster losses. As is evident in the Peru and India case studies, the authorities do not account for these developmental deficits in their calculations.

Bornstein et al. (2013) and Scott (1998) explain how states use different instruments such as cadastral maps, housing types or building codes to make society 'legible', simplified and standardised for easy functioning. As in Peru, for the sake of this simplicity and objectivity, the most tangible factors end up being considered in risk assessment frameworks and thereby policymaking processes: hazard risk exposure. Linder and Peters (2016) also suggest that the process by which these tools are chosen are important political considerations. They argue that the way state representatives perceive these instruments 'conditions their views of problem situations, biases their expectations of performance and shapes their choices … these perceptions operate within a complex ecology of contexts, beginning with the decision-maker's immediate organisational circumstances and extending to features of their political system' (Linder and Peters 2016, 1). Particular realities of people's lives are represented and homogenised, which helps consolidate a state's power.

The case studies of Peru and India exemplify how these understandings and definitions find their way into legal and policy frameworks, and how they play a consequential role in the conceptualisation and delivery of risk reduction interventions at scale. The processes of identifying 'unmitigable' or 'untenable' areas are based on a limited view of risk and risk mitigation options available. Once these laws are formulated, detailed context-specific economic, political and social feasibility studies are not undertaken to arrive at alternative risk management options such as infrastructure upgrading or in situ redevelopment (Correa 2011); the only means assumed to reduce hazard exposure is through resettlement and relocation. They also under-estimate adaptation strategies adopted by people living in hazard-prone areas. It is becoming increasingly common for development institutions and formal organisations to focus on the identification of 'at-risk' populations and the creation of vulnerability maps through participatory exercises. These exercises have a strong focus on the technical aspects in order to quantify reducing disaster risks, with little evaluation of the impacts of these efforts (Bowman and White 2012). In Uganda, the state does not exercise this power, which is partly due to the complexity of land tenure arrangements (see Chapter 9 by Marx in this book).

These laws are rigid and often place too much power in the hands of the few (Jain et al. 2017). They legitimise the actions undertaken by the state, even if they are used as a garb of risk reduction to pursue other agendas, including city 'beautification' by removing unwanted slums (for an example, see Chapter 14 by Jain, Singh and Malladi in this book). As has been the case in India, there is little scope built within them for people to deny, resist or affect such resettlement interventions. There are no meaningful transformative participation processes envisioned or undertaken as part of these frameworks (Chandrasekhar, Zhang and Xiao 2014). Unless the institutions involved have a strong long-term monitoring and evaluation framework and a knowledge system that informs their policies, these institutions continue with the same practices, with little learned from long-term outcomes of the previous investments.

Individual-level and collective risks: acceptability of risks and tipping points

There is a tendency among policymakers and practitioners to believe that 'more and better' hazard-based information could help people understand their risks 'better'. But O'Sullivan et al. (2012) find that this 'infor mation deficit model' for risk communication is insufficient and that the communications process needs to be multidimensional, taking into account people's own perspectives of risks. We also find in our case studies from Peru, India and Uganda that people tend to deal with a wider array of risks, and they see them differently from the siloed formal institutional approaches. People prioritise between these various risks based on their level of acceptability of living with them, informed by their perceptions and abilities (Correa 2011).

The levels of risk acceptability could be seen as a spectrum: acceptable, tolerable and unacceptable risks. To understand these conceptually, let's take the example of housing. According to the Office of the United Nations High Commissioner for Human Rights (OHCHR) and UN-Habitat (2014), 'adequate housing' is more than a physical shelter; it must also fulfil other functions including accessibility to services and livelihoods, security of tenure, physical safety and cultural adequacy, within the affordable means of the household. Our research in Uganda shows that poor and marginal households find it difficult to garner all these functions within their means, and are left with no choice but to make trade-offs. Considering that access to livelihoods is directly connected to their ability to afford, giving it up is an unacceptable choice. But in order to ensure access and affordability, they agree to tolerate a trade-off in the form of physical safety and security of tenure. This condition of making choices predisposes them to live with greater risks, including those due to hazard exposure.

Here, 'tolerability' must not be equated with 'acceptability'. Tolerability is the willingness to live with 'controllable' risk so as to secure certain benefits. This risk may not be negligible or something that could be ignored, but rather something to be kept under review and reduced further if possible. 'Acceptable' risk, on the other hand, is what one may be prepared to take as is, for maximising opportunities or benefits needed for the purposes of life or work (Correa 2011; Health and Safety Executive 1992). This distinction is based on the premise that in no condition is the risk absolutely zero and that there is always a certain level of risk everyone accepts living with: similar to the idea of 'risk appetite' as used in the insurance and banking industries (Deloitte 2014).

As such, trade-offs can be understood as a means with which different actors negotiate between the different acceptable and unacceptable risks, and eventually choose to live with a set of 'accepted' risks. But people's position within this spectrum of acceptability of risk is not a static one. Risk acceptability changes over time with experiences and choices available (Whittaker 1986). As is seen through the case study in Kampala, households can experience 'tipping points', owing to either sudden events or accumulation of losses over time, that change the way what they value is at risk. Therefore, people's acceptability of risk is informed by their perceptions of risks and what they value, and these perceptions are further influenced by many factors that vary widely situationally, across individuals (e.g. men and women) or as collectives.

So far research has investigated the evaluation, decision-making and trade-offs at an individual or a household level. However, collective patterns of risk perception at the community or even population level are far less explored (Moussaïd 2013). Research in this line of inquiry shows that while individuals' personal experience and existing socio-economic conditions play a major role in the perception of risk and how they respond to it (Gaillard 2008; Wisner et al. 2004), 'individual risk judgements tend to be correlated with the proximity of individuals in their social network' (Moussaïd 2013, 1). Collective perceptions of risk, and how people respond to it, seem to be linked to the social group within which these interactions are taking place. This is perhaps significant for how whole neighbourhoods in Kampala tolerate risks despite the presence of serious hazards.

Some such factors that influence perceptions of risk are explored by different disciplines. The 'social amplification of risk' framework proposed by Kasperson et al. (1988) suggests that informal dwellers face challenges on a daily basis to access basic services to build a livelihood. Hence, they see a 'disaster' as something that amplifies these challenges rather than as a single rare mega-event. Therefore, what formal institutions may see as an emergency/catastrophe is part of a continuum of everyday risks for the poor. According to this notion, although disasters are absolute, the knowledge of them and the way they are perceived is socially constructed. Certain aspects of the disaster interact with social, cultural and economic processes that may increase or decrease the perceptions of risk.

Environmental psychology literature suggests that people's relationship with place, in the form of dependence, attachment or identity, can shape their perception of risks associated with living in that place (Quinn et al. 2018). The longer someone lives in a place, the stronger the attachment is likely to be (Lewicka 2011). Although there is no consensus in the literature on the relationship between attachment and the perception of environmental risk, our research in India and Uganda suggests that longer-term residents seem to put less emphasis on hazard risk exposure than on other meanings they associated with the place, including social links, access to social services, etc.

Perception of risk and actors' ability to mitigate them informs their decision-making

Although the loss of life, injury and destruction of assets are the realities of a disaster, the question of 'what is at risk' is perceived differently by different actors. While government organisations and other formal institutions identify disasters as a risk to tangible assets such as property, life and economic resources, the people fear loss of safety and security of their homes, their social relations, and their livelihood opportunities which are at risk from the disaster. The two divergent perspectives of defining risk by the people and institutions ultimately inform their respective risk reduction actions.

Risk literature points out that perceptions of risk influence the adaptation or coping measures taken by people, including decisions to move or stay. But high perception of hazard risk does not prevent them from living in high-risk areas, because people's behaviour is influenced by both hazard- and non-hazard-related risk factors (Gaillard 2008). In addition, our study also points out that this decision-making is moderated by people's abilities, owing to their resource access and socio-economic conditions. Poorer people, despite their high level of perception of risk, do not have many alternative choices for risk-mitigating actions (see Chapter 15 by Kisembo in this book).

Some studies (largely based in developed country contexts) have attempted to look at the moderating effects of place attachment on risk adaptation behaviour in high-risk areas (Quinn et al. 2018; Lewicka 2011; De Dominicis et al. 2015). They point out that 'place attachment may function as a barrier for enacting preventive behaviours in order to cope with an environmental risk, especially when the perceived risk is higher due to the exposition to a higher objective risk' (De Dominicis et al. 2015, 72). These perspectives, although useful, do not include the role of the choices of adaptation available to the people as a limiting factor. Our case studies from the global South indicate a strong role of the 'abilities', or lack thereof, to take actions as a significant factor that affects people's choices and decision-making.

At the same time, we find through our research across all three regions that institutional approaches for risk reduction are narrowly focused on hazard risk reduction that directs them towards limited options for risk reduction approaches. Furthermore, the approaches taken tend to disrupt the already limited choices of actions available to people. Urban communities, such as those in Kampala who live along waterways, move out frequently, due to flooding. This sort of routine or pattern of coping behaviour helps them in reducing the construction and accumulation of risk. However, this routine is ruptured when communities are moved into 'stronger' structures elsewhere, and this rupturing of routine itself can be viewed as a risk.

Formal institutions tend to approach risk reduction from a position of 'better knowledge' and see themselves as the custodians of this knowledge and information. This information asymmetry, often including deliberate withholding of information from communities by the government, also creates greater risks for them, affecting their choice of coping mechanism. Communities are sometimes unaware of the risks they are exposed to objectively, whether they will be relocated or evicted, and their rights to stay, or even when and why are they being evicted. This renders them incapable of making decisions for their own risk reduction.

Shared understanding of resilience targets and pathways of action

In practice, there is value to both objective and subjective risk assessments. The former can enable a scientifically informed understanding of the issues, especially those due to changes likely to occur in the future, while the latter can facilitate consensus building and, in effect, promote political willingness among the people (Correa 2011). Eventually, the objective is not to calculate precisely the 'acceptable risk' or to create a no-risk condition; rather, it is to create the capacity to identify and mitigate processes which might impose unacceptable threats on part of society (Phillips, Jones and Thomas 2018; Brown 1970).

We found through our research and consultative exercises that there are ways these divergent understandings of risk and acceptable levels of risk could be aligned better, which in turn could affect the decision-making processes and therefore the outcomes on the people and the larger system. Sharing of 'technical' information with the people gives them a better perspective on their hazard risk exposure and decision-making opportunities. Consensus-building exercises to create a shared understanding of acceptable levels of current and future risk, agree on target resilience levels, and envision pathways for action could lead to better overall outcomes. These exercises can build a culture of more meaningful and transformative participatory processes (Chandrasekhar, Zhang and Xiao 2014). Overall, giving people the agency to affect their own risk reduction outcomes is likely to be one of the more sustainable approaches for development outcomes. At the same time, it is also critical for states to focus on improving overall development conditions and building systems that help people improve their own asset base, which can in turn widen their choices and abilities for adaptation.

Apart from more participatory methodologies available for preparing better preventative resettlements for risk reduction (Correa 2011), there is also evidence emerging from global South contexts that supports this approach for building consensus as a way for long-term sustainable and resilient outcomes. The well-known experiences from Thailand's Baan Mankong programme suggests the possibilities of building state institutions, like the Community Organizations Development Institute (CODI), which can work in close consensus with flood-affected low-income communities to arrive at mutually acceptable and more resilient solutions (Boonyabancha 2003; Castanas et al. 2016; Ratanawaraha 2016). Our study of the Odisha Disaster Recovery Project in rural Odisha (see Chapter 3 by Jain in this book) illustrates the potential of multi-level grievance redressal systems that can improve communication between the people and formal departments, which gives more agency not just to the communities but also to the front-line officers to take more measured and context-specific actions. Cases in Uganda (Vlaeminck et al. 2016) and India (see Chapter 3 by Jain in this book) suggest that giving people better incentives (such as higher compensation, better infrastructure at the relocation sites, closer locational choices, etc.), for instance even in resettlement interventions, could also improve people's own views and choices for decision-making.

Conclusion

This chapter has looked at how risk is perceived differently by residents than public agencies. It has tried to delve into the reasons behind this, looking at why government institutions or policymakers look at risk the way they do. We critiqued the narrow perspective that is often taken that blinds institutions to seeing wider criteria of livelihoods and services that are important to people's lives and to development. We have also looked at how communities and individuals see risk as integral to many decisions they take on a daily basis. One of the elements that became clear through the research is that the negotiation, education and communication about the different views and perceptions of risk needs to be an integral part of a multi-stakeholder deliberative process, thinking through the feasibility of different options. This is rarely applied in practice, but needs to be.

Notes

1. https://data.worldbank.org/indicator/EN.POP.SLUM.UR.ZS?locations=IN.
2. It mentions, 'In case of projects relating to Railway Lines, High-ways, Transmission Lines and laying pipelines wherein only a narrow stretch of land extending over several kilometres is being acquired, the Project Affected Families will be offered an ex-gratia amount of Rs. 10,000 per family, and no other Resettlement & Rehabilitation benefits shall be available to them.'
3. There has been one rural resettlement project undertaken from the slopes of Mount Elgon in Eastern Uganda, after a landslide in 2011 (Vlaeminck et al. 2016).

References

Barrow, Charlotte, Cassidy Johnson, Teddy Kisembo, Shuaib Lwasa and Colin Marx. 2016a. 'Uganda: cost & benefit analysis'. *Reducing Relocation Risk in Urban Areas*. https://www.ucl.ac.uk/bartlett/development/sites/bartlett/files/wp3_cost_benefit_dpu_report_rev.pdf.

Barrow, Charlotte, Cassidy Johnson, Shuaib Lwasa and Colin Marx. 2016b. 'Uganda: Site level report'. *Reducing Relocation Risk in Urban Areas*. https://www.ucl.ac.uk/bartlett/development/sites/bartlett/files/wp2_site_level_dpu_report_rev.pdf.

Bhan, Gautam, Geetika Anand and Swastik Harish. 2014. *Policy Approaches to Affordable Housing in Urban India: Problems and possibilities*. Bangalore: Indian Institute for Human Settlements. https://smartnet.niua.org/sites/default/files/resources/IIHS_Housing.pdf.

Boonyabancha, Somsook. 2003. *A Decade of Change: From the Urban Community Development Office (UCDO) to the Community Organizations Development Institute (CODI) in Thailand. Increasing community options through a national government development programme*. London: International Institute for Environment and Development.

Bornstein, Lisa, Gonzalo Lizarralde, Kevin A. Gould and Colin Davidson. 2013. 'Framing responses to post-earthquake Haiti: How representations of disasters, reconstruction and human settlements shape resilience'. *International Journal of Disaster Resilience in the Built Environment* 4 (1): 43–57. DOI:10.1108/17595901311298991.

Bowman, Luke and Paul White. 2012. '"Community" perceptions of a disaster risk reduction intervention at Santa Ana (Ilamatepec) volcano, El Salvador'. *Environmental Hazards* 11 (2): 138–54. https://doi.org/10.1080/17477891.2011.609880.

Brown, James M. 1970. 'Probing the law and beyond: A quest for public protection from hazardous product catastrophes'. *George Washington Law Review* 38 (3): 431–62.

Bull-Kamanga, Liseli, Kade Diagne, Allan Lavell, Esteban Leon, F. Lerise, H. MacGregor, A. Maskrey, M. Meshack, M. Pelling, H. Reid et al. 2003. 'From everyday hazards to disasters: The accumulation of risk in urban areas'. *Environment and Urbanization* 15 (1): 193–204. https://doi.org./10.1177%2F095624780301500109.

Cáceres-Martínez, José Delfín. 2017. 'Resettlement and risk perception in a post disaster context: The case of Lima in the aftermath of El Niño phenomenon', master's thesis, UCL.

Castanas, Nausica, Ploy Kasama Yamtree, Batan Yoswadee Sonthichai and Quentin Batréau. 2016. 'Leave no one behind: Community-driven urban development in Thailand'. London: International Institute for Environment and Development.

CENEPRED. 2014. *Manual Para La Evaluación de Riesgos Originados Por Fenómenos Naturales: 2da versión*. Lima: CENEPRED. https://www.cenepred.gob.pe/web/wp-content/uploads/Guia_Manuales/Manual-Evaluacion-de-Riesgos_v2.pdf.

Chandrasekhar, Divya, Yang Zhang and Yu Xiao. 2014. 'Nontraditional participation in disaster recovery planning: Cases from China, India, and the United States'. *Journal of the American Planning Association* 80 (4): 373–84. https://doi.org./10.1080/01944363.2014.989399.

Congreso de la República. 2012. *Ley No. 29869: Ley de Reasentamiento Poblacional para Zonas de muy Alto Riesgo no Mitigable*. Lima: CENEPRED. https://cenepred.gob.pe/web/wp-content/uploads/2018/06/ley_29869.pdf.

Congreso de la República. 2017a. *Ley No. 30556: Ley que Aprueba Disposiciones de Carácter Extraordinario para las Intervenciones del Gobierno Nacional frente a Desastres y que Dispone la Creación de la Autoridad para la Reconstrucción con Cambios*. Lima. https://busquedas.elperuano.pe/normaslegales/ley-que-aprueba-disposiciones-de-caracter-extraordinario-par-ley-n-30556-1514994-1.

Congreso de la República. 2017b. *Ley No. 30645: Ley que Modifica la Ley 29869, Ley de Reasentamiento Poblacional para Zonas de muy Alto Riesgo no Mitigable*. Lima. https://busquedas.elperuano.pe/normaslegales/ley-que-modifica-la-ley-29869-ley-de-reasentamiento-poblaci-ley-n-30645-1555415-5.

Correa, Elena. 2011. *Populations at Risk of Disaster: A resettlement guide*. With Fernando Ramírez and Haris Sanauja. Washington, DC: World Bank and GFDRR. https://www.gfdrr.org/sites/gfdrr/files/publication/resettlement_guide_150.pdf.

Counterview. 2015. 'Most of the slums can be considered tenable and hence must be taken up for in-situ upgradation'. 22 April 2015. https://counterview.org/2015/04/22/most-of-the-slums-can-be-considered-tenable-and-hence-must-be-taken-up-for-in-situ-upgradation.

De Dominicis, Stefano, Ferdinando Fornara, Uberta Ganucci Cancellieri, Clare Twigger-Ross and Marino Bonaiuto. 2015. 'We are at risk, and so what? Place attachment, environmental risk perceptions and preventive coping behaviours'. *Journal of Environmental Psychology* 43: 66–78. https://doi.org/10.1016/j.jenvp.2015.05.010.

Deloitte. 2014. *Risk Appetite Frameworks: How to spot the genuine article*. Sydney: Deloitte. https://www2.deloitte.com/content/dam/Deloitte/au/Documents/risk/deloitte-au-risk-appetite-frameworks-0614.pdf.

Gaillard, Jean-Christophe. 2008. 'Alternative paradigms of volcanic risk perception: The case of Mt Pinatubo in the Philippines'. *Journal of Volcanology and Geothermal Research* 172 (3–4): 315–28. https://doi.org/10.1016/j.jvolgeores.2007.12.036.

Goswami, Amlanjyoti. 2011. *Land Acquisition, Rehabilitation and Resettlement: Law and politics*. Bangalore: Indian Institute for Human Settlements. https://iihs.co.in/knowledge-gateway/wp-content/uploads/2017/05/Land-Acquisition.pdf.

Health and Safety Executive. 1992. *The Tolerability of Risk from Nuclear Power Stations*. http://www.onr.org.uk/documents/tolerability.pdf.

IPCC. 2012. *Managing the Risks of Extreme Events and Disasters to Advance Climate Change Adaptation: A special report of working groups I and II of the Intergovernmental Panel on Climate Change*. Edited by Chirstopher B. Field, Vicente Barros, Thomas F. Stocker, Qin Dahe, David J. Dokken, Kristie L. Ebi, Michael D. Mastrandrea et al. Cambridge and New York: Cambridge University Press.

Jain, Garima, Cassidy Johnson, Allan Lavell, Shauib Lwasa, Anthony Oliver-Smith and Emily Wilkinson. 2017. *Risk-Related Resettlement and Relocation in Urban Areas*. CDKN Essentials. https://cdkn.org/wp-content/uploads/2017/07/Risk-related-resettlement-CDKN.pdf.

Kasperson, Roger E., Ortwin Renn, Paul Slovic, Halina S. Brown, Jacque Emel, Robert Goble, Jeanne X. Kasperson and Samuel Ratick. 1988. 'The social amplification of risk: A conceptual framework'. *Risk Analysis* 8 (2): 177–87. https://doi.org/10.1111/j.1539-6924.1988.tb01168.x.

Kumar, Madhuresh, Samir Kumar Das and Paula Banerjee. 2004. *People On The Move: How governments manage moving populations*. Kolkata: Mahanirban Calcutta Research Group. http://www.mcrg.ac.in/pp1.pdf.

Lavell, Allan, Elizabeth Mansilla, Angel Chávez Eslava, Omar D. Cardona and Maria Pilar Perez. 2015. 'Colombia, Peru & Mexico: Diagnostic report'. *Reducing Relocation Risk in Urban Areas*. https://www.ucl.ac.uk/bartlett/development/sites/bartlett/files/diagnostic_flacso_english_spanish_v2.pdf.

Lewicka, Maria. 2011. 'Place attachment: How far have we come in the last 40 years?' *Journal of Environmental Psychology* 31 (3): 207–30. https://doi.org/10.1016/j.jenvp.2010.10.001.

Lichtenstein, Sarah, Paul Slovic, Baruch Fischhoff, Mark Layman and Barbara Combs. 1978. 'Judged frequency of lethal events'. *Journal of Experimental Psychology: Human Learning and Memory* 4 (6): 551–78.

Linder, Stephen H. and Guy Peters. 2016. 'Instruments of government: Perceptions and contexts'. *Journal of Public Policy* 9 (1): 35–58. https://doi.org/10.1017/S0143814X00007960.

Lwasa, Shuaib, M. Tenywa, G.J. Majaliwa Mwanjalolo, H. Sengendo and G. Prain. 2009. 'Enhancing adaptation of poor urban dwellers to the effects of climate variability and change'. *IOP Conference Series: Earth and Environmental Science* 6: 332002. https://doi.org/10.1088/1755-1307/6/33/332002.

Malladi, Teja, Garima Jain, Sunil Kraleti, Sushmita Ramoji, Aishwarya Balasubramanian and Grishma Hedge. 2016. 'India site report for urban risks and resettlements'. In *Reducing Relocation Risk in Urban Areas*, edited by Suresh Shyamala. https://www.ucl.ac.uk/bartlett/development/sites/bartlett/files/site_level_india.pdf.

Menon-Sen, K. and G. Bhan. 2008. *Swept Off the Map: Surviving eviction and resettlement in Delhi*. New Delhi: Yoda Press.

MoHUPA. 2011. *Guidelines for Preparation of Slum Free City Plan of Action (2013–22)*. http://mohua.gov.in/upload/uploadfiles/files/3RAYGuidelinesSFCP.pdf.

Ministry of Rural Development. 2007. *National Rehabilitation and Resettlement Policy, 2007*. https://dolr.gov.in/sites/default/files/National%20Rehabilitation%20%26%20Resettlement%20Policy%2C%202007.pdf.

Modesto, Gabriela. n.d. 'Lomo de Corvina protestó por constancias de posesión'. *Stereo Villa*. http://stereovilla.pe/pobladores-de-lomo-de-corvina-protestaron-frente-a-municipalidad.

Moussaïd, Mehdi. 2013. 'Opinion formation and the collective dynamics of risk perception'. *PLoS ONE* 8 (12): 1–8. https://doi.org/10.1371/journal.pone.0084592.

O'Sullivan, J.J., R.A. Bradford, M. Bonaiuto, S. De Dominicis, P. Rotko, J. Aaltonen, K. Waylen and S.J. Langan. 2012. 'Enhancing flood resilience through improved risk communications'. *Natural Hazards and Earth System Science* 12 (7): 2271–82. https://doi.org/10.5194/nhess-12-2271-2012.

OHCHR and UN-Habitat. 2014. *The Right to Adequate Housing*. Geneva: United Nations. https://www.ohchr.org/documents/publications/fs21_rev_1_housing_en.pdf.

Phillips, Michael R., Andrew L. Jones and Tony Thomas. 2018. 'Climate change, coastal management and acceptable risk: Consequences for tourism'. *Journal of Coastal Research* 85 (85): 1411–15. https://doi.org/10.2112/si85-283.1.

Presidencia del Consejo de Ministros. 2013. 'Decreto Supremo N° 115-2013-PCM: Decreto supremo que aprueba el reglamento de la ley N° 29869, ley de reasentamiento poblacional para las zonas de muy alto riesgo no mitigable'. *El Peruano*, 24 October 2013. https://cenepred.gob.pe/web/wp-content/uploads/2018/06/D.S.-115-2013-Rgto-Reasentamiento.pdf.

Quinn, Tara, François Bousquet, Chloe Guerbois, Elias Sougrati and Matthieu Tabutaud. 2018. 'The dynamic relationship between sense of place and risk perception in landscapes of mobility'. *Ecology and Society* 23 (2). https://doi.org/10.5751/ES-10004-230239.

Ratanawaraha, Apiwat. 2016. 'Inequality, fragility and resilience in Bangkok'. In *Building Resilience in Cities under Stress*, edited by Francesco Mancini and Andrea Ó Súilleabháin, 4–12. New York: International Peace Institute.

Scott, James C. 1998. *Seeing like a State: How certain schemes to improve the human condition have failed*. New Haven, CT: Yale University Press.

UNISDR. 2009. *Global Assessment Report on Disaster Risk Reduction: Risk and poverty in a changing climate*. Geneva: United Nations. https://www.undrr.org/publication/global-assessment-report-disaster-risk-reduction-2009.

Vlaeminck, Pieter, Miet Maertens, Moses Isabirye, Filip Vanderhoydonks, Jean Poesen, Seppe Deckers and Liesbet Vranken. 2016. 'Coping with landslide risk through preventive resettlement: Designing optimal strategies through choice experiments for the Mount Elgon region, Uganda'. *Land Use Policy* 51: 301–11. https://doi.org/10.1016/j.landusepol.2015.11.023.

Whittaker, John D. 1986. 'Evaluation of acceptable risk'. *Journal of the Operational Research Society* 37 (6): 541–47.

Wisner, Ben, Piers Blaikie, Terry Cannon and Ian Davis. 2004. *At Risk: Natural hazards, people's vulnerability and disasters*. London: Routledge.

5

A risk assessment framework for decision-making that transcends economic valuation: understanding why people choose to stay in disaster risk-prone areas

Shuaib Lwasa, Amir Bazaz and Garima Jain

Possible risk-mitigating options need to be examined before deciding on the most cost-effective strategy in the short, medium and long term. At the household level, factors including social attachment, connectivity and access to services in cities offer an extended value registry that needs to be incorporated into frameworks for assessing decisions about risk reduction alternatives. Any intervention (such as housing) results in both costs and benefits being incurred by the people. For instance, research reflects the fact that resettling people from high-risk areas eliminates the costs associated with the emergency and reconstruction phase (Correa 2011). However, certain non-monetary costs, such as the loss of livelihood opportunities, physiological and social consequences, and disruption of social cohesion are often overlooked, regardless of whether the intervention is beneficial or not.

Rightly, there is a global consensus underscoring the need for a comprehensive assessment of the economic, social and environmental costs prior to making any decision concerning resettlement (Cernea 1999; Ferris 2014). But what could form the basis for such an assessment? What risk is being reduced, for who, how and at what cost? In this chapter, we attempt to reimagine economic valuation, with alternative ways to think about 'risk values' which can inform decisions at various levels of actors. We draw upon empirical data from case studies of voluntary and involuntary resettlements in Uganda and India to illustrate this approach.

Valuing risk: household-level policymaking processes and systemic regional conditions

Risk can be defined and experienced in different ways. The first is that risk from flooding can be defined as a cost to the city, neighbourhoods, families and individuals, the environment, the conduct of business and/or livelihoods. This is the normative approach to risk in that it is seen as the potential for losses. However, we can also define risk as an opportunity, or making a trade-off for benefits (Chelleri et al. 2015). In this sense, risk-as-opportunity corresponds to a classic economic formula of 'the higher the risk, the greater the opportunity for profit'. In this understanding, 'risk' is an indicator of the potential for achieving greater gains than would otherwise be achievable and is to be embraced and actively engaged with.

'Costs' and 'risks' are related to 'value'. Here, 'value' is broader than financial measures and thus affords an opportunity to think of 'value', 'cost' and 'risk' in many different ways. Objects in the everyday environment and different configurations of location, infrastructure, flows of people, goods and resources can have different values for different people. These values can also change over time, for instance due to changing identities from a young person to an older parent. Values may also change due to changing registries of meaning: for example, land bought becomes an inheritance for children. In such a case, while the 'market value' has not gone away, the value of the land is understood within a different set of norms, expectations, obligations and relationships and affects what can and cannot be done with the land.

Household-level and project-level decisions play out within a wider regional and local dynamics of development (and not merely risk reduction). 'Value' is implicitly informed by the larger urban dynamics. These factors include histories of development policies, and urban land and economic dynamics (Sawada et al. 2018). At the same time, risks also need to be understood in the context of a changing climate, which may not be articulated as such at the time of 'valuing risk' due to lack of knowledge, but could potentially introduce new unknown risks in the future. It is, therefore, equally important to locate decision-making within the wider context of regional and city development agendas and to use the analytical reference of outcomes as a critical lens to examine the conditions and drivers of regional and local development trajectories which are often conveyors of systemic risk.

Economic assessments tend to estimate costs, often at an intervention level, using monetised factors translated into calculable costs and benefits, but this is not definitive since not all values, by different actors at various scales, get captured. Valuation is usually based on expenditure methodology, which is defensive expenditure that essentially relies on assessing the costs of undertaking activities aimed at offsetting anticipated impacts of the disasters. The second type of expenditure is the indirect costs that are estimates of expenditure associated with defensive mechanisms at a scale larger than the unit of analysis and anticipating future impacts. Indirect costs also involve expenditure associated with activities that relate to the direct costs but not the actual impact. But the value list is more than direct and defensive costs or benefits. Risk reduction can also offer an opportunity if seen through these lenses; the assessment of costs and benefits would require a different framework.

Framing our approach for evaluating risk

Asset accumulation and evaluation of risk

To understand what individuals and institutions value, we use the framework of asset accumulation (Sherraden 1991; Sherraden et al. 2011). Literature suggests that households follow a strategy of asset accumulation, which could be understood as an attempt at building their capabilities to deal with disaster impacts for the future (Dodman et al. 2017; Vatsa 2004; McKernan and Sherraden 2008). This becomes part of their coping strategy while living in areas exposed to hazards, be it accumulating housing options, access to livelihoods or receiving aid in the time of disasters. Households are likely to assess trade-offs based on these strategies. The households' ability (capabilities) to accumulate assets as well as to use a diversified asset accumulation strategy (innovative livelihood practices) clearly provides a social and economic buffer to resettled/relocated households (Dobson 2017). Hence it is important to understand decisions to move (or not) in the context of asset accumulation and its interface with disaster risk reduction and development.

Meanwhile, institutions play an important role in asset building by enabling or limiting households to accumulate assets. It is important to note here that asset building is different from asset accumulation. Social protection policies protect vulnerable people (Hulme, Moore and

Shepherd 2001) from adverse risks and against erosion of assets, and create more opportunities for asset accumulation. This creation of opportunities allows low-income families to accumulate assets and then build marketable/non-marketable assets on their own (Dani and Moser 2008; Moser 2011; Solimano 2006). In a way this goes beyond the mere concept of savings. In asset building, state-level institutional structures are quite important and dominant. This helps develop mechanisms of self-insurance and marketable skills among individuals and communities, enabling them to become more resilient, and ultimately making them less dependent on social insurance to protect themselves against negative shocks.

To see this in the context of climate change, asset accumulation could be regarded as a strategy for improving adaptation and coping capacities and building resilience. The asset-based approach protects the vulnerable against risks and helps in the reconstruction of assets. Assets are embedded within social processes, structures and power relationships, which help in mediating access and the accumulation of their value. This approach, therefore, provides them with an opportunity to renegotiate their entitlements during the reconstruction period, despite physical loss and damage (Dani and Moser 2008; Moser and Stein 2011). Over time, sound evidence has emerged that supports the view that increasing assets and capabilities is crucial to improving wellbeing (Moser and Dani 2008).

This approach, in the context of risk reduction interventions such as resettlement and relocation, therefore, plays out in how the state of assets and how localised economic and social networks facilitate asset accumulation. Using our case sites as settings, we chose, instead, to adopt a multi-scalar multi-actor asset accumulation strategy for assessing risk, while also addressing the larger risk-development narrative of the region.

In summary, our approach includes the following elements: first, situating the risk assessment (all costs and benefits) within the broader theoretical frameworks of urban poverty, asset accumulation strategies and the capability framework helps us understand structural and specific drivers of negative and positive outcomes and the interlinkages between them; secondly, assessing the interfaces between livelihoods, urban informality, climate impacts and regional development dynamics enables us to locate risk in a structural context; and third, the broader developmental pathways of transitions taking place in the urban and rural contexts. Here, disaster risk reduction (DRR) is viewed in the context of the changing climate, dynamics of changing settlements and in their relationship with the city and the region, including understanding the changing forms of the macro- and micro-narratives of development.

Cost–benefit analysis and evaluation of risk

This assessment of costs and benefits borne by different actors at different scales from an intervention could be understood from the perspective of the individual household or neighbourhood scale as well as from the perspective of the city scale (Jain and Bazaz 2020).

Individual household or neighbourhood perspective

As discussed above, households have a strategy to accumulate assets, and this could be understood as building their capabilities for the future (Moser and Stein 2011). Risk reduction interventions can be seen by them as an opportunity to accumulate (housing options, access to livelihoods or aid in the time of disasters, etc.) and they are likely to make some trade-offs based on this strategy. People may also have found ways of coping with various external hazards over time, and therefore may not consider those events as being risky. Their potential assets could be:

- social (health, education, social safety nets, networks, family extensions, community structures, cultural practices, etc.)
- physical (buildings, systems, land, public spaces, trees and natural capital, productive and non-productive assets, food, etc.)
- economic (livelihood options, access to financial services, investments, risk transfer and sharing mechanisms, etc.)
- environmental (quality and quantity of water, air, green cover, biodiversity, etc.)
- political (agency and voice)
- overall quality of life determined by their levels of access to the various assets.

It is in this context of assets and their strategies to accumulate that people's existing risks and opportunities need to be understood in the spatial contexts they are currently living in, which is best done with a participatory process to understand their individual and cumulative coping mechanisms and acceptable trade-offs. Further, for any potential intervention, the changes anticipated or experienced could be understood as costs and benefits: *reduction of existing risks* as benefits, loss of previously 'owned' assets or opportunities as *created risks* and therefore costs; on the other hand, *avoiding the creation of new risks* as benefits, *continuing risks* when previous developmental gaps continue to remain and therefore an *opportunity cost* that could have been avoided with alternate interventions. These created risks also need to be understood in the context of the changing climate, where the households may be exposed to future risks that we are uncertain about today. It is this overall comparison of the costs and benefits borne by them that could give an insight into the advantages and disadvantages of any potential intervention.

City perspective

The agency for institutional perspective is the municipality, city authority or government agency. Institutions always desire to maintain the functioning of services and infrastructure in relationship with the people. Any intervention, therefore, must also be based on an overall future vision for the city development, informed by the city's past. People may have a 'give and take' relationship with their environs in terms of flow of resources, livelihood extensions and other social and political dependencies, and any alterations to these must also be understood as costs for the city. The city's overall opportunity cost of land, pressures on infrastructure provisions and environment must also be understood as costs to the city when comparing the costs borne by people versus those borne by the city. City assets in terms of infrastructure are important to protect from risk, but this protection transcends the assets value. City jurisdictions also value the operations in the city, and their histories and functions, as well as the population. Thus, the smooth operation of city management is key in the evaluation of risk and risk-reducing measures. City authorities consider the opportunities of a well-functioning city with functional infrastructure to manage risk, including climate-induced disasters. The notion of value, then, broadens the valuation by city authorities beyond asset protection to include wellbeing, environmental services and social peace.

At city-wide scale, assessments can be made of the total costs of anticipated and or known risk such as climate-induced flooding. The costs have three elements: (1) the cost of mitigation, (2) the costs of adaptation, and (3) the cost of residual damage. The first refers to the cost associated with the reduction of the anthropogenic impact on the climate system, diminishing the extent of future climate change to which cities like Kampala or those in India contribute. The second refers to the cost of reducing the impacts of changes that are local to the city, in this case flooding in Kampala and India. The third refers to the cost of impacts that can be neither mitigated nor adapted to and that remain after such actions have been taken. As Markandya (2015) argues, the costs of the impacts of climate change can be defined as the sum of the costs of adaptation and the cost of residual damage. In this sense, two different economic assessments of the impacts of climate change can be accomplished. While estimates of damages refer to the total costs of the impacts of climate change, estimates of adaptation refer to only one part of them, as they do not consider the cost of residual damage. In a sense, if these costs are avoided by the intervention, they can be referred to as *avoided climatic costs*.

Valuation literature also points at costs and benefits based on an expenditure methodology undertaken to avoid exposure to hazards or costs of treatment. Defensive expenditure involves costs associated with impacts of hazard incidence (intensive or extensive) such as health, infrastructure repairs, maintenance and costs related to sustaining life or businesses despite impacts. It relies on assessing the costs of activities aimed at offsetting changes associated with flooding and other extreme events. Such costs can in turn be seen as a way of avoiding future costs. The second type of expenditure is indirect costs due to illness or costs in the future – for example, monetised time lost for a worker unable to access his or her workplace due to inundation by floodwaters. This relies on estimating expenditure associated with infrastructure or defensive mechanisms at a scale larger than the unit of analysis and anticipating future impacts. Indirect costs also involve expenditure on activities which relate to the direct costs but not the actual impact. By this method, benefits are considered as the savings that would otherwise be spent when there are defensive measures that deter the impacts of hazard incidence. This approach is illustrated below in the Kampala case, to show how institutional valuation of risk differs from households in applying the

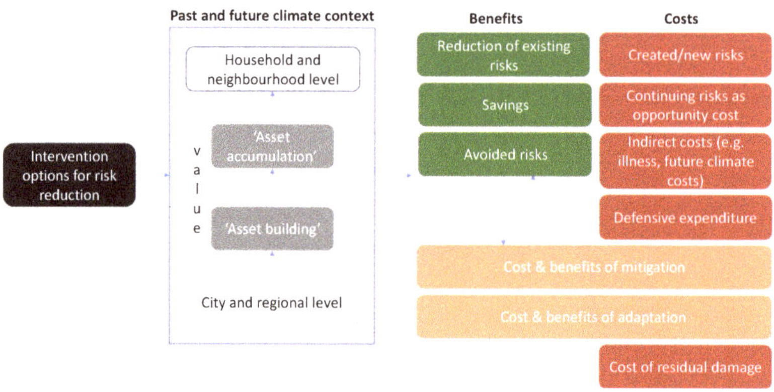

Figure 5.1 Conceptual framework to assess intervention options. The figure shows intervention options in the context of the city, past and future climatic changes, and household strategies for asset accumulation and resilience building, for the most equitable 'beneficial' outcomes. © Authors.

expenditure approach. These two approaches – value registry and the expenditure approach – enable us to situate risk in a historical and spatial context. These aids in understanding the costs and benefits of any intervention to achieve the goal of transformative development are also relevant when studying the impacts of a past intervention or counterfactuals, but most importantly they give insights that can direct policy, so that the overall quality of life of people and cities is improved in the process. A proof of concept is illustrated later in this chapter to show how these approaches are applied in a city setting at the levels of household, neighbourhood and city, and the decision to mitigate disaster risk. See Figure 5.1 that illustrates the framework described above.

Application of the framing and methods to two studies

The points made above are exemplified drawing on two of the country case studies from the 'Reducing Relocation Risk in Urban Areas' project: the city of Visakhapatnam in the state of Andhra Pradesh, India, and the city of Kampala, in Uganda.

Three resettlement sites from the city of Visakhapatnam are used: Sonia Gandhi Nagar, Sevanagar and Paradesipalem. The first two sites were located next to one another in the original locations, yet the first was an example of in situ redevelopment while the latter two settlements were moved on the grounds of 'untenability', i.e. the original slums were located in hazardous areas as defined by national affordable housing guidelines. A combination of methods was used, including stakeholder interviews with government officials, project coordinators, NGOs, community leaders and select disadvantaged individuals, and focus group discussions. Interviews with three types of household each corresponding to the three sites were considered: those who received in situ housing (n=12), those who moved involuntarily (n=16) and those who moved voluntarily (n=12). Field observations, geospatial analysis and a secondary review of programmes and policies were also conducted. Since the study was done post-intervention, it relies largely on people's memories and stated responses of how they perceived the changes from their previous locations and the process of resettlement.

In Uganda, the analysis draws on the data including 70 interviews with households and small enterprises in Bwaise and Natete and stakeholder interviews. Both Bwaise and Natete experience flooding. In addition, Bwaise has experienced an infrastructural intervention in canalising the main water channel as well as the compensated eviction of landowners and resettlement of people living near the channel. In Natete, infrastructural improvements were underway at the time the research was conducted in 2015–16 and compensated eviction for those affected landowners was due to begin.

In order to understand different responses, we analysed the data from the perspectives of individuals (household and small enterprise), 'small collectives' (neighbourhoods) and 'big collectives' (city). Our view that these different perspectives were necessary was not so much to cover different scales, but to understand different ways in which people come together (or not) in response to flooding phenomena that do not typically bear any relation to 'scales'. Although we were not able to shed insights on the 'small collective' activities within the scope of the project, it made it simpler to identify any gaps and/or overlaps between household- and small enterprise-level and city-level perspectives. Addressing the perspectives at the 'small collective' level is an issue that should be picked up in future research.

We began with the objective to understand how different actors from individual, collective and city-wide levels value the risks and benefits of relocation. The objectives were derived from two aims. First, to develop an approach that combines different methodological approaches to assessing risk and the benefits as well as costs of living and working in the hazard-prone areas (cyclones and floods in India, and floods in Uganda). Second, to generate evidence that transcends cost–benefit analysis from the different perspectives that tells us more about how different actors value or make trade-offs vis-à-vis living in hazard-prone areas.

In both cases, we pursue the approach as described above, albeit with slightly different methods of calculating costs and benefits. While the India case used the risks created and avoided and opportunity costs as a means, Uganda pursued the expenditure methodology. This demonstrates that this approach is adaptable depending on the context and relevance.

In both cases, we focused the analysis at two levels – household and/or small enterprise, and the city – for answering some more overarching questions. In Uganda, where the relocations were self-initiated by the households: why do people make decisions to relocate or stay? What are the costs and benefits for households and businesses of locating where they do? What shapes their decision-making? And in India, where the resettlements were done as a state intervention: what alternatives for risk reduction lead to outcomes that could be more beneficial in the short, mid and long term for people, communities and the city at large?

The costs are borne by different actors at multiple scales of city operations. The syntheses of economic assessments here are meant to give an insight into the valuation process and estimated costs but not to be definitive. While some elements at household level are included in assessment at the city-wide scale, other elements are unique to the neighbourhood and city-wide levels. This justifies the consideration of multi-level assessment or estimation of costs and benefits of climate-related hazards, as defined by the framework above.

Case study 1: Visakhapatnam, India

Using 23 indicators for socio-cultural outcomes, 31 for physical, 19 for economic, seven for environmental and six indicators for quality of life, the overall costs and benefit outcomes for the three settlements following the interventions were assessed and compared. The analyses showed that those who were provided in situ housing, such as Sonia Gandhi Nagar, faced the least costs and fewer new risks. While some of their previous challenges persist, they could be resolved with other policy measures going forward. On the other hand, in Sevanagar, where the residents had been moved by force, the wellbeing of residents worsened, and no amount of resources could bring back lost lives and reduce the trauma caused. The results could have been more beneficial, and costs could have been avoided, if people had retained and had been able to sustain their previous ways of living despite resettlement. This could have been possible by relocating them closer to their original location, not 25 km away.

The outcomes experienced at the settlement level reflected the development trajectory of the city. While the city has been sprawling and experiencing increased daily minimum and maximum temperatures over the last hundred years, new affordable housing resettlements continue to be located outside the city limits, further aiding this sprawl. While the city historically has had poor education and health indicators, the outcomes experienced by people post-resettlement included worsening health due to poorer waste and sanitation facilities and a higher number of school dropouts due to greater distances.

According to the census of India in 2011 (Directorate of Census Operations 2011), close to 56 per cent of Visakhapatnam's district population was not employed. The number of workers in 2011 decreased, compared to the percentage of workers in 2001. Female workers' participation decreased from 70.1 per cent in the 2001 census to 66 per cent in the 2011 census. Of those working, 3 per cent were involved in home-based industry. The experience in the two resettlement projects studied aligned with this trajectory. Many people had lost their jobs post-resettlement. Women, especially, indicated losing work, since travelling long distances was not considered safe. Of those working, many were employed in home-based industry, such as watch-repair work or metal-work, although even those had suffered because of a poorer customer base in these new locations.

Even though the city is a primary city for the state, and boasts of growing industrial, higher education and healthcare sectors, the overall human development indicators have remained poor for many years. In a way, two out of three resettlement interventions seemed to replicate or worsen these entrenched socio-economic vulnerabilities disproportionately for the poor and the marginalised. Such interventions, which seem to be perpetuating inequity, with the only clear benefit of hazard exposure reduction, raise questions for their overall contribution to sustainable development and wellbeing of people. (For more details on the case and the use of this methodology, please refer to Jain and Bazaz 2020.)

Experiences of risk valuation in Kampala, Uganda

Value registry and evaluation of risk

Kampala provides an example of how the framing explained earlier informed understanding how different actors evaluate risk at multiple scales. The two approaches applied to illustrate this example include the value registry on the one hand and the expenditure methodology on the other hand, applied at household and institutional levels. Both approaches tend to converge at the outcome – that is, the total cost (economic, social, environmental) and the benefits (asset protection, social networks, robust infrastructure) – although the detailed steps differ. At household level, the guiding issues included the actual stated costs associated with living in flood-prone areas in the context of a decision to relocate or resettle; the actual stated benefits associated with living in flood-prone areas in the context of a decision to relocate or resettle; the strategies implemented in managing trade-offs of not moving; and the processes of decision-making and how decisions affect outcomes, including who bears the costs and who gains the benefits.

Analysis of experiences at the household level shows that with both time and money in short supply, almost immediate access to the essentials of daily life – food, water, cleaning, transport to workplaces, energy supplies – is important for many poorer households, extending the value registry. At a more nuanced level, the unit cost of items sold in small quantities is convenient, though the total costs tend to be higher. This is because costs (time and money) saved accessing goods mitigate their higher per-unit price. People indicated several financial and opportunity costs of living in flood-affected areas. In two of the settlements studied in detail, Bwaise and Natete, households were coping with flooding by a variety of methods, including raising up furniture in the house when it rains, raising the height of the house, cleaning up after floods and staying home when it floods to protect children and property. Each of these activities has associated costs: for example, respondents in Bwaise said that they spend two days preparing for the floods. This preparation includes actions such as preparing sandbags, constructing embankments on houses, moving fragile property from the house and securing the house and property in case the household temporarily moves out.

This value registry varied across the two different groups of people surveyed. The first group relocated autonomously (although within the same areas) and the second was evicted by the state to make way for infrastructural improvements. For those moving autonomously, there were a range of reasons that combine to explain the evaluation and decision – not least the suffering and hardship caused by the flooding. One respondent was prepared to incur costs relating to changing from ownership to tenancy in order to escape the costs of dealing with the flooding. This reflects the effects of the fact that many residents have small houses that, they explained, poverty drove them to construct in flood-prone areas. In Natete, the costs are similar, with life-threatening events or death occurring occasionally due to flash floods. Effectively, for respondents that have moved within Bwaise and Natete, they have sought to retain the value of living in such central locations and when the costs of managing the risks became overwhelming, they relocated autonomously. For those moving as a result of eviction, this is a disruption to configurations of value, cost and risk that respondents were comfortable or satisfied with. The compensation provided was not sufficient for them to participate in the land market elsewhere. Since most of the evicted people continued to live in the same neighbourhoods, their costs for flood protection continued, and for those replacing assets destroyed and lost at the time of the evictions, costs were newly created. In sum, those respondents in Bwaise who had been evicted or those in Natete facing eviction appeared considerably worse off than they had been prior to the actual eviction or announcement of eviction. But eviction also reveals an institutional perspective on the value registry, which is the desire, in flood-prone areas, to protect the people from risk by relocation or resettlement. There are no examples of resettlements in Kampala, while in Uganda more broadly there have been only a few. Even with relocation, it is largely voluntary (King et al. 2014). Thus, for the institution, the value registry includes two elements. The first is to relocate using the market value of household assets to protect people's lives, while the second element is institutional asset accumulation by building flood-mitigating infrastructure robust enough to manage floods in the future.

Due to a focus on physical asset valuation, the land dynamics in Kampala greatly influenced decision-making at both the household and the institutional level. Within the complex and heterogeneous tenure types, 'people move between them in terms of their relations to land, or because a particular piece of land may lie between two systems which may be subject to conflicting rights and duties' associated with different value registers (Mukwaya, Sengendo and Lwasa 2010, 58). Market forces – influenced by private real estate companies, infrastructure development and expansion, residential housing and industrial development – further influence decision-making, whether people continue to stay or agree to move. The higher the cost of land, the more likely people are to be willing (or indeed be forced to) occupy high-risk land. The presence and grounding of the 'informal' underscores its role in the making of the city, in terms of both economic opportunities and housing. These economic undertakings are taking root and expanding fast in informal settlements, and people recognise they can easily make entry into the economy and labour market through these initiatives, furthering their intention to stay. At the institutional level, valuation of land rights as defined by a given type of tenure is used, on the one hand, to secure the easement for risk-reducing infrastructure, and on the other for motivating residents to consider relocation. Institutional securing of the easements implies asset accumulation for the institution; moreover, the constructed infrastructure is also valued for its sustenance of a robust response to disaster risk and thus the functional operation of the city.

Expenditure approach to risk decision-making

Using the expenditure approach, we again draw on experiences at household and institutional levels. At household level, the direct and indirect costs discussed earlier of living with and managing flood risk were estimated using the defensive mechanism. Treatment of water for drinking and domestic use was selected as a key defensive expenditure due to the importance of water to life and wellbeing. The treatment of water was coupled with estimates of actual treatment of illnesses associated with water and the indirect cost in terms of lost hours and wages due to ailments that keep households away from work. The inclusion of lost hours/wages was established as vital given that many households in the flood-prone areas work in low-skilled jobs either at home or nearby. The economic assessment results show that through defensive expenditure to treat water in Kampala, each household incurs an average cost of US$13.60 per month associated with flooding; given an average income of $62.80, the expenditure is just under a quarter of income. At neighbourhood scale, estimated household expenditure on flood-related costs is $17.4 million annually. This estimate, though not done by households, reflects some of the decision outcomes when evaluating the risk of living in flood-prone areas.

City-wide expenditure estimates considered a number of indicators, taking into consideration the future costs in view of climate change, including loss of life, affected people, infrastructure destruction, infrastructure damage and disaster relief, which are calculated as a proportion of GDP. The analysis in Kampala showed that on average three deaths have occurred per year due to floods between 1993 and 2014 and that floods were estimated to cost $0.22–5.7 million in life years lost, while effects on people were estimated to be $0.17–0.57 million per year. Destruction and damage to buildings due to floods was estimated to cost between $0.16 and $0.88 million per year. The future possible impact of increased flooding in Kampala utilised scenarios from the Intergovernmental Panel on Climate Change (IPCC). Three scenarios are considered. First is the current situation of flood events, with 2013 as the base year. The second is based on Representative Concentration Pathway (RCP) 4.5 and the third is based on RCP 8.5. With uncertainties notwithstanding, the costs are estimated to increase four-fold with an increase of 4.5°C and ten-fold with an increase of 8.5°C. The estimate runs from 2025 to 2050. The increase in temperature is likely to be associated with redistributed rainfall events, including extreme events that would affect assets. With respect to infrastructure, costs to climate-proof infrastructure in Kampala are estimated as significant: between $3,259 million and $3,699 million over the 2015–50 period, or between $560 million and $600 million over the period 2015–30. Costs increase with time, to a large extent due to population growth and associated infrastructure demands if the development trajectory continues with business as usual. Costs start out quite small but build up over the period to 2050. In 2020 they range from $11 to $13 million a year but by 2050 they are as high as $380–485 million. In terms of percentage of GDP, they go up from 0.03–0.04 per cent in 2015 to around 0.1 per cent in 2050.

Total costs vary considerably by socio-economic and climate scenario. With the more climate-friendly scenario, the total cost to 2050 is around $3.2 billion, while with the less friendly one, with little mitigation, it goes up to $3.7 billion (a 27 per cent increase). The calculation of current costs by the Kampala Capital City Authority and the government of Uganda was used to evaluate and inform risk-intervention measures for upgrading the drainage system. One element of this was the relocation or eviction of the residents to facilitate the widening and deepening of the primary drainage systems in the city. This example illustrates the differing indicators of evaluating risk by households and institutions, and further exemplifies how actors in disaster risk reduction arrive at decisions from their own perspectives. The downside of the expenditure approach taken by institutions is that the costs estimated are in respect to assets such as infrastructure. What is missing in this valuation are costs associated with relocation, breaking of social ties and community cohesion, business relocation and loss of proximity to workplaces or markets. These issues were raised by categories of people in the study sites as important and thus cannot be overlooked. These can be assessed as opportunities but also as costs of relocation. Distances to markets, customers and workplaces and the cost of housing are opportunities that the settlement offers which are not monetised. This disjuncture between the two levels of risk evaluation illustrates the convergence of the value registry and the expenditure approach methods in risk reduction decision-making.

Reflections

In both cases, we find:

- Clear evidence of collective action arrangements (informal safety net collectives, women's groups enabling the exercise of rights, local development committees) and their profound impact in terms of reducing risks.
- The factors that enabled the formation of innovative collectives and groups play a positive role by acting as a buffer against residual risk, most significantly in terms of negotiating the impact of economic or environmental shocks.
- Sufficient evidence to indicate the lack of social infrastructure provision (health and education) as a critical impediment to building adaptive capacities of households, particularly in the intergenerational context (lack of appropriate health facilities, greater prevalence

of health hazards, lack of safe access to educational opportunities). For example, the experience of poor health and education could seriously impair the adaptive capacities of young inhabitants of resettled/ affected households.

- The lack of access to employment opportunities within affordable distance, and the disruption of economic activities (many households rely on extended social networks to support profitable micro-enterprises) was a common problem experienced across settlements, except in cases where the distance was minimal. This is evidence of the inappropriate structural arrangements that can threaten the economic security of affected people and their livelihoods.
- Skill building (offered as a bundled product with relocation decisions) can help diversify livelihood opportunities for affected people. The provision of enablers such as skills training and access to financial services benefits affected communities in two critical ways: by improving their chances of asset and related accumulation strategies (through sustained income opportunities), and by strengthening their adaptive capacities, offering a much wider possibility of negotiating rights and opportunities and thereby contributing towards enhancing the political agency of the individual/household. Such skills make possible a better choice matrix and better negotiating terms.
- A clear linkage between the structural strength of new houses, environmental services (such as water and sanitation) and quality of life. While overall the new houses were structurally strong (and therefore able to provide protection in case of cyclonic storms), poor provisioning of environmental services led to poor quality of life outcomes. It is essential to recognise that the absence of appropriate provisioning of infrastructure services creates its own cycle of informal infrastructure provisioning – eating into the economic and asset base of households. This vicious cycle creates an endemic and endogenous poverty trap, which gets exacerbated through the larger, highly inequitable development trajectories. It is important to guard against a situation where economic opportunities that are created through larger development processes are left untapped by the vulnerable population because of their poor capabilities, such as poor asset and economic base.
- A strong correlation (in simple analogous terms) between effective official institutional frameworks (such as an efficient public food distribution system, accessible financial institutions, dedicated skills training programmes) and better economic, socio-cultural, political and environmental outcomes for affected households/settlements. It clearly follows from this insight that we need to redesign existing

institutional arrangements that focus on the eradication of urban poverty as their central mission (both structurally and non-structurally) and continuously reinvent them with the changing dynamics of regional development processes.

Conclusion

We argue that there are serious endemic deficits in key social, environmental and economic assets, which are largely driven by non-inclusive processes of development or the inability of the state to deal with risks (from a broader, regional perspective), partly driven by structural changes and the dynamic transitions involved (from agriculture to manufacturing to a services-led economy). We use the city framework to illustrate serious deficiencies in individual and systemic capabilities to address shocks or endemic stresses (such as poverty). We argue that, partly because of a lack of convergence in regional development and clustered economic development activity – and the imbalances in regional development – certain regions/cities will continue to be in a state of constant flux, with the creation of new risks as people migrate to the city in search of livelihoods, and the challenge of providing them with a decent quality of life.

The examples of Visakhapatnam and Kampala illustrate how city development processes (when faced with the challenges of supporting a higher than desirable human population) are unable to respond effectively in the context of risk management. We argue that asset accumulation cannot be looked at in isolation from the ability of individuals to do so, unless the city development process addresses the opportunity gap (in its various forms) through risk-focused development strategies. This, we argue, would result in serious erosion of the individual's and community's ability to respond to environmental stresses and shocks. Moreover, unless we address the fundamental blocks of development processes in the most inclusive manner, we will be unable to address risk-development exposure (which goes beyond hazard exposure) in an effective manner.

From the synthesis of the two case studies, it is clear that different actors make decisions to relocate based on various factors including health, economics, livelihoods and social ties. The extended costs and benefits framework combined with assets and non-monetised benefits provides an insight into why people choose to stay in risk-prone areas or resist relocation/resettlement or experience deteriorating experience of risk in both Kampala and India. Relocation decisions are not significantly influenced by disaster events unless their recurrence provides more evidence for the actors to decide on relocation or resettlement. Such evidence includes the destruction of livelihoods, inability to live in dignity, breakdown in social ties and lack of finances. Relocation is based on a decision made by individuals or households who are influenced by many interconnected factors. Individuals make decisions on their location and movements on the basis of their quality of life and the livelihoods of themselves and their families. Some people's inability to relocate is not significantly influenced by inadequate finances but rather by the proximity to education and health facilities as well as social ties. Thus, the issues of access to land, affordability, relocation costs and social ties are more influential on decisions around relocation. Inability to relocate leaves a trapped population with heightened vulnerability to extreme events and resultant floods. People with low to medium asset levels often become trapped in their homes during disasters, while inadequate social networks beyond their settlements also increase the possibility of people being trapped despite the desire to relocate.

References

Cernea, Michael M. 1999. 'Why economic analysis is essential to resettlement: A sociologist's view'. *Economic and Political Weekly* 34 (31): 2149–58.

Chelleri, Lorenzo, James J. Waters, Marta Olazabal and Guido Minucci. 2015. 'Resilience trade-offs: Addressing multiple scales and temporal aspects of urban resilience'. *Environment and Urbanization* 27 (1): 181–98. https://doi.org/10.1177%2F0956247814550780.

Correa, Elena. 2011. *Populations at Risk of Disaster: A resettlement guide*. Washington, DC: World Bank. https://www.gfdrr.org/sites/gfdrr/files/publication/resettlement_guide_150.pdf.

Dani, Anis A. and Caroline Moser. 2008. 'Asset-based social policy and public action in a polycentric world'. In *Assets, Livelihoods and Social Policy*, edited by Caroline Moser and Anis A. Dani, 3–41. Washington, DC: World Bank.

Directorate of Census Operations. 2011. *District Census Handbook: Visakhapatnam billage and town directory: Series 29*. Hyderabad: Directorate of Census Operations. https://censusindia.gov.in/2011census/dchb/2813_PART_A_DCHB_VISAKHAPATNAM.pdf.

Dobson, Skye. 2017. 'Community-driven pathways for implementation of global urban resilience goals in Africa'. *International Journal of Disaster Risk Reduction* 26: 78–84. https://doi.org/10.1016/j.ijdrr.2017.09.028.

Dodman, David, Hayley Leck, Maria Rusca and Sarah Colenbrander. 2017. 'African urbanisation and urbanism: Implications for risk accumulation and reduction'. *International Journal of Disaster Risk Reduction* 26: 7–15. https://doi.org/10.1016/j.ijdrr.2017.06.029.

Ferris, Elizabeth. 2014. *Planned Relocations, Disasters and Climate Change: Consolidating good practices and preparing for the future. Background document. Sanremo Consultation, 12–14 March, 2014*. UNHCR, Brookings-LSE and Georgetown University. https://www.unhcr.org/53c4d6f99.pdf.

Hulme, David, Karen Moore and Andrew Shepherd. 2001. *Chronic Poverty: Meanings and analytical frameworks*. Chronic Poverty Research Centre Working Paper No. 2. https://dx.doi.org/10.2139/ssrn.1754546.

Jain, Garima and Amir Bazaz. 2020. 'A multi-scalar approach for assessing costs and benefits of risk reduction alternatives for the people and the city: Cases of three resettlements in Visakhapatnam, India'. *Sustainability* 12 (15): 5958. https://doi.org/10.3390/su12155958.

King, David, Deanne Bird, Katharine Haynes, Helen Boon, Alison Cottrell, Joanne Millar, Tetsuya Okada, Pamela Box, Diane Keogh and Melanie Thomas. 2014. 'Voluntary relocation as an adaptation strategy to extreme weather events'. *International Journal of Disaster Risk Reduction* 8: 83–90. https://doi.org/10.1016/j.ijdrr.2014.02.006.

Markandya, Anil, Courtenay Cabot-Venton and Olivier Beucher. 2015. *Economic Assessment of the Impacts of Climate Change in Uganda*. Ministry of Water and Environment, Republic of Uganda.

McKernan, Signe-Mary and Michael W. Sherraden. 2008. *Asset Building and Low-Income Families*. Washington, DC: Urban Institute Press.

Moser, Caroline. 2011. 'A conceptual and operational framework for pro-poor asset adaptation to urban climate change'. In *Cities and Climate Change: Responding to an urgent agenda*, edited by Daniel Hoornweg, Mila Freire, Marcus J. Lee, Perinaz Bhada-Tata and Belinda Yuen, 225–53. Washington, DC: World Bank. https://doi.org/10.1596/978-0-8213-8493-0.

Moser, Caroline and Anis A. Dani, eds. 2008. *Assets, Livelihoods, and Social Policy*. Washington, DC: World Bank.

Moser, Caroline and Alfredo Stein. 2011. 'Implementing urban participatory climate change adaptation appraisals: A methodological guideline'. *Environment and Urbanization* 23 (2):463–85. https://doi.org/10.1177%2F0956247811418739.

Mukwaya, P.I., H. Sengendo and S. Lwasa. 2010. 'Urban development transitions and their implications for poverty reduction and policy planning in Uganda'. *Urban Forum* 21: 267–81. https://doi.org/10.1007/s12132-010-9090-9.

Sawada, Yasuyuki, Hiroyuki Nakata, Kunio Sekiguchi and Yoko Okuyama. 2018. 'Land and real estate price sensitivity to a disaster: Evidence from the 2011 Thai floods'. *Economics Bulletin* 38 (1): 89–97. https://econpapers.repec.org/RePEc:ebl:ecbull:eb-18-00022.

Sherraden, Michael W. 1991. *Assets and the Poor: A new American welfare policy*. Armonk, NY: M.E. Sharpe.

Sherraden, Michael, Mark Rank, Adam Carraso, Signe-Mary McKernan and West Coast Poverty Center. 2011. 'Asset-based policies and financial services: Toward fairness and inclusion'. In *Old Assumptions, New Realities: Economic security for working families in the 21st century*, edited by Robert D. Plotnick et al., 125–49. New York: Russell Sage Foundation.

Solimano, Andrés. 2006. *Asset Accumulation by the Middle Class and the Poor in Latin America: Political economy and governance dimensions*. Santiago: United Nations. https://repositorio.cepal.org/bitstream/handle/11362/5422/1/S0600971_en.pdf.

Vatsa, K.S. 2004. 'Risk, vulnerability, and asset-based approach to disaster risk management'. *International Journal of Sociology and Social Policy* 24 (10–11): 1–48. https://doi.org/doi:10.1108/01443330410791055.

6 Resettlement in Montserrat after the volcanic crisis: a consensus on tolerable levels of risk?

Emily Wilkinson

> While risk can be objectivized through metrics such as annual average loss (AAL) or probable maximum loss (PML) or through maps, these metrics only become useful if they are socially appropriated. Given that risk is socially constructed, this is a prerequisite for a transformation in how the social and economic constraints and opportunities facing households, businesses or governments are valued. What is considered acceptable or unacceptable risk, or what is an optimum strategy for risk management can only be understood in the relationship between the stakeholders and these opportunities and constraints (UNISDR 2015, 149).

Perceptions of risk reflect how individuals understand and experience a phenomenon. Many factors influence people's perceptions of risk, including familiarity with the source of danger (Ittelson 1978), control over the situation (Rachman 1990) and the intensity of the events (rare, extreme events tend to be over-estimated and more frequent events tend to be under-estimated; Lichtenstein et al. 1978). Much of the literature on risk perception focuses on the negative consequences of living in hazardous locations. Yet living in a specific hazardous location or context can also produce benefits; and this balance between risks and benefits, as estimated by individuals, can be a critical factor influencing risk perception (Wachinger and Renn 2010).

The benefits of taking risks are more often considered with respect to technology and technological hazards, and it is often the case that levels of what is considered an acceptable or tolerable level of risk varies between different social groups. Wachinger and Renn (2010, 16–17) describe the events surrounding the closure of a nuclear power plant in Valdecaballeros in Spain when a national nuclear moratorium came into force in 1993: 'Villagers actively protested against the dismantling of the power plant as it would have provided a substantial benefit for the town.' Hence non-economic considerations such as attachment to place, and even an emotional link with the hazard, also need to be balanced against any potential risk (Arranz-Lozano 2004).

This certainly appears to be the case for communities living close to volcanoes. As Kelman and Mather (2008) point out there are multiple benefits from populations locating themselves close to volcanoes, despite their negative impacts. These include good farmland and reliable water supplies. Robertson (1995) describes, for example, the benefits to agriculture, mining and tourism offered by La Soufrière volcano in St Vincent and the Grenadines. For local farmers, the 'pull' factor of sustainable livelihood activities close to volcanoes simply outweighs many of the threats. Similar pull factors were seen in the Philippines in 1998, when seven years after the eruption of Mount Pinatubo, and despite the fact that lahars had caused around 250 deaths triggered by rainfall in subsequent years, people chose to face the threat: '[The] cultural attachment to Bacolor … pulled people back to their native town … Perception of risk related to poverty and the loss of cultural heritage was actually higher than perception of risk linked to volcanic hazards' (Gaillard 2008, 324).

Disaster risk management (DRM) is unlikely to be effective without an understanding of different risk perceptions and preferences, and why these might vary between individuals facing multiple threats and those public officials charged with managing risks (Slovic 1987). Different people and cultures respond to disaster risk differently (Gaillard 2008; Heijmans 2001; Paton, Millar and Johnson 2001; Paton et al. 2010), and in the context of volcanic hazards, proximity to the hazard (Gregg et al. 2004), living memory of an eruption and level of impact (Paton, Millar and Johnson 2001) all shape levels of risk tolerance among individuals and groups. Even if risk perception is high, people may still put concerns about convenience and living costs ahead of their desire to lessen their exposure (Gaillard 2008). This suggests that the idea of an acceptable level of risk is inappropriate. Rather, people do not accept risks but tolerate them because they are associated with certain benefits (Pidgeon et al. 1992; Simmons and Walker 1999) and/or because risk management measures are able to control risks, allowing development to take place and people to thrive.

Continued investment in businesses and commercial activities despite frequent and sometimes significant economic losses associated with an active volcano reflect a level of risk tolerance among proximal communities. However, the values underlying any notion of tolerable risk may not be shared by everyone; in fact, much research on risk analysis and societal reactions to different threats highlights the differences between institutional responses (such as regulation) and public responses (Barnes 2002). In particular, the creation of new official rules to control risk, for example through the creation of exclusion zones and resettlement policies, may be considered inappropriate or excessive by those living in exposed areas and who may end up being resettled in 'safer areas' (Wilkinson 2015).

How these different values and preferences overlap, and the potential for their alignment and integration, is determined by broader risk governance arrangements. Risk governance is defined by the United Nations Office for Disaster Risk Reduction (UNDRR) as 'the system of institutions, mechanisms, policy and legal frameworks and other arrangements to guide, coordinate and oversee disaster risk reduction and related areas of policy'. One key aspect is the relationship between different decision-making units, from informal local institutions and local governments to tiers higher up the scale – including provincial governments (or states in federal systems of governance), national government and regional authorities like the European Union (EU). Incoherence in DRM often occurs because of poorly defined mandates across government agencies (where emergency management agencies are assumed to be responsible for all DRM), overly complex administrative structures, capacity and funding constraints, as well as centrist and paternalistic tendencies (Wilkinson 2012). Conversely, high levels of integration can help to promote more effective DRM. This includes not only the participation of actors from one level of decision-making processes at another but also institutions and knowledge produced at one level influencing processes at another (Pahl-Wostl 2009). More participatory forms of risk governance offer greater opportunity for different perceptions of risk and priorities for managing it (alongside other development and livelihood priorities) to be brought closer together.

Research methods

This research draws on focus group discussions and interviews conducted during a workshop held in Montserrat in September 2012 with

70 participants representing five stakeholder groups: scientists, UK government officials, Montserrat government officials (including disaster managers), regional agency staff and community representatives.[1] The aim was to explore components of resilience during and after the volcanic crisis as well as internal and external factors that have undermined it. Moderated focus group discussions on key events, tipping points and phases of change were held and recorded. In addition, 16 semi-structured interviews were conducted with local and UK government officials and community leaders. Workshop and interview recordings were transcribed and coded and analysed using Atlas-ti software.

The coding categories for this research capture data on: (1) risk management policies and key decisions taken during different time periods (before, during and after the crisis); (2) roles and responsibilities of different actors for DRM activities; (3) relationships between UK and local government authorities; and (4) public perceptions of government decisions on risk management policies (both UK and local). Interview and focus group data were also coded for issues of (5) risk perception, (6) trust, and (7) participation. Data was triangulated across the five stakeholder groups and with secondary literature, to help explain differences in judgements about decisions taken by local and UK authorities. Tensions arose as roles and responsibilities changed during and after the crisis, and these are highlighted, as are the contrasting views of citizens and formal institutions on levels of tolerable risk.

It is important to point out that primary data was collected from the focus group discussions and interviews to supplement existing data and analysis of the Montserrat crisis and recovery processes. This explains why only a few interviews were conducted. While this has its limitations, the research team felt that governance during the crisis and its immediate aftermath had already been studied in depth, albeit from the perspective of the science–policy interface (see, for example, Donovan, Bravo and Oppenheimer 2013; Donovan and Oppenheimer 2014). Further data was therefore collected to complement this and bring it up to date, situating the analysis of risk governance within broader decisions about development and the future of the island.

Governing risk in Montserrat, before the volcanic crisis

Montserrat is a UK Overseas Territory (UKOT) located in the eastern Caribbean (see Figure 6.1). The governance of UKOTs is unique because of their colonial history, although there are some similarities with

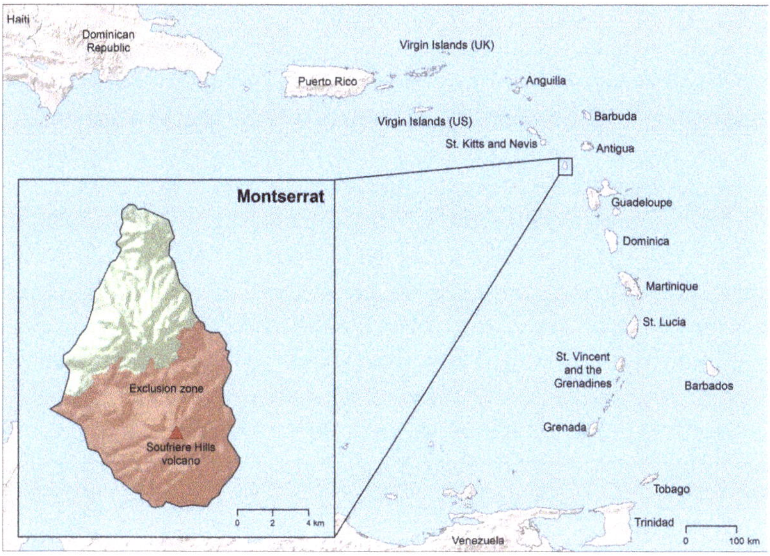

Figure 6.1 Map of Montserrat, locating the island in the eastern Caribbean. The map shows the Soufrière Hills volcano and the exclusion zone around the volcano. © Katy Mee, British Geological Survey. Based on data from multiple sources.

countries that have very decentralised public administration systems. Local governments in UKOTs have autonomy over day-to-day decision-making and planning with regard to social and economic policy, receiving some budget support to do so, but defer to central government over decisions regarding internal security and defence. This includes emergency management functions, if the capacity of the local government to respond is surpassed; but in pre- and post-disaster risk reduction decisions, local government are expected to play a dominant role.

From the 1960s up until the volcanic crisis in 1995–7, the local government in Montserrat enjoyed very high levels of autonomy from the UK. The 1960s saw a period of decolonisation in the Caribbean, and although Montserrat's leaders chose to remain part of Britain, the island became self-governing with the formation of a locally elected ministerial government. From then on, Montserrat, like the Turks and Caicos, Cayman Islands and Anguilla, was treated as a quasi-independent state. A new constitution in 1989 set the parameters for these governance arrangements, giving the local government close to full autonomy over decision-making within the territory. The governor of Montserrat, a UK government representative and civil servant in the Foreign and Commonwealth Office (FCO), was responsible for defence, external affairs and internal security but performed ceremonial roles, while the local government carried out most normal areas of government activity such as provision of health and education, policing and land-use planning, with relatively little interference from the UK government, requiring minimal budget support and even developing some infrastructure projects independently (Clay et al. 1999).

In terms of vertical coordination, a set of ad hoc and 'personalised' governance arrangements had evolved between the UK and its Caribbean Overseas Territories before the volcanic crisis. These reflected neither a sense of shared sovereignty (as in the French Caribbean) nor negotiated autonomy (as in the Dutch Caribbean), but rather an assumption by the UK government that these territories would become independent (Hintjens and Hodge 2012, 202). Even the constitution created ambivalence, recognising Montserrat's separateness, but maintaining the UK's constitutional power to invoke emergency orders and intervene directly in domestic affairs. In line with this broad level of independence, Montserrat was also able to design and implement its own policies in response to perceived disaster risks. However, limited local capacity to identify and analyse risk was a major problem, as were the concentration of political power within a few wealthy families, party politicking and personalised politics (Skinner 2002).

Like many of its Caribbean neighbours, Montserrat is prone to a range of geological and hydro-meteorological hazards, and yet risk management knowledge was not well developed and had not been incorporated into mainstream development (World Bank 2002). Knowledge of volcanic risk was extremely low among local politicians and UK government representatives on the island, despite the publication of the 'Wadge and Isaacs' report (Wadge and Isaacs 1986), which had been commissioned by the Pan-Caribbean Disaster Preparedness and Prevention Project (CDPPP). The report warned of volcanic activity and the potential impact that an eruption would have on the island's capital, Plymouth.

Disaster and resettlement in Montserrat

On 18 July 1995, the Soufrière Hills volcano became active after a long period of dormancy. Approximately six thousand people were evacuated from the capital Plymouth and nearby towns. They returned to their homes, were evacuated again, and on 3 April 1996 Plymouth was evacuated for the last time. From 4 to 8 August a series of large eruptions destroyed approximately 80 per cent of the capital, burying it under

1.4 metres of ash. By 1997 up to 1,600 people were housed in temporary public shelters, which suffered from overcrowding, lack of privacy, poor sanitation and lack of access to good nutrition. Many Montserratians left the island, supported by UK resettlement packages, family and friends. By 2011, the population of Montserrat had dropped by 60 per cent, from 11,314 in 1991 to 4,491 in 2001 (CARICOM 2009). Of those who stayed, some were still in shelters three years after the eruption. Those who decided to stay and resettle in the north of the island faced severe challenges in re-establishing their livelihoods (Rozdilsky 2001). Firstly, there was a shortage of available land in the north (Hicks and Few 2015). A few families owned the land and did not want to sell it, and this shortage meant that land prices rose sharply. While this had an effect on the government of Montserrat, who needed to purchase agricultural land from private landowners to start building housing developments, soaring prices particularly affected farmers, who could not afford to purchase replacement land:

> land was at a premium here [in the north] because people wanted places to build houses, they wanted places to establish businesses ... So the farmland started going at rates that were comparable to business leases (interview with local government official, 2 October 2012).

Secondly, the north of the island is much drier and less fertile than the south, and those who were able to rent land faced difficulties in cultivating in unproductive, infertile soils on small plots, resulting in low yields (Hicks and Few 2015). Consequently, few farmers could make a living solely from farming, so many had to obtain a second occupation such as fishing or construction (Halcrow Group and Montserrat National Assessment Team 2012).

Thirdly, one of the longer-term effects of the land shortages was the construction of housing in unsafe and unsuitable locations such as ravines. The north of the island is more exposed to hurricanes and flooding than the south, offering few affordable 'safe' relocation sites (Mitchell 2002). In one of the new housing developments, Lookout, some houses were built on steep, exposed slopes that have limited shelter against hurricanes, earthquakes and windborne salt (Mitchell 2002; Smith Warner International 2003). Another redevelopment in Little Bay is affected by regular coastal flooding (Mitchell 2002).

Resettlement in the south, meanwhile, has been controlled and in some areas prohibited. Exclusion zones have been set up to control access

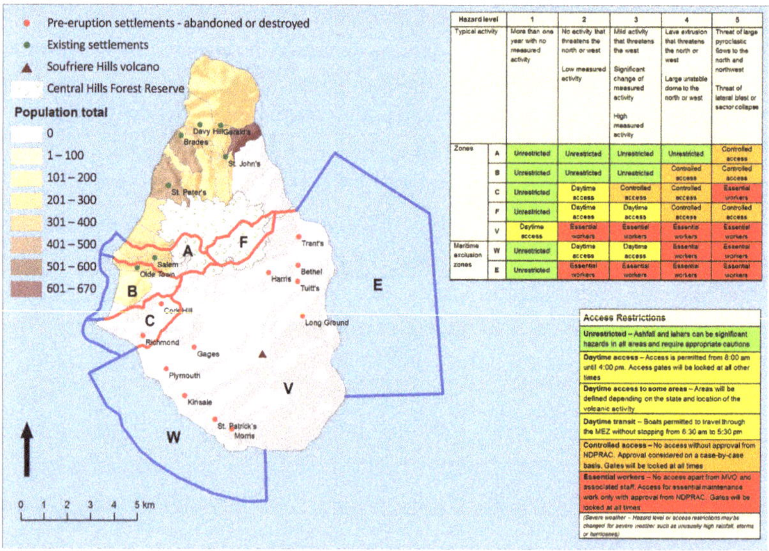

Figure 6.2 Map of the various Soufrière Hills volcano exclusion zones in 2011, showing where settlements used to be in those areas before the volcanic eruption. The key shows how access to different areas is related to the level of volcanic activity. © Katy Mee, British Geological Survey. Based on data from multiple sources.

to areas close to the volcano according to the level of volcanic activity (see Figure 6.2). The governance arrangements and relationships shaping these decisions and collective responses to volcanic risk are discussed below.

Post-disaster resettlement: an alignment of risk perceptions?

By the end of 1997, investment in infrastructure in the north was well underway, although people were still living in shelters and many of the investments needed for recovery were undertaken with only a short-term focus: the hospital was upgraded at the St John's site, not rebuilt; an emergency jetty was built at Little Bay instead of a harbour; and temporary government headquarters were set up in Brades (Sword-Daniels et al. 2014). These investments did not yet signal a reorientation in DRM. For many, it was not until 1999 that the emergency phase really ended. Eruptive activity continued, but a new governance regime was beginning to emerge, with a vision of the island's future development, and this 'co-governance' regime would continue to dominate central–local relations in Montserrat to the present day. The local government began to take the lead on day-to-day management functions, such as the procurement and supervision of development projects and some control over spending decisions, but with strong oversight and financial control from the UK.

Greater coherence between UK and local levels of risk tolerance can be observed from 2001 onwards, with the development of a strategy to sustain the on-island community and promote long-term investment in the north (Clay et al. 1999, 13). By restricting access to proximal areas (the boundaries of which have changed over time: see Aspinall et al. 2002) and investing in basic and road infrastructure, housing and services in the north, levels of exposure to pyroclastic flows and lahars have all been dramatically reduced (Sword-Daniels et al. 2014). For the Montserrat government these decisions marked an important turning point in the recovery process:

> In 2001 the economy began to recover and economic plans were made, based on scientific advice. The scientists said that the far north was of low negligible risk. Once that was said they set the foundations for serious thinking about investment for those who stayed. They realised it would have to be in the north (interview with local government official, 3 October 2012).

There was no formal public consultation process to establish how different actors viewed volcanic risk on the island (Haynes, Barclay and Pidgeon 2008), but perceptions of risk appear to have been broadly aligned at this point, with residents starting to consider the north their permanent home (interviews with local residents, 1–3 October 2012). Many had already left the island, prompted by the 'Boxing Day collapse' in 1997 (a major collapse of the old volcanic edifice and fresh lava dome), and facilitated by relocation packages offered in 1998; but even for those who stayed and had lost their houses, land and jobs, the north did not represent an 'acceptable option' in terms of levels of risk and livelihood options until housing reconstruction began (interview with UK government officials, 2 October 2012). This perception of the south being dangerous (approximately 60 per cent of the island) and the north being safe for habitation was broadly in line with the scientific assessments, through which areas were established as exclusion zones – some permanently, and others in accordance with the level of volcanic activity. Despite informal reports of people entering the permanent exclusion area (Zone V) without permission, the general perception among islanders is that this area will continue to be highly exposed to volcanic hazards and they will never be able to return (interview with local residents, 1–3 October 2012).

The volcanic crisis had uncovered some of the inherent contradictions in the autonomous system of governance in Montserrat, but it also prompted UK and local authorities to consider and make explicit their own views on acceptable levels of risk and their responsibilities for reducing exposure to volcanic hazards. UK and local government perceptions became more closely aligned in 1999, with both accepting that the future of the island would have to be in the north despite the disadvantages. This was endorsed through the definition of an exclusion zone and subsequent investment in the north.

More recent studies note, however, that these formal notions of tolerable risk may not be shared by the local population or even the local government (Haynes, Barclay and Pidgeon 2008). Exposure to high-impact events such as pyroclastic flows has been dramatically reduced through officially prescribed norms intended to reduce risk (relocation and establishing exclusion zones), but the north of the island was affected by ash fall and acid rain until recently, representing a low-level, intermittent but widespread risk that is given low consideration in development planning. Ash fall presents health risks, and asthma sufferers, in particular, have reported suffering respiratory problems from heavy ash fall (interview with local residents, 1–3 October 2012). Infrastructure built during the recovery period has also been affected and needs constant cleaning, replacement and repair. Most buildings (and homes) have tropical slatted windows, which allow ash to enter buildings because they cannot be properly sealed (Sword-Daniels et al. 2014).

The negative impacts of relocating people in the north of the island and of the social upheaval of Montserratians moving to the UK should not be overlooked. Most Montserratians on the island today are worse off economically than before the eruption. Farming activities are less lucrative, and farmers are reluctant to invest as they do not have security of tenure and are aware of the threat of future ash fall and acid rain (Halcrow Group and Montserrat National Assessment Team 2012). Land shortages in the north have meant that new houses have been erected in unsafe and unsuitable locations such as ravines (Hicks and Few 2015). Although resettlement has reduced exposure to volcanic hazards, these policies have created new vulnerabilities for the island population that may be more tolerable than volcanic hazard exposure for now, but this may not always be the case.

Examples of individuals not subscribing to official rules also demonstrate that the tolerability of risk varies among social groups and is not static. People entering the exclusion zone for livelihood reasons, such as tending to crops and illegal scrap metal collecting, as well as those building too close to the exclusion zone, are examples of this. Expatriate residents continue to live in Old Towne, which can become part of the exclusion zone with heightened volcanic activity, and have expressed their reluctance to evacuate and lack of confidence in the alert levels issued by the Montserrat Volcano Observatory and temporary evacuation decisions (interviews with local residents, 3 October 2012). Salem has a secondary school and a primary healthcare clinic and is home to a growing immigrant population and an ad hoc business district (Sword-Daniels et al. 2014). Rental housing is cheaper in this area and new arrivals appear to be less aware of the risks associated with volcanic activity than Montserratians (interview with local residents, 1–3 October 2012). Overall, the view that the future of the island is in the north appears not to be as unanimous as recent patterns of investment in housing and infrastructure suggest.

Another factor indicating that local authorities may not entirely endorse the idea of development in the north is the temporary nature of much of the island's vital infrastructure. Sword-Daniels et al. (2014) note that many of the buildings and essential services that were put up during the recovery period were not permanent structures. These facilities have been upgraded incrementally over time but the perception of sites as temporary has in some cases obstructed funding, leaving some buildings in an inadequate state. These 'quick fixes' need to be redressed to enable further progress of the island towards its development goals.

Discussion

The disaster risk governance regime in Montserrat has undergone a radical shift following the volcanic crisis of 1995–7 due to alterations in central and local perceptions of volcanic risk. Essentially, a longer-term view of DRM is now being taken, with new investments in vital infrastructure being made in safer locations further from the volcano and the UK government, local authorities, scientists and local communities agreeing that the future of the island is in the north. DRM in Montserrat is no longer concerned with when and how people will return to the south and how to protect them there. This represents an important shift in risk governance.

People's tolerance of risk is not static, however, and the analysis presented above demonstrates how new people coming into a high-risk volcanic area, as well as the passing of time, can change 'local' perceptions. Risk governance in Montserrat may become less effective if stakeholders no longer agree that development of the island should be based on low levels of volcanic risk. Without this convergence, policies for risk management will be ineffective at best, divisive at worst.

Many of the government-led relocation and resettlement cases described in this book reflect the very low levels of risk tolerance held by central and city government authorities. This contrasts sharply with the experiences and views of those living in hazardous places, who often tolerate these known risks because they have strategies to reduce them and because the risks associated with moving are even greater. Bringing these views closer together and achieving some consensus on the most appropriate risk management responses requires dialogue and risk governance systems that are well integrated, so this interaction can take place. In Montserrat this was partially achieved, but the dialogue needs to continue.

The Montserrat experience is atypical, and caution should be exercised in drawing lessons for other contexts. In particular, the relationship between the UK and its overseas territories is unique and different from French and Dutch overseas territories in the Caribbean, as witnessed in 2017 in these respective government responses to Hurricane Irma. Central governments elsewhere may not be so inclined to provide ongoing financial support to local governments after the recovery process is considered to have ended. Similarly, local governments with significant levels of autonomy in decentralised and particularly federal systems of governance elsewhere are likely to reject sustained central interference in local affairs following a protracted crisis. Governance reform in Montserrat was the product of conflict, but ultimately compromise, and in other contexts consensus between central and local assessments of risk may be harder to achieve. Notwithstanding these caveats, however, the transition to a system of co-governance and the reframing of disaster risk that have taken place in Montserrat provide useful examples of how transformations in disaster risk governance systems can occur following high-intensity, long-duration volcanic events.

The experience of Montserrat also provides useful insights for volcanic small island developing states (SIDS), and SIDS with disaster risks more generally. SIDS have few options for resettlement when significant parts of the territory are destroyed by a disaster, or when the pre-emptive decision is taken to move populations before a disaster to prevent loss of life. The benefits in terms of reducing disaster risk have to be weighed against loss of livelihoods for a significant proportion of the population, considerable social upheaval and often economic decline. In coastal areas, where managed retreat is being considered for many atolls and coastal cities around the world threatened by sea-level rise and storm surge, the impact of this resettlement on tourism and local economies could be huge.

Critical to the success and sustainability of these risk management decisions is the need for high levels of vertical integration in risk governance. In Montserrat, this has been partly achieved through its insertion into regional agreements and mechanisms such as the Caribbean Disaster Emergency Management Agency (CDEMA), and via the establishment of an economically dependent but politically autonomous system of co-governance with the UK. But unless communities are engaged in risk management decisions and consensus is built, the tacit state–society agreement to pursue a low-volcanic-risk development model could come unstuck. Small islands with large risks can learn from the Montserrat experience. They can anticipate and plan for how these dialogues might take place in the event of a major disaster.

Note

1. The Montserrat workshop was run by the STREVA programme as part of a 'forensic' research process, from 25 to 29 September 2012.

References

Arranz-Lozano, Mercedes. 2004. *Percepción de la Población en la Convivencia con los Riesgos Catastróficos*. Seminario Euro Mediterráneo sobre Nuevas Tecnologías Aplicadas a la Gestión de Desastres. Foro Euro Mediterráneo sobre Prevención de Catástrofes, Madrid. https://marranzl.webs.ull.es/Percepcion%20de%20poblacion.pdf.

Aspinall, Willy P., S.C. Loughlin, F.V. Michael, A.D. Miller, G.E. Norton, K.C. Rowley, R.S.J. Sparks and S.R. Young. 2002. 'The Montserrat volcano observatory: Its evolution, organization, role and activities'. In *The Eruption of Soufrière Hills Volcano, Montserrat, from 1995 to 1999*, edited by T.H. Druitt and B.P. Kokelaar, 71–91. London: Geological Society Publications. https://doi.org/10.1144/GSL.MEM.2002.021.01.04.

Barnes, Paul H. 2002. 'Approaches to community safety: Risk perception and social meaning'. *Australian Journal of Emergency Management* 1 (1): 15–23. https://eprints.qut.edu.au/606/1/Community-safety-riskperception.pdf.

CARICOM. 2009. *National Census Report Monserrat*. Georgetown, Guyana. http://statistics.caricom.org/Files/Publications/NCR%20Reports/Montserrat.pdf.

Clay, Edward, Christine Borrow, Charlotte Benson, Jim Dempster, Peter Kokelaar, Nita Pillai and John Seaman. 1999. *An Evaluation of HMG's Response to the Montserrat Volcanic Emergency. Volume 1*. London: Department for International Development. https://assets.publishing.service.gov.uk/government/uploads/system/uploads/attachment_data/file/67966/ev635.pdf.

Donovan, Amy, Michael Bravo and Clive Oppenheimer. 2013. 'Co-production of an institution: Montserrat volcano observatory and social dependence on science'. *Science and Public Policy* 40 (2): 171–86. https://doi.org/10.1093/scipol/scs078.

Donovan, Amy and Clive Oppenheimer. 2014. 'Science, policy and place in volcanic disasters: Insights from Montserrat'. *Environmental Science & Policy* 39: 150–61. https://doi.org/10.1016/j.envsci.2013.08.009.

Gaillard, Jean-Christophe. 2008. 'Alternative paradigms of volcanic risk perception: The case of Mt Pinatubo in the Philippines'. *Journal of Volcanology and Geothermal Research* 172 (3–4): 315–28. https://doi.org/10.1016/j.jvolgeores.2007.12.036.

Gregg, Chris E., Bruce F. Houghton, David M. Johnston, Douglas Paton and Donald A. Swanson. 2004. 'The perception of volcanic risk in Kona communities from Mauna Loa and Hualālai volcanoes, Hawai'i'. *Journal of Volcanology and Geothermal Research* 130 (3–4): 179–96. https://doi.org/10.1016/S0377-0273(03)00288-9.

Halcrow Group and Montserrat National Assessment Team. 2012. *Participatory Poverty Assessments*. London: Halcrow Group.

Haynes, Katharine, Jenni Barclay and Nick Pidgeon. 2008. 'Whose reality counts? Factors affecting the perception of volcanic risk'. *Journal of Volcanology and Geothermal Research* 172 (3–4): 259–72. https://doi.org/10.1016/j.jvolgeores.2007.12.012.

Heijmans, Annelies. 2001. *'Vulnerability': A matter of perception*. Benfield Greig Hazard Research Centre, UCL. https://pdfs.semanticscholar.org/04dc/68d70cd838108fb1793f69a3ca5d2634f58d.pdf?_ga=2.260839821.1055039297.1597177683-1818390683.1597177683.

Hicks, Anna and Roger Few. 2015. 'Trajectories of social vulnerability during the Soufrière Hills volcanic crisis'. *Journal of Applied Volcanology* 4 (1):1–15. https://doi.org/10.1186/s13617-015-0029-7.

Hintjens, Helen and Dorothea Hodge. 2012. 'The UK Caribbean Overseas Territories: Governing unruliness amidst the extra-territorial EU'. *Commonwealth & Comparative Politics* 50 (2): 190–225. https://doi.org/10.1080/14662043.2012.671604.

Ittelson, William H. 1978. 'Environmental perception and urban experience'. *Environment and Behavior* 10 (2): 193–213. https://doi.org/10.1177%2F0013916578102004.

Kelman, Ilan and Tamsin Mather. 2008. 'Living with volcanoes: The sustainable livelihoods approach for volcano-related opportunities'. *Journal of Volcanology and Geothermal Research* 172 (3–4): 189–98. https://doi.org/10.1016/j.jvolgeores.2007.12.007.

Lichtenstein, Sarah, Paul Slovic, Baruch Fischhoff, Mark Layman and Barbara Combs. 1978. 'Judged frequency of lethal events'. *Journal of Experimental Psychology: Human Learning and Memory* 4 (6): 551–78. DOI: 10.1037/0278-7393.4.6.551.

Mitchell, Thomas C. 2002. 'Discussion of "Second hazards assessment and sustainable hazards mitigation: Disaster recovery on Montserrat" by Jack L. Rozdilsky'. *Natural Hazards Review* 3 (2): 74–7. https://doi.org/10.1061/(ASCE)1527-6988(2002)3:2(74).

Pahl-Wostl, Claudia. 2009. 'A conceptual framework for analysing adaptive capacity and multi-level learning processes in resource governance regimes'. *Global Environmental Change* 19: 354–65. https://doi.org/10.1016/j.gloenvcha.2009.06.001.

Paton, Douglas, Marian Millar and David Johnston. 2001. 'Community resilience to volcanic hazard consequences'. *Natural Hazards* 24 (2): 157–69. https://doi.org/10.1023/A:1011882106373.

Paton, Douglas, Saut Sagala, Norio Okada, Li-Ju Jang, Petra T. Bürgelt and Chris E. Gregg. 2010. 'Making sense of natural hazard mitigation: Personal, social and cultural influences'. *Environmental Hazards* 9 (2): 183–96. DOI: 10.3763/ehaz.2010.0039.

Pidgeon, Nick, C. Hood, D. Jones, B. Turner and R. Gibson. 1992. 'Risk perception'. In *Risk: Analysis, perception and management*, 89–134. London: Royal Society Study Group.

Rachman, Stanley J. 1990. *Fear and Courage*. New York: W.H. Freeman.

Robertson, Richard E.A. 1995. 'An assessment of the risk from future eruptions of the Soufriere Volcano of St Vincent, West Indies'. *Natural Hazards* 11: 163–91. https://doi.org/10.1007/BF00634531.

Rozdilsky, Jack L. 2001. 'Second hazards assessment and sustainable hazards mitigation: Disaster recovery on Montserrat'. *Natural Hazards Review* 2 (2): 64–71. https://doi.org/10.1061/(ASCE)1527-6988(2001)2:2(64).

Simmons, Peter and Gordon Walker. 1999. 'Tolerating risk: Policy principles and public perceptions'. *Risk Decision and Policy* 4 (3): 179–90.

Skinner, Jonathan. 2002. 'British constructions with constitutions: The formal and informal nature of "island" relations on Montserrat and Gibraltar'. *Social Identities* 8 (2): 301–20. https://doi.org/10.1080/13504630220151584.

Slovic, Paul. 1987. 'Perception of risk'. *Science* 236 (4799): 280–5. https://doi.org/10.1126/science.3563507.

Smith Warner International. 2003. *Integrated Vulnerability Assessment of Montserrat*. Report submitted to the Government of Montserrat.

Sword-Daniels, Victoria, T.M. Wilson, S. Sargeant, T. Rossetto, J. Twigg, D.M. Johnston, S.C. Loughlin and P.D. Cole. 2014. 'Consequences of long-term volcanic activity for essential services in Montserrat: Challenges, adaptations and resilience'. *Geological Society, London, Memoirs* 39 (1): 471–88. https://doi.org/10.1144/M39.26.

UNISDR. 2015. *Global Assessment Report on Disaster Risk Reduction*. Geneva: UNISDR. http://www.preventionweb.net/english/hyogo/gar/2015/en/gar-pdf/GAR2015_EN.pdf.

Wachinger, Gisella and Ortwin Renn. 2010. *Risk Perception and Natural Hazards*. CapHaz-Net WP3 Report, DIALOGIK Non-Profit Institute for Communication and Cooperative Research, Stuttgart. http://caphaz-net.org/outcomes-results/CapHaz-Net_WP3_Risk-Perception.pdf.

Wadge, Geoffrey and Michael Isaacs. 1986. *Volcanic Hazards from Soufrière Hills Volcano Montserrat, West Indies*. Report to the Government of Montserrat and the Pan-Caribbean Disaster Preparedness and Prevention Project. Department of Geography, University of Reading, UK.

Wilkinson, Emily. 2012. *Transforming Disaster Risk Management: A political economy approach*. London: Overseas Development Institute. https://www.odi.org/sites/odi.org.uk/files/odi-assets/publications-opinion-files/7555.pdf.

Wilkinson, Emily. 2015. 'Beyond the volcanic crisis: Co-governance of risk in Montserrat'. *Journal of Applied Volcanology* 4 (1): 1–15. https://doi.org/10.1186/s13617-014-0021-7.

World Bank. 2002. 'Natural hazard risk management'. In *The Caribbean: Revisiting the Challenge*, Report No. 24166-LAC, 1. Washington, DC: Caribbean Group for Co-operation in Economic Development, World Bank.

Part 3
Protest and power: resistance to resettlement

The two chapters in this part discuss the practices, dynamics and reasons behind resistance to resettlement. Chapter 7, by Anthony Oliver-Smith, presents a wide-ranging and explanatory discussion of why protest is the dominant form of response to proposed resettlement. He points out that government entities are the agent of resettlement – enacting it – and that these entities usually have multiple agendas, not only moving people out of harm's way but also influenced by development projects, and often deep-seated race and class agendas. As many of the cases in this book show, those who are chosen as the subjects of resettlement are often less powerful or marginalised, and can therefore be politically expendable. Oliver-Smith also reminds us that decisions about managing climate change and disaster risks are always embedded in the political.

The lack of an accepted definition of uninhabitability means that decisions around managing risk can be interpreted by different actors, and that the proposal for resettlement often descends into bureaucratic chaos, even when there are clear definitions. Angel Wilson Chávez Eslava's chapter provides an excellent example of the bureaucratic chaos of resettlement, and how differing perspectives on the part of the communities to be resettled impact on the feasibility of the project. He shows how different interlocutors with their own agendas can influence the outcomes of the project. Both Chávez Eslava and Oliver-Smith remind us that people interpret the benefits of resettlement differently, or may perceive different levels of utility from what is offered in a resettlement package, and that these will influence whether resettlement is acceptable or not.

Chávez Eslava's chapter exemplifies how protest may be driven by individual rejection of the judgement and choices underlying risk interpretation, or of the compensation or resettlement package on offer.

Protest may also be influenced by interpersonal relations, or the need to confirm to dominant views within the community. However, the ability to resist resettlement depends largely on a number of factors, summarised by Oliver-Smith, including 1) the ability of communities to come together to protest, which must be enabled by a level of community organising; 2) the cause of resettlement and whether the location is inhabitable or not; 3) the importance of the place in people's lives, including emotionally and economically; 4) relation to the state – including trust in whether what is promised would be delivered and whether protest is politically possible; 5) the existence of allies, and their motivations to contribute to resistance; and 6) the quality of what is offered as a resettlement package.

So many resettlements are top-down propositions – communities being told they need to resettle, based on decisions that have been made by government powers, imposed on poor or marginalised communities. Community-led resettlement does exist, but is not the norm. Sometimes communities can successfully resist resettlement, and sometimes they are unable to wield enough power to stop the resettlement. Ideally, the proposition of resettlement needs to be negotiated, and protest is often about enforcing this ability to negotiate – to demand answers to complex questions such as: have all options for reducing risk in situ been exploited? Are the risks going to get worse in this location due to climate change? Should resettlement wait until such a time that the location becomes uninhabitable? What do I gain by resettling? How do I know that you will deliver on what is promised and when?

7

The choice of perils: understanding resistance to resettlement for urban disaster risk reduction and climate change adaptation

Anthony Oliver-Smith

While environmentally forced resettlement is a relatively new topic in the climate change literature, disaster risk-induced resettlement by governmental authorities has a long history. However, the topic of resistance to hazard risk and disaster displacement, despite a general focus on various forms of resistance over the last several decades (Scott 1985, 1990; Ortner 2011; Foucault 1978), has garnered significantly less attention than other types of protests such as resistance to displacement by infrastructural and other development projects. Protest and resistance to resettlement for disaster risk reduction (DRR)/climate change adaptation (CCA) are mentioned frequently in the media, but have infrequently been the focus of detailed study. Since the little detailed research that exists has focused on rural cases of resistance to resettlement for DRR/CCA, much of what follows will draw on the few urban cases that exist and much will be extrapolated from the findings of resistance to urban renewal/slum clearance (Ockey 1997; Mahadevia and Narayanan 1999; Perry 2004) and urban development-forced displacement and resettlement (Oliver-Smith 1982, 2010; Cernea 1988, 1997; Scudder 2005, 2009; De Wet 2006; Koenig 2009; Bennett and McDowell 2012). These processes share many similar characteristics with DRR/CCA resettlement in that the agent of displacement is some government entity, often operating with multiple agendas, including not only development projects, but racial and class agendas as well (Perry 2004).

Local and national governments have frequently resettled people affected by disasters in the past, but usually on an ad hoc, 'as needed' basis and usually as a post-disaster reconstruction project (Oliver-Smith 1991). However, the increasing exposure and vulnerability of urban populations today, compounded by the intensification of hazard risk from climate change, is now creating the need for resettlement as a policy option for DRR/CCA. National and sometimes local authorities are moving towards developing policy options that move people away from highly exposed environments as a strategy for reducing unmitigable risks of disaster. However, the tendency for people to resist resettlement, preferring to remain in or return to live in high-risk areas or locations that continue to be dangerous after disasters, has been noted, sometimes quite briefly, both today and in numerous cases in widely disparate cultures throughout history.

The case of Antigua, Guatemala is illustrative. Between the sixteenth and the eighteenth centuries the capital city of the colony of Guatemala, Santiago de los Caballeros de Guatemala, suffered eight serious earthquakes and a huge landslide, finally prompting the captain-general of the colony in 1773 to order the evacuation and relocation of the city to safer terrain. The citizens vigorously resisted the decision to relocate the capital, but the resettlement was undertaken, establishing the new capital, Nueva Guatemala de la Asunción. However, many citizens refused to abandon the old site, although the authorities forcibly closed down the city's remaining stores in 1779. Nevertheless, the old site was very quickly reoccupied and still exists today as the city of Antigua, one of Guatemala's major tourist attractions, famous for the beauty of its environment and colonial architecture (Tobriner 1980).

I first became aware of the importance of place in people's lives and their resistance to being uprooted in the aftermath of the Peruvian earthquake of 31 May 1970, one of the most devastating disasters in the history of Latin America. One of the central tragedies of that event took place in the city of Yungay, the capital of its province, which was destroyed by an enormous avalanche of ice, rock and mud shaken loose by the earthquake from Mount Huascarán, Peru's highest mountain, killing 95 per cent of its inhabitants. Several months after the disaster, I began a study of recovery and social reconstitution in Yungay that was to last for 10 years (Oliver-Smith 1986). The surviving Yungainos, grouped in a makeshift camp just north of the avalanche, faced the daunting task of constructing a new city and reconstituting a decimated community. To compound the losses experienced in the disaster, the government, for reasons of safety from further landslides, announced plans to resettle the survivors in the camp to a town called Tingua some 15 km to the south, which was intended to become the provincial capital.

The reaction to this project was an immediate and definite rejection on the part of the urban survivors residing in the camp, known as Yungay Norte. In addition to strong emotional ties to the location close to the old city, Yungaino leaders compiled an impressive list of practical reasons to oppose the move to Tingua (Oliver-Smith 1977). The reluctance of Yungainos to leave the general area of their destroyed city for an ostensibly safer location was based on a matrix of understandings, including deeply felt emotional ties to place and a solid grasp of the structural prerequisites of their urban socio-economic order. The Yungaino leaders reasoned that Yungay Norte would thrive because it was centrally located in the network of peasant villages of the district. These peasant villages were the life force of a town because they provided food as well as a market for commerce and administrative services in the town. Since Tingua did not have a large network of surrounding villages, any substantial urban settlement there would not be self-sustaining.

The importance of the peasant population in the decision to relocate the provincial capital of Yungay was clearly not understood by the authorities in charge of the programme. The primary motivation on the part of the authorities was to get the population moved to a safer area, out of the way of potential landslides. The risks of both alternatives were weighed, and removal to a safe but unpropitious site for urban growth was clearly rejected in favour of a site which, while less safe from geologic accident, was far better suited to the growth of a new city. Their resistance was successful and the city remains on the site of the survivor camp of 1970 now 50 years later.

This chapter will address the contexts and parameters of resistance to resettlement for DRR to gain a deeper understanding of the stakes that are at play for people faced with such an outcome. This issue needs to be addressed in the context of the rapid and essentially uncontrolled urban growth, not only of capital cities of the global South, but of secondary cities as well, although protest and resistance are not unheard of in industrialised nations such as Japan (Edgington 2010) and the United States (McPherson and Saarinen 1977). It further needs to be framed as a discourse about rights and risks, between expert and local knowledge, and between government and citizenry. After this introduction, the second section will briefly discuss the question of risk perception, with a particular focus on differential interpretations. The third section will then explore the evolving role of governance in risk and disaster management, focusing on changing state–local community relations in terms of expectations and obligations. The fourth section addresses the question of rights and the risks of resettlement. I then examine the choices made to accept or resist relocation or resettlement. As a conclusion, the final section will speak to the basic issues that people bring up as part of resistance as keys to improving resettlement policy and practice.

The question of threat: perception and interpretation of risk

Resistance to resettlement for DRR is based on assessments of a variety of threats and risks, as well as resources. The question of threat entails the apprehension of an indication or warning of the possibility that something unwanted will happen.[1] It is the assessment of the likelihood of a threat that constitutes the degree of risk that is presented. Risk generally refers to variable processes with degrees of predictability (or unpredictability) of probable dangers or harms (Tucker and Nelson 2017). In our context, risk comprises both external and internal characteristics that affect the propensity to put people at risk. To the degree that natural and technological hazards are systemic features of socio-ecological systems, threats and hazards are generally recognised, but rarely part of daily consciousness. People are usually more occupied in coping with and adapting to the micro-threats and risks of daily life, but low-predictability, high-impact threats are ignored, denied, in some cases minimally prepared for, or seen as the purview of larger political and administrative systems. Every society has to adapt to its total environment, including the local natural environment with its resources and hazards, but also its social environment, with its own resources and hazards, which are in fact derived both locally and from sources often very distant from their local contexts. For the poor and marginalised, daily life is consumed with adapting much less to environmental hazard than to the multiple systemic social hazards, many of which are a consequence of the location of their homes and/or livelihoods that are imposed on them by the society at large.

Although originally informed by the formal logic of rational choice theory, with individuals assessing risk on the basis of available information, studies of risk perception and interpretation now approach the problem from a more holistic perspective that encompasses not only information (or lack thereof), but also the social, cultural and psychological sources of attitudes and beliefs that are often inflected by such emotional variables as degree of trust in such sources. The choices to act or not are made in the context of uncertainty, a condition that can refer to the recognition of incomplete knowledge, a prioritisation of values, an assessment of probabilities or simply an existential condition of life. According to Eiser et al. (2013), whose work largely informs the approach adopted in this chapter, people's interpretations of risks are shaped by their own experience, personal feelings and values, local knowledge, cultural beliefs and interpersonal and societal dynamics. More importantly, however, risk arises not just from some description of a future event, but from the uncertainty, actual or perceived, that characterises that description. It is because the consequences of choices are uncertain, and may have positive or negative outcomes, that 'risk' becomes a factor in how decisions are made.

It is clear that risk, however, is interpreted differently by different individuals and groups, particularly in terms of how the outcomes of choices they make or are made on their behalf by other decision-makers are anticipated. These choices are based on interpretations of forms of information that come from many different sources. Uncertainties often lead people to depend on others to provide information, but acceptance of information in turn will depend on the level of trust that is inspired by such sources. The interpretation of risk in specific contexts requires understanding the values people assign to different kinds of outcomes. Moreover, individuals influence and are influenced by one another in social and institutional contexts. In point of fact, people tend to behave 'less like utility calculators and more like puzzle decryptors, simplifying cues and sorting options using heuristic algorithms' (Gigerenzer and Selten 2002, cited in Tucker and Nelson 2017, 163).

When interpreting risk on the basis of experience, people attend to multiple characteristics of risks: the severity of the threat, the magnitude of potential consequences, their ability to do something about the risk, uncertainties and ambiguities about the risk, and what they know about the hazards creating the risk in question. Experiences provide a perspective, but any learning derived from experience is always partial because evidence may be uncertain and incomplete. It is also important to consider the interactions between the decisions made by several actors rather than those of individuals considered singly, as well as groups of individuals who interact and communicate with one another, thus creating social networks that may determine responses to resettlement for hazard mitigation.

The judgements and choices underlying risk interpretation and action, then, are not merely personal, but also interpersonal, both within communities and between a community and its larger socio-political authority structure across a range of risks, environmental, social and political. In the context of resettlement for DRR/CCA, therefore, resistance is ultimately based on a choice of perils. In framing those risks, it is common for people's interpretations to differ markedly from those of formal governmental assessments. Since protection from hazards is generally framed as a techno-scientific problem best managed through rational approaches to management, governments tend to assess risks through formal methods, calling on the technical expertise of engineers, geologists, urban planners, architects and social workers. In effect, the tools of these specialised fields, assessing risk on the formal basis of degrees of probability, tend to disguise or elide socio-political causes and solutions by foregrounding technical solutions instead (Tucker and Nelson 2017). Local people, on the other hand, must take into account a host of variables that comprise the resources and risks of their total environment.

Politics and governance in DRR/CCA implementation

Resistance to resettlement for DRR/CCA is fundamentally a statement about rights and power relations. The political nature of hazards and disasters is long established in social science research. Groups, interests and institutions interact to make decisions, often intertwining with other expressions of power and wealth, about the use of public resources in preparing for and responding to extreme natural events. Moreover, disasters and their management, both before and after such events, become part of unfolding political histories (Pelling and Dill 2009). While much of the research on the politics of disasters deals with their potential for bringing about social change (e.g. Olson and Gawronski 2003), displacement and resettlement, and any resistance to those processes, are in many senses simply part of the day-to-day business of urban politics of growth and development. Cities are constantly changing, demolishing structures, building others in a process Harvey (2007) calls 'creative destruction' which, he posits, provides the basis for 'accumulation by dispossession', a process that has often seemed possible to people facing displacement for disaster risk reduction. Indeed, efforts to resist displacement and resettlement are deeply enmeshed in local issues of race, ethnicity and class as well as broader issues of development, human rights and specific political issues and goals regarding the wellbeing of the poor and the marginalised.

Displacement and resettlement policies, practices and projects are generally constructed in the institutional, legislative and legal contexts and agendas of the state, although other interests may sometimes impinge on the process. The state gains authority over a particular territory and simultaneously that territory becomes identified with that authority. This association enables the state to assume the role of holding exclusive authority over territory and, by virtue of that authority, exclusive grantor and guarantor of rights, particularly in the relationship of people to territory (Sassen 2008, 1, 6). A fundamental component of such governance is the social contract. In theory, a contract is drawn between government and a civil community that defines the rights and responsibilities of each party. In exchange for accepting certain obligations (taxes, obeying rules and regulations, etc.), citizens are afforded certain benefits and protections (maintenance of order, safety, wellbeing, etc.) by the state (O'Brien, Hayward and Berkes 2009).

We are at an interesting moment in the existence and evolution of the state, particularly as regards the social contract between the state and its citizenry. Various aspects of the relationship are undergoing significant change, altering rights and responsibilities of the parties in ways that have profound implications for displaced and resettled peoples (Sassen 2008). On the one hand, over the last three to four decades the current form of capitalism known as neoliberalism has enacted a number of basic shifts in fundamental relationships. Specifically, there has been a shift in the relationship between capital and government from one in which government played a role in regulating the economy and provided social programmes for general welfare to one in which the role of government is basically reduced to ensuring strong individual private property rights, the rule of law and the institutions of freely functioning markets and free trade (Ortner 2011). The transfer of public assets to private interests as well as the deregulation of social, political and economic processes is fundamental to this ideology, allegedly to improve efficiency and productivity and reduce costs and taxes (Harvey 2007). Further, the state's contract regarding the security of the citizenry is seen to be achieved most efficiently through the functions of the market and individual solutions to structural problems (Lampis 2016; Zeiderman 2016).

However, on the other hand, the same three to four decades have also seen a significant shift in the way disasters are conceptualised that has profound implications for disaster policy and practice, particularly as regards the state. The shift from seeing disasters as unfortunate accidents or acts of nature (or God) to framing them as the outcomes of social processes set in motion by human priorities and decisions has begun to alter the role of the state from disaster response in emergency management, which continues to be necessary, towards disaster reduction through prevention. In effect, as Zeiderman (2016) argues, disaster risk management becomes a feature of governance through which the state establishes and maintains authority and legitimacy and intervenes in the lives of citizens in the city and how they in turn address the state.

In the context of disaster management these two trends produce at best ambiguous responsibilities for the state, and at worst outright contradictions with varying consequences. On the one hand, interests and forces are freed up to pursue unrestricted gain with diminishing regard for social or environmental impact, and on the other, greater understanding of disaster causation has increased participation by the state in disaster prevention by increasing regulatory constraints, for example in land use and building codes, as well as active interventions, such as resettlement for DRR. However, many of the processes that create risk and vulnerability are standard development strategies that actually constitute drivers or compound them (Cannon and Müller-Mahn 2010). For example, Pelling notes in the case of Barbados that the post-independence modernisation project has generated an economic surplus, much of which was invested in environmental infrastructure to enhance security at the same time that it degraded the environment (Pelling 2003).

Moreover, globalised norms are pressuring the state role towards greater responsibility and intervention. Under international human rights law, states have legal responsibilities towards other states, individuals who are their own citizens, people under their jurisdiction, international organisations (e.g. the United Nations) and the international community as a whole. In the case of disasters, states normally provide humanitarian relief and reconstruction and resettlement assistance, although there are no international legal requirements binding them to these functions. However, United Nations covenants and conventions establish the human rights to health, a decent existence, work and occupational safety, an adequate standard of living, freedom from hunger, an adequate and wholesome diet, decent housing, education, culture, equality and non-discrimination, dignity, harmonious development of the personality, security of person and of the family, peace and development. These rights are considered the ideal that all governments should strive for. They are the basic life requirements to which all human beings are entitled.

However, in terms of resettlement, many states currently do not have the required legislation, responsible institutions and trained personnel to carry out resettlement in an effective, humanitarian and developmental way (Jain, Singh and Malladi 2017; Nalau and Handmer 2018). There are few agreements as yet on guidelines for anticipatory resettlement (that is, resettlement in *advance* of significant impacts), or indeed by what criteria such resettlement might be deemed necessary. Ferris (2012) notes that the lack of a clear internationally accepted definition of uninhabitability of a location, and the probability that such conditions are due to multiple factors makes it difficult to determine both causality and responsibility. Furthermore, it is unclear whether residents of a risk-prone area should be moved in advance of potential impacts, even given uncertainties concerning timing and magnitude, or whether it is best to wait until after a major disaster occurs (Kelman 2008).

In general, when confidence in government is low, there is likely to be more community resistance (Oliver-Smith 2010). However, in some contexts resistance has discouraged governments from considering relocation as a DRR option (Nalau and Handmer 2018). Resistance demonstrates that there is a need to reconcile the ethics of policies that remove people from high-risk areas with the potential that they will undermine historical freedoms and long-standing cultural patterns of settlement, mobility and livelihood (Johnson 2012). This risk that vacated lands might be appropriated for financial gain or that resettlement might be used as a tool against politically marginalised peoples suggests that criteria and guidelines are needed. Further, the lack of appropriate legislation on resettlement at the state level often leads to bureaucratic and administrative confusion, often resulting in internally inconsistent, contradictory and costly projects. Because jurisdictional and administrative responsibilities are not clearly articulated in laws and regulations, many resettlement projects result in bureaucratic chaos (Marino and Schweitzer 2009; Bronen 2008).

Rights and risks in urban resettlement for DRR

It can be reasonably argued that depriving people of access to safe and secure locations and the corresponding conditions in which to live sustainably is violating human rights since it infringes on the basic principles asserted in the Universal Declaration of Human Rights (Robinson 2003). Specific rights that are placed at risk are articulated in Article 11(1) of the 1966 UN International Covenant on Economic, Social and Cultural Rights, which affirms the right to an adequate standard of living, including food, clothing, housing and steady improvement of living conditions. Therefore, urban resettlement for DRR/CCA can be rights violating if it destroys, and does not replace, communities where people have developed livelihoods, social institutions and networks, and a meaningful context in which to live their lives. By the same token, such resettlement can become rights affirming if it supports and enables people to improve their living conditions, with better food, improved shelter and adequate livelihoods (Koenig 2009). Moreover, the state has the obligation to deal with the injustices generated by the reigning neoliberal development model. In effect, the balance of proof ultimately lies in implementation. As such, it can also be reasonably argued that the state's purpose is to address its failure to protect the basic rights of populations at risk of disaster, and that resettlement for DRR is actually a recognition of their equality and rights as citizens and a fulfilment of its obligation, thereby integrating the marginalised more fully into the larger society (Lampis 2016; Zeiderman 2016).

Before the risks of resettlement are considered, a distinction must be drawn between the refusal to evacuate in emergencies, resistance to resettlement and rejection of actual resettlement projects. There is a clear temporal dimension to each. Refusal to evacuate is either prior to or just after a disaster and may be followed by return or subsequent relocation. Resistance to resettlement is prior to project implementation, and rejection is the refusal to occupy or reside in the constructed settlement, which in the final analysis signifies project failure. Each occasions specific kinds of losses and risks. The losses of people displaced for DRR/CCA are similar to those experienced by people uprooted for infrastructure development projects. Displacement and resettlement generate a wide range of impacts that encompass both socio-cultural and psychological losses and economic and material losses. Both kinds play important roles in conditioning people's perceptions of, and reactions to, post-disaster resettlement (Oliver-Smith 1982, 1986). Regardless of the nature of their concerns, it is clear that in many cases, affected people both perceive and interpret resettlement as more of a threat than a solution.

It is either the risk or the substance of losses that energises the protest and resistance of citizens to resettlement for DRR/CCA. Many settlements that have suffered a disaster that makes their location completely insecure or those similarly exposed to risks that cannot be mitigated are the result of long and arduous processes of occupation, often in opposition to national or local governments, as migrants seek to escape rural poverty to gain a foothold in the urban environment. People risk a great deal to establish themselves as communities (often through carefully planned campaigns of occupation), regardless of the hazardous conditions in which they are obliged to live. Over time in such settlements, despite the hazards and hardships that residents face, deep connections to place are established. Further, dense networks of social relations are formed that enable people to access necessities, jobs and services that would otherwise be out of economic reach in pure market transactions. Although residents lack legal title, holdings can often be multigenerational, as families establish themselves throughout the community. In effect, such communities sink deep roots in the place they occupy and form close ties with the people they live with. Removal from these social resources and foundations of identity is both materially and emotionally experienced as loss.

In addition, urban resettlement also may bring concrete economic losses in terms of decreased access to employment, markets and clientele. The displacement and resettlement of communities also occasions a loss of social and political power in local affairs, and, if people are moved into an existing community, conflict with original residents over access to resources may result. Features of the resettlement project itself are often the cause of protest and resistance as well. The mechanisms by which expropriation and compensation are enacted, subsidies, the cost of new housing and eligibility criteria frequently elicit protest and fuel resistance by individuals, groups and entire communities.

Resettlement project-affected people, regardless of cause, are confronted with a complex, cascading sequence of events and processes most often involving risks of dislocation, homelessness, unemployment, the dismantling of families and communities, adaptive stresses, loss of privacy, political marginalisation, a decrease in mental and physical health status and the daunting challenge of reconstructing one's ontological status, family and community (Oliver-Smith 2005; Cernea 1988, 1977; Scudder and Colson 1982; Colson 1971). All may suffer the endangerment of the formulation of a sense of meaning and identity, and all must mobilise social and cultural resources in their efforts to re-establish viable social groups and communities and to restore adequate levels of material and cultural life (Bennett and McDowell 2012). Given the risks of disruption and trauma that may be generated by displacement, it is not surprising that it often generates significant protest and resistance.

Claiming rights and confronting risks

When confronted with DRR/CCA resettlement, people must decide which risks require their immediate attention: those associated with natural hazards, those that issue from the societal context (crime, poverty, health, etc.) or those that are posed by a resettlement project from a government that has rarely served them well. For marginalised people, the projects of governments are often met with a scepticism borne of a long record of unfulfilled promises and, in their eyes, dubious motives. Many people in Colombian resettlement projects for DRR thought, for example, that the risk designation for their community would cause property values to fall, thereby generating speculation for land appropriation for more profitable uses (Zeiderman 2016). In that context the record of resettlement projects itself does little to inspire confidence. Post-disaster projects have led not only to greater impoverishment but also to increased vulnerability (Birkmann et al. 2013). Moreover, in post-disaster contexts, people may be less able to resist resettlement because the disaster has skewed the power dynamics in favour of the government (Jain, Singh and Malladi 2017). Therefore, in contexts in which resettlement is being considered for people in high-risk situations, dealing with the risks of daily life by remaining in place may be afforded a higher value than reducing the risk of a low-probability/high-impact event by resettling. Indeed, even when the probability of an event is high, its unpredictability may reduce the value of taking precautions because resettlement is seen as presenting more immediate risks and losses.

The forms and modalities of resistance to DRR/CCA resettlement can be both individual and collective, legal or illegal, non-violent or violent. Not all people included in such projects will be opposed, since they may be attracted by benefits of better housing and services that have been promised. Sometimes a proposed resettlement project can be the cause of significant dissension in a community between those who favour and those who oppose. Resettlement is almost always a contentious issue. While a project may not elicit full-blown resistance, complaints, arguments over eligibility for participation, disputes over benefits, refusals to participate, foot-dragging and other delays characterise to one extent or another most resettlement projects. Chapter 8 in this volume by Chávez Eslava provides an excellent example of the kinds of conflicts that resettlement for DRR/CCA will increasingly elicit in the future. It is for that reason that many resettlement project guidelines call for conflict resolution mechanisms, complaints handling mechanisms and/or grievance procedures to be included in implementation plans.

The potential for conflict and resistance lies in the experiential basis of human cognition, which relies on past understandings for the formulation of actions with higher probabilities of predictable results. In effect, the known is preferable at some basic level to the unknown, because it is thought to provide greater accuracy in predicting the future. In that sense, then, one of the most significant dimensions of change is the degree of understanding and control which human beings can exert in dealing with the forces of change. Consequently, where understanding and control are diminished, we may expect change to be characterised by conflict, tension and resistance. At some fundamental level, all change, even positive change, in human affairs may involve a difficult process of negotiation and transition between the old and the new (Marris 1975).

Resistance to uprooting and resettlement not only involves the cognitive predisposition for order and predictability, but also implies a rejection of the imposition of superior forces or power to control either choice of action or resources (Mack and Snyder 1973, 75–6). It is in this sense that resettlement is seen as a violation of rights. The involuntary nature of the migration and resettlement process involves a loss of control over both choices and resources. The record of resettlement strategies and schemes in general is at best uneven in affording the affected populations sufficient information to reassert satisfactory control and understanding over the changed circumstances of their lives, much less the restoration of control over equal or similar resources. In a single stroke, resettlement can create a 'community which does not effectively control its own affairs ... and in which a feeling of powerlessness is pervasive', or, as Kushner goes on to characterise it, 'an administered community' (1988, 29). This loss of control and understanding is more than compounded by the often extremely negative material impacts of resettlement projects on affected peoples as motivation for resistance. More important, however, is the fact that such resettlement schemes are the direct result of purposive policies and actions, and consequently are seen as open to contestation and rejection, or alteration and improvement.

Drawing on research on resistance from development-forced displacement and resettlement and slum clearance/urban renewal, a number of factors have proven to play important roles in the ways that resistance is decided upon, organised and carried out. Clearly, a major factor in the decision to resist resettlement is the community or group's capacity to mobilise itself for organised resistance. The existence, or lack thereof, of patterns of internal differentiation based on ethnicity, class or race may undermine or enhance the establishment of the necessary levels of solidarity and cooperation for effective resistance to a resettlement project (Gans 1962). A history of internal coherence and solidarity, long-term effective leadership, pre-existing local organisations and previous successful defence of interests may also affect the community's ability to mount serious resistance efforts (Waldram 1980).

A second factor which influences the decision to resist is the cause of resettlement. The nature of the force or forces threatening resettlement will affect resistance in that some forces are clearly resistible, others permit the possibility of resistance, and still others preclude resistance entirely. Disasters associated with earthquakes, floods, hurricanes and avalanches result in circumstances in which dislocation takes place by sheer destruction. Survivors must often be relocated because their previous locale has become uninhabitable. However, disaster-affected people often are among the most contentious and resistant to further subsequent relocation, and have been known to 'invade' their devastated home sites (Oliver-Smith 1982, 1986).

A third major factor influencing resistance to resettlement is the multifaceted relationship of the target population to its environment. This relationship is based on a number of elements. In urban contexts, access to employment, political factors such as territoriality and intergroup relations, and cultural factors such as the intimate connections between components of the built environment and individual and cultural identity may all play significant roles in the relationships of a society to its general environment. Ultimately, such ties lie at the core of both individual and collective constructions of reality, and the threat of removal from their most basic physical manifestation may elicit deeply rooted resistance efforts.

A fourth factor affecting resistance to resettlement is the target population's relationship to the resettlement agent, which today is generally the nation state. As previously discussed, the relationship between the state and the diverse peoples under its control is crucial in the decision to resist resettlement. In numerous cases, this relationship is complicated by ethnic or class differences between those in control of the state apparatus and those subjected to its authority. Clearly, the general democratic or authoritarian character of the state will set a 'climate' for resistance or acquiescence, but even in authoritarian regimes with poor human rights records, resistance to resettlement has taken place. The past performance of the state in other contexts on behalf of the target population may also affect the reaction of people to proposed resettlement projects. Where the state's record is non-existent or bad, trust and confidence may be low, conditioning the response to resettlement projects (Drucker 1985; Waldram 1980).

A fifth factor in the decision to resist resettlement may be the availability of local and non-local allies. Local allies in urban areas may include non-affected neighbourhoods, co-ethnics, or non-governmental organisations (NGOs) working in the local context (Cernea 1988). International NGOs – particularly those concerned with environmental and human rights issues – may also get involved. Other potential allies include opposition political parties, student organisations, labour unions and spontaneous groups which form to combat the resettlement project for a variety of environmental or human rights causes. Allies in the media become particularly valuable in a resistance struggle. However, it must be recognised that allies generally have their own interests in mind and they may not always coincide perfectly with those of the affected population, as the chapter by Chávez Eslava (in this volume) clearly demonstrates.

A final major factor in the choice to resist or accept resettlement will be the quality of the resettlement project itself. As mentioned earlier, a resettlement project which does not enhance control and understanding, or, in other words, provide relocatees with a significant role in design and implementation, will not inspire much confidence in a population facing such a challenge to its lifeway. An ill-considered or hastily drawn up resettlement plan which does not attend to such crucial factors as employment opportunities, local housing and settlement patterns, interethnic relations, physical security, leadership and local authority institutions, among other dimensions, will be likewise unconvincing. A plan which is vague or obtuse about these or other issues of importance to the target population will engender only doubt. Conversely, a plan which is extravagant in its claims may also provoke distrust particularly if such claims can be easily disproven.

One further dimension of resettlement plans which will only be mentioned here is the resistance to the project which may be engendered in host populations. Projects which do not adequately plan for the impact of the resettled group on a host region risk provoking the resistance and hostility of the host population (Cernea 1988; Nalau and Handmer 2018). Ultimately, a relocation project not only has to be well designed and entirely adequate to the task, but it also has to be well presented and communicated in terms which permit comprehension and stimulate discussion among the affected population (Cernea 1988).

Strategies of resistance

At such time that people decide to resist resettlement, they are faced with a major strategic decision, namely whether to resist the resettlement project or to accept it as a fait accompli and put their efforts into improving it. Such a decision is often the source of much conflict within the population threatened with resettlement and between the affected population and its real and potential allies at both local and international levels. In such contexts, resistance to resettlement in reality becomes resistance to bad resettlement. Such resistance in fact signifies the adoption of a strategy of negotiation in which varying tactics of resistance are used to acquire bargaining chips in the effort to secure better terms and conditions for resettlement, such as improved replacement land, compensation for losses, housing allowances, better urban services such as transportation or better public facilities such as medical clinics or schools.

Resettlement resistance tactics

The repertoire of tactics available to people threatened with resettlement is broad, ranging from passive forms of resistance to extremely active options. Much depends on where and when tactics are initiated in the resettlement process. Tactics appropriate to early stages of planning a resettlement may not be appropriate for resistance at the implementation stage. The choice of tactics at any stage, however, will be a function of both local culture and the political space created by relations between the resettlement agent and the group facing resettlement. Generally, resisters are operating at a distinct disadvantage in terms of power and resources. However, they may seize a moral advantage based on violation of their rights as citizens which may be difficult for the state to combat or deflect. A primary and obvious distinction which must be drawn is between legal and illegal tactics. A second important distinction in resistance tactics is between non-violent and violent tactics.

Some tactics, particularly under authoritarian political regimes, employ personal connections, such as patron–client ties to influence government decision-makers (Ockey 1997). The Yungainos, for example, facing a military dictatorship, recruited prestigious professionals from their migrant community in Lima to advance their case before the government (Oliver-Smith 1986). Other initial tactics are more direct, if it is politically feasible, such as letters of appeal to the resettlement agent, which, if ignored, may be followed by letters of protest. In democratic regimes, elected officials may also be recruited to assist. In some contexts in which implementation has already begun, resistors may take more active measures by removing designations assigned to houses to be removed or uprooting stakes that mark terrain to be excavated or prepared for construction.

An important organisational tactic may be the election of a special commission or delegation of representatives of the group to visit the offices of the resettlement agent, deliver letters of appeal and present the case against resettlement in person. Crucial allies include the media, particularly if the resettlement agent is sensitive to its public image in human rights issues. Indeed, communication is always a crucial resource for a resistance movement, both in disseminating information about their struggle or in acquiring information about the resettlement project, which is often carefully controlled by planners. Establishing linkages with other causes, most notably environmental and human rights organisations, is also an important tactic. Other NGOs concerned with such issues as healthcare, nutrition, housing and water resources have also proved to be extremely helpful allies, particularly in legal matters (Cernea 1988).

Public non-violent demonstrations at the project site, the offices of the resettlement agent or the offices of funding agencies, which in urban contexts are easily accessible, are also effective in focusing attention on the cause of resistance. Such demonstrations serve to gain the attention of the public about the determination of the resistance. These events are also important in creating and maintaining solidarity in that they constitute ritualised expressions of resistance goals. In addition, these demonstrations may be the vehicle of expression for a variety of public messages of resistance, including threats of escalation in tactics, which may gain further media attention. Such escalation may include various forms of passive resistance, such as halting project progress by placing people in the path of machines, blockades at strategic entry points to the neighbourhood or community, or a simple refusal to move, even under the threat of armed troops. In that vein, there have been open physical confrontations between police or troops and people resisting resettlement.

Conclusion

Several years ago, I was invited to give a talk at a workshop in Bogotá on resettlement for DRR/CCA. Expecting a small gathering of specialists, I was surprised on arriving at the workshop venue to see a large room with perhaps as many as 250 people, both women and men, young and old, in attendance. My talk was the first on the programme and was followed by two presenters from government agencies associated with current DRR/CCA resettlement programmes in Bogotá. I gave my talk, focusing on the complex challenges that resettlement presents to affected people. It was politely received and I then sat down to follow with interest the presentations on prospective plans and projects from the government agencies. As soon as the second government presenter finished, hands instantly shot up around the hall as members of the audience began to loudly assail the government presenters, protesting the resettlement programmes with angry accusations ranging from corruption to land usurpation to destruction of community.

Their fierce rhetoric was met initially by stoic silence from the government presenters. The anger of the public was palpable and their concerns were clearly deeply felt, as were their feelings that their basic rights were being violated by an undemocratic and authoritarian government. Not only were they rejecting the risk assessment and interpretation of the city government, but they were clearly aware of and ready to accept the risks of their location rather than abandon their hard-won foothold in the urban environment for what they saw as a dubious project with an uncertain future. They appeared to hold no illusions about their current locations, fully aware of their marginalised condition within the larger political economy of the city and the nation, but feared resettlement would constitute a further infringement of their rights, yet one more manifestation of the problems of the society in which they lived. Subsequent attempts by the government presenters to respond to the protests were met with further outcries. In effect, the frictions, struggles and contestations that energised their resistance signalled eloquently that they saw contemporary urban development in Bogotá as following paths that clearly place people at risk (Allen, Lampis and Swilling 2016). Their resistance to resettlement for DRR/CCA demonstrated both a declaration and defence of their rights as citizens and at the same time, their outrage pointed to their sense of injustice and the desire to address the serious problems in their society.

Note

1. Definition from the Cambridge Dictionary online, http://dictionary.cambridge.org/us.

References

Allen, Adriana, Andrea Lampis and Mark Swilling. 2016. 'Introduction: Why untamed urbanisms?' In *Untamed Urbanisms*, edited by Adriana Allen, Andrea Lampis and Mark Swilling, 1–15. Oxford: Routledge.

Bennett, Olivia and Chris McDowell. 2012. *Displaced: The human cost of development and resettlement*. New York: Springer.

Birkmann, Jörn, Matthias Garschagen, Nishara Fernando, Vo Va Tuan, Anthony Oliver-Smith and Siri Hettige. 2013. 'Dynamics of vulnerability: Relocation in the context of natural hazards and disasters'. In *Measuring Vulnerability to Natural Hazards*, second edition, edited by Jörn Birkmann, 505–50. Tokyo: United Nations University Press.

Bronen, Robin. 2008. 'Alaskan communities' rights and resilience'. *Forced Migration Review* 31: 30–2. https://www.fmreview.org/climatechange/bronen.

Cannon, Terry and Detlef Müller-Mahn. 2010. 'Vulnerability, resilience and development discourses in context of climate change'. *Natural Hazards* 55 (3): 621–35. https://doi.org/10.1007/s11069-010-9499-4.

Cernea, Michael M. 1988. *Involuntary Resettlement in Development Projects: Policy guidelines in World Bank-financed projects*. Washington, DC: World Bank. https://doi.org/10.1596/0-8213-1036-4

Cernea, Michael M. 1997. 'The risks and reconstruction model for resettling displaced populations'. *World Development* 25 (10): 1569–87. https://doi.org/10.1016/S0305-750X(97)00054-5.

Colson, Elizabeth. 1971. *The Social Consequences of Resettlement*. Manchester: Manchester University Press.

De Wet, Chris. 2006. 'Risk, complexity and local initiative in forced resettlement outcomes'. In *Development-Induced Displacement: Problems, policies and people*, edited by Chris de Wet, 180–202. Oxford: Berghahn.

Drucker, Charles. 1985. 'Dam the Chico: Hydropower development and tribal resistance'. *The Ecologist* 15 (4): 149–57.

Edgington, David W. 2010. *Reconstructing Kobe: The geography of crisis and opportunity*. Vancouver: UBC Press.

Eiser, Richard J., Ann Bostrom, Ian Burton, David M. Johnston, John McClure, Douglas Paton, Joop van der Pligt and Mathew P. White. 2013. *Risk Interpretation and Action (RIA) Report No. 1*. Beijing: Integrated Research on Disaster Risk. http://www.irdrinternational.org/2013/01/25/ria-report-1.

Ferris, Elizabeth. 2012. *Protection and Planned Relocations in the Context of Climate Change*. Geneva: UNHCR. https://www.unhcr.org/protection/globalconsult/5024d5169/27-protection-planned-relocations-context-climate-change-elizabeth-ferris.html.

Foucault, Michel. 1978. *The History of Sexuality, volume 1: An introduction*, translated by Robert Hurley. New York: Pantheon.

Gans, Herbert J. 1962. *The Urban Villagers: Group and class in the life of Italian-Americans*. New York: Free Press of Glencoe.

Gigerenzer, Gerd and Reinhard Selten. 2002. *Bounded Rationality: The adaptive toolbox*. Cambridge, MA: MIT Press.

Harvey, David. 2007. 'Neo-liberalism as creative destruction'. *Annals of the American Academy of Political and Social Science* 610 (1): 21–44.

Jain, Garima, Chandni Singh and Teja Malladi. 2017. *Rethinking Post-Disaster Relocation in Urban India*. London: IIED. https://pubs.iied.org/pdfs/17430IIED.pdf.

Johnson, Craig A. 2012. 'Governing climate displacement: The ethics and politics of human resettlement'. *Environmental Politics* 21 (2): 308–28. https://doi.org/10.1080/09644016.2012.651905.

Kelman, Ilan. 2008. 'Island evacuation'. *Forced Migration Review* 31 (20): 20. https://www.fmreview.org/sites/fmr/files/FMRdownloads/en/climatechange/kelman.pdf.

Koenig, Dolores. 2009. 'Urban relocation and resettlement: Distinctive problems, distinctive opportunities'. In *Development and Dispossession: The crisis of forced displacement and resettlement*, edited by Anthony Oliver-Smith, 119–40. Santa Fe, NM: SAR Press.

Kushner, Gilbert. 1988. 'Powerless people: The administered community'. In *Human Rights and Anthropology*, edited by Theodore E. Downing and Gilbert Kushner. Cambridge, MA: Cultural Survival.

Lampis, Andrea. 2016. 'Lost in translation: Social protection and the search for security in Bogotá, Colombia'. In *Untamed Urbanisms*, edited by Adriana Allen, Andrea Lampis and Mark Swilling, 93–106. Oxford: Routledge.

Mack, Raymond W. and Richard C. Snyder. 1973. 'The analysis of social conflict: Toward an overview and synthesis'. In *Conflict Resolution through Communication*, edited by Fred E. Jandt, 25–87. New York: Harper and Row.

Mahadevia, Darshini and Harini Narayanan. 1999. *Shanghaing Mumbai: Politics of evictions and resistance in slum settlements*. Ahmedabad: Centre for Development Alternatives. http://gbgb.in/docs/articles/Shangaisation%20of%20Mumbai%20D%20Mahadevan.pdf.

Marino, Elizabeth and Peter Schweitzer. 2009. 'Talking and not talking about climate change in northwestern Alaska'. In *Anthropology and Climate Change: From encounters to actions*, edited by Susan A. Crate and Mark Nuttall, 209–17. Walnut Creek, CA: Left Coast Press.

Marris, Peter. 1975. *Loss and Change*. Garden City, NY: Anchor.

McPherson, Harold J. and Thomas F. Saarinen. 1977. 'Flood plain dwellers' perception of the flood hazard in Tucson, Arizona'. *Annals of Regional Science* 11 (2): 25–40. doi:10.1007/BF01287852.

Nalau, Johanna and John Handmer. 2018. 'Improving development outcomes and reducing disaster risk through planned community relocation'. *Sustainability* 10 (10): 3545.

O'Brien, Karen, Bronwyn Hayward and Fikret Berkes. 2009. 'Rethinking social contracts: Building resilience in a changing climate'. *Ecology and Society* 14 (2): 12.

Ockey, James. 1997. 'Weapons of the urban weak: Democracy and resistance to eviction in Bangkok slum communities'. *Sojourn: Journal of Social Issues in Southeast Asia* 12 (1): 1–25.

Oliver-Smith, Anthony. 1977. 'Traditional agriculture, central places, and post-disaster urban relocation in Peru'. *American Ethnologist* 4 (1): 102–16. https://doi.org/10.1525/ae.1977.4.1.02a00060.

Oliver-Smith, Anthony. 1982. 'Here there is life: The social and cultural dynamics of resistance to resettlement in post-disaster Peru'. In *Involuntary Migration and Resettlement: The problems and responses of dislocated people*, edited by Art Hansen and Anthony Oliver-Smith, 83–104. Boulder, CO: Westview Press.

Oliver-Smith, Anthony. 1986. *The Martyred City: Death and rebirth in the Andes*. Albuquerque: University of New Mexico Press.

Oliver-Smith, Anthony. 1991. 'Successes and failures in post-disaster resettlement'. *Disasters* 15 (1): 12–24. https://doi.org/10.1111/j.1467-7717.1991.tb00423.x.

Oliver-Smith, Anthony. 2005. 'Communities after catastrophe: Reconstructing the material, reconstituting the social'. In *Community Building in the 21st Century*, edited by Stanley E. Hyland, 45–70. Santa Fe: SAR Press.

Oliver-Smith, Anthony. 2010. *Defying Displacement: Grassroots resistance and the critique of development*. Austin: University of Texas Press.

Olson, Richard Stuart and Vincent T. Gawronski. 2003. 'Disasters as critical junctures? Managua, Nicaragua 1972 and Mexico City 1985'. *International Journal of Mass Emergencies and Disasters* 21 (1): 3–35.

Ortner, Sherry B. 2011. 'On neoliberalism'. *Anthropology of This Century* 1 (2011). http://aotcpress.com/articles/neoliberalism.

Pelling, Mark. 2003. *The Vulnerability of Cities: Natural disasters and social resilience*. London: Earthscan. https://doi.org/10.4324/9781849773379.

Pelling, Mark and Kathleen Dill. 2009. 'Disaster politics: Tipping points for change in the adaptation of sociopolitical regimes'. *Progress in Human Geography* 34 (1). https://doi.org/10.1177/0309132509105004.

Perry, Keisha-Khan. 2004. 'The roots of black resistance: Race, gender and the struggle for urban land rights in Salvador, Bahia, Brazil'. *Social Identities* 10 (6): 811–31. https://doi.org/10.1080/1350463042000324283.

Robinson, W. Courtland. 2003. *Risks and Rights: The causes, consequences, and challenges of development-induced displacement*. Washington, DC: Brookings Institution-SAIS Project on Internal Displacement. https://www.brookings.edu/research/risks-and-rights-the-causes-consequences-and-challenges-of-development-induced-displacement.

Sassen, Saskia. 2008. *Territory, Authority, Rights: From medieval to global assemblages*. Princeton, NJ: Princeton University Press.

Scott, James C. 1985. *Weapons of the Weak: Everyday forms of peasant resistance*. New Haven, CT: Yale University Press.

Scott, James C. 1990. *Domination and the Arts of Resistance: Hidden transcripts*. New Haven, CT: Yale University Press.

Scudder, Thayer. 2005. *The Future of Large Dams: Dealing with social, environmental, institutional and political costs*. London: Earthscan.

Scudder, Thayer. 2009. 'Resettlement theory and the Kariba case: An anthropology of resettlement'. In *Development and Dispossession: The crisis of forced displacement and resettlement*, edited by Anthony Oliver-Smith, 25–48. Santa Fe: SAR Press.

Scudder, Thayer and Elizabeth Colson. 1982. 'From welfare to development: A conceptual framework for the analysis of dislocated people'. In *Involuntary Migration and Resettlement: The problems and responses of dislocated people*, edited by Art Hansen and Anthony Oliver-Smith, 267–87. Boulder, CO: Westview Press.

Tobriner, Stephen. 1980. 'Earthquakes and planning in the 17th and 18th centuries'. *Journal of Architectural Education* 33 (4): 11–15.

Tucker, Bram and Donald R. Nelson. 2017. 'What does economic anthropology have to contribute to studies of risk and resilience?' *Economic Anthropology* 4 (2): 161–72. DOI:10.1002/sea2.12085.

Waldram, James. 1980. 'Relocation and political change in a Manitoba native community'. *Canadian Journal of Anthropology* 1 (2): 173–8.

Zeiderman, Austin. 2016. *Endangered City: The politics of security and risk in Bogotá*. Durham, NC: Duke University Press. https://doi.org/10.1215/9780822374183.

8
Resistance and resilience of the community of Belén, Iquitos, Peru, to resettlement

Angel Wilson Chávez Eslava

It is important for Peru to generate a broad debate about the importance of population resettlement under conditions of disaster risk in a context where historical alterations in the equilibrium between humans and the environment have increasingly led to the proposed relocation or resettlement of the population from high-risk areas, where their personal security and livelihoods cannot be guaranteed. One such case is the ongoing resettlement of population from the Lower Belén Flood Zone (LBFZ), a non-mitigable high-risk[1] sector located in the district of Belén, in the city of Iquitos, Province of Maynas, Department of Loreto, which is part of the Amazon region of Peru.[2] The LBFZ comprises a riverside community, accustomed to regular annual flooding, principally between March and July. This community has more than fifteen thousand people living under conditions of very high disaster risk and extreme poverty. The human–environment balance in which they live has been severely altered due to the inadequate historical occupation of the flood plain of the River Itaya (a tributary of the Amazon), and a recent increase in the number and recurrence of extreme flood events, usually attributed to climate change.

Faced with this situation, the national government of Peru decided to implement measures to help reduce the disaster risk of the population. The New City of Belén project, implemented by the Ministry of Housing, Construction and Sanitation (MHCS) since 2014, is the most significant resettlement experience in Peru. The present chapter aims to examine the resilience to floods of the LBFZ population and the resistance to the New City of Belén resettlement project, and thereby contribute to further analysis and debate on resettlement in Peru. The study on which the chapter is based employed a method of participatory action research, using both qualitative and quantitative methods, including fieldwork, participatory observation, questionnaires and interviews with key informants from the affected population and government authorities at a local and national level (see Table 8.1).

The chapter has eight sections. The first provides a brief history of urban disaster risk in Peru. Second, the disaster risk from flooding in Iquitos city is reviewed. A third section considers urban growth and flood risk in the LBFZ. Fourth, the two major alternatives proposed as solutions to disaster risk are reviewed. A fifth section provides an analysis of stakeholders and examines their level of interest and influence on the resettlement project. The sixth section presents an analysis of conflicts between the different actors and the power relations among them. Seventh, a reflection on resilience and its impact on culture is carried out. Eighth and last, a summary conclusion is provided.

Table 8.1 The sample of surveys, interviews and focus groups in high-risk zones and in the areas of the resettlement and with government authorities and employees at a national, regional and local level.

Zone	Condition	Surveys	Focus groups	Interviews
Lower Belén	Population under conditions of non-mitigable risk	55	2	10
Calipso resettlement	Resettled	51		2
Stakeholder	Key informants	38		5
Villa Olímpica resettlement	Refuge	36		
Varillalito: the new resettlement area with few people there at time of study	Resettled voluntarily	0	1	5
Total		180	3	22

Background: disaster risk in Peru

The diverse geological and hydro-meteorological phenomena that threaten Peru expose more than fifteen million people, four million homes and thirty-four thousand population centres to hazard.[3] An estimated 10 per cent of the population is located in very high unmitigable risk areas, where their lives and heritage are in danger. The National Water Authority (ANA) has recently identified 563 urban settlements located in hazardous flood plain areas (ANA 2016). During the El Niño event in summer 2007, all the important northern, central and southern coastal cities were severely affected by flooding and landslides, including Lima, Piura, Chiclayo, Trujillo, Huarmey and Arequipa.

Accelerated processes of urbanisation occurred in Peru from the mid-twentieth century onwards, which was mainly associated with agrarian reform and political violence, particularly in rural areas. These processes led to migratory waves from the countryside to the city, to such an extent that today 79.3 per cent of the national population lives in towns and cities (INEI 2018). Many unplanned urban settlements were then built in highly hazard-prone zones. Small settlements subsequently became cities and metropolises, driven by the housing boom at the beginning of the twenty-first century. As a result of modern technology and infrastructure, the old human–nature relationship was modified and a new, more risk-prone human–environment relationship was established.[4]

Disaster risk due to flooding in Iquitos city

In the Department of Loreto, where Iquitos is located, more than sixty-five thousand homes are at very high risk. This number has been arrived at considering the number of houses that were lost or damaged in the most recent extreme flooding in 2012 and 2018 (see Figure 8.1). Iquitos city itself is almost an island, bordered on three sides by the Itaya, Nanay and Amazon rivers, with flood zones along all the rivers.

The absence of land-use planning, accompanied by high levels of poverty and a historical culture of riverine flood plain occupation, has led to large numbers of people settling in flood-prone areas (the Belén area, the subject of this chapter, is euphemistically referred to as the Venice of Peru).

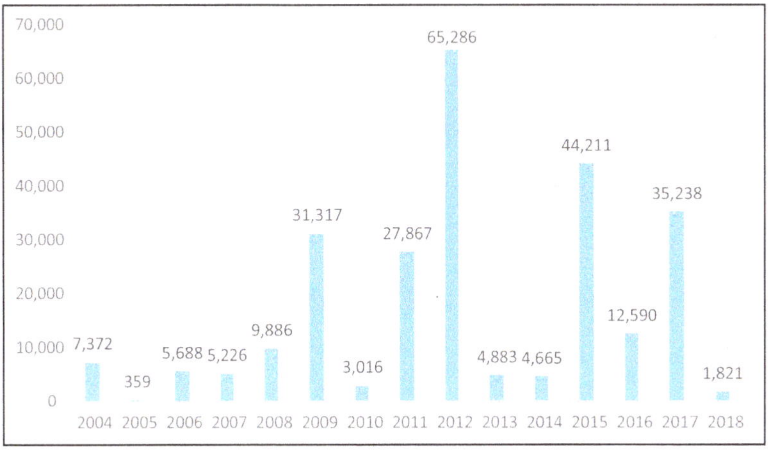

Figure 8.1 Number of houses in the Department of Loreto destroyed and affected by flooding between 2004 and 2018. © Angel Wilson Chávez Eslava, with data from INDECI.

Studies carried out by the Peruvian Navy report that the Amazon is migrating closer to the Itaya river and that in approximately 30 years it will occupy and permanently flood the LBFZ sectors of Muyuy and Aguajal (Dirección Nacional de Hidrografía y Navegación 2015). The Amazon is the largest river in the world and contains more water than the Nile, the Yangtze and the Mississippi together. This means that when the waters of the Amazon reach the Itaya it will be impossible to reduce, in situ, the flood hazard for the LBFZ population, thus making resettlement unavoidable (Chávez 2016).

In 2012 Iquitos suffered the most extreme floods in decades, severely affecting the LBFZ. That same year a large urban fire also consumed a large sector of the LBFZ. Both disasters increased the already precarious living conditions of the population and placed Belén firmly on the national disaster risk agenda. In 2015 the city and the LBFZ were once more affected by severe flooding, increasing pressure for remedial actions.

In the past, the extreme rainfall that Iquitos suffered every year was discharged through natural channels that functioned as a rainwater drainage system. However, these natural drains were destroyed by urban growth, causing an increased level of flood hazard during regular seasonal rainfalls. Despite their potential use for flood drainage, no inventory of natural drains is available, nor is there any political will to recover them.

Urban growth and flood risk in the LBFZ

More than a century ago, the LBFZ was the port area of Iquitos and an access point for agricultural products to the Belén market. The market generated economic activities in the area of Belén, such as fishing, river and land transport services, agriculture, retail trade, informal street traders, and commerce in stolen and used items, among others. Currently the market is in the process of relocation within the same district of Belén, a process widely accepted by the local government.

The Belén municipality was founded in 2002. This led to the mobilisation of population demanding basic services, such as electricity, telecommunications, healthcare and education. The authorities attended to many of these demands. However, the severe environmental conditions did not facilitate the provision of some basic services. Potable running water, sewerage services and solid waste management are pending in many places. Moreover, the levels of poverty and exclusion mean that families do not pay municipal taxes for basic services. It is a challenge for the municipality of Belén to finance and execute basic service projects in the LBFZ given the adverse environmental and social conditions that exist due to the floods.

The original settlers of Belén did not severely suffer the effects of floods because they lived on raft-houses that floated during flooding. However, these rafts were built with local materials which have been over-exploited, making them difficult to find any more. Over time, the city's population occupied more and more land in the flood plain of the Itaya river, changing the pattern of land use and consolidating residential urban areas. Building raised houses with stilts avoided flooding. The local authorities also provided the floodable area with health clinics, schools, churches and parks, among other things, without considering risk. In this way they institutionalised disaster risk. Some houses in the LBFZ were built with brick and concrete, imitating big-city, non-flood-zone building practices because the use of the more adequate, albeit rustic materials was not seen as 'progress'. This population did not value the past culture of the riverine settlers, who constructed using the available local materials which were more adaptable to the flood season.

Although rivers are a source of life for riverine populations, the city of Iquitos is highly deficient in the management of solid waste. It disposes tonnes of garbage into its rivers, causing dangerous levels of environmental contamination. This has a substantial impact on the health of its inhabitants. Lethal diseases such as dengue and leptospirosis have high incidence rates in the LBFZ and elsewhere. Although for decades the people of Belén have lived under threat of pollution and flooding, the conditions have now grown worse. Today the higher contamination includes fecal coliforms, toxic residues and heavy minerals, which are all detrimental to the health and quality of life of the riverine inhabitants and greatly aggravate the problem of floodwaters.

At present, the LBFZ is a type of ghetto, an underworld of formal society. Made up of a culturally defined, socially excluded group of people, it comprises an economically poorer population, dedicated in good part to illicit activities under the guise of informality. In addition, the illegal activities of certain sectors of the population legitimate and support grave conditions of exclusion, such as in the trafficking of persons and child slavery. Many inhabitants want to leave the zone and start over again elsewhere. However, for others any such relocation would seriously affect their economic status and lifestyle. These two opposing views are expressed in the project proposals developed to favour the LBFZ population.

The alternatives

Faced with flooding, the city has a history of small-scale, intermittent relocations to safer areas during the 1990s, beginning with the Los Delfines resettlement project and later the Calipso resettlement project. These and other attempts were largely unsuccessful due to insufficient planning and political commitment. The relocated population does not yet own the land they occupy and still lacks some basic services. This has increased the possibility of them abandoning the areas and returning to their old sites. During the 2012 flooding, the more seriously affected population of the Iquitos city districts of Belén, San Juan Bautista, Punchana and Maynas were temporarily relocated to the Fuerte Vargas Guerra and Olympic Village areas. The affected population was provided transitional shelter and other basic services. With the end of support to the shelters, the LBFZ population agreed to leave if they were transferred to Varillalito, the new resettlement site for the LBFZ population planned by government (see below). This occurred in mid-2016, initially with 70 families.

The critical situation of the LBFZ has led to two disaster risk reduction proposals. The first focused on an in situ urban renewal solution. A second option, now underway, involves the implementation of a large-scale resettlement project.

Urban renewal in situ: Sustainable Belén Project

The historic floods in Belén in 2012 came to the attention of the national authorities because of the unusually high critical conditions faced by the population. The government of President Humala (2011–16) made the political decision to search for a solution for families living in the LBFZ. A so-called Presidential Promise for finding a solution was made to the local population. The Ministry of Housing, Construction and Sanitation (MHCS) developed an on-site improvement programme called the Sustainable Belén Project. This consisted of urban renewal in the LBFZ with new stilt homes, installation of sanitation services, aerial drainage systems, roads, sidewalks and parks. Technical aspects were based in part on models used in South-East Asia.

The project managers found it very difficult to comply with construction demands due to technical difficulties installing houses and adapting basic services in the area subject to flooding. The project was cancelled after approximately a hundred of the planned 2,600 houses had been constructed. High costs and technical difficulties were used to explain the cancellation of the project. However, the reasons were never openly presented or discussed with the population. Despite the constant demands by the people of LBFZ for the reactivation of the Sustainable Belén Project, the environmental conditions made the proposal unfeasible. A second catastrophic flood in 2015 confirmed this conclusion.

The New Belén Resettlement Scheme

As a measure of the political will to solve the existing problem in Belén, in December 2014 the national government promulgated Law No. 30291. This action was for the relocation of the Lower Zone of Belén, and it proposed a completely new resettlement scheme. With the enactment of the law, known as the New Belén City Project, the Sustainable Cities Programme (SCP) of the MHCS was created. This project planned to resettle nearly 2,600 families to Varillalito, an area to the south of the city of Iquitos on the LO-103 road located in the district of San Juan Bautista, 13 km from Iquitos (Cruzatt 2014).

The project proposed a new city with the potential to become an economic development pole. A 50-hectare plot of land bought by the government was divided into 120 m^2 lots. On each lot, a free housing module of 40 m^2 will be constructed. Potable water, sanitation, flood drainage and electricity will be provided. In addition, public areas will have sidewalks, sports areas, parks, gardens, schools, health centres, a market and a police station (Cruzatt 2014).

The beneficiaries include people from the nine Lower Belén communities of October 6, August 30, Prolongación Santa Rosa, Belén III Stage, Pueblo Libre, Sachachorro, Zona Belén de Belén, Caserío and Nuevo Liberal. Unfortunately, five years after the law was enacted, the project had only built 400 of the 2,600 homes, and the promised services (water, sewage, education, etc.) are not properly functional. Because of this, some of the relocated family groups have chosen to keep their houses in the LBFZ.

Analysis of actors: level of interest and influence on the project

The slow overall progress made in implementing the New City of Belén project has been one reason for the existing levels of organised support or opposition for the scheme by different stakeholders. With the change of national government in July 2016, project implementation slowed even more, given that the current MHCS authorities do not have the same political interest in executing the project as the previous administration had. The delays have permitted different stakeholders to develop a strategy for defending or opposing the project. The nature of the power relations, as well as the structure of stakeholder support and opposition, are analysed below in order to help understand the projects' governance context and the types of difficulty large-scale resettlement of well-consolidated population groups may signify.

The dynamic of the relationship between stakeholders

With the cancellation of the Sustainable Belén Project and the subsequent passing of Law No. 30291 for the relocation of Lower Belén, a significant part of the population grew distrustful of the government. The rejection of the resettlement project was inevitable. Local actors mobilised against the project and formed a tacit alliance with leaders of neighbourhood councils, local merchants, the tabloid press, NGOs, the municipality of Belén, various opposition political parties, and regional and national social movements.

However, another group of leaders of the LBFZ accepted and promoted the project and joined with the MHCS in its promotion of the benefits of the project. The previous mayor of the municipality of San Juan Bautista had also supported the project with its economic and developmental benefits, because the 2,600 families would have been resettled in an area under his jurisdiction.

For the population to widely support the project, a strategy that results in a win–win situation is required (Flint 2001). This option would exist if the families were able to take full ownership of the housing in the New City of Belén and in turn managed to retain property in the LBFZ. However, this strategy is not feasible because the law of relocation for Belén clearly establishes that the abandoned land must be expropriated by the state and that the area may only be zoned for purposes other than urban uses. The lack of a favourable alternative for all those involved may be expressed using the prisoner's dilemma analogy. If all the options are unfavourable, which one is furthest from a zero-sum solution? The position taken by the population, social organisations, politicians and economic interest groups to the New Belén Project depends on positive results for all those deriving benefits from the alternatives offered.

Another positive alternative for a large sector of the population of Belén would be on-site improvement, that is to say, a project similar to the Sustainable Belén Project, but this time with feasible technical proposals. This option is one of the most popular among the inhabitants of the LBFZ but is not acceptable to the state. The state notes the projected movement of the Amazon towards the Itaya, along with the predicted future of unmitigable flooding in the Belén area no matter what technical solutions are sought.

Families in favour of the resettlement project consider it beneficial to search for better living conditions outside the flood zone of Belén. However, for the much larger group that does not want to leave the flood zone, the project means being uprooted and fracturing the existing social, economic and political power relations. If the New Belén City project were cancelled, villagers who rejected the project would maintain their status quo on-site, while people who are affected by the flood would miss an opportunity to generate other development opportunities away from the high-risk areas.

The opposition group to the project may employ legal and illegal, violent and non-violent tactics and has voice, determination and magnitude (Tilly 1995). Voice is expressed in the ability to put the issue on the local and national political agenda, while determination is demonstrated in the sacrifice that people are willing to make to oppose the project, including the sacrifice of their own lives. Magnitude refers to the number of settlers that can be mobilised by the protest movement. These three factors do not exist in the group that favours the project. They only have voice and leadership, but they do not have determination and magnitude. If they did, it would be expressed in far greater social pressure on the authorities to accelerate the execution of the project. People who do not reject the project have a contemplative attitude, not a belligerent attitude. They are only waiting for the project to be implemented in order to support and defend it.

The opposition group, which is highly organised and consolidated, has an ideology that fosters radical opposition to the project. All radical groups recreate their own history of battles and heroes, rewriting stories to depict them as winners (although they are not) and allow them to generate bonds of union within the group. The settlers who do not reject the project outright are neither cohesive nor pragmatic. They do not fully trust the state, and their support and confidence in the authorities depends on the level of progress of the works at the new city site. Given this, they do not offer any real opposition to those who openly oppose the project.

Based on interview results with 54 people, Figure 8.2 reveals certain contradictions. For example, many who protest daily are not necessarily against the project. One faction of daily protesters supports the

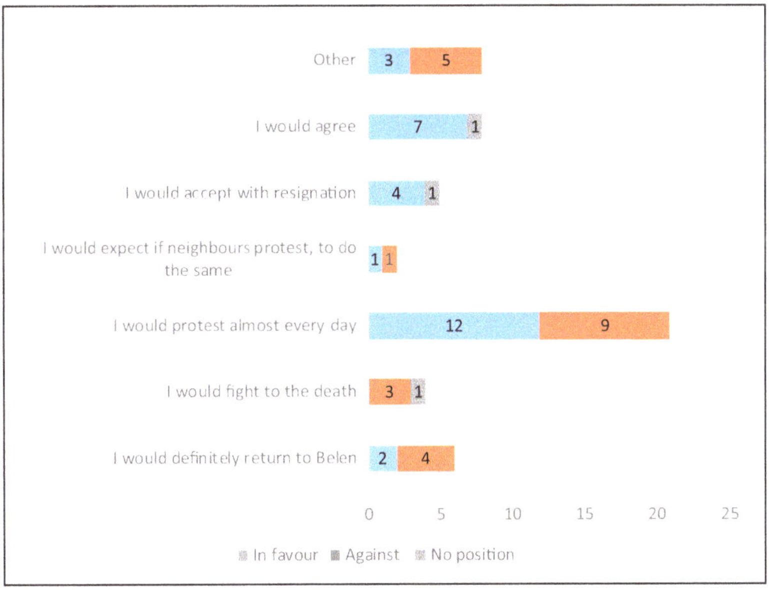

Figure 8.2 People's reactions to obligatory resettlement: results from interviews conducted with 54 people. © Angel Wilson Chávez Eslava.

project, despite their actions to the contrary. They protest because of social pressure to do so, and they know that if they do not protest, they will be recriminated against by the opposition group. On the other hand, there is a very small radical group who would fight to the death to reject the project, or they would accept resettlement with resignation. Finally, there is a group who would return to their place of origin later if they were forced to relocate.

The possibility of the opposing group weakening its collective position will depend on the extent to which a 'free rider' effect is generated. This measures when a protest is losing its efficacy, and when more and more residents obtain individual benefits produced by the opposition group without having to protest themselves. That is to say, free riders grow within the group. Such people reject the project, but do not mobilise to protest, because they feel that those inhabitants already mobilised are sufficient to sustain the goals and benefits expected by resistance (Paramio 2005). To the extent many free riders are created in the opposition group, mobilisation will lose voice, magnitude and determination.

Another factor that generates free riders is the high transaction cost of social mobilisation that leads to project failure. The benefits of staying in the flood zone may be superior to those expected at the new location, but if the costs of staying in the flood zone are higher, the free rider effect will spread and collective mobilisation against the project will be weakened. There has been a significant increase in the number of free riders as the project has proceeded and infrastructure has been built. This has meant that radical groups have attacked many free riders and accused them of being traitors, thus generating conflict in neighbourhoods.

Positive and negative resilience

Resilience is the ability of society to absorb the impacts of dangerous phenomena and recover to a normal state (UNISDR 2009). Resilience is a supplement to the human–environment relationship, helping to prevent it from breaking down under stress. However, resilience can be harmful if it supports a perverse relationship between poor humans living in unhealthy environments.

Adaptation to climate change can be expressed as maladaptation if a perverse relationship is established between humans and the environment. Unlike resilience, adjustments to climate change are slow and occur in the short, medium and long term, such that the population may not perceive them. Resilience includes not only adjustments to environmental changes, but also resistance and recovery when encountering climate variability, particularly when faced with the effects of extreme events. The settlers of Belén meet this definition of resilience because they survive under conditions of extreme poverty, underemployment and lack of opportunities, pollution and periods of flood. They have made informal activity a way of life, and this allows them to maintain their families. They know of no other viable option in life and they remain averse to change. They have made Belén their territory, a place where they establish their own rules for coexistence. This form of resilience is negative because the informality in which they live forces them to coexist without complaint with crime, violence and impunity, as well as the destruction of their own environment. The settlers are highly tolerant of living standards well below those that would be considered decent and salubrious under other circumstances. This type of resilience perpetuates and legitimises discrimination and exclusion.

It is difficult for the population of Belén to trust the state and its promises, or to imagine living in another area in the future when nowadays they barely manage to survive and to maintain their families on a day-to-day basis. The ability to project to the future is not part of the resilience of this population. This means that resettlement is not a credible option for them. Thus, their resistance to the resettlement process is strengthened.

As the population struggles to survive in the flood zone, a form of positive resilience is expressed when people have hopes of improving their living conditions (work, health, education, water, sanitation and drainage), and care about their children's education, especially for preventing them from joining any of the local gangs. During flood periods, these families lock themselves in their homes to prevent their young children from drowning or contracting lethal diseases. For them, if the strategy to improve their condition of life happens to be relocation outside of Belén, they are willing to accept it. In Figure 8.3, one can see the position of the settlers of the LBFZ with regard to relocation.

Local politicians and the inhabitants believe that high exposure to flooding is normal. The romantic view held by some actors about a 'culture of water' among those living in flood zones impedes them from considering how flooding is a problem for the security of the society. Moreover, a sector of the population of the LBFZ does not want to be relocated, preferring instead to accept the risks to their health and physical integrity.

According to Michel Foucault, 'normalisation' is the process by which certain behaviours and ideas are made 'natural' through coercion

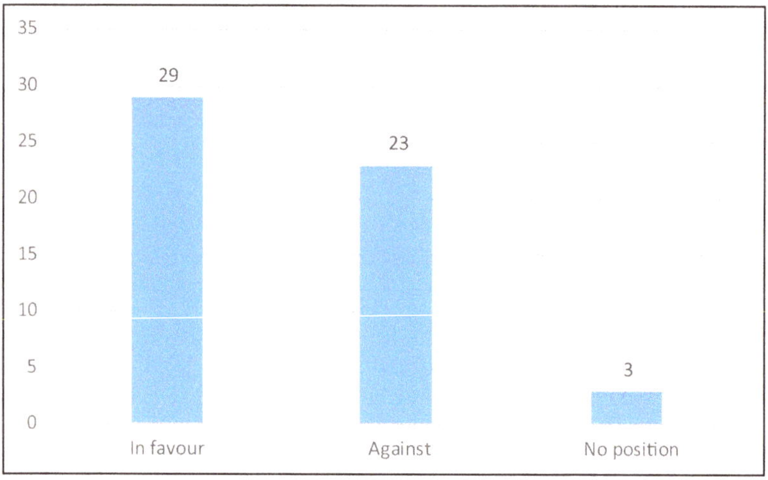

Figure 8.3 Do you approve of the New Belén project in Varillalito? Reactions of people of Belén to relocation are mixed. Those who believe that moving will improve their conditions of living and safety approve of it, while those who do not trust the state to keep its promises and anticipate difficulties after moving resist. © Angel Wilson Chávez Eslava.

mechanisms expressed in sanctions, discipline, ideology, education or other means. Normalisation formalises social differences and exclusion, which does not allow for further questioning (Foucault 2010). Poverty, inequality and living in constantly flooded areas of the LBFZ are very common. This has been 'normalised' in such a way that the actors consider that such living conditions are socially acceptable. Those accepting such normalisation do so without exerting pressure on the authorities to generate change.

Conclusion

The state has created a hyper-centralism of power in Lima, causing the cities of the Andes and Amazonia to be systematically excluded, thus generating a constant mistrust of the elites among local populations. In this institutional context, the resettlement project has been implemented, with high levels of distrust on the part of the community and the radicalisation of political opponents. Since the change of national government in 2016, the political will for the project has diminished. As a result of these factors there is now evidence of a slowdown in the execution of the work. This delay gives more time for opponents to design new strategies and plan sabotage against the project. Although the project has not been cancelled, the situation does create greater distrust in the population and weakens support.

The human–environment balance has been profoundly altered by the inadequate occupation of territory and a recent increase in catastrophic climatic events. Resilience, a mechanism that allows society to face extreme conditions of life, has been surpassed by the destructiveness of recent events. Decent living conditions, and above all the mitigation of or adaptation to disasters in situ, is now a very difficult challenge to face. On the other hand, resilience contributes to legitimising marginality and exclusion and is especially important in generating incentives for resistance to resettlement.

The resettlement project places the population in a difficult position because it is not the typical situation where the state uses force to impose an abrupt relocation of the population. Even though there is resistance and opposition to the project, there is also support for it. Therefore, bipolarity in the population means that if the project fails or succeeds there will always be losers and winners. The prisoner's dilemma exists here, as does the free rider effect. The endgame of political mobilisation is not yet decided, and this will depend on the results of each group's strategies.

Disasters during the last decade have shown that secure conditions cannot be achieved in situ with the implementation of mitigation measures. Damage and loss caused by disasters have revealed to the public the need to develop population resettlement processes for cities facing high risks. In this sense, the New Belén City Project is crucial for decision-makers because it is needed in order to validate a model of successful resettlement policy for the country. Also, future land use and territorial planning must ensure that risk is not reconstructed in any new locations which are highly prone to flooding.

Beyond the power game and protest by actors, the Belén project opened a door of opportunity for a sector of the population that does not wish to continue living in conditions of exclusion and marginalisation. Assuming the project is not cancelled, it will be a challenge for project implementers to sustain the limited trust already gained among an increasing part of the population. The state may not have the political appetite to continue taking concrete actions during the remainder of the project.

Notes

1. Zones of very high, unmitigable risk are defined in the 2012 Law on Population Relocation (Law 29869) as those where the implementation of mitigation measures in situ is more expensive and complex than a process of human resettlement.
2. See Chapter 7 in this book by Oliver-Smith, who comments on one of the first processes of resettlement in Peru associated with the destruction of Yungay in 1970 due to an avalanche caused by the Ancash earthquake.
3. According to a 2014 report of the Commission for Housing and Construction of the National Congress, based on official data of the National Statistics Office for 2007.
4. Another form of expressing this relationship is environment = technology – infrastructure + nature.

References

ANA. 2016. *Identificación de Poblaciones Vulnerables Por Activación de Quebradas 2015–2016*. Lima. https://hdl.handle.net/20.500.12543/198.

Chávez, Angel. 2016. *Reasentamiento Poblacional En Zonas Urbanas Por Impacto de Fenómeno Hidro-Meteorológicas, Incluyendo Efectos Del Cambio Climático: Caso Belén*. Lima.

Cruzatt, Sandra. 2014. *Estudio de Análisis Micro Social de Involucrados*. Iquitos.

Dirección Nacional de Hidrografía y Navegación. 2015. *Informe Técnico: Variación Del Rio Amazonas en relación al Río Itaya*. Loreto.

INEI. 2018. *Perú: Perfil Sociodemográfico*. https://www.inei.gob.pe/media/MenuRecursivo/publicaciones_digitales/Est/Lib1539/libro.pdf.

Flint, Pinkas. 2001. *Negociaciones Eficaces: Implemente las mejores estrategias y tácticas*. Lima: El Comercio.

Foucault, Michel. 2010. *Vigilar y Castigar: Nacimiento de la prisión*. Mexico: Siglo XXI.

Law 29869. 2012. *Ley de Reasentamiento Poblacional Para Zonas de Muy Alto Riesgo No Mitigable*. Peru.

Law 30291. 2014. *Ley Que Declara En Emergencia y de Necesidad Pública La Reubicación de La Población de La Zona Baja Del Distrito de Belén, Provincia de Maynas, Departamento de Loreto*. Peru.

Paramio, Ludolfo. 2005. 'Teorías de la decisión racional y de la acción colectiva'. *Sociológica (México)* 20 (57): 13–34. http://www.scielo.org.mx/pdf/soc/v20n57/2007-8358-soc-20-57-00013.pdf.

Tilly, Charles. 1995. 'Los movimientos sociales como agrupaciones históricamente específicas de actuaciones políticas'. *Sociológica (México)* 10 (28): 13–36. http://www.sociologicamexico.azc.uam.mx/index.php/Sociologica/article/view/667/640.

UNISDR. 2009. *Terminología Sobre Reducción Del Riesgo de Desastres*. Geneva. https://www.unisdr.org/files/7817_UNISDRTerminologySpanish.pdf.

Part 4
Land issues in resettlement

The four chapters in this part are concerned with understanding how land tenure and property rights influence risk and resettlement. They also look at the growing rate of evictions in urban areas. Land dynamics are a primary driver of risk accumulation in certain areas – some people cannot afford safe places to settle so they build where it is inexpensive and convenient, in flood plains and coastal areas, along rivers and slopes, many of which are becoming more at risk due to climate change. Risk-related resettlement may be a knee-jerk reaction that tries to mitigate the risk in a city where populations have informally settled on exposed sites – thus, as is mentioned in the introduction to this book, resettlement is a response to failed development planning, and should be a last-resort option.

The chapters in this part all use a rights-based approach, essentially building on the definitions of relocation and resettlement set out in the introduction to this book, and argue for people to have the right not only to housing (which may be provided in resettlement), but to the full spectrum of land, property and livelihood rights. The cases examined in this part make clear that resettlement is not voluntary and for the most part would be classified as a forced eviction, firstly because people did not choose to be moved, and secondly because they are denied the rights to property and livelihood at the resettlement sites. Furthermore, as is pointed out in Chapters 10 (by Yves Cabannes), 11 (by Giovanna Astolfo) and 12 (by Bill Flinn and Holly Schofield), the resettlement usually results in a second market-based eviction, as families are not able to keep up payments or meet the criteria to remain eligible for the new housing – amounting to a second eviction and the ultimate denial of housing rights.

Chapter 9, by Colin Marx, puts forward the idea that property rights have an influence on risk reduction measures – using the notions of *insulating* and *isolating* effects on people. For example, in Kampala, Uganda, those people who were perceived to hold bona fide property rights to settle in low-lying areas were not seen a being 'at fault' for causing the flooding problems – they were insulated from being held accountable for degradation of the wetlands. Also, the perceived lack of property rights insulated the authorities from having to worry about individual loss from disasters, i.e. if they were not owners then the authorities were absolved from needing to offer assistance.

In Chapter 10, Yves Cabannes outlines how climate change and risks tend to be used as a key 'rational discourse' to justify either forced or market-driven evictions, by putting into perspective climate-induced relocation and resettlement with other forms of land and housing eviction that have increased in scale, number and brutality over the last 40 years. He outlines how climate change and risk-related displacements are among many causes of evictions that are intrinsically linked with one another, and gives examples of this snowball effect or chain reaction. Drawing on David Harvey's concept of accumulation by dispossession, Cabannes argues that Harvey's concept needs to be nuanced as a socially and spatially selective accumulation by dispossession process, affecting primarily the most vulnerable groups and globalised territories that can absorb massive amounts of capital and offer the most lucrative investments. This chapter also lays out how current UN frameworks show a regressive attitude through weak wording and exclusion of key phrases, which are making people more exposed to eviction and insecurity of land rights, and offers some glimmers of hope with positive examples of securing rights.

As an example of the need for a nuanced argument of accumulation by dispossession, Giovanna Astolfo, in Chapter 11, takes us through the genealogy of land systems in Cambodia and relates the current round of evictions to the making of the global city, and foreign investment, and traces how this process has been enabled by the history of land expulsions in the country. She explains how the evicted communities lack knowledge (no maps, no clear plans, no information) and resources to enforce their rights. This links to Oliver-Smith's outlining, in Chapter 7, of the ability for community resistance to evictions.

Chapter 12, by Bill Flinn and Holly Schofield, looks at the tensions that land tenure security brings up for international and national NGOs supporting families with recovery after disasters. They compare NGO approaches in two areas affected by Typhoon Haiyan in 2013: one rural area where families have relatively secure tenure status, and an urban area of Tacloban in the Philippines, where families were forced by the government to resettle on the outskirts of the city, where their rights to livelihoods, social connections and education were impossible to maintain. Thus, in urban areas of Talcoban, the NGOs found themselves faced with either supporting household recovery in a way that the households did not choose (resettlement), or illegally supporting households to recover in the No-Build Zones. They conclude that in these situations, supporting indirectly can be much more pertinent – through advocacy, mediation, legal support on tenure issues, services and infrastructure improvement, access to markets and more.

9
Land, property rights and risk

Colin Marx

This chapter starts from the assumption that the intensity of weather variability associated with climate change is likely to make some cities more hazardous – and specific population groups within them more vulnerable. Thus, innovative and equitable actions are needed that go beyond current mainstream responses. Among these actions, developing an understanding of our collective complicity in creating the vulnerabilities, and hence the need for collective responses, will be necessary to add to more individually based responses. Put more bluntly: it is evident that dominant representations of collective responsibility for creating hazards currently do very little to offer progressive ways of addressing the unequal distribution of the burdens of hazards.

There are many analyses of why and how disasters are created, and unequally so. This chapter builds on the seminal work of Wisner et al. (2004), Oliver-Smith (2013), Lavell (2012) and the recent Urban ARC project (Adelekan et al. 2015), among many others, which has established that disasters are not 'natural' and that disasters are created and accumulate through the interaction of systemic issues. Disaster risk emerges, in these accounts, as one way of accounting for the exposure to configurations of vulnerability and hazards where vulnerability is already an outcome of systemic inequalities and hazards are not natural. In these accounts, risk serves as a golden thread of analysis into the ways people are differentially exposed to hazards and the effects of disasters.

In a similar way, this chapter uses risk as a guiding thread into analyses of the unequal distribution of the burden of disasters. However, it draws on a different aspect of risk to think about social accountability for events and processes threatening societies: in this case, for the collective creation of disasters. The logic of the argument is that analysing risk can help to understand how accountability for the creation of disasters is commonly understood. Furthermore, because understandings of accountability for problems are related to action to address these problems, if we have further insights into how accountability is constructed, it can alert us to what might need to be engaged with to generate different actions.

To ground the chapter, I explore urban flooding in Kampala and the way notions of urban flood risk are shared across different groups and institutions. The focus on sharing is important because it is one way in which accountability for floods comes to be constructed and agreed upon across different social groups and institutions. There will be many ways in which accountability can be shared and agreed, but I look at the effects of property rights on how notions of risk are shared in the context of resettlement from flood risk. Property rights are useful because they are fundamental to the financial compensation provided for resettlement in Kampala, as in many other countries. If the logic of my argument holds up, then the sharing of risk through property rights should tell us a little about the social construction of common perceptions about the creation of disasters: specifically, that they tend to obscure the ways that an important part of being together in a city is a relational experience that is always already unequal.

The idea that one of the functions of 'risk' is to offer a social way of working out accountability for threatening events is developed by Douglas (1990). In this view, risk is shared and mediated through cultural activities to protect valued social institutions. In other words, how risk is understood and how these understandings are shared can offer insights into what societies consider valuable and who should be responsible for dealing with threats. In relating to accountability, assessing questions relating to risk is about interrogating solidarities – renewing the solidarities of old or questioning them. When it comes to attributing accountability for actions, questions of justice come to the fore because such social mechanisms work out 'who is most at risk, who will suffer the risk, and who will be held accountable for exposing the others to risk' (Douglas 1990, 17). Such questions are even more urgent in the context of highly unequal cities where disaster risks are unevenly distributed.

As understandings of risk are shared, there are two interlinked representations that could concern people: the probability that something will happen and the consequences of that happening (the loss). Understandings and forms of accountability will vary depending on whether people are thinking about the probability or the consequence.

Anticipating some of the evidence provided later in this chapter, it seemed as if policymakers in Kampala tended to focus on the probabilities of risk existing, while people (and without sophisticated modelling resources) relate more strongly to the losses. In this chapter, the assumptions underlying these two ways of representing risk are used as clues to sketch out people's world view and, in such a world view, what might prove threatening, and what steps could be taken to mitigate such risks. Despite people having differing world views, all world views share a belief in a particular form of order and what can threaten this order. In this way, 'risk' is also constitutive of particular understandings of the world (see Chapter 4 by Johnson et al. in this book). It is this point that I return to in the concluding sections of the chapter.

The chapter begins by describing the context and the principal axis of 'location–settlement–property rights–compensation' that relates to resettlement from disaster risk in Kampala. This axis establishes the importance of perceptions of (private) property rights and leads to two sections which detail how property rights have effects that simultaneously work in different ways. The data that the section draws on relates to thematic analysis of semi-structured, open-ended interviews conducted in 2015–16 with policymakers in Kampala Capital City Authority (KCCA) and Uganda's National Environmental Management Authority (NEMA), residents of Bwaise III who had been evicted and compensated, those from Natete who were awaiting eviction and compensation, and civil society organisations working in urban development (Lwasa et al. 2016). The final section then looks at the effects of property rights on understanding how disasters are collectively created in the city.

The context

The city of Kampala is built on a series of hills and wide wetland valleys that drain away into Uganda's river and lake systems. Historically, the wetland valleys were used for low-intensity agriculture. However, with increasing urbanisation, more of the wetlands have been settled on, thus degrading their drainage system functions. The degradation, and the consequent inability of the wetlands to perform their ecosystem functions of absorbing higher rainfall, are due to a number of factors. In Kampala's context, the people settled in the wetland areas tend to be poorer residents availing themselves of cheaper land that is relatively well located with respect to work and services, or people who historically settled in the areas before they became flood prone (and now find themselves increasingly impoverished as they own an asset of decreasing value). The combination of the wetlands no longer being able to fulfil their ecosystem function of absorbing excess rainfall, and greater rainfall due to weather variability associated with climate change, has meant that those living in the wetlands face greater and more prolonged flooding events (Kabesiime et al. 2015; UN Habitat 2013).

The Constitution of the Republic of Uganda (1995) groups property rights under four different forms of tenure – customary, freehold, *mailo* and leasehold. The simplicity of the statement in the Constitution belies the complexity and ambiguity of interpreting property rights in practice (Lwasa 2010). Overlap these tenure forms with a diverse series of informal practices and discerning 'legitimate' property rights becomes exceedingly complicated (Nkurunziza 2007, 2008). This process of discernment is also often politically fraught as large areas of Kampala are considered to be part of the Buganda Kingdom (Meinert and Kjær 2016). The value and control of land are a central feature of the kingdom's political, cultural and social claims (Médard and Golaz 2018). The legal complexity of property rights makes compensation especially difficult in Kampala, and this form of complexity often absorbs all the attention.

Beginning in the mid-1990s, the Kampala City Council[1] began investigating ways of managing flood risk – typically in the form of upgrading drainage infrastructure – and the financial resources provided to do so usually came as a package requiring institutional reforms. A good example is the various phases of the World Bank-funded Kampala Institutional and Infrastructure Development Project (KIIDP).[2] KIIDP is conceived, inter alia, as 'drainage system improvement' to contribute to public confidence which, in turn, relates to the economic and commercial development of the city.[3] As part of this sectoral trajectory of upgrading and institutional reforms in KCCA, this chapter focuses on the drainage, transport and sanitation upgrading in two areas: Bwaise III (in 2006) and Natete (2015/16). See also Chapter 15 by Kisembo in this book. In both cases, the infrastructure upgrading induced resettlement of residents and commercial enterprises. The rationale for the resettlement was that people and businesses were located in an area where the city wanted to build risk-reducing infrastructure even though the people living there were experiencing flooding. In Kampala, the approach to resettlement is governed by the Land Act (1998) and works through financial compensation to people who are evicted. The responsibility for finding a new place to live rests with the evictees.

The axis

In this section, I identify a 'settlement–location–property rights–compensation–resettlement' axis and the importance of perceptions of property rights in this axis. These perceptions equate settlement in specific (flood-prone) areas and ownership of land with private, individual property rights. Most importantly here, because resettlement is facilitated by compensation and compensation turns on property rights, the role of property rights is central.

In most countries, land may be acquired by the state for public purposes. In Uganda, acquisition can be in the interests of defence, public safety, public order, public morality or public health (Articles 26(2) and 237(2) of the Constitution of the Republic of Uganda 1995). The process of acquiring land for public purposes and providing compensation (as a resettlement measure) is governed and bolstered by a series of national laws and, in this case, funding conditionalities. Here I single out four that relate most directly to resettlement compensation.

First, the Constitution provides for the taking of privately owned land on condition that prompt and fair compensation is paid prior to the taking of the property (Article 237(2)). Second, the Land Acquisition Act (1965) provides for compensation as the only remedy for eviction. There is no requirement to move people or buy or make available alternative land. Receipt of compensation extinguishes any claim to the land – a point that will become crucial in our consideration later in the chapter on how understandings of risks are shared. Third, the Land Act 1998 (amended 2004) Section 77 provides for valuation principles of open market value for customary land, replacement value for buildings and disturbance allowances. Fourth, the World Bank's Policy on Involuntary Resettlement (OP/BP/4.12) also applied because the projects involved World Bank funds. This policy stipulates that people who are displaced should be compensated at full replacement cost and assisted with relocation or resettlement. The policy encourages the implementing agency to offer replacement land, especially when any residual land holdings are not economically viable. The policy broadens the support to include support for any impact on livelihoods.[4]

Uganda's national laws do not require compensation to tenants, squatters (unlawful tenants) and residents or land users on land that was identified and gazetted for public purposes prior to people's use of the land. Under national laws, tenants and squatters can only be compensated if they have resided on the land for longer than 15 years. However,

World Bank guidelines require compensation regardless of how long they have stayed, provided that they fall within the stipulation of any project cut-off date. In the event, a socio-economic survey of affected persons commissioned by the Kampala City Council revealed that the majority of respondents (94 per cent) preferred (among a list of options that did not allow for continued residence in the same location) 'fair, adequate and prompt compensation' and not resettlement to an alternative location (Geomaps Africa et al. 2006).

Thus, the following property rights were recognised as eligible for compensation[5] in Bwaise III and Natete:

- Registered landowners with either leasehold or private *mailo* land titles.
- Bona fide occupants – persons sitting on registered land, having been settled by the government or its agents and those having settled on the land between 1983 and 1995 without interference by the registered owner.
- Lawful occupants – persons who came onto the registered land with the permission of the registered owner.
- Licensees – persons without legal claim to the land but with the permission of the landowner to carry out activities on the land.
- Squatters – persons using the land without the permission of the landowner and having no legal nor traditionally recognised claim to the land.

The aim of this section has been to identify the 'settlement–location–property rights–compensation–resettlement' axis. It is clear that property rights interpreted as ownership are one of the clearest determinants of eligibility for compensation as a resettlement remedy. It is also worth highlighting here that property rights (as a basis for eligibility) work as an individualising logic – matching a single owner to a single property right – even if one of the hallmarks of *mailo* tenure is that it creates the possibility of there being overlapping single ownership of property rights. It is the individualising logic that I will return to, after considering the effects of property rights on risk.

The effects of property rights on risk

In this section, I draw together a few of the ways in which risk was being considered from the point of view of the local authority and residents in flood-prone areas of the wetlands. One of the most important ways in which risk was conceived, by the local authority, for the city, was as the probability of risk to the city's commercial development, as most succinctly expressed in World Bank funding motivations (World Bank 2014). In this view, risk threatened future growth through the probability of more flooding and loss to city assets in seeking to ensure a risk-free investment environment. The authorities thought of it in terms of 'flood protection' for the delivery capabilities of the city. This view has emerged as part of what the World Bank and Overseas Development Institute (ODI) have termed the triple dividend from disaster risk management (see Tanner et al. 2015). One dividend is reducing existing risk, another is avoiding risk and thus encouraging investment and development in non-hazard-prone areas.

From the perspective of the people living in the risk-prone wetlands, they conveyed the flood risk not as a probability – as people were painfully resigned to the inevitable fact that floods would come – but as actual loss; in other words, as the other component in ways of conceiving risk: loss of assets, loss of work days, loss of loved ones, loss of comfort and security (Barrow et al. 2016). Although such a simple representation is a caricature of a complex reality, the simplicity provides a means of capturing the dominant positions and their internal logics repeated most commonly by the different respondents. With this representation, it is possible to consider the two effects of property rights in relation to how understandings of risk are shared.

Insulating effects

The first effect was how people living in the flood-prone areas and considered as legitimate property owners (i.e. those with eligible property rights) tended to be insulated – that is, protected from the harshest social criticisms – from being held accountable for the degradation of the wetlands.[6] Certainly, a wide range of actors, from different institutional positions, including people who had settled in the wetlands, recognised that settlement degraded the wetlands and increased the chance of flood risk. In addition, any land transactions and settlement were in contravention of Uganda's national laws protecting wetlands. As a representative from the National Environmental Management Authority pointed out, ignorance of the law was no defence (interview, 5 November 2015). Yet the same representative (as well as other senior officials from Kampala Capital City Authority) pointed out that bona fide landowners could be considered legitimate, legal land users.[7] As noted above, the Constitution defines legitimate property rights where the land belongs to the people of Uganda. Arguably, if people were not insulated from accountability, their presence would not be tolerated and they could be summarily evicted without compensation.[8] This is brought into even greater focus for those residents who are/were extremely poor and who, traditionally, often become scapegoats for wider social ills.

However, simultaneously, the very same function of insulation worked in different ways and less advantageously for those living with the floods. For the most part, it would seem that the understandings of risk that came to be imposed from the authorities were those that are focused on the probability of disaster happening and not so much on the immediate loss to households. In part, this is because property rights insulated the authorities from having to worry about individual loss. Because it is private property, the (public) authorities have neither the basis nor the power to intervene and are thus absolved of responsibilities for loss.

Isolating effects

This section identifies how the very same property rights had another effect in isolating the residents from receiving assistance for their losses and ways of mitigating risk. With the local authority insulated from having to provide support, households were isolated from any support to recover their losses from disaster. In this sense, property rights cut households off from any meaningful assistance. That is, respondents in the settlements could only ever recall one instance when they had been supported after a flood, which had been in 2007 (just prior to the Commonwealth Heads of Government Meeting hosted by the Ugandan government in Kampala; Barrow et al. 2016). Isolated from any significant support, households repeatedly endured actual losses.

In this way, the effect of property rights is to prevent the possibility that risk, either as probability or as actual loss, could be shared across different contexts – despite individuals in households wishing that KCCA would pay more heed to their plight, and individuals in the local authorities wishing they could be of more assistance. It is only when the possibility of compensation – which could extinguish property rights – arises through KIIDP that owners of property rights can be connected to assistance and this can enable them to resettle away from the flood risks without incurring considerable loss.[9] Moreover, the local authorities can connect their perceptions of risk as probability to households in order to evict/resettle them and make way for the implementation of drainage improvement projects.

These effects are significant in explaining why local institutions struggled to manage settlement in the wetlands and mitigate the risks of floods for people living there. Property rights clearly play a broader role than simply being the basis upon which compensation can be calculated in a resettlement process. However, more than this, these effects point to the significance of an individualising logic in understanding the construction of broader world views and how risk is generated in the first place. By individualising logic, I refer to a system of categorising and classifying people and events based on how they can be associated with separately identifiable units. From such an approach, the collective tends to be understood as an aggregation of individual units.

Understanding the creation of risk

I now shift the focus from the effects of property rights on how understandings of disaster risk might be shared (or not) to how they also work to restrict the ways in which the creation of disaster risk is understood: in other words, how notions of risk are constitutive of broader world views and what is of value in such social orders. The effect of property rights on not allowing risk to be shared is shown above, as it is that these effects emerge primarily from the perception that property rights are fundamentally individual and belong to a person or persons. Despite the different effects of property rights as insulating and isolating from risk, they share a common foundation in mapping risks against individual units – whether these be individual households or people. If disaster risk is commonly understood through property rights then it is inevitable that an individualising logic of perceptions of property rights will imperceptibly slide into an individualising logic for risk: risk belongs to the identifiably separate owners of property rights (because property rights are essentially *private*).

There will, of course, be many cases where the straightforward aggregation of individual behaviours and actions in relation to flood risk will be relevant and important. An example might include the aggregated effects of certain forms of (individual) development decisions to reduce hard surfaces that are associated with higher rainfall run-off. Critics might also point out that sharing a common belief, that property rights are private and individual, binds together all those who hold this view and offers a common platform for understanding cumulative or compound effects. However, I would argue that the logic of this approach is still to understand risk as aggregations of individuals making it difficult to conceive of the creation of risk in other, collective ways. It also means that there is a danger that risk is limited in playing its social function of attributing responsibility 'correctly' and equitably.

A collective understanding of how risk is created in the first place relates to the complex interplay of relational processes that drive poorer households to settle in hazard-prone areas. Borrowing from the idea of relational poverty, where someone's impoverishment is likely to be another's gain (Mosse 2010), a collective understanding of the creation of disasters opens the possibilities to see how individuals' ways of being in the city always have relational consequences – even before they are aggregated. Such relations work through processes including rural–urban migration, land markets, infrastructure provision, livelihoods and cultural and economic values, among other things. Importantly, these processes go beyond aggregating the actions of certain groups to consider the interactions of different processes and the way they differentiate the opportunities open to people to make their way in the city (Adelekan et al. 2015).

Thinking only through (individual) property rights restricts the analysis from accounting for these relational interactions. It prohibits analysis of *all* urban residents' complicity in the production of a world view in which disaster risk is created through their unequal everyday and unwitting engagements with the systemic features listed above. It tends to limit the development of a world view in which relational features can come to be considered as part of the cumulative and compound flood risks generated by the city. Put differently, is the risk the probability of flood and consequent loss (or costs) to the city, or is the risk that people can only afford to own land in flood-prone locations and compensate for this by developing livelihood options under such conditions?

Conclusion

At issue is how the property rights in a resettlement process function to either facilitate or slow down the sharing of understandings of disaster risk. Thinking about risk as a thread to guide analysis has shown that the property rights in this case both slowed down and made possible shared understandings of risk and how accountability for disasters could be shared across different social groups. These effects are important in terms of issues of social justice. However, the individualising logic on which they are based also has effects on limiting the emergence of collective understandings of the creation of disasters.

The limitations arise because of the way the individualising logics of private property rights tend to be asocial and disregard the way that being together in cities is always already an unequal relational experience. Considering that activities and relating to others are a fundamental aspect of urban life opens up possibilities to see how individuals' activities and ways of being in the city always have relational consequences – even before they are aggregated. By only thinking in aggregated terms, we miss the possibilities of collectively accounting for the ways these activities operate unequally and create disasters.

Thus, in the case of Bwaise III and Natete, people considered to have legitimate property rights tended to be insulated from being identified as solely responsible for causing disasters by degrading the wetland and settling in places that were flood prone. But the local authority was also insulated from having to respond with significant resources, and property rights holders were isolated from being able to make claims. It was only when the property rights could be extinguished that understandings of disaster risk could be shared or imposed – depending on the viewpoint. In this process, accountability for the causes of resettlement from risk are seen through the particular lens of the individualising logic of private property rights. It would appear that this offers a stunted understanding of the requirements of resettlement. Compensation for resettlement should consider not only the (individual) market value of land and assets in determining the amounts but also the nature of risk-prone residents' relations to urban processes. The basis for enhanced solidarity that affords such support lies in recognising the common accountability for the creation of urban disasters.

Acknowledgements

This chapter was prepared with the valuable assistance of Armando Caroca Fernandez. I am extremely grateful for his diligence and thoughtful insights in analysing the data.

Notes

1. The Kampala City Council was replaced by the Kampala Capital City Authority in 2011.
2. KIIDP was preceded by earlier initiatives to reduce flood risk in Kampala through improved drainage infrastructure, such as the Nakivubo Channel Rehabilitation Project.
3. This is important because the increased probability of flood risk would jeopardise this development, and Kampala's ability to provide the resources to address poverty and underdevelopment elsewhere in Uganda.
4. Other relevant national laws that were applicable in Bwaise III and Natete were: the Land Acquisition Act (1965), the Land Act (1998), the Roads Act (1949), the National Environment Act (1995) and the Town and Country Planning Act (1951)
5. The chapter is not concerned with the amount, acceptability and timely payment of compensation, nor with how compensation filtered down (or did not) from principal property claim holders and those holding other, 'lesser' claims to the land. I also do not deal with the inevitable questions of how to compensate for 'non-measurable' losses such as proximity to family, neighbourhood networks and employment opportunities.
6. In some ways, this is to be expected. One of the perceived prime advantages of the (private) ownership of property rights is that they offer high levels of protection and security from the actions of neighbouring land users.
7. In a legally plural society, it is arguable as to which legal system is more significant in people's lives.
8. The fact that even legitimate and reasonable evictions in the public interest required presidential approval is further evidence in support for the argument that property rights insulated people.
9. Some respondents reported that other people had been able to sell their land and move to less risky locations without waiting to be evicted and compensated.

References

Adelekan, Ibidun, Cassidy Johnson, Mtafu Manda, David Matyas, Blessing Mberu, Susan Parnell, Mark Pelling, David Satterthwaite and Janani Vivekananda. 2015. 'Disaster risk and its reduction: An agenda for urban Africa'. *International Development Planning Review* 37 (1): 33–43. DOI:10.3828/idpr.2015.4.

Barrow, Charlotte, Cassidy Johnson, Teddy Kisembo, Shuaib Lwasa and Colin Marx. 2016. 'Uganda: Cost and benefit analysis'. *Reducing Relocation Risk in Urban Areas*. London: UCL. https://www.ucl.ac.uk/bartlett/development/sites/bartlett/files/wp3_cost_benefit_dpu_report_rev.pdf.

Douglas, Mary. 1990. 'Risk as a forensic resource'. *Daedalus* 119 (4): 1–16.

Geomaps Africa, Delta Partnership, Interface Consulting and RESCO. 2006. *Resettlement Action Plan. Volume 1. Kampala Institutional Infrastructure Development Project (KIIDP).* Kampala: Ministry of Local Government and Kampala City Council. https://www.kcca.go.ug/media/docs/Final%20Drainage_RAP_Report.pdf.

Kabesiime, Edith, Charles Owuor, Margaret Barihaihi and Tracy Kajumba. 2015. *Monitoring and Evaluating Climate Change Adaptation and Disaster Risk Reduction in Uganda: TAMD appraisal study*. London: International Institute for Environment and Development. https://pubs.iied.org/10116IIED.

Lavell, Allan. 2012. 'Reflections: Advancing development-based interpretations and interventions in disaster risk: Some conceptual and contextual stumbling blocks'. *Environmental Hazards: Human and Policy Dimensions* 11 (3): 242–6. https://doi.org/10.1080/17477891.2012.698845.

Lwasa, Shuaib. 2010. *Urban Land Markets, Housing Development and Spatial Planning in Sub-Saharan Africa: The case of Uganda*. New York: Nova Science Publishers.

Lwasa, Shuaib, Teddy Kisembo, Colin Marx, Charlotte Barrow and Cassidy Johnson. 2016. 'Uganda: Diagnostic Report'. *Reducing Relocation Risk in Urban Areas*. London: UCL. https://www.ucl.ac.uk/bartlett/development/sites/bartlett/files/wp1_diagnostic_dpu_28_pp.pdf.

Médard, Claire and Valérie Golaz. 2018. 'Entwined values: Protecting and subdividing land in Buganda'. *Critical African Studies* 10 (1): 47–66. https://doi.org/10.1080/21681392.2018.1491802.

Meinert, Lotte and Anne Mette Kjær. 2016. '"Land belongs to the people of Uganda": Politicians' use of land issues in the 2016 election campaigns'. *Journal of Eastern African Studies* 10 (4): 769–88. https://doi.org/10.1080/17531055.2016.1274251.

Mosse, David. 2010. 'A relational approach to durable poverty, inequality and power'. *Journal of Development Studies* 46 (7): 1156–78. https://doi.org/10.1080/00220388.2010.487095.

Nkurunziza, Emmanuel. 2007. 'Informal mechanisms for accessing and securing urban land rights: The case of Kampala, Uganda'. *Environment and Urbanization* 19 (2): 509–26. https://doi-org.libproxy.ucl.ac.uk/10.1177%2F0956247807082833.

Nkurunziza, Emmanuel. 2008. 'Understanding informal urban land access processes from a legal pluralist perspective: The case of Kampala, Uganda'. *Habitat International* 32 (1): 109–20. https://doi.org/10.1016/j.habitatint.2007.08.004.

Oliver-Smith, Anthony. 2013. 'Disaster risk reduction and climate change adaptation: The view from applied anthropology'. *Human Organization* 72 (4): 275–82. https://doi.org/DOI 10.17730/humo.72.4.j7u8054266386822.

Tanner, Thomas, Swenja Surminski, Emily Wilkinson, Robert Reid, Jun Rentschler and Sumati Rajput. 2015. *The Triple Dividend of Resilience: Realising development goals through the multiple benefits of disaster risk management*. London and Washington, DC: Overseas Development Institute and the World Bank.

UN Habitat. 2013. *Flood Risk Assessment, Strategies and Actions for Improving Flood Risk Management in Kampala: Final report of integrated flood management project Kampala*. Nairobi: UN Habitat.

Wisner, Ben, Piers Blaikie, Terry Cannon and Ian Davis. 2004. *At Risk: Natural hazards, people's vulnerability and disasters*, second edition. London and New York: Routledge.

World Bank. 2014. *Project Information Document: Appraisal stage. Kampala Institutional & Infrastructure Development Project 2*. Washington, DC: World Bank. http://documents1.worldbank.org/curated/en/639331468317685743/pdf/PID-Appraisal-Print-P133590-01-20-2014-1390199862749.pdf.

10

Climate change, land and housing-induced evictions: another round of accumulation through dispossession?

Yves Cabannes

The number of women, men and children reported displaced by sudden-onset extreme weather disasters is overwhelmingly dramatic: Oxfam (2017) reports 21.8 million each year between 2008 and 2016. The impact on people of sudden-onset disasters including floods, storms, wildfires, extreme weather conditions, earthquakes, volcanic eruptions and landslides will keep rising. Despite strong variations according to sources and scenarios, by 2050, it is likely that such events will affect between twenty-five million and one billion people, with two hundred million being the most widely accepted number (according to the International Organization for Migration).

The starting point for this chapter comes from a woman's testimony during the fieldwork of the 'Reducing Relocation Risk in Urban Areas' project: 'When they speak about relocation and resettlements, they really mean eviction.' It raises in simple words several research questions: who are 'they'? Do climate change-induced resettlements and relocations, in their multiple forms, actually lead to evicting dwellers from the place they were occupying? If so, what are the drivers for such evictions, and their overarching logic?

After a conceptual clarification of the concepts of relocation, resettlements, forced and market-driven evictions, under a rights-based approach, this chapter puts in perspective climate-induced relocation and resettlements with other forms of land and housing evictions that have increased in scale, number and brutality over the last 40 years. It explores to what extent they relate to each other and highlights their very specific links, the central argument being that depending on the situation, climate change often worsens, speeds up or scales up other forms of evictions. The climate change imperative also acts as a pretext for multiple forms of eviction, but conversely, climate change-induced evictions might result from forced displacements under various motives.

In order to better understand the drivers behind this, and the underpinning logics, I discuss David Harvey's concept of accumulation by dispossession (Harvey 2004) as the 'hallmark of what the new imperialism is about' (Harvey 2003) and explore to what extent the concept is sufficient to explain the breadth, the depth and the variety of evictions taking place worldwide, and primarily those that are climate change-induced. The chapter then explores the role played by the United Nations system and argues that various UN agencies have shifted over the last 20 years from being a land rights and anti-evictions defender to an accommodative force, avoiding conflict with dominant eviction processes, or even avoiding playing a mediating role to find solutions that would benefit citizens and their multiple rights.

Despite an apparently rather dark future, the final section brings to the fore how market-driven, forced and climate change-induced evictions are currently addressed and challenged. Multiple community-led struggles, innovative programmes and actions are taking place in different locales and some innovative ones are briefly introduced, paving the way for future anti-hegemonic practices and signalling hope for all those who challenge the current economic (dis)order in favour of spatial and social justice.

Conceptual and analytical debate on relocation, resettlement and forced evictions: introducing a rights-based perspective

This chapter takes into account the overall definition given in the introduction to this book that seeks to differentiate between the concepts of resettlement, relocation and rehabilitation. Resettlement is a major integrated, comprehensive movement of people and families which normally involves significant distance between the original and new location. Resettlement involves not only new housing and services but also new social and economic relations, and new challenges such as access to work and social cohesion (Ferris 2014). Relocation, meanwhile, refers to non-systematic movements of families or individuals from hazard-prone locations to nearby areas. Relocation, therefore, would involve less upheaval in terms of access to work and social networks (Ferris 2012). Rehabilitation is an overarching term about processes of restoration of housing and urban conditions. It could be either relocation or resettlement, but could also mean in situ upgrading or a host of other kind of interventions.

Displacement Solutions and the participants in the Peninsula Declaration (Leckie 2013b), which focused precisely on climate change displacements, embrace both concepts of resettlement and relocation as defined previously under the notion of relocation, and bring in essential complements for our exploration in this chapter: '*Relocation* means the voluntary, planned and coordinated movement of climate displaced persons within States to suitable locations, away from risk-prone areas, where they can enjoy the full spectrum of rights including housing, land and property and livelihood rights and all other livelihood and related rights' (Leckie and Huggins 2016, 179). The first complement is a clear rights-based approach, not limited to housing but embracing it; the second is the reference to livelihoods. This is of prime importance, as displacements in most cases, even if they provide a safer roof, mean losing livelihoods and falling lower in the spiral of poverty. The third complement refers to the voluntary (or involuntary) dimension of people's movement, which stands at the core of what forced eviction is about.

When referring to forced evictions, the definition adopted in 1997 by the United Nations will be used: 'The permanent or temporary removal against their will of individuals, families and/or communities from the homes and/or land which they occupy, without the provision of, and access to, appropriate forms of legal or other protection and with or without State sanction.'[1] The definition echoes the previous one as it insists on the voluntary dimension as a marker ('removal … against their will'). It encompasses the individual, family or community dimensions that evictions can entail, and that effectively are a second marker, and it insists on the responsibility of the state. This global definition needs to be complemented with another UN resolution that allows us to link forced evictions with a broad range of human rights, far beyond adequate housing:

> The practice of forced evictions constitutes a gross violation of a broad range of human rights, in particular the right to adequate housing, the right to remain, the right to freedom of movement, the right to privacy, the right to property, the right to an adequate standard of living, the right to security of the person, the right to

security of the home, the right to security of tenure and the right to equality of treatment.[2]

The United Nations definition, when referring to evictions, considers only 'forced' ones as defined before and remains blind to market-driven evictions, which tend to occur through foreclosures, for example, resulting primarily from the financialisation of housing and the subprime crisis, mass touristification of some cities or gentrification of entire neighbourhoods. These processes are much less visible as they tend to be individual instead of collective and are conducted within national legal frameworks, and are much more difficult to defend, one of the reasons being that international human rights definitions remain blind to them. In this chapter, 'evictions' will refer to both forced and market-driven ones under the assumption that they are intrinsically related and refer to the same logic.

Previous analysis of forced and market-driven evictions processes[3] led to the differentiation of five different stages:

1. Threat – when local or central governments have designated a site as a renewal area or for mega-projects such as commercial centres, highways, golf courses, etc. However, the plan has not yet been officially approved.
2. Planning process underway – when a plan for renewal of the neighbourhood has been approved or is likely to be approved. Negotiations with owners and purchasing of properties are taking place. Evictions may not have started but will likely begin soon.
3. Demolition ongoing – some residents have been evicted and some houses have been destroyed. Such processes might last for years.
4. Demolition completed – the residents have been evicted and the houses have been destroyed.
5. Repeated evictions – people are displaced. However, they might be forced to leave their new homes because they cannot afford to pay their monthly loan repayments or other costs, or are too far from any services and jobs, or simply because they cannot make a livelihood any more. They are not forcibly evicted (as per the UN definition), but subject to what is considered here market-driven evictions.

In summary, from a rights-based perspective, relocation should be the exception and not the rule, 'an option of last resort' (Oxfam 2017), and in situ rehabilitation preferred to resettlement and/or relocation, whenever possible.

Climate change-induced displacements: one among many causes of evictions

This section explores the specific links between displacements and evictions resulting from climate change-related hazards with the multiple other forms that exist globally. I argue that climate change displacements are one among many causes of evictions that are intrinsically linked. Before highlighting some of these links and exploring in the next section to what extent they answer the same underpinning logics, a typology of the most frequent causes of evictions will be briefly summarised (International Alliance of Inhabitants 2013).[4]

Simplified typology of frequent causes of evictions

1. Urban regeneration, neighbourhood improvements, smart cities and their destructive impact on smaller human settlements and rural villages

The regeneration of central and historic districts, the beautification of cities and the eradication of favelas are often synonymous with forced eviction processes, particularly when such districts enjoy a good urban location. Technical reasons might be to lower housing densities, improve hygiene or security or to expand internal circulation systems, through opening streets, avenues or car parks. Very few of these 'improved' neighbourhoods will benefit the population that might have lived there for generations. Usually, urban regeneration results in gentrification, attracting wealthier people looking for centrality, pushing away the poorest inhabitants, for example the elderly or the young who will not be able to meet the costs of housing, services, shopping, car parks, etc. Gentrification also affects tenants, particularly those without formal contracts, another form of eviction, via the market, which affects millions of people (see category seven below).

2. Major urban works, to promote the global city

Malls and shopping centres, automobile racing circuits, giant sports stadiums, shopping centres, central business districts, marinas, stellar international or national hotels and golf courses, constitute some of the most land-consuming pages of the global city catalogue. As a whole, they tend to transform cities into places of spectacular consumption, mostly destroying the remaining productive industries, local markets and livelihood-based locales for the benefit of a limited number of inhabitants. Again, they are altogether a major threat and cause of forced evictions.

3. Infrastructures and large industrial projects: circulation and distribution of goods, transport and communication to facilitate the import and export of products at a global level

Urban highways, modern ports adapted for containers or international tourism (cruise ships, tourism ports), heliports, inter-nodal communications hubs, metropolitan highway networks and airports for an increasing volume of low-cost traffic constitute land-consuming elements necessary to interconnect the constitutive elements of the globalised city: the airport with the regenerated historical centre, or the stadium with the stellar hotels. These large infrastructures of the city of the fluxes (Castells 1989) also allow the flow of goods and services (water, sanitation, water drainage), as well as the connection of the global city with other globalised spaces. They also constitute a major source of the forced eradication of spaces, as referred to by Castells (1989), and more importantly of their inhabitants.

4. Mega-events impact on evictions

Major events in the sports industry such as the Olympic Games, World Cup, Inter-American or Commonwealth Games, World Expo and major events of the recreation industry (Miss World, Miss Universe, beauty pageants, competitions, etc.) serve in many cases as a pretext to 'modernise' and 'uplift' cities. During the preparation stages, a kind of building state of emergency is practised, during which urban planning regulations and basic rights, in particular the right to adequate housing, are not taken into account, in the name of fast-track processes and the imperative of the deadline of the event. The international and national investments that attract these events are of such magnitude that entire neighbourhoods are destroyed and mass evictions occur. These occurrences are relatively well documented and have generated large mass protests (e.g. relating to the World Cup in Brazil, and the Olympic Games in Tokyo), sometimes capturing media attention.

5. Market-driven evictions

The speculative production of housing, 'financialisation', housing bubbles and subprimes, and the touristification of heritage cities (Barcelona, Lisbon, Seville, for instance) are responsible for large market-driven evictions, within national legal frameworks, as in Spain, where nearly half a million cases of evictions resulted from a law (*hipotecaria*) from the dictatorship period (Duval and Martín 2015). Legal procedures against defaulting tenants, primarily those without formal contracts, resulting in evictions fall under the market-driven category and concern millions of people: as an example, in France alone, more than fifteen thousand home evictions were conducted by the authorities in 2016, the highest recorded number over the last 15 years. Since this modality deals with individuals or single families, it is tremendously difficult to compute numbers, to make them visible and to form an organised defence movement.

6. Land and water grabbing, mining expansion, dispossession of the planet's scarce non-renewable resources

Mining sites, forests, biosphere reserves (such as springs, groundwater, rivers and their surroundings) increasingly constitute territories of fierce struggle between international and national capital (International Alliance of Inhabitants 2015b) and populations opposing such a depletion. Such an uneven battle results most of the time in forced evictions. According to the United Nations Environment Programme, 'over the last 60 years, 40 percent of all internal conflicts have been linked to the exploitation of natural resources' (UNEP 2015, 10).

As a result of a growing world food crisis with more than two billion over-fed and under-fed people, countries with high financial reserves such as China or several oil-producing countries tend to acquire land in developing countries to grow their own food industrially for the sake of their own food security. Small and family farmers, agro-pastoralists, nomads and indigenous peoples are thus dispossessed of thousands of hectares of land. On the other hand, uncontrolled urban expansion means for thousands of urban inhabitants, usually the poorest, the loss of the few metres of land they cultivated for their own consumption or as a source of income. These evictions are probably the least defended today.

7. War and conflicts, internal and international displacements

Ethnic conflicts, wars and political conflicts leading to internal displacements are probably the most dramatic cases in terms of scale and deprivation of rights and affect millions every year. Evictions of Roma and/or Gypsy populations, evictions of ethnic minorities in some cities, such as Istanbul's historic districts (where Roma and Kurds were the first to suffer from so-called urban renewal), or Dalits in India, or migrants in some European cities are a few among numerous urban cases (Internal Displacement Monitoring Centre 2017).

In general terms, according to UNHCR, the world counted at the end of 2018 at least 70.8 million persons displaced by force, a 2.3 million increase in relation to 2017 (see Breteau 2019). An explosive increase occurred over the last 20 years: the number of people being cared for grew from 20 million people[5] to 74.8 million in 2019.

Relations between climate change displacements and other causes of evictions

Snowball effect and chain reaction

In some cases, the causes just identified that led to forced evictions might have disastrous effects on the environment, increasing vulnerability to climate change effects and leading to further climate change displacements. Such a chain effect relation can be anticipated on a larger scale in the future.

For example, in the name of urban regeneration (category one of the typology), residents of the Boeung Kak Reservoir area in Phnom Penh, Cambodia, were forcefully evicted, despite a long and exemplary mobilisation and struggle by the population. As a result, about 12 hectares were left to the inhabitants, while 144 hectares were 'cleared' and given to private developers. Importantly, in relation to the issues debated here, this vast piece of land originally acted, as its name implies, as a reservoir, regulating water levels, primarily in the case of heavy rains. The reclaiming of the reservoir and its transformation into tenements for the upper and upper-middle classes will probably bring dramatic impacts not only for the people who have been evicted but also for the environment: floods are likely to occur, and in the case of climate change hazards, the neighbourhoods around Boeung Kak Reservoir will probably be affected, and climate change displacement can be anticipated. The whole point is that these new evictions are resulting from other causes (profit-oriented urban regeneration), and therefore mirror another aspect of forced evictions.

Similarly, illegal wood extraction in the Amazon forest (category six of the typology) leads to forced evictions, as happened for instance with a thousand families of the Asháninka nation in Peru.[6] The result is not only the evictions of people but at the same time the devastation of large areas of prime forest, which will lead to an increased vulnerability of the Amazon to the effects of climate change. Will the next people affected be considered climate change displaced?

These two examples, chosen among many, illustrate that climate change displacements are intrinsically linked to environmental plundering provoked by multiple causes, suggesting that they are part of a single system. This consideration remains central to addressing not only the consequences of climate changes but also its origins: once the floods reach Phnom Penh's low-income areas or remote Amazonian settlements, climate change might be pointed out as the cause, when it is in fact the consequence of forest grabbing and profit-based urban regeneration.

Climate change as a pretext and an opportunity

My argument is that climate change is being used and will be used to speed up multiple eviction processes, increase their size and make them more organised. They tend to become a key justification for displacement. In other words, the climate change rationale tends to be used as a key 'rational discourse' to justify either forced or market-driven evictions. This is nothing new as, ironically, environmental reasons such as the protection of watersheds, preventing people from being flooded or being exposed to earthquake-prone areas, have been largely used as a justification for wholesale evictions and displacements (e.g. the massive displacement in Mumbai in 2008 of a population settled on watersheds).

The land and water grabbing in Morocco (see Box 10.1) resulting from a project selected as part of the UN Green Climate Fund highlights the way the Moroccan government takes advantage of the climate change rationale to evict nomadic tribes from their ancestral lands.

Box 10.1 Land and water grabbing in Morocco

This same logic of 'accumulation by dispossession', which consists in closing public goods to the benefit of private for-profit interests, is at work in the projects submitted by Morocco to access the UN Green Climate Fund, the financial mechanism of the United Nations Framework Convention on Climate Change (UNFCCC), created in 2009. The objectives of this fund are to limit or reduce greenhouse gas emissions in developing countries and to help vulnerable communities adapt to the impacts of climate change.

One of the projects currently selected for Morocco, in the Boudnib region in Tafilalet, poses enormous problems. It provides irrigation to cultivate 5,000 hectares outside the oasis in a public–private partnership. This is only possible by pumping into the groundwater. The planned area can only be secured by evicting the nomadic tribes from the collective lands where they practise extensive livestock farming, a process that has already begun.

The project will also lead to a significant disruption of ancestral traditions of water management and distribution in the oasis, especially since it is foreseeable that the distribution of water between the 'modern' and 'solidarity' [= traditional] sectors will be to the detriment of the latter, which has little power and a weak capacity for pressure and negotiation. Thus, this project, which is supposed to contribute to the struggle against climate change, and in particular against desertification, and to help the most vulnerable populations, is based on:

- The eviction of indigenous communities from their collective lands and pastoral activities.
- The diversion of part of the water supplying the oases to artificial irrigated areas benefiting foreign investors in the region for intensive export-oriented production.
- The inaccessibility of traditional water points for livestock and the enclosure of the remaining grazing trails and areas.

Extracts from Daumas 2017. Translation by author.

Climate change-related projects as a means to avoid forced, legally condemnable evictions and introduce market-driven evictions

The award-winning Pluit Reservoir revitalisation project[7] in Jakarta is one among various climate change-related initiatives that deserve critical attention. On the one hand it undoubtedly introduced impressive and bold approaches. Its aim was to 'restore and improve the coastal reservoir's performance as one of the vital drainage retention basins' (C40 Cities n.d.). Among the most tangible results, three thousand families living in floodable kampongs were displaced and relocated to high-rise tenement buildings, the water reservoir capacity was improved by over 6 million m^3 and a 20 hectare park and city forest were developed, with around ten thousand trees newly planted, contributing positively to climate change mitigation for absorbing carbon dioxide (C40 Cities n.d.). In order to convince reluctant families to be relocated into high-rise buildings, when traditionally they had lived close to the land and the water, a rental/loan subsidy was offered for a limited number of years. What remains unclear is what will happen when the subsidy ends. Experience suggests that many of these relocated families will not be able to stay and will probably have to find once again a place to stay, which is likely to be further away from the Pluit Reservoir area.

The other preoccupying consequence of this project, again relatively common, was to transform communities and their cohesive strength into isolated and individual renters and loan-takers, who sooner or later will be exposed to market-driven evictions. In other terms, the project avoided forced evictions, which would have fallen under international and national criticism, but introduced market-driven eviction possibilities, perfectly legal and much more difficult to address. Most probably, after one or two decades, and possibly much sooner, a gentrification of this area will take place, and a fifth stage of eviction (see the stages described earlier in this chapter) will occur for those families who cannot pay. Once again, this case illustrates the close links existing between climate change and non-climate-change-induced evictions.

Theoretical debate: accumulation by dispossession

In this section we discuss David Harvey's concept of accumulation by dispossession as the 'hallmark of what the new imperialism is about' (Harvey 2004, 82) and explore to what extent the concept is sufficient to explain the breadth, depth and variety of evictions taking place worldwide, primarily those that are climate change-induced.

According to Harvey, a central argument to understand the centralisation of wealth in the hands of a shrinking number of few people and institutions relates to neoliberal capitalist policies, to 'global capitalism that has experienced a chronic and enduring problem of overaccumulation' (Harvey 2004, 64) and to the dispossession of the public of their wealth or land. Fundamentally, when the excess of capital exists in a given nation and cannot be absorbed, then 'they must be sent elsewhere to find a fresh terrain for their profitable realization' (Harvey 2003, 117). These neoliberal policies are guided by privatisation, financialisation, management and manipulation of crises, and state redistributions.

Since Harvey developed his theory in the early 2000s, the creation of money and the subsequent excess of capital has exploded. Global financial liquidity represented less than 10 per cent of global GNP in 2004, but reached an unprecedented 30 per cent in 2018. In absolute numbers the amount of liquidities increased over ten-fold. Two main factors explain this increase: the decision of some central banks to increase their currency reserves, notably China and more recently Japan (Arthus 2017), and the creation of currency through quantitative easing[8] practised by the United States and the European Central

Bank as a response to the 2008 financial crisis. This policy has injected hundreds of billions of dollars and euros, which were made available at a very low rate for banks, transnational companies and investors, which could look for new land and territories to dispossess. The current international financial system will lead, as various economists are alerting us, to new financial bubbles and crises. Meanwhile, though, the availability of low-interest capital remained the key driver to acquiring new profitable lands in a new cycle of unprecedented accumulation by dispossession processes.

Climate change-induced displacements and relocations, and the difficulty for displaced dwellers of settling back on their lands, need to be examined within this context. Our central argument is that climate change displacements emerge as a new fix, in Harvey's double meaning of a short-term remedy for capitalism and of 'localised' processes (that are physically 'fixed' somewhere). However, this fix, instead of a short fix, could become a longer-term one, as climate change displacements will expand in the next decades. Disasters destroying homes, entire neighbourhoods and cities turn out to be an opportunity for massive channelling of surplus capital available internationally and a massive transfer of assets, primarily land, from their original owners and users to international banks and funds. Our observations indicate that people are effectively, as underlined by Harvey, dispossessed from common and public lands. However, dispossession is not limited to common and public lands but also takes place on private lands. When they are hit by a disaster these are not spared by international investors either, whenever they offer a possibility of profitable investments – very rarely for the benefit of original dwellers, especially when they are poor. Therefore, from a theoretical point of view, accumulation by dispossession in a climate disaster context goes beyond Harvey's proposition of public and common lands and embraces private ones as well.

A second adjustment needs to be made to Harvey's argument when referring to the assets that are dispossessed when referring to climate change displacements. Our argument is more restrictive than Harvey's: acquiring land is central, followed by water, as both are needed for any new profitable development. New lands, easy to develop for building smart cities, commercial centres, housing and international tourism developments, or for export-oriented agriculture, are among the most profitable assets to be captured in the short term. Dispossession of land can absorb huge amounts of capital and open up even larger amounts for profitable investments.

Accumulation by selective dispossession

As rightly underlined in Oxfam's occasional paper *Uprooted by Climate Change* (Oxfam 2017, 25), 'no country is immune from the impacts of climate change'. However, one needs to differentiate those territories that are of interest for international capital, and that are able to absorb gigantic amounts of capital and labour, from those that offer much less potential for profit. Harvey's theory seems too generic, and should be nuanced as an accumulation by *selective* dispossession. In 2004 I identified, in the case of Latin America, at least four categories of globalised territories (Cabannes 2004) of prime interest for international capital and for the expansion of capitalism. As a consequence, they tend to be the first target for accumulation by dispossession. Climate change hazards will have a much higher probability of resulting in massive displacements with little chance for the displaced to regain their land in:

- City states – corresponding to the majority of the capitals and metropolises that are part of the globalised economy.
- Enclave cities – the economic base of these cities is similar to that of seventeenth- and eighteenth-century colonial enclaves. Three types of cities fall into this category:
    - International tourism cities.
    - Highly profitable mining areas and cities. In general, they are being privatised, as in the case of the concessions of oil companies in Ecuador or the Vale do Rio Doce company in Brazil.
    - Free trade zones that offer low production costs, reduced wages, import and export facilities and access to modern services. The cities that host *maquiladoras* on the Mexico–United States border are a good example of this situation (Gun Cuninghame 2007).
- Cities on the nodes of the global market – airport and port cities in particular.
- Cities located in ecological biospheres and raw material reserves.

Fifteen years later, at least a fifth category of territory should be included, corresponding to land and spaces that are needed to secure a cheap food supply for the richest countries. The food security imperative implies land and water grabbing as a necessity and at the same time can absorb huge amounts of excess capital (see for instance how Singapore's food security is assured thanks to land grabbing in Malaysia or the expansion of their food supply companies, such as for poultry in Vietnam). The Moroccan case previously analysed is another illustrative example.

Evictions, whether forced or market-driven, provoked or not by climate change impact, cannot be explained systematically by an accumulation by dispossession. Evictions, including climate change-related ones, go well beyond the accumulation by dispossession argument. As argued previously, in non-globalised territories in poor countries, displacement tends to benefit a bourgeois comprador or petty bourgeoisie for a very limited form of primitive accumulation, not only with national capital but, depending on the case, also with aid money, corruption or sheer repression. However, in most cases, these new disaster-related settlements (e.g. Canaan in Haiti, with 200,000+ inhabitants), climate refugee camps or transit camps housing war refugees but exposed to climate change hazards (e.g. Zam Zam in Darfur, South Sudan, with 165,000+ inhabitants) are usually left to their fate and no international capital threatens them. This being said, these camps might be closed or threatened with closure (stages one and two in our typology) for other reasons, well beyond accumulation by dispossession. This is the case in Kenya for Dadaab transit camp, which has a population of about 350,000 Somalis according to UNCHR and is quite vulnerable to climate change hazards. It faces an uncertain future as the Kenyan government announced its closure, allegedly for being a base for radicalised Muslims active in Somalia and Kenya. The new massive eviction of hundreds of thousands of mostly children and women (stage five of our typology) cannot be considered 'accumulation by dispossession'.

Selective social dispossession

In a similar way as for spatial selective dispossession, the analysis of multiple cases of evictions clearly indicates that the most vulnerable groups have the most chance of being evicted, or of becoming climate change refugees after a climatic hazard (Oxfam 2017): women and children are disproportionately high in number, as are ethnic minorities. Evictions are highly discriminatory. This was particularly the case in Istanbul, where Roma people occupying a neighbourhood were the first to be evicted, as in Sulukule neighbourhood for instance. Similarly, those historically inhabited by Greek or Kurdish people were the ones that suffered most from evictions (Cabannes, Asan and Baysal 2009). The situation in Istanbul is far from unique and can be observed repeatedly. Displacements and evictions occur for non-economic reasons such as ethnic ones (e.g. repeated evictions from Bedouin villages in Israel, constantly exposed to climate change hazards – see International Alliance of Inhabitants 2015a). Operation Murambatsvina ('Move the Rubbish') in Zimbabwe was launched by President Mugabe in 2005 and led to brutal evictions and the destruction of the homes of at least seven hundred thousand people. The reason, beyond the official eradication of illegal housing was, as explained by the opposition party, political revenge and punishment of those who dared to vote against Mugabe. In India, the growing difficulties of Muslim street hawkers to keep their activities in Ahmedabad's main central market in Gujarat mirrors the growing nationalism in India and the exclusion suffered by non-Hindu believers (Oriard 2018).

In summary, Harvey's accumulation by dispossession theory explains largely forced and market-driven evictions, as well as those resulting from climate change, particularly so as the amount of liquidity at global level has dramatically increased over the last decade. Climate change displacements and relocations are, and will be for years to come, a new fix to capitalism, and an additional opportunity of accumulation by dispossession, primarily of land.

However, Harvey's theory needs to be nuanced: accumulation by dispossession is a socially and spatially selective process, affecting above all the most vulnerable groups and globalised territories that can absorb massive amounts of capital and that offer the most lucrative investments. In addition, a large number of evictions, including those resulting from climate change impact, can be driven by other factors, be they ideological, ethnic, nationalist or religious.

Losing ground over the last 20 years

While the New Imperialism expanded and evictions, under multiple forms, reached an unpresented scale, the United Nations as a whole shifted over the last 20 years from a land rights and anti-evictions defender to an accommodative force, avoiding conflict with dominant eviction processes, or even playing a mediating role to find solutions that would benefit citizens and their multiple rights. This seems understandable as the UN is controlled by central governments and funded by the most powerful ones that at the same time facilitate market-driven and forced evictions and support land and asset dispossession worldwide. Such an evolution, if it continues, is a prime concern for climate change-induced displacements and evictions, as they will become even more difficult to address from a government and rights-based perspective.

New Urban Agenda

The New Urban Agenda (NAU; see UN-Habitat 2016), approved in 2016 during Quito Habitat III summit, is a regression when compared to the declarations and agendas of Habitat I (Vancouver, 1976) and Habitat II (Istanbul, 1996), if one considers housing and land rights or forced evictions, which are scarcely mentioned, without a single measure to address them. Two key elements need to be discussed in light of paragraph 25 of the Agenda – see Box 10.2 below.

First, the shift from the realisation of the right to adequate housing as a universal right identical for all, to its 'progressive' realisation only. This substantial change was introduced in 1996, under the coordinated lobby of nations such as the United States, Iran and the Vatican, for varying reasons. This means that any progress, however minimal, is considered a realisation of the right, and it also means that its normative universal value was largely lost. The regressive shift introduced at the last minute in 1996 unfortunately remained in 2016's agenda, confirming a regressive trend that started over 20 years ago.

Box 10.2 The New Urban Agenda

We commit to promote national, sub-national, and local housing policies that support the *progressive* realisation of the right to adequate housing for all as a component of the right to an adequate standard of living, that address all forms of discrimination and violence, prevent *arbitrary* forced evictions, and focus on the needs of the homeless, persons in vulnerable situations, low income groups, and persons with disabilities, while enabling participation and engagement of communities and relevant stakeholders, in the planning and implementation of these policies.

New Urban Agenda 2016, paragraph 25 (italics my emphasis).

Second, and more importantly in relation to the discussion on evictions in the present chapter, the prevention of forced evictions became (articles 25, 103 and 106) 'the prevention of *arbitrary* forced evictions' (my emphasis; see Box 10.2). Such a significant conceptual turn raises a couple of unanswered questions: what is 'arbitrary'? Who defines what is arbitrary? How will this arbitrariness be monitored and enforced and by whom, and how will people threatened by evictions be able to make a case with such a notion? A second significant consequence is that each country or each city will have the freedom to use their own perception of arbitrary forced evictions, leaving aside universal value. A third observation is that no mention is made of market-driven evictions that have become dramatically significant over the last 20 years, or of climate change-induced displacements and evictions that will become dominant in the future.

In summary, both notions – *arbitrary* forced evictions and right to *progressive* housing – turn the New Urban Agenda, supposedly the city agenda for the next 20 years, into quite a weak tool for the defence of the access to land for all, and a powerful tool to facilitate all sorts of evictions anywhere in the world.

Structural limits of the Sustainable Development Goals

The Sustainable Development Goals (SDGs), which were approved and endorsed one year before the New Urban Agenda, illustrate a similar direction. This is primarily the case for SDG 11, 'Make cities and human settlements inclusive, safe, resilient and sustainable', which is blind to evictions and security of right to land and other assets. None of the seven targets of this goal refer to security of land tenure, or stopping forced evictions, be they unlawful, market-driven or induced by climate change. Unfortunately, very clear targets addressing an increase of secure rights of land were eliminated during the formulation process. They were included in the original document (UN-Habitat 2013, 5) but were omitted along the way and not included at the end:

> By 2030, increase by x% the share of women and men, communities and businesses with secure rights to land, property, and other assets.
>
> By 2030, ensure equal right of women to own and inherit property, sign a contract, register a business and open a bank account.

This evidences once again the dismissal of the UN system in relation to preserving or improving secure land rights for both men and women, which have been deleted from the two main agendas. This tends to leave the gates open to evictions of all kinds and to a system of insecure rights to land.

Millennium Development Goals and slum index

The deconstruction of the protection against evictions within a rights-based approach did not start recently with the SDGs and the NAU, but can be traced back to around 15 years ago, in the context of the monitoring of the Millennium Development Goals (MDGs), the predecessor to the SDGs. The operational measurement of slum improvement (Target 11: 'By 2020, achieve significant improvement in the lives of at least 100 million slum dwellers') included as one of its five indexes secure tenure, defined as 'the right of all individuals and groups to effective protection by the State against forced evictions' (UN-Habitat 2007, iv).

As per a recommendation made at the Expert Group Meeting on Urban Indicators – in which I participated – held in Nairobi in November 2002, and fully documented by UN-Habitat (2003, 7, 10, 11) the measurement of slum improvement, called the slum index, should consider five key dimensions, each of which is measured with indicators:

- Access to safe water
- Access to sanitation
- Secure tenure
- Durability of housing
- Sufficient living area

The secure tenure sub-index was measured with the following indicator: proportion of individuals who have secure tenure, i.e. who have: (1) evidence of documentation that can be used as proof of secure tenure status, and (2) either de facto or perceived protection from forced evictions. Three component indicators were recommended for this measurement:

- Proportion of urban households with documents can be used as evidence of tenure
- Evictions: proportion of men and women who are evicted from their residence in the past 10 years
- Perception of security of tenure: proportion of households' heads who believe that they will not be evicted from their present residence within the next five years

Unfortunately, and despite its relevance, the secure tenure sub-index was simply deleted by UN-Habitat reports on the MDGs (see for instance UN-Habitat 2007). Hence, the most important source of data that qualified evictions on a global scale was lost and the issue became invisible. In addition, if a slum was 'improved' by its original dwellers, whether renters or owners, being forcibly evicted, there was no way to count them in, and such an 'improved slum' would meet target 11.

Dismantling of the Advisory Group on Forced Evictions to the executive director of UN-Habitat

During its nineteenth session (2003), UN-Habitat's Governing Council 'requested the Executive Director, in line with the recommendations of the World Urban Forum to establish an advisory group to monitor and identify, and if so requested, to promote alternatives to unlawful evictions' (Resolution 19/5). As a result, 15 pro bono independent members were appointed by the executive director as an Advisory Group on Forced Evictions (AGFE) to provide him with advice, with a clear set of responsibilities: to monitor acts of forced evictions; facilitate learning; advocate and support research, training and capacity building. The country missions that were supposed to document forced evictions and propose actions and solutions to the UN were always problematic and they were scarcely attended to by UN-Habitat's executive director, Anna Kajumulo Tibaijuka.[9] Her successor, Joan Clos, decided to dismantle it, and in doing so, stopped meeting the request made by the Governing Council. As a consequence, one of the very few independent mediation channels at international level was closed and has not been reopened since, despite the request from the Governing Council still being present. This clearly indicates that the decision was taken by the UN bureaucracy and not so much by government representatives.

OHCHR and the Special Rapporteur on Adequate Housing

When considering more specifically climate change-induced displacements and evictions, a similar 'permissive' evolution can be observed at the UN Office of the High Commissioner on Human Rights (OHCHR), including the Office of the Special Rapporteur on Adequate Housing. For instance, the OHCHR's *Key Messages on Human Rights and Climate Change* (OHCHR n.d.) highlight the essential obligations and responsibilities of states and other duty-bearers, but do not include a single word on addressing as a priority climate change-related displacements and subsequent potential evictions. The problem is simply ignored. When referred to, the recommendations made are particularly mild and simply indicative: 'States should engage in cooperative efforts to respond to climate-related displacement and migration and to address climate-related conflicts and security risks.'

From the early 2000s, the OHCHR Office on Adequate Housing had been one of the most influential bodies to deal with forced evictions and displacements. In 2012, the second Special Rapporteur on Adequate Housing drew attention to the effects of climate change on the right to adequate housing (OHCHR 2012), particularly on women and girls. She confirmed the trends observed with respect to rehabilitation and reconstruction following natural disasters, i.e., that women encounter problems related to their lack of tenure and property rights and are frequently ignored in the process of rebuilding livelihoods.[10] Unfortunately, since that date and the appointment of the third Special Rapporteur, very little attention has been devoted to these issues, which might be interpreted as regressive trend similar to that seen in the UN as a whole, with no goals or targets on secure land tenure in the SDGs, and the New Urban Agenda position on arbitrary evictions and the progressive right to housing that followed the dismantling of AGFE and the deletion of the indicator on eviction and land tenure security. The next section will highlight some positive actions taken by different actors, challenging the new imperialist dispossession currents and the UN's regressive attitude.

The way forward

How to face market-driven, forced and climate change-induced evictions remains a challenge for the years to come, and proposals made by the defunct AGFE might still be a contribution (Cabannes 2005). However, on the positive side, multiple community-led struggles, resistance and initiatives are taking place that deserve much more documentation (see Cabannes, Guimarães-Yafi and Johnson 2010, 6), reflexive research and dissemination. In this concluding section some of them are briefly introduced, as being of direct interest for climate change and paving the way for future anti-hegemonic practices.

Knowledge and advocacy: the need for local and global observatories

The last global survey on forced evictions dates from 2009 and was published by the Centre on Housing Rights and Evictions (COHRE), covering the 2007–8 period (COHRE 2009). Eviction reports were provided for 53 countries and 835 cases, concerning over four million people and covering actual evictions, threatened and planned ones and a meagre five experiences where evictions could be averted. Since that date no global data are available, and gradually the type of evictions, their scale and the rights they are violating became more and more invisible, and therefore more difficult to be advocated for. Even if not focused on climate change-induced displacements or eviction cases, local observatories have been founded in different parts of the world in order to partially fill the void. The São Paulo Observatory on Removals in Brazil is an interesting case for the tools and methods it designed; for its multi-actor partnership, closely related with social movements, and spearheaded by various laboratories from two local universities; and for its capacity to produce accessible knowledge (Rolnik et al. 2017).

Advocacy: local and regional tribunals on evictions

As a reaction to the growing difficulty of advocating for housing and local evictions, and in the aftermath of the dismantling of AGFE, the International Alliance of Inhabitants established an annual International Eviction Tribunal that allowed the identification of numerous cases at global level. For instance, in 2016, 86 cases were filed by organisations from 31 countries, concerning 1.8 million people. An annual one-day session allowed some of the claimants to introduce their case to an international jury that was producing recommendations. The limitation of the tribunal, under its current format and given its institutional isolation, lies in its incapacity to provide any support to desperate residents who are threatened by evictions or have recently been evicted; just as importantly, it has been unable to mobilise the media to raise awareness on the issue and change the situations. During the Quito habitat summit in 2016, the session was attended by a few dozen people despite the thirty thousand visitors to the various conferences, and its media impact was almost nil.

Local and regional tribunals on evictions, independent from the International Alliance of Inhabitants, have encountered a more sustained success and impact. In Cameroon in particular, the People's Tribunal on Evictions (*Tribunal Populaire des Evictions*) finalised its second edition as part of the Cameroon Network of Inhabitants (RNHC) triennial meeting, where thousands of community delegates from the whole country were present and strongly mobilised. The eviction cases are usually documented and introduced by volunteers from an associated NGO, ASSOAL, or by the concerned communities. In addition, the tribunal is only one among various land and housing activities carried out by the national network. Interestingly, some of the cases filed result from climatic hazards, such as heavy rains and flooding. Cameroon's People's Tribunal on Evictions remains a source of inspiration and an example for other countries.

Emergence of locally grounded innovative practices

Various successful projects and programmes have been reaching a significant scale and gained international recognition. Each one of the examples below, selected from among a significant number, highlight in their own right some paradigm shift, and they demonstrate that climate change-induced displacements can be avoided and are not an automatic fate. They challenge the dominant selective land dispossession trend through in situ solutions. They deserve to be better disseminated and better known, and would benefit from peer-to-peer exchanges of knowledge and knowhow.

Preventing typhoon damage to housing

In Central Vietnam, a country exposed to sea-level rise and its associated hazards, Development Workshop France has supported the large-scale programme Preventing Typhoon Damage to Housing since 2000 to strengthen the capacities of families, communities and grassroots organisations to make their homes and communities safer, in the context of participatory commune Damage Action Plans. Collaboration with and the involvement of commune people's committees and local and national authorities remains a distinctive and positive feature (World Habitat Awards n.d.; Development Workshop France and Viêt Nam 2010). One key lesson learned is that 'the preventive strengthening of the houses is viable and efficient in terms of cost, performance and social acceptability' (World Habitat Awards n.d.; Development Workshop France and Viêt Nam 2010): for instance, the houses and public buildings strengthened through the programme withstood the impact of a major typhoon in 2016, and none of them were displaced, while thousands of others were severely damaged.

Bridging the gap between participatory budgeting and climate change

Lisbon, Portugal, another country particularly exposed to sea-level rise, floods and fire hazards, was the first European capital city to introduce in 2008 a participatory budgeting (PB) process for the citizens to decide on a portion of the public budget. Since 2018, the Lisbon Climate Citizenship

Commitment aims at integrating climate projects into its PB and at creating a platform that materialises 'Lisbon's Commitment for Resilience to Climate Change'. In 2020–1 'Green' PB will dedicate five million euros exclusively to proposals that contribute to climate change and environmentally friendly projects. Considering the five thousand or more PB experiences in more than 45 countries and the massive amount of public resources at stake, this dedicated approach to climate change, from a citizen and local government perspective, will be a significant measure to prevent the effect of climate hazards at neighbourhood level and at the same time to reinforce the capacities of citizens and their communities to resist and avoid climate change-induced displacements.

Community, collective and cooperative forms of land tenure

Caño Martin Peña Community Fideicomiso de la Tierra is:

> an innovative community land trust [CLT] designed by residents of historically disenfranchised and underserved informal settlements at the heart of San Juan, Puerto Rico, to secure land rights and prevent displacement as an unintended consequence of an environmental restoration project that, by reconnecting several inland bodies of water, will transform the city (personal communication from Lyvia N. Rodríguez del Valle, November 2018).

This large-scale programme, on 78 hectares and concerning over sixteen thousand inhabitants, is one among hundreds of collective, communal and cooperative forms of land tenure that are mushrooming in various countries, as a successful resistance to dispossession, foreclosures and evictions (Cabannes and Baysal 2012; Cabannes 2014; United Nations 2012).

Directly related to the debate in this chapter, when an exceptionally strong typhoon hit the island in 2017, Caño Martin Peña Community was not spared, but demonstrated a remarkably higher level of resilience and recovery when compared to other communities. Importantly, no families were relocated outside the neighbourhood and no dispossession occurred, because of collective ownership and the social cohesion resulting from the CLT process (Rodríguez del Valle 2016).

Self-recovery, on-site rehabilitation and build back better

The Post-Haiyan Self-Recovery Housing Programme in the Philippines illuminates various paradigm shifts in relation to how to approach massive climate change hazards.[11] In 2013, Typhoon Haiyan, the strongest tropical cyclone ever recorded, destroyed approximately one million homes and four million people were displaced. Through the Post-Haiyan Programme, CARE Philippines helped about sixteen thousand families made homeless to rebuild their homes themselves (World Habitat 2017). The concept of shelter self-recovery can be summarised as a 'process of households making use of their own resources to repair and rebuild their homes' (Schofield and Flinn 2018); it remains at the heart of this innovative approach, which provided guidance on 'building back safer'. Another key element was focusing on people working together to rebuild their homes, reactivating the community spirit,[12] and fostering the importance of resilience as a collective asset. Through on-site reconstruction, the programme preserved families' access to their livelihoods, where possible, and maintained access to health and education services when they existed, an asset considered more important than the house itself (Twigg et al. 2017; World Habitat 2017).

Conclusion: land-based solutions and human rights-based improvements

I fully agree with Scott Leckie's conclusions and beliefs (Leckie 2013a, 77): 'that many aspects of climate displacement can be resolved with land-based solutions and human rights-based improvements in domestic housing, land and property law and policy'. I also agree with his concluding remark referring to the centrality of land in addressing climate displacements challenges: 'At the core of all solutions will be land. Identifying this land, accessing it, acquiring it and, ultimately, allocating it remains the challenge of the era of climate displacement in which we live' (Leckie 2013a, 81). As Leckie rightly states, this will effectively depend on political will, and the Peninsula Principles on climate displacement within states (Leckie 2013b) seem a good way to start. However, what still remains to be underlined is the necessity of facing with bold determination the new imperialist logic of dispossession through selective accumulation competing precisely for the same pieces of land. This competition is harsh, and will be harsher in the future, and it is not only through political will and good policies that land will be secured for people displaced by climate change. It is through mobilisation, education, organisation and struggle, too. Challenging the current economic (dis)order remains at the core of the problem, as does the need to support grassroots organisations, tenants' families with and without formal title[13] in their initiatives and struggles for survival, for not being 'climate evicted' and for the respect of their multiple rights.

Notes

1. Committee on Economic, Social and Cultural Rights (CESCR), General Comment 7: The right to adequate housing – forced evictions, 20 May 1997.
2. Resolution 1998/9 on Forced Evictions, E/CN.4/SUB.2/RES/1998/9 (20 August 1998).
3. Typology adapted from Cabannes, Asan and Baysal (2009, 7).
4. For a longer version see the International Alliance of Inhabitants' typology on evictions and Cabannes 2016.
5. This number includes people forcibly displaced, internally displaced or assisted by UNHCR after they have been able to return home.
6. International Tribunal on Evictions, file on Pueblo Asháninka eviction, November 2015, unpublished material, International Alliance of Inhabitants.
7. Among the various international recognitions for this project, see C40 Cities n.d.
8. In theory, quantitative easing can be summarised as consisting of four phases: (1) In agreement with the treasury, the central bank creates money. This currency is not physically created, it is simply a credit line to the central bank account. (2) To inject this newly created money, the central bank buys sovereign bonds from financial institutions (banks, insurance companies, pension funds). (3) Banks therefore end up with more cash, which can be lent more easily (and at a lower rate) to companies and households, in order to boost investment and consumption. (4) Once growth is restored through increased investment and consumption, the Central Bank should in theory sell the previously purchased sovereign bonds (or wait for the bonds to mature), and destroy the currency that has been created. If the intervention is totally sterilised, the currency created at the time of the crisis to boost investment must then be destroyed to avoid inflationary pressures. Translated from French by the author, from Captain Economist, 6 April 2012.
   However, the last phase that consists of the destruction of the money injected, might happen… but only after the cheap money permitted to acquire new lands, and after therefore dispossession has taken place for the benefit of few banks, hedge funds and international investors and a massive dispossession of many families and individuals.
9. Testimony by the author as AGFE convenor for both mandates, until the dismantling of the group.
10. A/64/255, paras. 15 and 59.
11. As Chapter 12 by Bill Flinn and Holly Schofield in this volume is dedicated to this approach, the programme and its lessons learned will be only briefly referred to here.
12. Locally called *bayanihan*.
13. Tenants, with or without formal titles, deserve a much longer discussion, as they are the prime losers in any resettlement, relocation or displacement of any kind. They are often the most deprived, least protected and the first to be hit by the consequences of climate change.

References

Arthus, Patrick. 2017. 'La liquidité mondiale continue à augmenter'. *Flash Économie NATIXIS*, 2017. https://www.research.natixis.com/GlobalResearchWeb/Main/GlobalResearch/GetDocument/EEQOsP3z4qWu3krxvo1CXQ==.

Breteau, Pierre. 2019. 'Vers quels pays ont fui les 74,8 millions de personnes contraintes à l'exil?' *Le Monde*, 20 June 2019. https://www.lemonde.fr/les-decodeurs/article/2019/06/20/ou-ont-fui-les-74-8-millions-de-personnes-contraintes-a-l-exil_5479071_4355770.html.

C40 Cities. n.d. 'Jakarta: Socially inclusive coastal protection today and for 2030'. https://www.c40.org/profiles/2014-jakarta.

Cabannes, Yves. 2004. 'Réponses des villes latino-américaines aux défis posés par la planification urbaine participative'. In *Quels plans pour la ville? Gouvernance, gestion et politique urbaines*. UNESCO MOST Discussion Paper 69.

Cabannes, Yves. 2005. 'Forced evictions: Reflection on some innovative solutions and the way forward'. In *Forced Evictions: Towards solutions? First report of the Advisory Group on Forced Evictions (UN AGFE) to the Executive Director of UN-Habitat*, 138–55. https://reliefweb.int/report/world/forced-evictions-towards-solutions-first-report-advisory-group-forced-evictions.

Cabannes, Yves. 2014. 'Cooperative, communal and collective forms of land tenure and their contribution to the social function of land and housing'. In *Take Back the Land! The social function of land and housing, resistance and alternatives*, 137–44. http://www.citego.org/bdf_fiche-document-1364_en.html.

Cabannes, Yves. 2016. 'The challenge of slum evictions in a neo liberal world'. In *Who Owns the City? Exclusion and inclusion – some global perspectives*, 16–24. Oslo: Habitat Norway. http://habitat-norge.org/wp-content/uploads/2016/10/Who-owns-the-city-summary-report.pdf.

Cabannes, Yves, Arif Asan and Cihan Uzuncarsili Baysal. 2009. *Forced Evictions in Istanbul: Report from the Advisory Group on Forced Evictions to the Executive Director of UN-Habitat*. https://mirror.unhabitat.org/downloads/docs/10008_1_593995.pdf.

Cabannes, Yves and Cihan Uzuncarsili Baysal. 2012. 'When national policies stand against human and housing rights: Lessons from Istanbul'. *Passerelle* 7: 122–7. https://www.coredem.info/IMG/pdf/housing_in_eurp.pdf.

Cabannes, Yves, Silvia Guimarães-Yafi and Cassidy Johnson, eds. 2010. *How People Face Evictions*. Development Planning Unit, UCL. https://www.ucl.ac.uk/bartlett/development/sites/bartlett/files/how_people_face_evictions_eng.pdf.

Castells, Manuel. 1989. *The Informational City: Information technology, economic restructuring, and the urban-regional process*. Oxford: Blackwell.

COHRE. 2009. *Global Forced Evictions Survey 2007–2008*. Geneva. https://issuu.com/cohre/docs/cohre_forcedevictions_globalsurvey2_17a2f1db41a915.

Daumas, Lucile. 2017. 'Accaparement des terres et de l'eau au Maroc'. Committee for the Abolition of Illegitimate Debt (CADTM), 21 October 2017. https://www.cadtm.org/Accaparement-des-terres-et-de-l.

Development Workshop France and Viêt Nam. 2010. *Impact Study on Developing Local Capacity to Reduce Vulnerability and Poverty in Central Viêt Nam*. https://www.preventionweb.net/files/submissions/20274_dwfimpactstudyofdwfprogrammeinvietnambshf2011.pdf.

Duval, Jérôme and Fátima Martín. 2015. 'Casi medio millón de desahucios producto de una ley hipotecaria franquista'. *America Latina en Movimiento*, 17 December 2015. https://www.alainet.org/es/articulo/174318.

Ferris, Elizabeth. 2012. *Protection and Planned Relocations in the Context of Climate Change*. UNHCR Geneva. https://www.unhcr.org/protection/globalconsult/5024d5169/27-protection-planned-relocations-context-climate-change-elizabeth-ferris.html.

Ferris, Elizabeth. 2014. *Planned Relocations, Disasters and Climate Change: Consolidating good practices and preparing for the future. Background document. Sanremo consultation, 12–14 March 2014*. UNHCR, Brookings-LSE and Georgetown University. https://www.unhcr.org/53c4d6f99.pdf.

Gun Cuninghame, Patrick. 2007. 'Globalisation, maquiladoras and transnational identities at the US-Mexico border: The case of Ciudad Juarez-El Paso'. *Revue Interventions Économiques* 35. http://journals.openedition.org/interventionseconomiques/648.

Harvey, David. 2003. *The New Imperialism*. Oxford and New York: Oxford University Press.

Harvey, David. 2004. 'The "new" imperialism: Accumulation by dispossession'. *Socialist Register* 40 (1): 63–87.

Internal Displacement Monitoring Centre. 2017. *Global Report on Internal Displacement*. Geneva: Displacement Solutions. https://www.internal-displacement.org/sites/default/files/publications/documents/20170522-GRID.pdf.

International Alliance of Inhabitants. 2013. *Guia Popular Cero Desalojos y para la Defensa del Territorio*. https://www.habitants.org/content/download/199298/2594789/version/10/file/%28Espa%C3%B1ol%29+Guia+Popular+Cero+Desalojos+y+para+la+defensa+del+territorio.pdf.

International Alliance of Inhabitants. 2015a. Archive file on Bedouins eviction case in Israel.

International Alliance of Inhabitants. 2015b. Archive file on Pueblo Asháninka Eviction.

Leckie, Scott. 2013a. *Finding Land Solutions for Climate Displacement: A challenge like few others*. Geneva: Displacement Solutions. https://environmentalmigration.iom.int/finding-land-solutions-climate-displacement-challenge-few-others.

Leckie, Scott. 2013b. *The Peninsula Principles on Climate Displacement within States*. Geneva: Displacement Solutions. http://displacementsolutions.org/wp-content/uploads/2014/12/Peninsula-Principles.pdf.

Leckie, Scott and Chris Huggins, eds. 2016. *Repairing Domestic Climate Displacement: The Peninsula Principles*. London: Routledge.

OHCHR. n.d. *Key Messages on Human Rights and Climate Change*. https://www.ohchr.org/Documents/Issues/ClimateChange/KeyMessages_on_HR_CC.pdf.

OHCHR. 2012. *Women and the Right to Adequate Housing*. https://www.ohchr.org/Documents/Publications/WomenHousing_HR.PUB.11.2.pdf.

Oriard Colin, Lila. 2018. 'Street vending from the right to the city approach: The appropriation of Bhadra Plaza'. In *Cities in Asia by and for the People*, edited by Yves Cabannes, Michael Douglass and Rita Padawangi, 259–82. Amsterdam: Amsterdam University Press. https://doi.org/doi 10.5117/9789462985223/ch10.

Oxfam. 2017. *Uprooted by Climate Change, Responding to the Growing Risk of Displacement*. https://www-cdn.oxfam.org/s3fs-public/file_attachments/bp-uprooted-climate-change-displacement-021117-en.pdf.

Rodríguez del Valle, Lyvia N. 2016. 'El caso del Caño Martin Peña en Puerto Rico: Fideicomiso de la tierra para asegurar el derecho a la ciudad'. *America Latina en Movimiento: Las agendas del Hábitat* 519: 25–6. https://www.alainet.org/sites/default/files/alai519.pdf.

Rolnik, Raquel, Karina Leitão, Francisco Comaru and Regina Dulce Lins. 2017. 'Observátorio das remoções 2015–2017: Relatorio final do projeto'. São Paulo: FAUUSP. http://www.labcidade.fau.usp.br/wp-content/uploads/2017/12/1707OR_publicacaofinal_revDigital_menor.pdf.

Schofield, Holly and Bill Flinn. 2018. 'People first: Agency, choice and empowerment in the support of self-recovery'. In *The State of Humanitarian Shelter and Settlements*. International Federation of Red Cross and Red Crescent Societies, United Nations High Commissioner for Refugees. https://www.sheltercluster.org/resources/documents/state-humanitarian-shelter-and-settlements-2018pdf.

Twigg, John, Emma Lovell, Holly Schofield, Luisa Miranda Morel, Bill Flinn, Susanne Sargeant, Andrew Finlayson et al. 2017. *Self-Recovery from Disasters: An interdisciplinary perspective*. London: ODI. https://www.odi.org/sites/odi.org.uk/files/resource-documents/11870.pdf.

UNEP. 2015. 'UNEP marks international day for preventing the exploitation of the environment in war and armed conflict'. Press release, 6 November 2015. https://www.unenvironment.org/news-and-stories/press-release/unep-marks-international-day-preventing-exploitation-environment-war.

UN-Habitat. 2003. *Improving the Lives of 100 Million Slum Dwellers: Guide to monitoring target 11*. https://unhabitat.org/improving-the-lives-of-100-million-slum-dwellers-guide-to-monitoring-target-11.

UN-Habitat. 2007. *Enhancing Urban Safety and Security: Global report on human settlements 2007*. https://www.un.org/ruleoflaw/files/urbansafetyandsecurity.pdf.

UN-Habitat. 2013. *Revised Compilation for Sustainable Cities and Human Settlements in the Sustainable Development Goals (SDGs) within the post-2015 Development Agenda*. https://sustainabledevelopment.un.org/content/documents/2913Revised Cities SDG Compilation 20 Dec 2013.pdf.

UN-Habitat. 2016. *New Urban Agenda*. Quito Declaration on Sustainable Cities and Human Settlements for All. http://habitat3.org/wp-content/uploads/NUA-English.pdf.

United Nations. 2012. *Report of the Special Rapporteur on Adequate Housing as a Component of the Right to an Adequate Standard of Living, and the Right to Non-Discrimination in This Context, Raquel Rolnik*. https://documents-dds-ny.un.org/doc/UNDOC/GEN/G12/189/79/PDF/G1218979.pdf?OpenElement.

World Habitat. 2017. 'Self-recovery housing programme in the Philippines wins World Habitat Awards 2017'. Press release. https://world-habitat.org/news/press-releases/self-recovery-housing-programme-philippines-wins-world-habitat-awards-2017.

World Habitat Awards. n.d. 'Preventing typhoon damage to housing in Central Viet Nam'. https://world-habitat.org/world-habitat-awards/winners-and-finalists/preventing-typhoon-damage-to-housing-central-viet-nam.

11

Relocation, expulsion and risk in Phnom Penh, Cambodia

Giovanna Astolfo

> The machinations of global capital have left a deep scar on the country, as land grabbing, forced eviction and environmental destruction have ensured the perpetuation of Cambodia's encounter with violence (Brickell and Springer 2016, 2).

For a long time, Phnom Penh was an unmapped land, with no land policy, planning or registration system as the French *cadastre* was destroyed during the Khmer Rouge period (Diepart and Sem 2015; Fauveaud 2016). Starting from the 1990s, and following the clichéd patterns of newly emerging nations, Cambodia opened its markets to foreign investment (Clerc 2016). The Phnom Penh strategic orientation masterplan developed during the mid-2000s and a number of corollary local development plans attracted investments from foreign companies (Connell and Grimsditch 2016; Percival 2016). With the ambition to resemble a collage of fragments from Singapore, South Korea and China, Phnom Penh follows the trend of what Percival terms 'intra-Asian urbanism' (Percival 2016, 186; see also Nam 2012). The masterplan paved the way for the acquisition of 5,000 hectares of reclaimed urban marshlands for the building of satellite cities and consumption spaces (Clerc 2016). Taking advantage of a weak state and widespread corruption, satellite cities represented the globalisation of capital, while urban development was monopolised de facto by the market. As Shatkin would put it, this represented the 'transfer of power over and responsibility for the visioning of urban futures and the exercise of social action for urban change from public to private sector actors' (2008, 388).

Satellite cities, however, are not the only developments and real estate dynamics characterising Phnom Penh's mixed-use periphery, as they are paired with small resident projects that nurture the informal land market (Percival 2016; Fauveaud 2016). Such a market, though, is not accessible to marginalised communities, who continue to occupy public or private interstitial land along canals and unused infrastructure, mostly vulnerable and prone to flooding, while gated communities and satellite cities are growing in number (Goad 2012; Fallavier 1999, 2002).[1] Given that half of the urban population is below the poverty line, who can afford these houses? Gated communities and residential projects are probably aimed at a middle class or, better, at foreigners and officials who are part of a highly corrupted political system. As marginalised dwellers are not involved in decision-making and planning, the city transforms beyond their control. In the face of aggressive commercialisation of land markets, and market-oriented tenure reforms, they struggle to secure a place (Asian Coalition for Housing Rights [ACHR] 2004; Springer 2013, 2016, 2020; Flower 2018). Most of them lack basic knowledge and sufficient resources to enforce their rights, while the government and the private sector take advantage of the regime of uncertainty, provisionality and informational opacity.

Like several other Asian cities, Phnom Penh developed beyond the intentions of its dwellers (Satterthwaite 2008). In this light, this chapter examines involuntary resettlement as a mode of urban production, pursued by the state as a deliberate strategy of exclusion and expulsion and engineered through economic and land reforms (Springer 2013; Brickell 2016; Flower 2018), deregulation and informational opacity.

A satellite pattern of displacement: some numbers

> Relocating communities is fraught with difficulty. In the past 20 years, more than 300 million people have been resettled as a result of conservation, urbanisation or development schemes, including dam and road-building, mainly in developing countries. Most moves faced local resistance and were detrimental to livelihoods, health and wellbeing. Remuneration for lost income, land and jobs rarely compensated for reduced access to resources, fractured social networks and emotional trauma (López-Carr and Marter-Kenyon 2015, 8).

Resettlement in Phnom Penh is extremely well documented in multi-disciplinary literature – rightly so, given the scale of the phenomenon. Resettlements took place from the 1990s to, officially, the early 2010s. According to Amnesty International (2008, 7), in 2008 there were around 150,000 Cambodians at risk of displacement. According to Land and Housing Working Group (LHWG), 'in total, at least 26,600 Phnom Penh families, approximately 133,000 residents or 11 per cent of the city's population of 1.2 million, have been evicted since 1990' (LHWG 2009, 3). According to the Cambodia Office of the United Nations High Commissioner for Human Rights (OHCHR), 120,000 individuals in Phnom Penh have been evicted since 1990, and thousands more face the risk of being forcibly displaced in the coming years (OHCHR 2012, 2). Finally, according to the local NGO Sahmakum Teang Tnaut (STT), the number of families evicted between 1990 and 2014 in Phnom Penh was 29,715 (STT 2014, 9).

According to the most recent report by STT (2020), the largest number of evictions and relocations was carried out between 2001 and 2010 as a result of the 2001 law. After 2010 there was a slowdown, but evictions still happen, including during the Covid-19 outbreak in 2020.

Although the figures do not match, the number of people forcibly displaced as a consequence of urban development is set above one hundred thousand. The scale of the expulsion had little precedent in history, except for the evacuation ('exurbanisation') that took place during the Democratic Kampuchea regime of 1975–9. Counting the displaced is difficult, as the government has never released official data, and figures entirely rely on unsystematically recorded surveys conducted by NGOs and international agencies (Connell and Grimsditch 2016, 226).

Interestingly enough, there is no available holistic cartographic material that documents the designation of resettlement land. Only the maps elaborated by STT (2012a, 2012b, 2014) can actually help us to grasp the physical scale of the resettlement process. Over the period 1998–2012 the number of resettlement sites grew exponentially (STT 2020, 16). Early in 2004, ACHR argued that 'since 1998, more than 8,100 people have relocated to 18 sites across rural Phnom Penh' (ACHR 2004, 10). The number doubled in a few years. According to STT, in 2007 there were more than 40 resettlement sites in and around Phnom Penh (LHWG 2009, 4); in 2012 the number increased to 50, while the sites were, for evident reasons, increasingly distant from the city (STT 2012b, 1). By December 2014, the resettlement sites numbered 54 (STT 2014, 14); see Figure 11.1.

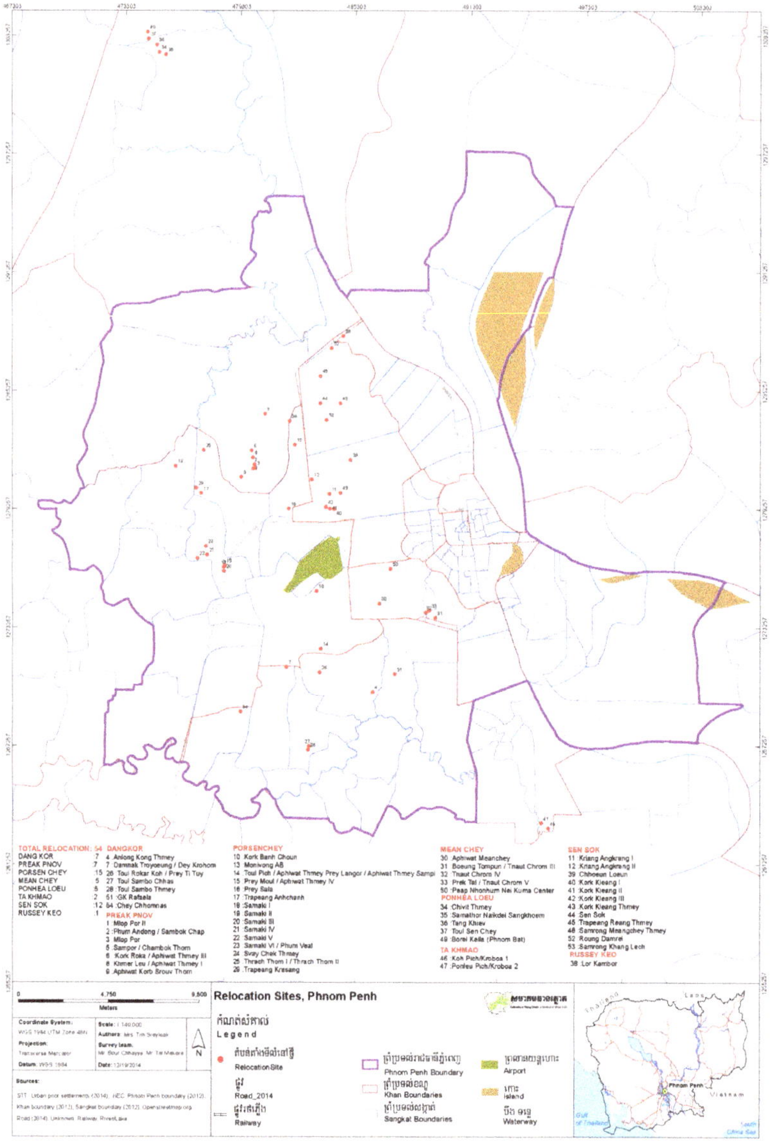

Figure 11.1 Map of resettlement sites in Phnom Penh, 2014. © Sahmakum Teang Tnaut.

Three years of engagement with relocated communities in Phnom Penh

A study over a number of resettlement sites[2] conducted by ACHR (2004), Community Architects Network Cambodia (CAN CAM) and Community Development Foundation (CDF) since the 2000s formed the starting point of our three years' engagement and action research within the MSc Building and Urban Design in Development (BUDD) programme at the Bartlett Development Planning Unit at UCL.

During our work with relocated communities in and around Phnom Penh between 2014 and 2016, we listened to numerous testimonies that referred to a condition of non-belonging from individuals and families who were both displaced and dispossessed. A dire sense of uncertainty, suspension and temporariness pervaded our informal conversations. Tenure security was the most sought-after asset – although amid wide confusion and disagreement around old and new titles and their validity before the law. In some settlements there were multiple typologies of tenure, reflecting unchanged complexity compared to Payne's (2002; Khemro and Payne 2004) earlier research; but in truth, I cannot cite a single interviewee who said he/she had received a title after resettlement, not even after many years. Mobility between former and new sites was a common mechanism for coping that emerged during our survey visits to the many unoccupied houses. As the neighbours explained to us, the owners were travelling. Land and titles transactions, as well as rapid turnover within the same resettlement site, were also very common, resulting in mixed populations and a high proportion of renters.

The presence of multiple coping mechanisms, including mobility and title transactions, mitigated the way in which everyday risk – of eviction and flooding – was perceived, though interviews clearly revealed the extent to which people were more highly exposed to risk in the resettlement sites compared to the original ones. The loss of a job following resettlement was a principal factor that could potentially undermine familial stability and produce indebtedness, as is also widely documented in the literature (STT 2020; Connell and Grimsditch 2016; OHCHR 2012). The poorest group seemed to be less able to absorb or mitigate the shock as they were still struggling to save even a number of years after resettlement. As a result, they were suffering a greater risk of being relocated again. However, people who were slightly better off at the time of resettlement, or were part of a community that was resettled en bloc, seemed to have better managed to adapt to the new conditions. With the support of ACHR and CAN CAM, they have started saving groups and are now involved in upgrading efforts.

An overview of the literature on resettlement in Phnom Penh

> The process has interrupted and seriously modified the existing livelihood options and the types of access to existing services with the substantial disruption of social relations and habitat (Lavell 2017, 23).

In the case of Phnom Penh, resettlement is referred to in various ways in the literature, including 'involuntary resettlement',[3] 'displacement' and 'development-induced displacement' (Connell and Grimsditch 2016, 223). There is wide agreement that it is related to development activities and particularly to infrastructure projects, urban beautification, private development and land speculation (Durand-Lasserve 2007; STT 2014, 2–9; Connell and Grimsditch 2016, 223; OHCHR 2012; LHWG 2009, 4; ACHR 2004, 11). Resettlement happened in the form of large-scale relocation of households from one location to another at a considerable distance, following forced evictions. In most cases resettlement was undertaken in violation of basic human rights, without consultation, notice or adequate compensation (Mgbako et al. 2010; STT 2012a, 2012b). The only documented case of participatory resettlement dates back to the late 1990s (ACHR 2004, 11; LHWG 2009).

Some forms of resettlement brought a resource bundle with them, including land, housing and service provision, albeit meagre or inadequate, but in most cases displaced people did not receive assistance (Nop and Thornton 2019; STT 2020). In some cases the resettlement sites sat on virgin land, without housing or services of any sort (Talocci and Boano 2015, 16; LHWG 2009, 4; Mgbako et al. 2010).

There is unanimous agreement that resettlement has been a large-scale failure, in terms of the reproduction of inequality and an increase in poverty, as living conditions for relocated families after resettlement were worse than before (Khemro and Payne 2004; Grimsditch and Henderson 2009; STT 2012a, 2014; Bugalski and Medallo 2012; Connell and Connell 2016; OHCHR 2012; ACHR 2004; LHWG 2009; Durand-Lasserve 2007; Tyskerud and Linsdtrom 2013).

Financial stress, the increasing cost of transport and uncertainty related to income adversely impacted relocated families. Connell and Grimsditch (2016) argue that resettlement resulted in further impoverishment even when compensation was in place, and highlight that there is no statistical evidence that the condition of resettled people improved over time. According to STT (2012b), the increased distance of the resettlement sites resulted in higher costs for electricity and water for each household and this led to the creation of debt. Additionally, resettlement stress contributed to marriage difficulties, family separations resulting from men leaving or both parents migrating (STT 2012a, 2014). Homelessness, indebtedness and social and family disruption increased settlers' dependency on NGOs, as families did not receive any support from the government according to the OHCHR report (2012).

The lack of assistance and services, the loss of jobs and increased indebtedness, and the disruption of existing social networks forced many people to abandon the resettlement site shortly after. Some returned to the city to squat in even more precarious conditions.[4] Others started moving between new and old sites as a coping mechanism (Connell and Connell 2016). Most people were promised tenure security on the new land, but the status granted for the plot was conditional and temporary. Years after resettlement, tenure security remains the main issue, as the lack of tenure increases the risk of further eviction. Monvilaite (2014) and Connell and Grimsditch (2016) highlight how in response to insecurity, people tried to sublet or sell the land, starting markets of temporary titles to cope with unemployment.

Connell (2015) mentions how resettlement tends to split groups and reduce intra-community solidarity, although social integration mechanisms in resettlement sites have not yet been thoroughly studied. According to Talocci and Boano (2016), resettlement is fundamentally a 'process of pacification and de-politicisation' to undermine people's cohesion and the possibility of mobilisation, while relocated subjects are stripped of any rights. However, the emergence of women leading protests is highlighted in some literature (STT 2012a, 2014; Brickell 2016; Cambodian League for the Promotion and Defense of Human Rights [LICADHO] 2016). Early forms of resistance are also documented, particularly in the paradigmatic cases of Borei Keila and Boeung Kak Lake.[5]

Resettlement undertaken to support policies targeted at disaster risk reduction, environmental conservation and climate change adaptation are more recent, and very little is known and researched about resettlement induced by climate change in Phnom Penh, although there is evidence that risk related to climate change affects resettled people more severely. In the case of Phnom Penh, resettlement happened in un-urbanised peripheral low land which is more exposed to the effects of climate change; in many cases development, accompanied by landfilling, exposes contiguous communities to the risk of resettlement due to the combined effect of land development and climate change.

Similarly, there is a paucity of literature that looks at the phenomenon of involuntary resettlement at scale, in historical and political terms (Diepart and Sem 2015; Dwyer 2015; Simone 2008; Talocci and Boano 2015, 2016). In the following section, this chapter attempts to look at resettlement as urbanism, its historical roots and drivers.

Resettlement as urbanism

> A moto taxi driver, the man compared Phan Imex's action to the Pol Pot era, which he was old enough to remember clearly. The comparison, extreme as it is, seem apt (Greenwood 2012).

The scale of involuntary resettlement in Phnom Penh suggests it is a radicalised mode of urban production rooted deeply in the urban history of the city and sustained by the legal apparatus (Springer 2013; Brickell 2016; Flower 2018). With thirty thousand families displaced since the 1990s (STT 2014), the resettlement process has become the main way of producing the city (STT 2020, 8). However, there are two long-standing narratives that need to be corrected. The first relates to the anti-urban bias of the Khmer Rouge period, which Shawn (2007) and Bishop and Clancey (2004) have defined as the most paradigmatic 'urbicide' in history (Tyner et al. 2014); the second is related to how a 'land issue' has been aptly constructed in order to favour the resettlement process and how land law enforcement, rather than the supposed lack of a legislative framework, has historically legitimised violent dispossession (Springer 2013; Dwyer 2015; Brickell 2016; Flower 2018).

> In present-day Cambodia such violence is palpable, as the tenor of accumulation by dispossession is shot through the various processes of neoliberalisation that the country has implemented under international tutelage since the United Nations-sponsored transition of the early 1990s (Springer 2013, 609).

Springer (2013) continues:

> In other words, property is impossible without accumulation by dispossession and both are impossible without organised violence. Accordingly, Blomley (2003) recognised law as the glue that binds this bloody trinity of property, accumulation by dispossession and violence together and argues that violent geographies must be recognised at all three levels of legal formation: origin, legitimation and enforcement (Springer 2013, 617).

The concept of urbicide[6] has been employed in a number of different cases of violence specifically directed to the destruction of an urban area. In this chapter I argue that urbicide was in fact a process of construction through destruction and that it occurred multiple times in the urban history of Phnom Penh following analogous patterns. Although they occurred within substantially different timeframes and contexts, the evacuation ('exurbanisation') of the capital city that took place in the 1970s under the Khmer Rouge and the current resettlement process following the economic reform in the 1990s and early 2000s are forms of urbicide, acts of extreme violence towards the city and what it represents for its people. Both were major factors of poverty-creation in the city.

Although there is no clarity on numbers and the scale of the phenomenon, during the Pol Pot regime, a vast majority of the urban population was forcibly deported to the countryside, in order to fulfil the utopia of a rural Kampuchea and a classless agrarian society, and urban public buildings, cultural and institutional symbols were emptied, abandoned and eventually destroyed (Shawn 2007; Bishop and Clancey 2004; Beng Hong 1984). According to a more recent study conducted by Tyner et al. (2014), while Phnom Penh was evacuated and many buildings destroyed, a simultaneous reconstruction process took place, and old administrative functions were replaced with new ones closer to the regime. Such an intentional destruction/construction process is not the reason but rather the model for the resettlement process that happened 20 years later, in the 1990s. In other words, we could argue that the current neoliberal production of the city entailing the expulsion of the poor is a reproduction of a socialist schemata:

> The city had to be remade from scratch following the evacuation … Phnom Penh had to rapidly accommodate a population that was in essence a residue of its former self (Simone 2008, 2).

At the end of the war, after the fall of the Khmer Rouge regime, people returned to Phnom Penh. Again, there exists little evidence of such movement (see Desbarats 1995), but it is plausible to assume that the large majority of the displaced population was reunited with their old communities. As refugees in their own city, they occupied abandoned buildings or settled in vacant land, particularly around lakes and along water channels (Khemro and Payne 2004). As already stated at the beginning of this chapter, for a long time after the war the land remained unmapped. There was no cadastral or formal property system in place, as during the Khmer Rouge period all land ownership was dissolved and land titles destroyed; tenure was simply regulated by social consensus (Grimsditch and Henderson 2009). When in the 1990s Cambodia opened to the global market and foreign investment flooded into the city, the central, informally regulated land became attractive to new developers (Percival 2016; Clerc 2016; Connell and Grimsditch 2016; Nam 2012). The lack of regulations, planning and policy became handy. Not only did the local government make little effort in resisting the land grabbing, it largely and intentionally favoured it through land reforms – and later planning tools – that encouraged investment (Khemro and Payne 2004; Percival 2016; Flower 2018; STT 2020). The timely construction of a 'land issue' served the purpose.

In order to justify other agendas, informality became a problem to be urgently fixed. The long-lived dual tenure system, based on possession and ownership, was no longer acceptable. A legal tool and a large-scale campaign for land registration and titling were vital. The 2001 Land Law was widely supported by the Royal Government of Cambodia, financially and technically by the World Bank and German Technical Assistance (GTZ) as well as foreign governments (Grimsditch and Henderson 2009; Khemro and Payne 2004). Officially aimed at the formalisation of the property system to ensure poor people's access to land and pave the way out of poverty, in reality the reform ended up legalising land grabbing through the removal of precedent titling and the customary tenure system in order to fulfil the 'Hun Sen neo-liberal path of marketisation' (Springer 2016, 3; see Dwyer 2015; Fauveaud 2016).

In Cambodia, land was and still is the most highly sought-after asset and a central issue deeply rooted in the history of the country. Contrary to the common narrative, conflict over land was not born after the Khmer Rouge, but rather earlier, during the colonial period. The French made the first attempt to formalise land tenure and create a cadastral system, though the formalisation process was left incomplete, leaving customary systems – based on possession – unreconciled with the newly introduced ownership system. The result was a dual system that laid the foundations for many problems to follow. The 2001 Land Law – based on French regulations – took responsibility for completing the job by entirely suppressing the customary system, making existing tenure forms unlawful and land certificates illegal. In simple words, the law promoted evictions (STT 2020) and produced more informality and illegality than before (Diepart and Sem 2015).

> Consequently, the preoccupation with strengthening the legal system in Cambodia is not a benevolent act for the betterment of Cambodian society. Rather, its primary function is the imposition of a 'grid' of property rights (Blomley 2003) that serves to legitimise the violences of property and thus reinforce a 'trilateral of logics' (Springer 2013, 610).

Additionally, despite nearly two decades of efforts to provide titles to Phnom Penh urban dwellers, at least 200 communities continue to lack tenure security, according to STT (2020, 8). Land registration and titling have failed people, while the legal provisions have resulted in increased informal tenure and exposure to eviction. As Flower (2018, 2408) puts it, 'insecurity in Phnom Penh was perpetuated by laws, rather than their absence or the circumventing of laws'.

The construction of a 'land issue'

In their genealogy of tenure systems in Cambodia, Diepart and Sem (2015, 15) remind us that in the traditional Khmer rural codes, the king owned the land and the farmers were the users; the right to land (possession) could be claimed by settling and cultivating it. During the colonial period, the French attempted to replace possession with ownership, officially in an effort to 'modernise' land tenure regimes by introducing land title and registration (*cadastre*), but in reality, in order to secure the alienation of a large portion of land for investment. While only a tiny percentage of the land was actually titled, leaving customary systems unchanged, the high cost for land registration triggered indebtedness and landlessness among farmers. It is at this point that the two systems – possession and ownership – started coexisting and the confusion between them, responsible for many contemporary land difficulties, began.

During the Democratic Kampuchea period, both systems were abolished, all land was nationalised, cadastral administration stopped functioning and documents were destroyed (Grimsditch and Henderson 2009). In the years that followed the regime, a de facto land reappropriation took place, in spite of the government's attempt to redistribute it.

Starting from the 1990s, Cambodia embarked on a series of reforms that laid the foundations for the 2001 Land Law.[7] Its objective was to reinstate the French cadastral and titling system, to improve tenure security through market-based access to land. From a government perspective, the law was useful to incentivise taxation and stimulate investment. In the eyes of international organisations and donors, the law was the right approach to reduce inequality and protect people from unlawful evictions (Diepart and Sem 2015; Biddulph and Williams 2016; Khemro and Payne 2004; Durand-Lasserve and Royston 2002).

Evidently, it missed the point.

The new law recognised possession, but only if it commenced before 2001. Any form of customary tenure that started after that date was rendered illegal by law (Royal Government of Cambodia 2001, articles 30, 31; Grimsditch, Leakhana and Sherchan 2012, 25). The first land titling campaign started soon after the law was passed, and by November 2011, 1.7 million titles had been issued. Titling targeted only conflict-free cases and did not happen in a fair and even way (Grimsditch, Leakhana and Sherchan 2012, 25; Biddulph and Williams 2016; Grimsditch and Henderson 2009). New campaigns for land titling in disputed areas[8] and further laws tried to address the issue, including the well-known Circular 03 targeting informal settlements (Royal Government of Cambodia 2010).

Overall, the formalisation process did not improve tenure security; on the contrary, it destabilised it, ultimately legitimising land grabbing and violent dispossession (Diepart and Sem 2015, 99; Dwyer 2015; Springer 2013). Entire communities were brutally evicted and forced to move to peripheral resettlement sites (Connell and Grimsditch 2016).

Dispossession was globally justified as a poverty alleviation strategy (Neef and Touch 2012), while in the eyes of the evictees, it was presented as the only way to be granted land tenure. Motivated by such a conditional promise, thirty thousand families moved out of the city, making little or none resistance. The promise was never fulfilled, as the government never had any intention of giving up the peripheral land, especially in light of potential future development. After many years of deceptive relocation, the displaced families are still waiting for the promised title, while in the meantime their political agency and ability to organise and resist have been completely neutralised.

Once again, the Cambodian government's strategy has kept the urban poor in a state of 'intentional insecurity' (Monvilaite 2014, 53). Not only did resettlement never translate into tenure security, it also generated greater precariousness (Connell and Grimsditch 2016). Either due to the consequent urban growth (and renewed appetite for land) or the increased vulnerability of some areas (consequent to landfilling of lakes and water networks), some communities underwent relocation again or are currently facing relocation risk again.

The process of expulsion has become potentially endless, and resettlement is getting radicalised and becoming a structural feature of the city, to the point that its scale and modality are analogous – rather than antithetical – to the evacuation and destruction/reconstruction process that the Khmer Rouge regime engineered 40 years ago.

Conclusion

After reflecting on the literature as well as the discourses and actions of those involved in our three-year engagement and action research – both NGOs and community members – it is worth concluding with a few points learned from the resettlement process in Phnom Penh. Firstly, although resettlement is increasingly acknowledged as a legal weapon to fulfil projects of expulsion, a large portion of the population is still very much excluded from such knowledge. People are intentionally kept uninformed or receive contradictory information regarding the future development of their land; maps, documents and information are not shared; when shared, they are not explained and therefore not understood. The production and sharing of knowledge therefore becomes a central issue to be addressed.

Secondly, resettlement has proved very rarely to be 'necessary', especially in relation to development. Its necessity is a discursive construction and a propagandistic tool to cover other agendas. Options such as on-site upgrading and re-blocking are equally if not even more feasible, although they are rarely presented to the people. Furthermore, and particularly in the case of Phnom Penh, when landfilling operations are involved, resettlement is less cost effective than upgrading, even in cases where no compensation is offered – leaving aside, of course, the social cost.

Finally, there can hardly be a successful resettlement process without the involvement of the people at the different stages. To return to Simone's idea of 'remaking' Phnom Penh, people can adapt, find ways, circulate knowledge and create relationships of trust. As he argues, inclusiveness is not a matter of policy, but rather a by-product of residents having access to rights and knowledge: 'even under siege, [inclusiveness] is their exemplification of how the ambivalence of urban life can be managed' (Simone 2008, 10).

Notes

1. This is also where living conditions are the harshest: in makeshift shelters under the level of flooding for a large part of the year, in areas very difficult to reach, in the alleys and corridors of dilapidated buildings, or on their rooftops (Fallavier 1999).
2. Including Pong Ro Senchey and Steung Kombot, two relocation sites located on narrow strips of public land between privately owned land; Andong, probably the largest and most contested resettlement in Phnom Penh; Borei Keila, a very conflictual case of on-site relocation and land sharing; and Kompong Thom village, in Kompong Thom Province, the only participatory relocation case we have been part of, with the local community engaged in land negotiation with local government.
3. Heterogeneous typologies of resettlement are documented, including direct resettlement (with and without compensation); induced or secondary relocation (without compensation); and post-resettlement displacement (Hall, Hirsch and Li 2011; Grimsditch, Leakhana and Sherchan 2012; LHWG 2009). As Connell and Grimsditch (2016, 225) remind us, there are countless nuances between direct and induced relocation, as people might get slowly displaced by economic, political and environmental dynamics that 'gradually reduce their livelihood'; yet secondary relocation is the most difficult to record. In the case of Phnom Penh, many communities were secondarily affected by development either because of flooding consequent to landfilling (see for instance the case of Boueng Kak Lake discussed by Mgbako et al. 2010, 52), or the increase in land price over time; as they were not deemed affected, they were not compensated (STT 2012a).
4. 'Many relocation sites, such as the notorious Andong relocation site, were barren fields in peri-urban areas, without proper housing, potable water or sanitation. Access to basic facilities such as schools and hospitals was hampered by the distance of these sites from inner Phnom Penh. Perhaps most troubling was the diminished access to employment opportunities by the remoteness of the sites – the cost of traveling to jobs in the city often exceeds daily average earnings. As a result, many were forced to return to the city centre and rent or squat in order to continue their livelihoods. Often titles were not issued to households at the relocation sites, creating renewed situations of tenure insecurity and the possibility of further forced evictions as Phnom Penh continues to sprawl' (LHWG 2009, 13).
5. 'Renters at Boeung Kak have protested against the government and demanded the same offers of compensation that those with soft-title have received, but the arrest of one renter on October 15, 2008, whom the government accused of leading the protests, has halted the demonstration for renters' rights and resulted in an increase of "voluntary" departures of Boeung Kak renters' (Mgbako et al. 2010, 51). The Boeung Kak Lake case (four thousand households evicted in 2007) serves as a pertinent example of the dangers of uneven implementation of the existing regulatory framework, and apparent manipulation of the land classification system in order to serve powerful interests, as residents have been unlawfully evicted and barely compensated (Grimsditch and Henderson 2009).
6. The term urbicide was first used by a former mayor of Belgrade, Bogdan Bogdanovic, in 1993, in relation to the deliberate physical destruction and ethnic cleansing of the city of Vukovar in Croatia by Serbian forces in 1991–2. What is involved in urbicide is the negation of all normal urban existence, both literal – in physical terms – and even more significantly symbolic – in terms of such values as liberty, civility, diversity and coexistence (Safier 2001, 422). For Bogdanovic, the term urbicide came into existence where the entire city, all its citizens and the symbols of their humanity, civility and diversity were under attack by superior armed forces animated by a determination to kill or cleanse those very qualities of civilised city living.

7. According to the first Land Law (1992), all land belongs to the state and all Cambodians have possession rights. However, the law does not reflect the 'three main tenure regimes inherited from history: the acquisition "by plough", state and private ownership promoted by the French and the socialist ideology' (Diepart and Sem 2015, 29). The dualisation of the land tenure regime between possession (socially recognised) and private ownership (acquired through cadastral procedure) has become conflictual. In fact, the latter can invalidate the former, and therefore can cause dispossession. In other words, land reforms starting from the 1990s paved the way for landlessness.
8. A new titling campaign occurred in 2012 – further to Hun Sen's announcement of the freezing of economic land concessions (ELC) when it became clear to the world that the government was involved in land grabbing through concessions and to recognise rightful claims by people within areas of ELCs (Diepart and Sem 2015; Dwyer 2015; Biddulph and Williams 2016; Percival 2016). ELCs can be traced back to the French system of enclosures; reshaped and retooled over time, ELCs are currently the main *instrumentum regni*. They have largely contributed to land dispossession and induced the emergence of land struggle (Diepart and Schoenberger 2016, 157).

References

ACHR. 2004. 'Negotiating the right to stay in the city'. *Environment and Urbanization* 16 (1): 9–26. https://doi.org/10.1177%2F095624780401600103.

Amnesty International. 2008. *Cambodia: Rights razed: Forced evictions in Cambodia*. www.amnesty.org/en/documents/ASA23/002/2008/en.

Beng Hong, Kry. 1984. 'Survey of the housing and infrastructure of Phnom Penh'. Phnom Penh: State of Cambodia.

Biddulph, Robin and Shaun Williams. 2016. 'From chicken wing receipts to students in military uniforms: Land titling and property in post-conflict Cambodia'. In *The Handbook of Contemporary Cambodia*, edited by Katherine Brickell and Simon Springer, 169–78. London and New York: Routledge. https://www.routledgehandbooks.com/doi/10.4324/9781315736709.ch14.

Bishop, Ryan and Gregory Clancey. 2004. 'The city-as-target, or perpetuation and death'. In *Cities, War, and Terrorism: Towards an urban geopolitics*, edited by Stephen Graham, 54–74. Malden, MA: Blackwell. https://doi.org/10.1002/9780470753033.ch3.

Blomley, Nicholas. 2003. 'Law, property, and the geography of violence: The frontier, the survey, and the grid'. *Annals of the Association of American Geographers* 93 (1): 121–41.

Brickell, Katherine. 2016. 'Gendered violences and rule of/by law in Cambodia'. *Dialogues in Human Geography* 6 (2): 182–5.

Brickell, Katherine and Simon Springer, eds. 2016. *The Handbook of Contemporary Cambodia*. London: Routledge. https://doi.org/10.4324/9781315736709.

Bugalski, Natalie and Jocelyn Medallo. 2012. *Derailed: A study on the resettlement process and impacts of the rehabilitation of the Cambodian railway*. Phnom Penh: Bridges Across Borders Cambodia. https://data.opendevelopmentmekong.net/dataset/4db84e8a-498b-41f4-bf8f-b993a655b17f/resource/5ad5d2c0-1751-4056-84c4-61db5f21eac3/download/6190da0f-53f5-44ff-b450-b5acdd193504.pdf.

Clerc, Valerie. 2016. 'A competition for land policies towards informal urban settlements in Cambodia, from regularization to eviction'. In *Learning from the Slums for the Development of Emerging Cities*, edited by Jean Claude Bolay, Jérôme Chenal and Yves Pedrazzini, 173–87. Cham: Springer.

Connell, Jessie. 2015. 'Resettlement and borderlands: Adapting to planned population resettlement on the Cambodian–Thai Border'. In *Global Implications of Development, Disasters and Climate Change: Responses to displacement from the Asia Pacific*, edited by Susanna Price and Jane Singer, 142–58. London: Routledge.

Connell, Jessie and John Connell. 2016. 'Development-induced displacement, adaptation and mobility in Cambodia'. *Migration and Development* 5 (3): 413–30. https://doi.org/10.1080/21632324.2014.984900.

Connell, Jessie and Mark Grimsditch. 2016. 'Forced relocation in Cambodia'. In *The Handbook of Contemporary Cambodia*, edited by Katherine Brickell and Simon Springer. London: Routledge. https://www.routledgehandbooks.com/doi/10.4324/9781315736709.ch19.

Desbarats, Jacqueline. 1995. *Prolific Survivors: Population change in Cambodia, 1975–1993*. Tempe, AZ: Arizona State University Program for Southeast Asian Studies.

Diepart, Jean-Christophe and Laura Schoenberger. 2016. 'Concessions in Cambodia: Governing profits, extending state power and enclosing resources from the colonial era to the present'. In *The Handbook of Contemporary Cambodia*, edited by Katherine Brickell and Simon Springer, 157–68. London: Routledge. https://www.routledgehandbooks.com/doi/10.4324/9781315736709.ch13.

Diepart, Jean-Christophe and Thol Sem. 2015. *The Cambodian Peasantry and the Formalisation of Land Rights: Historical overview and current issues.* Groupe de Recherches Asie de l'Est et du Sud Est. https://orbi.ulg.ac.be/bitstream/2268/186135/1/DIEPART-SEM_2015_Cambodian-Peasantry-Formalization-Land-Rights.pdf.

Durand-Lasserve, Alain. 2007. 'Market-driven eviction processes in developing country cities: The cases of Kigali in Rwanda and Phnom Penh in Cambodia'. *Global Urban Development* 3 (1): 1–14. https://www.globalurban.org/GUDMag07Vol3Iss1/Durand-Lasserve.htm.

Durand-Lasserve, Alain and Lauren Royston, eds. 2002. *Holding Their Ground: Secure land tenure for the urban poor in developing countries*. London: Earthscan.

Dwyer, Michael. 2015. 'The formalization fix? Land titling, land concessions and the politics of spatial transparency in Cambodia'. *Journal of Peasant Studies* 5 (42): 903–28. https://doi.org/10.1080/03066150.2014.994510.

Fallavier, Pierre. 1999. *Poverty Analysis in Phnom Penh: Laying basis for strengthening participatory urban development – An identification of the most vulnerable and excluded population.* Action Nord Sud (ANS) and United Nations Centre for Human Settlements (UNCHS). https://www.academia.edu/19523974/Fallavier_P_1999_Poverty_Analysis_in_Phnom_Penh_pp_57_Phnom_Penh_Action_Nord_Sud_United_Nations_Centre_for_Human_Settlements.

Fallavier, Pierre. 2002. 'Urban slums report: The case of Phnom Penh, Cambodia'. Global Report on Human Settlements 2003. https://www.researchgate.net/publication/200538441_Urban_Slums_report_The_case_of_Phnom_Penh_Cambodia.

Fauveaud, Gabriel. 2016. 'Real estate productions, practices, and strategies in contemporary Phnom Penh: An overview of social, economic, and political issues'. In *The Handook of Contemporary Cambodia*, edited by Kathrine Brickell and Simon Springer, 212–22. London: Routledge. https://www.routledgehandbooks.com/doi/10.4324/9781315736709.ch18.

Flower, Benjamin. 2018. 'Legal geographies of neoliberalism: Market-oriented tenure reforms and the construction of an "informal" urban class in post-socialist Phnom Penh'. *Urban Studies* 56 (12): 2408–25.

Goad, Hallam. 2012. *Phnom Penh and Its Informal Settlements: A chronological overview of key events (1992–2012).* https://cityofwater.files.wordpress.com/2014/03/phnom-penh-informal-settlements-1992-2012-main-text-jan2014goad.pdf.

Greenwood, Faine. 2012. 'Borei Keila evictees shunted aside to inhumane refugee camp'. http://faineg.com/tag/relocation-sites.

Grimsditch, Mark and Nick Henderson. 2009. *Untitled: Tenure insecurity and inequality in the Cambodian land sector*. Phnom Penh: Bridges Across Borders Southeast Asia, Centre on Housing Rights and Evictions, Jesuit Refugee Service. https://data.opendevelopmentmekong.net/library_record/untitled-tenure-insecurity-and-inequality-in-the-cambodian-land-sector.

Grimsditch, Mark, Kol Leakhana and Depika Sherchan. 2012. *Access to Land Title in Cambodia: A study of systematic land registration in three Cambodian provinces and the capital.* Phnom Penh: NGO Forum on Cambodia. https://www.academia.edu/3859491/Access_to_Land_Title_in_Cambodia_A_Study_of_Systematic_Land_Registration_in_Three_Cambodian_Provinces_and_the_Capital.

Hall, Derek, Philip Hirsch and Tania Murray Li. 2011. *Powers of Exclusion: Land Dilemmas in Southeast Asia*. Singapore: NUS Press.

Khemro, Beng Hong Socheat and Geoffrey Payne. 2004. 'Improving tenure security for the urban poor in Phnom Penh, Cambodia: An analytical case study'. *Habitat International* 28 (2): 181–201. https://doi.org/10.1016/S0197-3975(03)00067-5.

Lavell, Allan. 2017. 'Colombia, Peru and Mexico: Closure report'. *Reducing Relocation Risk in Urban Areas.* https://www.ucl.ac.uk/bartlett/development/sites/bartlett/files/wp4_closure_rep_flacso_eng.pdf.

LHWG. 2009. *Land and Housing Rights in Cambodia Parallel Report 2009*. https://tbinternet.ohchr.org/Treaties/CESCR/Shared%20Documents/KHM/INT_CESCR_NGO_KHM_42_9415_E.pdf.

LICADHO. 2016. *Human Rights 2015: The year in review.* http://www.licadho-cambodia.org/reports/files/217LICADHO_YearInReview_2015.pdf.

López-Carr, David and Jessica Marter-Kenyon. 2015. 'Human adaptation: Manage climate-induced resettlement'. *Nature* 517 (7534). https://www.nature.com/news/human-adaptation-manage-climate-induced-resettlement-1.16697.

Mgbako, Chi, Rijie Ernie Gao, Elizabeth Joynes, Anna Cave and Jessica Mikhailevich. 2010. 'Forced eviction and resettlement in Cambodia: Case studies from Phnom Penh'. *Washington University Global Studies Law Review* 9: 39–76.

Monvilaite, Gabija. 2014. 'Phnom Penh: Towards comprehensive resettlement planning post-resettlement land transactions and tenure insecurity'. Thesis, Kungliga Tekniska Högskolan. https://www.diva-portal.org/smash/get/diva2:730002/FULLTEXT01.pdf.

Nam, Sylvia. 2012. 'Speculative urbanism: The remaking of Phnom Penh'. PhD thesis, Berkeley, University of California. https://escholarship.org/uc/item/5nt8h7mz.

Neef, Andreas and Siphat Touch. 2012 'Land grabbing in Cambodia: Mechanisms, narratives, resistance'. Paper presented at the Global Land Grabbing Conference II at Cornell University, Ithaca, NY, 17–19 October 2012.

Nop, Sothun and Thornton, Alec. 2019. 'Urban resilience building in modern development: A case of Phnom Penh City, Cambodia'. *Ecology and Society* 24 (2): 23.

OHCHR. 2012. *Eviction and Resettlement in Cambodia: Human costs, impacts and solutions. A study on selected urban resettlement cases.* Phnom Penh: OHCHR. https://cambodia.ohchr.org/sites/default/files/Thematic-reports/Resettlement_Study-28_Feb_2012_Eng.pdf.

Payne, Geoffrey. 2002. *Land, Rights and Innovation: Improving Security of Tenure for the Urban Poor*. London: ITDG.

Percival, Tom. 2016. 'Urban megaprojects and city planning in Phnom Penh'. In *The Handbook of Contemporary Cambodia*, edited by Katherine Brickell and Simon Springer, 181–90. London: Routledge. https://www.routledgehandbooks.com/doi/10.4324/9781315736709.ch15.

Royal Government of Cambodia. 2001. *The 2001 Land Law*. Phnom Penh: Royal Government of Cambodia.

Royal Government of Cambodia. 2010. *Circular on Resolution on Temporary Settlements on Land which Has Been Illegally Occupied in the Capital, Municipal and Urban Areas*. Phnom Penh: Secretariat of Council for Land Policy, Royal Government of Cambodia. http://countrysafeguardsystems.net/sites/default/files/KH%20Circular%203%20Resolution%20Temporary%20Settlements%20on%20Land%202010.pdf.

Safier, Michael. 2001. 'Confronting "urbicide": Crimes against humanity, civility and diversity, and the case for a civic cosmopolitan response to the attack on New York'. *City* 5 (2): 416–29.

Satterthwaite, David. 2008. 'Understanding Asian cities: A synthesis of the findings from eight city case studies'. *Global Urban Development Magazine* 4 (2): 1–24. https://www.globalurban.org/GUDMag08Vol4Iss2/Satterthwaite.htm.

Shatkin, Gavin. 2008. 'The city and the bottom line: Urban megaprojects and the privatization of planning in Southeast Asia'. *Environment and Planning A* 40 (2): 383–401.

Shawn, Martin. 2007. *What Is Genocide?* Cambridge: Polity Press.

Simone, AbdouMaliq. 2008. 'The politics of the possible: Making urban life in Phnom Penh'. *Singapore Journal of Tropical Geography* 29 (2): 186–204. doi:10.1111/j.1467-9493.2008.00328.x.

Springer, Simon. 2013. 'Violent accumulation: A postanarchist critique of property, dispossession, and the state of exception in neoliberalizing Cambodia'. *Annals of the Association of American Geographers* 103 (3): 608–26.

Springer, Simon. 2016. 'Homelessness in Cambodia: The terror of gentrification'. In *The Handbook of Contemporary Cambodia*, edited by Katherine Brickell and Simon Springer, 234–44. London: Routledge. https://www.routledgehandbooks.com/doi/10.4324/9781315736709.ch20.

Springer, Simon. 2020. 'The violence of homelessness: Exile and arbitrary detention in Cambodia's war on the poor'. *Asia Pacific Viewpoint* 61 (1): 3–18. https://doi.org/10.1111/apv.12273.

STT. 2012a. *Losing the Plot: Rapid assessment of household debt in Trapeang Anhchanh*. Edited by Nora Lindstrom. http://teangtnaut.org/wp-content/uploads/2012/07/Losing-the-Plot_STT-2012_FINAL.pdf.

STT. 2012b. 'Resettling Phnom Penh: 54 – and counting'. *Facts and Figures* 21: 1–14. http://teangtnaut.org/wp-content/uploads/2013/01/20121218_FF21_relocation-sites_vsFINAL1.pdf.

STT. 2014. 'Phnom Penh's history of displacement: Evicted communities from 1990 to 2014'. *Facts and Figures* 23: 1–11. http://teangtnaut.org/wp-content/uploads/2014/12/FactFigures23_Evicted-Communities-PP-1990-2014_VsFinal.pdf.

STT. 2020. 'Eviction and relocation: Research on the process of eviction and relocation in Phnom Penh'. https://media.business-humanrights.org/media/documents/files/documents/STT-Eviction-and-Relocation_ENG_Final.pdf.

Talocci, Giorgio and Camillo Boano. 2015. 'The politics of urban displacement practices in Phnom Penh: Reflections from Borei Santepheap Pi and Oudong Moi'. *Pacific Geographies* 43: 15–20. http://www.pacific-geographies.org/wp-content/uploads/sites/2/2017/06/PG43_Research_Note_Talocci_Boano.pdf.

Talocci, Giorgio and Camillo Boano. 2016. 'Phnom Penh's relocation sites and the obliteration of politics'. In *The Handbook of Contemporary Cambodia*, edited by Katherine Brickell and Simon Springer, 245–56. London: Routledge. https://www.routledgehandbooks.com/doi/10.4324/9781315736709.ch21.

Tyner, James A., Samuel Henkin, Savina Sirik and Sokvisal Kimsroy. 2014. 'Phnom Penh during the Cambodian genocide: A case of selective urbicide'. *Environment and Planning A* 46 (8): 1873–91. https://doi.org/10.1068%2Fa130278p.

Tyskerud, Yani and Nora Lindstrom. 2013. *End of the Line: Impacts of resettlement under the railway project in Phnom Penh*. Phnom Penh: STT. http://teangtnaut.org/wp-content/uploads/2013/07/EndofthelineHIGHRES.pdf.

12

Stay or leave? The dilemma of typhoon survivors in urban Tacloban, Philippines

Bill Flinn and Holly Schofield

For an international humanitarian aid worker, visiting the site of a recent cyclone can be a salutary and humbling experience. Within days the community is restoring vital infrastructure, families are rebuilding their homes and the incipient recovery process has begun. Astonishingly, after the unprecedented destruction caused by Typhoon Haiyan in 2013, severely damaged schools were reopened within a few weeks and many families had rebuilt and repaired their homes.

Generalisations are rare in the world of humanitarian response, but the Filipino experience is far from unique. On the island of 'Eua, in the Kingdom of Tonga, houses were being repaired, roofing sheets nailed back on, within a day or two of the passing of Tropical Storm Gita in 2018 – long before the humanitarian system had mobilised. There are many other recent examples: on the tiny island of Aniwa in the Pacific island nation of Vanuatu, not only had the community prepared extensively for Cyclone Pam in 2015 by strengthening their homes and evacuating to known safe buildings, but they had also rebuilt many of their pole, reed and thatch houses within a week.

It has long been recognised that survivors are the first responders. In 1982, the United Nations Disaster Relief Organisation (UNDRO) Guidelines for Assistance, *Shelter after Disaster*, stated that 'the primary resource in the provision of post-disaster shelter is the grass-roots motivation of the survivors, their friends and families. Assisting groups can help, but they must avoid duplicating anything best undertaken by survivors themselves' (UNDRO 1982). Much more recently, the Global Facility for Disaster Risk Reduction's *Safer Homes, Stronger Communities* handbook has as one of its guiding principles: 'Reconstruction begins the day of the disaster ... Owners are almost always the best managers of their own housing reconstruction; they know how they live and what they need' (Jha et al. 2010). Indeed, self-organising, voluntary groups and individuals are a common but under-recognised feature of disasters, responding to immediate needs long before formal organisations are able to mobilise (Twigg and Mosel 2017). In recent years, the term self-recovery has been coined to describe this process of rebuilding that relies on the mobilisation of the family's own resources, and there is much interest in developing humanitarian responses that recognise the inevitability of this process and actively seek to support it (Parrack, Flinn and Passey 2014; Twigg et al. 2017; Schofield et al. 2019).

This developing interest is a welcome departure from the sector's conventional product-based approach that has tended to target the most vulnerable. While the principle of leaving no one behind, and especially society's most vulnerable, must be upheld, the practice of providing a whole house – often temporary, sub-standard and not intended to last more than a year or two – has been much criticised (Ashdown 2011; Davis 2012).

This chapter explores the notion of self-recovery in Tacloban, Philippines following the devastating impacts of Typhoon Haiyan in 2013. It focuses on the notions and perceptions of safety in post-disaster housing within the context of differing levels of insecure tenure. The discussion is based on qualitative, interdisciplinary research involving social scientists and geo-scientists, engineers and humanitarian shelter practitioners, which took place in April 2017[1] and June 2018.[2] These two research projects studied the recovery trajectories of families that lost their homes in the typhoon, which overwhelmed the Visayas region of the Philippines. The first focused on the largely rural *barangays* (a formal division roughly equating to a village or parish) on the island of Leyte, while the second concentrated on poor urban areas of the city of Tacloban that were severely affected by the storm. The research centred on the concept of self-recovery, investigating what this meant for the relatively secure rural population compared to the very insecure urban dwellers who were, and still are, facing eviction and relocation. This is complemented by observations from other disaster responses that the authors have been involved in (Twigg et al. 2017).

Self-recovery

It is often stated that humanitarian shelter assistance only ever reaches between 10 and 20 per cent of the need (Parrack, Flinn and Passey 2014; Miranda-Morel 2018). The conclusion that can be drawn is that, one way or another, 80 to 90 per cent of households recover their homes using their own resources, coupled with assistance drawn from the community itself, remittances from the national diaspora living overseas or government subsidies. They self-recover. The data, and the observational evidence from Philippines, Tonga, Vanuatu and in common with many disaster-affected communities in the global South, shows that this is a powerful and inevitable force for recovery, and one that has been conventionally under-valued and little understood. Moreover, it shows that people exercise agency and choice, and set their own recovery priorities (see Figure 12.1). These two factors – the inevitability of self-recovery and the primacy of agency – are central to the thinking behind the development of response approaches that support self-recovery (Schofield and Flinn 2018).

Figure 12.1 Signs of self-recovery within a few weeks of Typhoon Haiyan. Many houses were rebuilt or repaired within days of the storm. © Bill Flinn.

Supporting this process of self-recovery has been characterised as a combination of cash transfers, in-kind assistance in the form of building materials and technical assistance (Maynard, Parker and Twigg 2016). This approach has met with considerable success in rural areas, and indeed was recognised by the World Habitat Awards (WHA): the CARE Philippines post-Typhoon Haiyan shelter programme won the global South award in 2018 expressly for its self-recovery project (WHA 2017; Flinn and Echegaray 2016). In this instance, CARE Philippines and its national NGO partners recognised the self-motivation of the families and communities. Almost sixteen thousand houses were built, but each one was unique, tailored to the needs, priorities and choices of the family. Other major international agencies took similar approaches, making a significant impact on the post-Haiyan recovery process. However, investigating self-recovery in the cities of Chautara and Bhaktapur in Nepal, and Tacloban in Philippines, showed that this 'three-pronged' approach of cash, materials and technical assistance was far from adequate for the diverse needs and circumstances of urban contexts (Schofield and Flinn 2018; Schofield et al. 2019). Helping to develop an enabling environment that can support the process of self-recovery in these complex contexts demands a strategy that lifts barriers such as land tenure, infrastructure, access to markets and community mediation as well as directly supporting families in the process of informed decision-making.

The proponents of self-recovery advocate the pre-eminence of people's choice and agency, and their right to decide their own priorities and needs and to define the rate and direction of travel of their recovery pathway. This presents a challenge to the humanitarian shelter sector, which conventionally prioritises structural safety and often makes this a condition of support. It calls for a better definition of what is considered a 'good house', with structural safety being just one element alongside improved health, sanitation, space standards, durability, livelihood opportunities (through the construction of small household stores, for example), and even simply a home that is dignified, beautiful and loved (Flinn 2019, 2020).

Supporting self-recovery has now been accepted as part of the humanitarian shelter discourse and it aligns well with a more bottom-up and participatory, flexible approach. The Global Shelter Cluster recognises supporting self-recovery as one of its strategic approaches (Global Shelter Cluster 2018). The Grand Bargain agreement, ratified by the 2016 World Humanitarian Summit, endorses the wide use of cash and an increase in 'localisation' (Inter-Agency Standing Committee 2016). It also calls for a 'participation revolution'. One of the four priority areas of action of the Sendai Framework for Disaster Risk Reduction 'is to enhance disaster preparedness for effective response, and to "Build Back Better" in recovery, rehabilitation and reconstruction' (UNDRR 2015). These strategic approaches, now being promoted by international bodies, all point to the need for increased flexibility and this is reflected in an acceptance of the need for 'adaptive management', a recognition that needs and priorities change with time in a way that is impossible to predict at the outset. Finally, there is a current interest in unconditional multi-purpose cash transfer programming that, in a world of increasing need and decreasing resources, is likely to become a standard ingredient of future humanitarian programming (Overseas Development Institute and Centre for Global Development 2015). Assisting people in their inevitable self-recovery pathways fits well with each of these current humanitarian concerns, especially the need for a flexible, reflective, participatory and agile response that recognises changing needs and the primacy of the agency of the affected population.

Typhoon Haiyan

Typhoon Haiyan, known locally as Yolanda, devasted large parts of the Philippines in November 2013. The largest typhoon ever to make landfall, Haiyan displaced more than four million people, and damaged or destroyed 1.1 million homes. While the Philippines is battered by several severe typhoons each year, Haiyan was exceptional in its strength and destructive power as well as for striking an area of the country less accustomed to such powerful storms. The city of Tacloban was particularly badly affected, with very significant loss of life, because of the unexpectedly high storm surge.

The severity and extent of the destruction and suffering prompted a generous global outpouring of support. Donors and aid agencies committed to both immediate emergency relief and medium-term recovery. Shelter, or the provision of housing, was seen as a high priority, along with water and sanitation and the recovery of livelihoods. Coastal towns were particularly affected by calamitous devastation to coconut plantations and the fishing industry.

Rural Philippines: secure enough

Rural, agricultural Filipino society remains largely feudal. The land is owned by large landowners and many poor families are sharecroppers, paying an annual rent in-kind through a proportion of their harvest. Householders would say that they own their house, but not the land it is built on. One man, observing a coconut tree that had been blown down by the storm, said that although he himself had planted the tree many years ago, he couldn't use the timber to rebuild his house because it was the property of the landowner. Those with no access to farmland tend to be day-labourers depending on the agricultural cycle, which can, of course, be disrupted by typhoons. Increased mechanisation also threatens their livelihood: a group of women described the new rice harvester as an 'enemy' of the day-labourer. However, the rural families are inventive, spirited and determined. Backyard farming of pigs, chickens and ducks is commonplace, families join together to buy a water buffalo that they rent to neighbours, small convenience stores attached to their houses proliferate.

The housing typology reflects this reality. Most families do not feel that there is an immediate threat of eviction, despite their security of tenure being largely informal and essentially tenuous. They feel secure enough. However, landowners sometimes forbid them from building in durable materials such as concrete blocks, and families themselves feel reluctant to invest too heavily in their homes in case the landowner has a change of heart, or perhaps his or her inheritors might take a less benevolent stand. So many homes are built of timber or bamboo; and of course, the simple matter of affordability also forces many poor families to build in these relatively economic materials. Nonetheless, these houses are invariably beautifully designed and constructed, with intricate woven bamboo screens and an astonishing array of pot plants and shrubs.

Those able to observe the extraordinary devastation of Typhoon Haiyan in the week following the storm witnessed first hand the immediate self-recovery process as families repaired and rebuilt with no outside assistance at all. The first needs assessments were carried out to the background sound of chainsaws and hammers. Contrary perhaps to expectation, the Filipino example shows how poor landless rural families can in fact have more resources to fall back on than their urban counterparts.

> We stayed the first night with my aunt. Then my father built us a house. He is not a carpenter, but he became a carpenter that day (interview with female resident, 30, of Estancia, Pannay by Bill Flinn, November 2013).

Many post-Haiyan housing projects recognised the potential benefit of supporting families in this very evident self-recovery process. The

Philippines Shelter Cluster prepared a series of Build Back Safer (BBS) messages that were used to guide the training of carpenters. Compliance with these messages was frequently used to condition the release of second and third instalments of cash. A small cash grant (for example the amount given by CARE was just £43) was complemented by some basic high-value materials – typically corrugated metal roofing sheets, fixing straps (hurricane straps) and tools. The government did provide a grant for families with destroyed houses called the ESA (Emergency Shelter Assistance) that was worth about £450, but this often came very late. Many aid agencies supported 'roving teams', two to three people from the community with extra training who provided advice and encouraged the rebuilding efforts of the families.

> We started by building a temporary house, then every time we got cash support we added a little. That's how we built. It took a year to get ESA and we used it to expand our house. That is why it has two rooms now (interview with female resident, 30, of Cambucao by Bill Flinn, April 2017).

With this support families rebuilt according to their own needs, priorities and resources. They were able to complement the assistance by reusing materials and sharing labour between families. The cash alone was clearly not enough, and some invested extra money through loans, savings or remittances from the Filipino diaspora. In most communities, where the practice of *bayanihan* was strong (this is a traditional system of community cooperation that is embedded in the Filipino culture), it was unusual for anyone to be left behind as the community prioritised the elderly, the infirm or those living on their own.

Technical quality and the consequent robustness of the houses was sometimes patchy – and this is something that the sector needs to keep in mind and improve. However, in general, programmes that adopted this approach of supporting self-recovery resulted in a high level of satisfaction, very considerable coverage and therefore high value for money (CARE 2014).

Urban Philippines: day-to-day safety

The city of Tacloban, on the island of Leyte, is built at sea level. The San José neighbourhood is a spit of low-lying land that stretches out to the airport, with sea to the east and west. A five-metre storm surge swept across the whole of this peninsula, resulting in considerable loss of life. The residents do not count the number of destroyed and damaged houses: they describe it as a washout, with just floor slabs left in place and debris scattered far and wide. All the low-lying areas of Tacloban suffered a similar fate, with the destruction of more than twenty-eight thousand houses (Iuchi and Maly 2016). Invariably these were poor settlements, many of them squatters, some paying rent to a landowner. All were living in the most precarious circumstances, some of the homes built out over the sea (see Figure 12.2):

> My house was washed out because the water was so strong and it also brought the containers from the port on the other side of the bay. My house before Yolanda was bigger and made of cement but now we built a small one just to have somewhere to sleep because I'll be given a permanent shelter in the relocation site. Because of that we wouldn't build a bigger or nicer house. The government will remove us from here (interview with female resident, 37, of Anibong by Bill Flinn, June 2018).

Figure 12.2 The informal settlement of Anibong, just outside downtown Tacloban. The houses are built out over the sea and accessed via dangerous planks. © CARE UK/Bill Flinn.

On presidential recommendation, the municipality very quickly declared a 40-metre 'no-build zone' (NBZ) along the coastal strip, later altered to a 'no-dwelling zone' (NDZ). It was estimated that at least fourteen thousand families would have to be relocated from within Tacloban (Stodart 2016). Nonetheless, five years on, the area remains home to thousands of Tacloban's poorest families, who depend for their livelihood on fishing, small-time buying and selling in the markets and pedicab (rickshaw) driving. A daily income of 200 pesos (£2.90) is normal, less than the national minimum wage. The city's land use map, which pre-dates the typhoon, zones most of this land as commercial and recreational.

The residents of these *barangays* have lived in these locations for decades. Despite the designation of 'no-dwelling zone', most have rebuilt on the site of their previous homes. At the time of writing, five and a half years after the 2013 Typhoon, these *barangays* remained bustling and dynamic communities (see Figure 12.3). However, while before the storm they felt they had relatively secure tenure, they now face the imminent possibility of eviction and relocation:

Figure 12.3 Self-built housing and the lively community spirit of an informal settlement in a *barangay* in San José, close to the centre of Tacloban city. © CARE UK/Bill Flinn 2018.

> The government have said they will implement the no-dwell zone policy. This is a squatter area. We won't have a choice. If we had the choice we would stay here. It's better for us because our livelihoods are here. Although it is not safe, we prefer it here (interview with male resident, 52, of Anibong by Bill Flinn, June 2018).

The official policy is one of relocation to purpose-built sites some considerable distance, over 10 km, to the north of the city. The area where this new housing is being built is referred to as a new economic zone and is quite close to the bridge to the neighbouring island of Samar. The National Housing Authority (NHA) initially proposed the building of thirteen thousand units over several new sites. As well as the NHA, private companies, church groups and national and international NGOs have also been engaged in the development of some sites. The character of the sites varies from single-room dwellings with a separate bathroom to slightly more spacious one-up, one-down two-storey houses. Many were still under construction at the time of the research (2018), but some were partially occupied. All are terraced, or row, housing. The

Figure 12.4 One of the relocation sites over 10 km outside Tacloban, far from people's original community and their livelihoods. The plants, gates and fences show the Philippine home-making spirit. © CARE UK/ Bill Flinn 2018.

construction quality is very variable indeed. Residents complain of a lack of community facilities such as schools, the absence of water and power, and a general absence of community cohesion. At times the allocation of houses was done by lottery, so families were fractured and communities scattered. This apparently random relocation of families was seen as very detrimental to the cohesion of the neighbourhood communities that had been established over many decades. Universally, families mentioned the high cost of public transport back into the city where their livelihoods are located (see Figure 12.4).

> I'm worried that the houses there are substandard. The walls are not strong. We went to look and we saw the unfinished houses and the materials that they were using. The steel was thin, and the blocks were cracked. The toilets were already clogged (interview with female resident, 50, of San José by Bill Flinn, June 2018).
>
> I prefer it here [downtown] because my grandchildren are at school here in Anibong and I want to spend my time with my neighbourhood before the last relocation site is finished and everyone gets evicted. My neighbours all come back here [during the week] from their relocation sites too, we all come back together. We're all being broken up. Even my daughters have houses at different sites. Relocation is good but the 'raffle process' has broken my family and my community up (interview with female resident, 66, of Anibong by Bill Flinn, June 2018).

Although the mechanism varies and there are conditions attached, most families will one day take ownership of these new houses. Clearly this is very attractive to a family that has never had the opportunity to own an asset, and is especially so given the ever-present fear of eviction from their homes in downtown Tacloban. Nonetheless, there is a reluctance to relocate. A number of different factors explain this. The most notable is the absence of livelihood opportunities and the impossibility of continuing normal economic activity closer to town. The shortage of schools and the loss of community spirit and cohesion are also important.

Many families spend weekends in the relocation sites, and weekdays in their original homes in the no-dwelling zones. Once a house has been allocated there is an obligation to occupy it; failure to do so can result in that house being given to another family. Some families are split between the two sites, typically with older, retired members staying in the new houses. While eviction remains a threat and is not yet a reality, this dual residence can work in the family's favour: a home in the city near to their source of livelihood; and a 'weekend home' that will one day provide them with an asset.

> I was given a government house but it got taken away as I wasn't going there frequently enough. It is hard to go because of the bus fare. I only make 250 pesos [less than £4] a day from selling lemons (interview with female resident, 51, of Anibong by Bill Flinn, June 2018).

Regardless of where the family lives – under threat of eviction near the city centre, or over 10 km away in a relocation site – their homes always display a strong sense of pride and place. The outsides are painted, shrubs are planted, fences and gates are constructed, and pot plants multiply.

At the risk of being seen as complicit in a policy that was not viewed favourably by the affected population, very few international and national NGOs became involved in the design, location and construction of the relocation projects. There were a few exceptions, notably a Catholic Relief Services site and Pope Francis Village, a site funded by a coalition of church-based organisations. Both had a consultative and participatory approach, notably lacking in the other sites. While these relocation sites epitomise a contractor-driven process, by contrast in San José, and in the other Tacloban urban *barangays* destroyed by the typhoon, the individual houses were rebuilt by the residents themselves in a process of self-recovery. Compared with rural families, there was less support from international agencies for these families, and indeed permanent shelter support to people living in the NBZs was not permitted. Nonetheless, there were some interventions in informal settlements outside the NBZs and the Build Back Safer messages were promoted. However, there is little evidence of this guidance being followed, despite an acknowledgment that the Build Back Safer messages had been disseminated and training conducted. Nonetheless, residents rank safety as a very high priority. But when this question is probed, it transpires that the families do feel safe – on a day-to-day basis – as they are familiar with the procedure in the case of a storm warning, when to evacuate and where to go. During Tropical Storm Urduja, which passed through in 2017, they evacuated and later returned to find minor damage to their homes.

Eviction and relocation loom real for the residents of these marginal areas of Tacloban. Under the circumstances, their reluctance to invest in durable materials, and the cross-bracing and hurricane straps recommended by the humanitarian shelter sector, is entirely understandable. They feel safe in this day-to-day manner, and have found ways of managing such risks as repeat flooding. Meanwhile the real threat of being moved on hangs over them.

> What I like about my house is that it is my own ... We had to rebuild here as there was no other option, we are not in the NBZ and so couldn't apply for a relocation house. I have no plans to make any further changes to my house, as we don't own the land and it would be a waste if [we were] evicted ... When the creek floods, there is 18 inches of water in the house. We just stay here; that is why the bed has such long legs (interview with female resident, 39, of Barangay 83C by Bill Flinn, June 2018).

Discussion

It is clear that an insistence on structural safety as a condition for shelter assistance would not be appropriate for the residents of these communities in Tacloban. They feel 'safe enough'. They do, however, have many other needs and priorities that are shelter-related and have a direct bearing on their recovery. If we adhere to the principle of the primacy of the family's right to choose and have agency over their recovery, then these priorities should be given equal, or higher, consideration than the shelter professional's understandable desire to increase structural safety and robustness against the next storm. It is hard for a shelter practitioner, often an architect or engineer, to accept that the appearance or size of the house can be as important as its strength. Less contentious is a family's need to include a small store, or a latrine, or a concrete floor – and their decision that this is more important than the strength of the house.

Although this argument – that assistance should not be conditional on structural safety measures – can also hold good for rural families, it is much more evident in the informal settlements of urban Tacloban where land tenure is so insecure. Observation and talking with the residents make it clear that making their house a 'home' is more important than making it safer. People are well aware that no amount of strengthening will make their homes strong enough to withstand a Haiyan-type storm surge, and the regular annual storms cause light damage that can be repaired. Besides, eviction is more than likely to result in the demise of their house and home before the next Haiyan comes along.

In Tacloban, the humanitarian shelter sector is caught in a double bind: on the one hand relocation is almost always seen as the option of last resort; on the other, supporting the construction of permanent houses on unregistered, and frankly precarious, land is seen as inappropriate and risky. Assisting families in rural Filipino locations was generally less risky, and more straightforward. Frequently this conundrum puts the sector at odds with its mandate to support the most needy without discrimination (Stodart 2016). While this can be true of both rural and urban Filipino contexts, there is a stark distinction between the 'secure enough' position of the rural families, and the acutely insecure tenure of the urban dwellers.

Moreover, supporting families in the process of moving to the relocation sites is particularly problematic and challenging, especially in a way that holds true to the principles of self-recovery. While it is acknowledged that families may choose to relocate, residents essentially fall victim to the push-pull of the threat of forced eviction and the carrot of an asset, and cannot really be said to be exercising genuine agency or choice. It could be said that they have no choice at all; and this is starkly highlighted by the random process of allocating houses – referred to as a lottery – and the lack of provision of services and livelihoods.

Nonetheless, the reality is that families will relocate, and many already have. Once they have moved, the process of making their new house into a home is akin to self-recovery. Within the very tight confines of a small contractor-built terraced house, there is almost no scope to physically adapt or expand. Despite this limitation, by 2018 small businesses were seen to be emerging in the few areas that were already occupied. These ranged from taking in laundry and photocopying to small shops and bakeries, demonstrating the industrious spirit of Filipino families.

Supporting both the family and community self-recovery processes in the circumstances of forced relocation requires an approach that recognises the variety and complexity of the issues, the limitations of a constrained site and the power of the community to self-organise. A report written through the eyes of local Filipino NGOs emphasises the importance of community organisation in any self-recovery approach (CARE 2019).

There are clear differences between the 'secure enough' situation of rural families and the precarious tenure of urban Tacloban residents. However, even within the urban context the contrast between supporting families remaining in their original urban context and those that have relocated, or will relocate, is every bit as extreme. While direct support to rural families has a high beneficial impact, it will be the indirect support of advocacy, livelihoods, mediation and legal aid that can be of most benefit to those who relocate.

Assisting families in the construction of their homes in the relocation sites is clearly impossible given the contractor-driven approach to the provision of identical housing units. However, even in rural areas, assisting organisations were reluctant to build permanent houses without a contractual agreement with the landowner stating that the family would have the right to remain for a given number of years, typically between five and ten. Programmes that supported the process of self-recovery were able to avoid this barrier, simply providing cash, materials and technical assistance in a process that accompanied families and allowed them to make their own choices and take their own risk with respect to security of tenure. This also proved to be efficient and appropriate and resulted in a high level of satisfaction and some delightful houses (Flinn and Echegaray 2016). Although the approach may struggle to meet the needs of the most vulnerable families, which some housing programmes target precisely because of their lack of capacity to self-recover, some agencies were able to overcome this by providing these families with top-up grants and through the promotion of systems of *bayanihan*.

The same approach had little traction in urban Tacloban. Supporting reconstruction in the NDZs through cash and with permanent housing material was not permitted, although there were occasional projects that assisted repair and strengthening in settlements outside the NDZs with mixed formal and informal status. While all poor urban residents of Tacloban might share similar economic circumstances, the precarious nature of their tenure did vary from one location to another. The residents of the coastal strip of Anibong, to the north of downtown Tacloban, live in very crowded makeshift shacks, built on stilts out into the ocean. Their latrines are over the water and accessed by dangerous narrow planks. Residents talk of the planned highway construction project that will oblige them to relocate. Across the existing road and up a steep hillside, the houses are no longer in the NDZ, are protected from the storm surges, and the threat of eviction is diminished. Somehow, however, some of these families had successfully registered for a new relocation house.

> All my eleven children live here, more than 50 grandchildren and 16 great grandchildren. That represents more than 50 votes (interview with resident of Anibong, a great-grandmother, by Bill Flinn, June 2018. The family was allocated several new relocation houses).

Generally, an inverse law applies: the greater the need, the more difficult it is to effectively support the family's shelter and recovery needs. This perhaps presents a substantial challenge to the humanitarian sector: simply opting to support rural families, where the impact is more apparent, is not adequate. The sector is rising to the challenge with very significant interest in urban post-disaster shelter and a shift away from a product-based approach to a wider use of cash and more emphasis on 'software'.

Does the success of a self-recovery approach in rural Philippines give an indication that a similar approach would be equally successful in urban Tacloban? The answer is both yes and no. Support to self-recovery can be both direct and indirect. The approach adopted in the rural *barangays* was almost entirely direct. Support was given to the families and communities in the form of cash, materials and technical assistance. Little was done, in these rural areas, in the form of indirect support that would lift or mitigate the barriers that hinder a family's recovery. For urban families, where direct support was sometimes not allowed and investment in durable housing seen as risky in light of the threat of eviction, supporting indirectly could be much more pertinent. In practical terms this can be in the form of advocacy, mediation, legal support on tenure issues, services and infrastructure improvement, access to markets and more. Understanding the shelter-related priorities of the urban Tacloban families as they juggle the uncertainties of eviction and difficulties of a new life away from livelihoods and community can translate into a self-recovery programme that can provide permitted direct support and appropriate indirect support. The people of urban informal settlements in Tacloban, caught between living in their traditional communities and relocation to new sites, have real shelter priorities and are just as in need of support as the rural population.

Conclusion

Advocates of self-recovery recognise the right of people to exercise their own agency, but also point to the ability of a self-recovery approach to support those who really have no choice at all. This could be the residents of San José and Anibong, caught as they are between the rock of insecure tenure and the hard place of unwanted relocation; but it equally applies to the most vulnerable in our global society living on the slopes of ravines, flood plains and informal settlements in major cities around the world. By working both directly with the families and indirectly with the barriers that hinder their recovery, a self-recovery approach allows them to make the decisions that best meet their needs and priorities. The lack of formal secure land tenure should not be an obstacle to helping the most vulnerable – an increasing number of whom are now found in poor and very vulnerable urban settings.

Notes

1. Funded by the Global Challenges Research Fund via Natural Environment Research Council. Grant ref: NE/PO16200/1.
2. Funded by the Global Challenges Research Fund via British Academy Cities and Infrastructure Programme.

References

Ashdown, Lord Paddy. 2011. *Humanitarian Emergency Response Review*. https://www.preventionweb.net/files/18663_herr1.pdf.

CARE. 2014. *CARE Philippines: Typhoon Haiyan shelter recovery project evaluation*. https://reliefweb.int/sites/reliefweb.int/files/resources/CARE%20Philippines%20Typhoon%20Haiyan%20Shelter%20Recovery%20Programme%20Evaluation_1.pdf

CARE. 2019. *Soaring High: Self-recovery through the eyes of local actors*. https://world-habitat.org/publications/soaring-high-self-recovery-through-the-eyes-of-local-actors.

Davis, Ian. 2012. *What Is the Vision for Sheltering and Housing in Haiti: Summary observations of reconstruction progress following the Haiti earthquake of January 12th 2010*. https://reliefweb.int/sites/reliefweb.int/files/resources/Situation_Report_215.pdf.

Flinn, Bill. 2019. *Humanitarian Shelter and the Ethics of Self-Recovery*. https://insights.careinternational.org.uk/publications/humanitarian-shelter-and-the-ethics-of-self-recovery-a-discussion-paper.

Flinn, Bill. 2020. 'Defining "better" better: Why building back better means more than structural safety'. *Journal of Humanitarian Affairs* 2 (1): 35–43.

Flinn, Bill and Marta Llorens Echegaray. 2016. *Stories of Recovery: CARE Philippines post Haiyan/Yolanda shelter response*. https://insights.careinternational.org.uk/media/k2/attachments/CARE_Stories-of-recovery__Post-Haiyan-Yolanda-shelter-report_2016.pdf.

Global Shelter Cluster. 2018. *Shelter and Settlements: The foundation of humanitarian response. Strategy 2018–2022*. https://reliefweb.int/report/world/shelter-settlements-foundation-humanitarian-response-strategy-2018-2022-executive.

Inter-Agency Standing Committee. 2016. 'The grand bargain'. https://interagencystandingcommittee.org/grand-bargain.

Iuchi, Kanako and Elizabeth Maly. 2016. 'Residential relocation processes in coastal areas Tacloban city after Typhoon Yolanda'. In *Coming Home After Disaster: Multiple dimensions of housing recovery*, edited by Alka Sapat and Ann-Margaret Esnard. London: Routledge.

Jha, Abhas K., Jennifer D. Barenstein, Priscilla M. Phelps, Daniel Pittet and Stephen Sena. 2010. *Safer Homes, Stronger Communities: A handbook for reconstruction after natural disaster*. Washington, DC: World Bank. https://www.gfdrr.org/sites/gfdrr/files/publication/SaferHomesStrongerCommunitites.pdf.

Maynard, Victoria, Elizabeth Parker and John Twigg. 2016. *The Effectiveness and Efficiency of Interventions Supporting Shelter Self-Recovery Following Humanitarian Crises: An evidence synthesis protocol*. https://oxfamilibrary.openrepository.com/bitstream/handle/10546/605179/rr-effectiveness-interventions-shelter-self-recovery-130416-en.pdf;jsessionid=1324F00C1BA6123960D525394DA29824?sequence=1.

Miranda-Morel, Luisa. 2018. *Shelter Assistance: Gaps in the evidence*. https://insights.careinternational.org.uk/media/k2/attachments/Shelter-assistance_gaps-in-the-evidence_Discussion-Paper_November-2018.pdf.

Overseas Development Institute and Centre for Global Development. 2015. *Doing Cash Differently: How cash transfers can transform humanitarian aid*. https://www.odi.org/sites/odi.org.uk/files/odi-assets/publications-opinion-files/9828.pdf.

Parrack, Charles, Bill Flinn and Megan Passey. 2014. 'Getting the message across for safer self-recovery in post-disaster shelter'. *Open House International* 39 (3): 47–58.

Schofield, Holly and Bill Flinn. 2018. 'People first: Agency, choice and empowerment in the support of self-recovery'. In *The State of Humanitarian Shelter and Settlements 2018*, edited by David Sanderson and Anshu Sharma, 29–34. Geneva: IFRC. http://unsworks.unsw.edu.au/fapi/datastream/unsworks:55062/bin61bc3bd2-1071-4244-ae32-17568a5340be?view=true&xy=01.

Schofield, Holly, Emma Lovell, Bill Flinn and John Twigg. 2019. 'Barriers to urban shelter self-recovery in Philippines and Nepal: Lessons for humanitarian policy and practice'. *Journal of the British Academy* 7 (s2): 83–107. https://www.thebritishacademy.ac.uk/documents/934/JBA-7s2-04-Schofield-Lovell-Flinn-Twigg.pdf.

Stodart, Victoria. 2016. 'Regulatory barriers and the provision of shelter in post-disaster situations: Housing, land and property (HLP) issues in the recovery of Tacloban, the Philippines, after 2013 Typhoon Haiyan'. In *Urban Disaster Resilience*, edited by David Sanderson, Jerold Kayden and Julia Leis, 123–37. New York: Routledge. https://doi.org/10.4324/9781315725420.

Twigg, John, Emma Lovell, Holly Schofield, Luisa Miranda-Morel, Bill Flinn, Susanne Sargeant, Andrew Finlayson et al. 2017. *Self-Recovery from Disasters: An interdisciplinary perspective*. https://www.odi.org/sites/odi.org.uk/files/resource-documents/11870.pdf.

Twigg, John and Irina Mosel. 2017. 'Emergent groups and spontaneous volunteers in urban disaster response'. *Environment and Urbanization* 29 (2): 443–58. https://doi.org/10.1177%2F0956247817721413.

UNDRO. 1982. *Shelter after Disaster: Guidelines for assistance*. https://reliefweb.int/sites/reliefweb.int/files/resources/E4FE896AFFF16709C1256CB10056558E-undro-shelter1-jul82.pdf.

UNDRR. 2015. *Sendai Framework for Disaster Risk Reduction 2015–2030*. https://www.preventionweb.net/files/43291_sendaiframeworkfordrren.pdf.

WHA. 2017. 'Post-Haiyan self-recovery housing programme'. http://www.world-habitat.org/world-habitat-awards/winners-and-finalists/post-haiyan-self-recovery-housing-programme.

Part 5

Natural resource and human occupation issues

Continuing from the previous part that dealt with land-related concerns, the three chapters in this section further explore the relationships between human occupation and resettlement interventions on the environment, within the context of urbanisation and land pressures. Natural resources such as wetlands are among the most valuable assets that can help mitigate climate change, and at the same time, are also the most fragile to human interventions. The three cases from Mexico, India and Uganda presented in this part foreground the urbanisation pressures on the limited available land, forcing the settlements to occupy environmentally fragile and hazard-exposed areas. While they also illustrate the disproportionate impact of these risks on the marginalised poor communities, they bring to the fore some important insights for the future of risk and people's habitations.

Mansilla, in Chapter 13, explores the particular case of people living in natural protected areas in Las Charcas, where degradation and 'illegal' occupation of environmentally sensitive flood-prone areas over two decades are a consequence of a lack of planning and demographic dynamics. The settlement's formalisation over the years through service provisions further ignored its environmental consequences, until recently when the losses due to floods and increased climate risks began to be seen as untenable by the authorities. The decision to resettle the communities came without due assessment of alternatives or dialogue with the people, raising some critical questions for the potential of co-habitation of humans and natural resources for the benefit of both, versus making these resources 'untouchable'.

Jain, Singh and Malladi, in Chapter 14, describe the history of development of the city of Chennai, where state and local authorities have systematically built tenements on 'under-utilised' environmentally sensitive marsh areas, classified as 'wastelands', using funds from centrally sponsored schemes for affordable housing. With increasing urbanisation pressures, the state began using these 'wastelands' instead of otherwise expensive urban land for purposes such as affordable housing, sewage treatment plants and landfills, with a persistent lack of concern for the environment and marginalised sections of the society. Despite large investments, hazard exposure and experiences of losses continue to increase. This is locking the city's growth into an unsustainable and inequitable pathway. The case demonstrates how long-term socio-economic and ecological risks are created for the people as well as the city at large as a consequence of poorly planned interventions.

Kisembo, in Chapter 15, describes the conditions of the two settlements in Kampala, located on low-lying areas along the natural drainage channels. In this case, in contrast with the Chennai case, the authorities' attempt to scale up greening of all open spaces to deter flood incidences is faced with the challenge of lack of land. Despite several attempts at incorporating water management systems at site level, there are few incentives for private developers to comply. In an attempt to protect the wetlands, the authorities are pursuing either technical solutions of widening of the water channels, or legal approaches of deregistration of land titles. The logic behind the cancellation of titles is not for 'flood risk reduction' directly, but rather the protection of ecologically important areas of the city by stopping the degradation of wetlands. In either case, these actions are forcing people (mainly the poor) to relocate themselves in lieu of compensation.

Mansilla and Jain et al. further highlight that the adverse effects of environmental degradation can go beyond the local geography and affect more extensive territories. But scarcity of land for growth and urbanisation, and the interest in environmental conservation and the population's right to both adequate housing and sources of income, are various reasons for conflict between the communities and authorities. The three chapters together point to the underlying challenges of governing the commons, while ensuring the wellbeing of the people (especially the most marginalised) and conserving the environment.

Important questions arise from this part which are relevant for not just the cases in point, but more broadly for resettlement cases that are considered within the context of environmental conservation. Is it possible to reimagine resettlements as developments based on comprehensive management of the environmental, social and urban challenges? Can there be a holistic risk-informed development planning such that future hazard and socio-economic risks are mitigated, and the wellbeing of the people and urban systems be achieved?

13
Population resettlement in the Ría Celestún Biosphere Reserve: an opportunity for development?

Elizabeth Mansilla

In Mexico, the resettlement of populations from risk areas has become popular in recent years. During the last few decades a significant number of such interventions have been identified throughout the country, mainly in post-disaster circumstances. Even though evidence exists at the international and national levels about the complexity of these processes – whether with development projects or in post-disaster situations – and despite the failure of most experiences worldwide (Inspection Panel 2016, 18–20), most interventions are still made uncritically and with inadequate information and knowledge on the part of decision-makers and those responsible for implementing them.

The resettlement of populations living in natural protected or conservation areas is even more complex. In these cases, the right of possession, occupation and exploitation of land (sometimes ancestral), safety from future disaster risk, and the need to preserve or restore areas with significant environmental value are all important, and at times competing, issues. These processes also imply land tenure conflicts that are sometimes irresolvable.

In such areas, the need for urban growth and the scarcity of land suitable for urbanisation are often the most common triggers of conflict between authorities and populations, as well as between the interest in environmental conservation/restoration and the population's right to both adequate housing and sources of income. Conflicts between authorities at different levels of government are also frequent, since they necessarily intersect in the management of these areas, as are those derived from the interests of private individuals in the exploitation of natural resources and the development of tourism projects with a high environmental impact.

This contradiction between desired development and required conservation leads to a clear paradox in natural protected areas. On the one hand these are among the most valuable natural assets the planet has and provide a mechanism for cushioning the possible adverse effects of climate change. On the other hand, they are extremely fragile ecosystems susceptible to the unplanned action of humans. In natural protected areas where human settlements exist with little planning and uncontrolled levels of exploitation, the benefits of nature often convert into risk factors. Indeed, the adverse effects of development in such places can transcend the local geography and affect more extensive territories. Such is the case, for example, with mangrove destruction, which reduces the landscape's capacity to absorb intense hurricanes and extreme wave action, leading to great effects on populations that may be relatively far from the site of impact.

There are around nine hundred Natural Protected Areas (NPAs) in Mexico, and in 2005, 279 of these had human settlement, with a population of over 3.4 million inhabitants (Bezaury-Creel and Gutiérrez-Carbonell 2009, 387–8). During the last 15 years, there has been steady pressure on the NPAs. By 2005 half of the population living in these areas was urban (population centres of more than fifteen thousand inhabitants) or mixed rural/urban (in centres with from 2,500 to fewer than fifteen thousand inhabitants). In at least 73 NPAs under federal jurisdiction there was significant demographic pressure, despite the fact that the General Law of Ecological Equilibrium and Environmental Protection establishes, in article 46, that new population centres cannot be authorised in the NPAs and the growth of existing ones should be monitored (Garcés-Fierros and Ruiz-Guzmán 2010, 210–11).[1] Despite the wide availability of natural resources, an estimated 83 per cent of these populations are highly to very highly marginalised (Garcés-Fierros and Ruiz-Guzmán 2010, 222), clearly manifesting the contradiction between natural wealth and human poverty, or more specifically, between social development and natural conservation.

It is in the former contexts that we may fully appreciate that population resettlement projects in NPAs – whether for the purpose of risk reduction, recovery of areas with environmental value or for any other reason – cannot be implemented through isolated or specific actions. They must be analysed in the framework of genuinely integrated development projects and with no clear dividing line between nature and society.

In the framework of the 'Reducing Relocation Risk in Urban Areas' project, two resettlement experiences were studied in depth in the Ría Celestún Biosphere Reserve (RCBR), located in the Mexican state of Yucatán and part of the state of Campeche. The first of these cases, concluded several years ago, was a small post-disaster project that involved the relocation of 83 families – the FONDEN project. The second is a major ongoing project for the resettlement of more than seven hundred families covering about one-third of the inhabitants of the town of Celestún in the area known as Las Charcas.[2]

This second case is this chapter's focal point. It synthesises the contradictions of development manifested in the previous paragraphs and allows a rich analysis of those processes that must be creatively contemplated in the search for comprehensive and sustainable development. This is helped by the fact the project is ongoing. I must note that the research resulted in more questions than answers; however, it is a good beginning and allows issues to be put on the table, for them to be considered in an integrated manner, and for options for future progress to be assessed. The orientation of the analysis is futuristic given the incipient nature of the scheme I analyse in depth. That is to say, as opposed to identifying problems with the enactment of a finished resettlement scheme, I take advantage of the incipient nature of the Las Charcas scheme so as to identify needs and challenges for the future and for the implementation of non-conventional, holistic resettlement initiatives.

Celestún: the transition from a fishing village to a biosphere reserve

Physical and social context

Celestún is internationally renowned as a winter refuge for pink flamingos and other species of birds and protected wildlife. Surrounded by a large mangrove swamp, it is one of the largest and best-preserved wetlands in Mexico and the world (Villalobos Zapata 2004, 398; Secretariat of Environment and Natural Resources [SEMARNAT] 2002, 5–6). Due to its importance, it was declared a Wildlife Refuge Zone and in November 2000 declared the Ría Celestún Biosphere Reserve.[3] Covering an area of 81,482.33 hectares, it is located within the municipalities of Celestún and Maxcanú in the state of Yucatán, and Calkiní in the state of Campeche (SEMARNAT 2002, 5; CONANP-RBRC n.d.).

The rural/urban mixed area of Celestún, located in the heart of the reserve has about eight thousand inhabitants (National Institute of Statistics and Geography [INEGI] 2015), and although this is a relatively small population, it exerts a high pressure on natural resources and generates a significant impact on the physical environment. The town, for which pre-Hispanic origins can be traced, became the head of the municipality in 1918. Since then, salt extraction and fishing have been the primary employment and income sources, with seasonal tourism growing in more recent years. Salt extraction has been important for more than two centuries and to a large extent determined the demographic and urban dynamics of the settlement (CONANP-RBRC n.d.).

When the salt industry declined in the late 1940s and, above all, when the state government promoted a policy of peasant migration to coastal communities, as a result of a drop in the demand for henequen fibre – the most relevant productive activity in the Yucatán peninsula in the 1970s, and especially in the 1980s – the population of Celestún began to grow steadily. It rose from 476 inhabitants in 1900 to 7,836 in 2015; population projections estimate that by 2020 there will be 8,745 inhabitants in the area (INEGI n.d.; see Figure 13.1). Despite rapid relative population growth in recent decades, the locality has no legal instruments for the adequate planning of urban growth and land use. At the socio-economic level, the National Council for the Evaluation of Social Development Policy (CONEVAL) estimates that 83.6 per cent of Celestunians live in poverty, with 26.4 per cent living in extreme poverty (CONEVAL 2010).

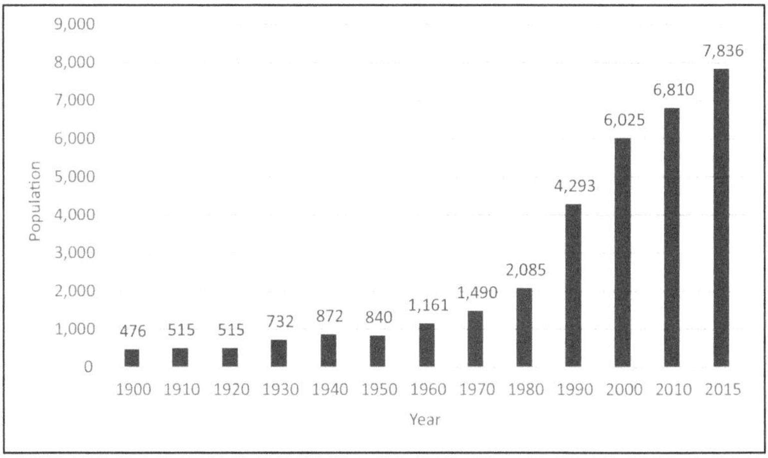

Figure 13.1 Population growth in Celestún. © Author, based on data from INEGI.

Urban dynamics and increased risk

Population growth has forced urban development to occupy environmentally fragile and unsuitable areas (see Figure 13.2). With the scarce land available for human settlements being exhausted or earmarked for more profitable purposes, families have opted to infill wetlands or so-called 'salt ponds' with garbage and waste material in order to build houses. Some houses are precariously constructed using lightweight materials and others are consolidated homes of one or even two storeys. Currently, more than 60 per cent of dwellings are located in flooded areas (SEDUMA-SEDATU-AXIS 2015, 36; SEDUMA 2015). The effects of unplanned urban sprawl, poor solid waste management, and the lack of adequate and sufficient drainage systems result in severe sanitary problems and environmental and groundwater contamination, with serious effects on the environment and the health of the inhabitants (Villalobos Zapata 2004, 404).

Due to the physical characteristics of the land and the process by which it was occupied, the population is susceptible to flooding and subsidence, suffering constant damage and loss during the rainy

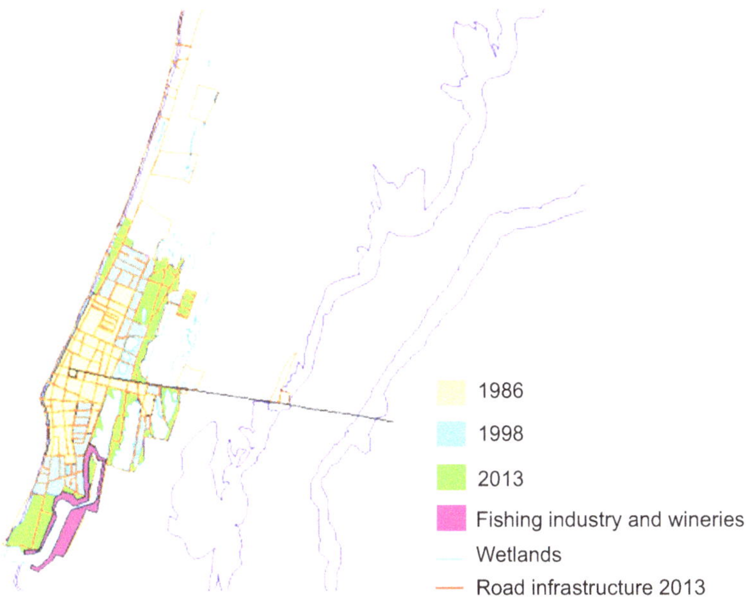

Figure 13.2 Urban sprawl in Celestún. © Author, based on information from CONANP-RBRC.

season and the passing of tropical cyclones. Although losses – with some exceptions – have been relatively moderate to date, risk construction processes are prevalent in the area, and may increase the potential for damage both among the population itself and in the vicinity. More recurrent extreme events, intensified by the effects of climate change, are to be expected. Hurricanes Gilbert in 1988, Isidore in 2002, Emily in 2005 and Dean in 2007, as well as Tropical Storm Alex in 2010, and a series of lesser storms, provide recent experiences of severe direct damage to the population and economic activity in the area. This also shows that a recurrent pattern of considerable damage can be observed every two or three years over the last few decades. Here it should be noted that given the high levels of exposure and vulnerability that exist, no extraordinary events are required to cause significant damage to the population. During the astronomical phenomenon known as the 'supermoon' on 14 November 2016, the increase in the tide produced floods of up to 60 cm, affecting a considerable number of houses and streets in the town, in addition to direct damages to the fishing activity.[4]

Resettlement experiences in the area

Recent cases

The government of the state of Yucatán, motivated by the occurrence of disasters and the availability of federal funds for the resettlement of at-risk populations, has implemented a series of projects over time, with diverse results.[5] Two of these cases involve the town of Celestún.

The FONDEN neighbourhood, as it is known among residents, is a scheme implemented following the floods caused by Hurricane Dean in 2007. This relocation of 83 homes provided houses for families from different flooded parts of the same urban area. Atypically, the relocation of the families was carried out without conflict. A register of affected people was made, land was acquired within the urban area and housing was constructed and directly allocated to beneficiary families. This was undertaken with resources from the Natural Disasters Fund (FONDEN) and was operated by authorities from the Yucatán state government. The land is located in the central area of the town, very close to the affected area. Because of this the beneficiary families offered no resistance to the move. This was reinforced by the fact that the houses were given for free and the population was allowed to retain ownership of their original dwelling.

Such conditions do not exist in the second project – the central object of analysis in this chapter. This project consists of the resettlement of irregularly settled families in the El Arenal area, better known among residents as 'Las Charcas', and is being promoted by the Yucatán state government's Ministry of Urban Development and Environment (SEDUMA). This project is currently underway and differs markedly in magnitude when compared to the FONDEN project, since in this case, about one-third of the total population of Celestún is to be resettled. All families come from informally occupied areas and to resettle this population on a single site close by requires a large plot of land, which would necessarily affect another part of the reserve since the municipality does not have sufficient territorial reserves for such an allocation. Such a move would also involve a process of environmental restoration of the old occupied areas and a strong programme that prevents them from being invaded again.

Las Charcas: the current settlement and the resettlement project

Characteristics of the current settlement

The settlement subject to intervention is a product of the demographic dynamics suffered in the municipality in recent decades and a consequence of the lack of planning by the local authorities and the federal authorities responsible for the RCBR. Both have allowed the illegal occupation of this flood-prone federally protected area for over two decades. It is only now, with increased risks of flooding and other environmental disadvantages, along with projections for climate change, that such a situation is considered untenable.

The area is occupied by low- to middle-income families who, lacking access to better land, have established their dwellings by invading federal lands adjacent to the salt ponds and wetlands on the periphery of the town centre. By infilling with garbage or riverine bank materials, villagers have gained ground and built houses ranging from the most precarious, made with cardboard and other waste materials, to more consolidated homes involving greater relative investment in financial and temporal terms. The neglect for years by several municipal administrations and federal authorities has brought the problem to a critical state: currently, 2,298 people occupy 763 dwellings in the threatened Las Charcas wetlands area (SEDUMA-SEDATU-AXIS 2015, 58).

The paradox is that some of the villagers have documentation that 'proves' the legal estate of the land they occupy, despite them being national lands under federal protection.[6] However, this estate has been improperly granted by the municipality, since the occupied areas have not been 'dissociated' and urbanisation has not been authorised by the Agrarian Attorney's Office or any other appropriate instance, as established by Mexico's current Agrarian Law.[7]

Although the settlement was established illegally, over the years it has been 'formalised', to the point that today it has a relatively broad coverage of basic services. According to the feasibility study carried out by SEDUMA for the resettlement project, 89.7 per cent of the dwellings have piped water and 55.9 per cent have electricity, while 76.9 per cent of the houses have sanitary facilities. As for urban services, most are in bad condition, but 90 per cent of households have access to street lighting; 57 per cent of the houses are consolidated buildings and 28 per cent semi-consolidated, while only 15 per cent of the total houses located in the area are precarious constructions. About 70 per cent of the homes have some degree of overcrowding and only 1.94 per cent have drainage, which means that much of the wastewater is directly discharged to the land on which the dwellings are located (SEDUMA-SEDATU-AXIS 2015, 30–55).

The intervention proposal

With the interest of reducing poverty and the environmental impact that the occupation of these lands causes, the state government, through SEDUMA, began an evaluation process in order to undertake the eventual relocation of this population to safer lands, the sanitation of the area, and its active reinsertion in the RCBR. Using federal funds available from the Ministry of Agrarian, Territorial and Urban Development (SEDATU), SEDUMA commissioned a feasibility study (SEDUMA-SEDATU-AXIS 2015). This provides a diagnosis of the general situation of the area and resettlement options are evaluated.

The results of the study suggested that the resettlement of the population was the only real option. Three alternatives were offered for the new settlement:

1. Infill and protect one of the ponds inside the existing risk zone and relocate the whole population to that area.
2. Resettle the population outside the urban area, in a sector located approximately 30 km east of Celestún, near the town of Kinchil. This distance was required in order to respect the mangrove area

and associated vegetation as well as the floodplain, which must be preserved.

3. Relocate the population to an area north of the existing population nucleus, within the existing urban area, on a single piece of land with the appropriate dimensions and characteristics to support the necessary housing.

Beyond the dubious technical quality of the feasibility study, it is between these three options that the authorities are deciding the resettlement issue, and the population will only be informed of the final decision when this is taken. More relevant here, however, are the economic, social and political realities of the area, which are not even considered in the feasibility study.

Resettlement as the only solution and under a unique model

The authorities have considered the resettlement of more than seven hundred families living in Las Charcas using a conventional model of single resettlement as the only option. Alternative and differentiated intervention options according to individual risk exposure and habitation conditions have not been offered. As in many other cases, the target population is seen as a monolithic block that can be uprooted and placed elsewhere, even if this is 30 km away from its source of employment and livelihood. But not all the families settled in Las Charcas respond to the same pattern or live in the same conditions of risk exposure, nor are all homes the same. Usually, the more recently settled families have built using precarious materials, while the longer-rooted families have built more consolidated houses that have involved significant investment. Among the latter, greater resistance to change can be seen. On the other hand, property status is also not the same for all families. Some of them have a legal estate granted by the municipality or have a written authorisation to settle there, even though the land has been urbanised on a landfill or in federal areas over which the municipality has no legal jurisdiction.

Proposing 'mono-solutions' to such diverse situations can only hinder the process and does not guarantee that the intervention meets its proposed objectives. It fuels conflict and opposition from the population and completely cancels out any possibility of transforming this process into a true development option. This is especially true when the project is based on an incomplete and insufficient diagnosis and a narrow-minded intervention proposal. The solution to these problems is not always technical and requires imagination and the art of negotiation. The inhabitants of Las Charcas are well aware of the risks and the conditions under which they live and, like any family, would like to have legal certainty about their tenure. That is why a significant number of them are willing to be resettled under negotiated conditions that positively affect their employment opportunities. From interviews with the population it would seem they have access to secure plots within the municipal area that could be used for resettlement. This would be based on the option of not being resettled in one place but rather being relocated to different areas of the same town, according to opportunity and need.

Another aspect that should be considered is that at minimum, housing similar to the original housing should be provided. Among those consulted, the average house has an area of 60 m^2. There is no additional land given that houses are raised on a cluster of garbage and stones. Even when there are cases that differ from those described above, the investigation shows that resettlement is viable and that the requests by the population are reasonable, although everything will depend on how the authorities decide to carry out the process.

Up until now, the authorities have not consulted the families that will eventually be resettled, and although the resettlement process is forthcoming, it has not been officially announced. It is, however, already an open secret that runs throughout the village. Would it not be better, in this case, to start from an objective diagnosis and more imaginative and better-informed intervention proposals? Is it possible that with appropriate intervention this resettlement project could become an authentic development opportunity for the families of Las Charcas? Knowing that a good number of the families would agree in principle to resettlement, would it not be more appropriate to report truthfully, to consult the affected population and to involve them in the process from the beginning, so that negotiations flow better and the proposed objectives are achieved? The reasons for the secretive, unilateral approach are not overly clear.

The conflict of authority and the right to the land

Although there are families in Las Charcas that have migrated from other states of the country, most of them are Celestunians. In general, they are young families, second- or third-generation descendants of the original population. With the intention of owning their own dwellings, they invaded the area after not being able to find land in better and more accessible conditions. Neither did they have the option of being included in state or federal housing programmes.

The housing crisis in the municipality involves not only the inhabitants of Las Charcas, but also a large part of the total population. This is manifested in a severe housing deficit that has led to 55 per cent of existing housing being overcrowded in different degrees, according to the Municipal Development Plan for 2015–18 (Ayuntamiento de Celestún 2015, 18). There is little land suitable for urbanisation, given the physical conditions of the area, and because suitable land is monopolised by private individuals, who use it for holiday homes, hotels or shops, or simply keep it as vacant lots.

According to the RCBR Management Programme, land tenure is as follows: 89 per cent of the area covered by the reserve is under federal jurisdiction, 7.5 per cent is *ejido* (collective lands without the possibility of being sold or divided), 1.7 per cent is private property, and 1.8 per cent has unknown property status (SEMARNAT 2002, 29–30).[8] On the other hand, the city has no territorial reserves to meet the demands of urban growth. In fact, urban growth is being promoted by the municipal authorities on land to the north-west of the town, which is under federal jurisdiction and has not been disassociated: therefore, there is no authorisation for its use. However, at least one access road has been opened in the area and the relocation of a school that is constantly flooded in its present location has been contemplated. The mayor has granted legal estate or written authorisation to some residents to occupy lots. For several years they have demanded a home. They have been recommended to delimit 'their land' with bushes and plants as a means of continuing the process of urbanisation while the disassociation of the land by the federation is achieved.

This clearly constitutes an illegal act and promotes the informality of urban growth. It is, in general terms, a formal authorisation to invade land. The question is, however, what options remain for both local authorities and the population, when the vast majority of the land has been devoted to environmental conservation, less than 8 per cent is under productive use and less than 2 per cent has potential for building but is in the hands of private hoarders?

It is within this framework that a debate should occur on the rights of native populations to occupy the lands they have inhabited for centuries and the undeniable need to conserve the natural wealth of the area. Celestún already existed as a settlement long before the biosphere reserve was created, so a management programme should not have been established without considering that a population already existed there, has needs and will eventually grow in number and territorial extension. The current management programme has not been updated since 2002, the year in which it was created, and although it acknowledges the problem of urban growth, it offers no solutions. Nor is it known whether the reserve authority has undertaken any economic or social development initiatives to prevent the problems of disordered urban growth and increases in the population's poor living conditions, resulting in even more severe environmental impacts.

Based on the former arguments, the key question would then be: does a human presence automatically imply environmental degradation or are there options for resource conservation through controlled exploitation? Should populations living in NPAs benefit from the natural wealth of their environment in order to achieve better living conditions or should natural resources be untouchable? Is it possible to improve the living conditions of the population and at the same time conserve natural resources? A research report published by various academic institutions shows that under appropriate conditions, communities can maintain forest coverage and conserve the biodiversity of the forests they manage, even better than what can and has been achieved with the NPAs. An example of this are the community forests in the centre of the state of Quintana Roo, where the lowest deforestation rate in all of south-east Mexico has been registered, including regions where NPAs occupy most of the territory (Bray et al. 2007, 36). In addition, the use of community forests contributes to poverty reduction. Would not it be better to base new initiatives on the search to resolve problems instead of ignoring them?

The different visions of development

The lack of communication between different levels of government and between the government and the population, the vision of 'conservation by decree' and the lack of institutional coordination have led to the improvisation of public policies. Each of the authorities involved has its own vision of what development should be. On the one hand, the federal authorities, through the National Commission of Natural Protected Areas, maintain a bureaucratic vision of conservation, ignoring any other problems that fall outside this domain. On the other hand, the vision of the municipal authorities is mediated by the pragmatism required when a government lasts for three years, with no opportunity for the re-election of mayors. And finally, there is the vision of the intermediate level of government (state government), which has no jurisdiction over the area and whose intervention in any conservation or development project can only be implemented in agreement with the local authority, but mainly with the federal level.

Thus, at the governmental level, three different development ideas prevail for the area and these are not necessarily complementary. At the national level, the federal authority expresses its interest in the preservation of natural resources, both flora and fauna, while in terms of management practice social and urban problems are ignored, communication with the mayor is very limited and with the population it is simply non-existent.

At the opposite extreme is the vision of development at the municipal level, based on the promotion of tourism: the only activity that successive mayors suppose can be profitable. Parallel to the promotion of tourism, the construction of a coastal boardwalk throughout the reserve for the enjoyment of visitors is planned (Ayuntamiento de Celestún 2015, 38). This is, of course, planned without considering the environmental impact of construction or the large-scale arrival of tourists on a natural area that is intended to be conserved and that does not even have the basic infrastructure necessary for its inhabitants.

Finally, for its part, the state government, through SEDUMA, has a vision that is closer to that of the federal government, based on resource conservation. In fact, although the resettlement project of Las Charcas is apparently motivated by the need to reduce flooding and improve sanitary conditions, it may in fact be explained by the interest in recovering the wetlands and restoring them to the reserve. The problem with this initiative, however, is that the resettlement project is not being seen as an opportunity to redirect urban growth in the area and to foster real development for Celestunians by preventing poor families from continuing to cause harmful effects on the environment due to the lack of other options. Nor does it contemplate, for example, actions to avoid the vacated and restored areas in the reserve being occupied again, or to develop different productive options for those affected in the case of resettlement some 30 km distant – much less the environmental impact that a new settlement of more than seven hundred houses in a protected area could have.

But to these three visions a fourth must be added: that of the population itself. For generations, Celestunians have lived from fishing and salt extraction from ponds that are close to where they currently live. And although a good proportion of them also provide services, mainly in the flamingo observation tours, income from tourism is marginal because it is seasonal and the offer of service providers surpasses demand by far. That is why all the settlers, at least those who were consulted during the investigation, continue to bet on fishing as the main source of income in spite of the restrictions that the reserve authority imposes on them. But they are also eager to receive proposals on different productive options that complement their incomes and enable them to improve their living conditions. They are well aware of the fact that it is necessary to conserve natural resources because their income depends on them and, ultimately, they do not wish to live on a garbage dump, nor for their children to be exposed to attack by crocodiles when the tide rises. The problem is that they have no options. For them, the federal authority only signifies prohibition on developing their activity, the local authority acts for personal benefit and for the good of relatives, and the state government, which could eventually act as interlocutor and mediator, ignores them. Proof of this is the census that was taken as a basis for the feasibility study. The population was never informed as to why the census was being taken.

Conclusions: is the resettlement an opportunity for development?

In this context, it is questionable whether this resettlement project can represent a real opportunity for the development of the area. It is possible that a positive result could be achieved, but there are a number of obstacles that must be overcome.

A starting point is to move from a conventional vision of resettlement[9] to a more imaginative idea of development, based on a comprehensive management of the environmental, social and urban challenges prevailing in the area. The conservation of natural resources is undoubtedly important, but it is also a fact that those who live there are not going to leave. On the contrary, the town will continue to grow and it will become increasingly difficult to control growth if the relevant measures are not taken now. For that reason, the first thing is to plan the use of the territory with a vision that includes not only wild flora and fauna but also the human urban area. It is essential to start from a serious and careful study that determines the lands that can be objectively urbanised – obviously with acceptable levels of security – and to initiate a legal and orderly process of dissociation so that they can be incorporated as urban lots. At the same time, options should be explored for the creation of 'development poles' outside the reserve, so new generations of Celestunians are attracted by profitable economic activities different from those currently offered by the town. This would help avoid further invasions of land in already recovered areas, so pressure from the reserve can be removed.

On the other hand, distrust between different government authorities and between these and the population must be overcome. It is undeniable that among the settlers there is a sense of having been stripped of their territory when the biosphere reserve was created. To some extent they are right, since there are few productive options left, in the name of 'natural resources conservation'. Hence poverty in the municipality continues to increase. In addition, the reserve authority must recognise that it does not have the capacity to monitor compliance with all the prohibitions established in the regulations – including non-invasion of lands under federal jurisdiction. Human and financial resources are limited.

A different situation would exist if the reserve's authority established direct and permanent contact with the population in the search for and implementation of productive activities that benefit the citizens of Celestún and at the same time allow for resource conservation. This would not only create a link between them but would also help prevent municipal authorities from acting at a discrete level, while the same population would be the main proponent of conserving resources.[10] Most of the population is fully aware of the great environmental value of the land, but people also have daily needs to solve for themselves and their families. A balance between the two would be ideal to ensure a good future for the area and the fulfilment of the objectives of any intervention project. In this, SEDUMA could play an important role as mediator within the contemplated relocation project framework. SEDUMA could still take advantage of local capacities and avoid a project decided and executed from above, unplanned and with little consideration for those affected. It would also avoid another failed project.

Celestún is at a point where it is still possible to solve problems, because the magnitude of its difficulties is very small compared to what happens in other NPAs. Such is the case of the Montes Azules Biosphere Reserve in Chiapas, for example, where there are more than five hundred dispersed human settlements with more than half a million people demanding a solution to their land tenure problems. Agrarian conflicts have prevailed there for more than 40 years, and plundering of land, forced resettlements, and violent and prolonged social conflicts have occurred. All this has been aggravated by the arrival of Guatemalan refugees since 1981, conflicts between communities and the emergence of the armed conflict in Chiapas since 1994 in the Reserve (Secretariat of the Environment, Natural Resources and Fisheries [SEMARNAP] 2000). Unlike Montes Azules, in Celestún the population is relatively small, concentrated in a single urban centre, quite friendly and well disposed to resettlement, so it is unnecessary to start a process of removing distrust.

In short, the project that the state government has commenced can become a real opportunity for development by ordering urban growth in the area and encouraging sustainable productive activities that do not go against resource management. This is a resettlement initiative for a third of an urban centre. This may be small in absolute terms, but its impact could be significant and it could establish a precedent of good practice. In an area like the RCBR, everyone loses with the destruction of the environment, and everyone gains from its conservation. However, the key to the success of an initiative of this kind is to recognise that in Natural Protected Areas where human settlements are present, more than anywhere else, there is an indissoluble link between society and nature.

Notes

1. It is worth noting the scarcity of updated demographic and social information on the NPAs in Mexico since the last demographic study was carried out by the National Population Council (CONAPO) in 2010. Other relevant studies on the problem of human settlements in these areas date from 2009, although they use demographic information from 2005 (Bezaury-Creel and Gutiérrez-Carbonell 2009).
2. I use the term 'relocation' to refer to population movements to sites close to the original location and where substantial changes in terms of employment, access to services, etc. are not implied. 'Resettlement' refers to more complex processes of population movement involving greater distances from original sites, changes in livelihoods (source of employment, access to services, longer-distance transport, etc.). For greater precision on both terms, see Chapter 1 in this book on the concept of resettlement. For more details on the area of study and the method of research, consult the research reports at https://www.ucl.ac.uk/bartlett/development/reducing-relocation-risk-urban-areas.
3. *Diario Oficial de la Federación*, 27 November 2000.
4. According to the testimony of Celestún settlers and several journalistic articles (in *La Jornada*, *Milenio* and *Unión Yucatán*, 15 November 2016).
5. For further details on resettlement experiences in the state of Yucatán see Lavell 2016 and Lavell et al. 2016.
6. According to the *Glossary of Legal-Agrarian Terms of the Agrarian Attorney's Office* (Procuraduria Agraria 2009), the 'legal estate' is a portion of land destined for the foundation and construction of a village. At the moment it is regulated by agricultural regulations, as well as by federal or state provisions related to human settlements.
7. See Mexico's Agrarian Law (Cámara de Diputados n.d.), in particular articles 63, 64 and 65 relating to human settlements on ejidal lands. The last reform of this law was published in the *Diario Oficial de la Federación* on 9 April 2012.
8. These figures refer only to the land area of the reserve; although I have no figures for the current status of land tenure, I assume that it has not changed significantly.
9. The most widely applied conventional model consists of moving the target population as a whole to a new site, usually far from the place of origin, as a single settlement that is built for this purpose. This does not involve wider intervention to solve problems in the community that go beyond the explicit reason for resettlement: for example, to improve the living conditions of

poor populations with alternative productive options, housing improvements, urban reorganisation, etc.

10. In 2017, residents of Celestún tried to lynch the mayor, Leonel Rosado Meda, for the alleged sale to a private consortium of a 5 hectare beach that is part of the reserve. The mayor had to flee the municipality for several days and the intervention of the state police was necessary. It is not the first conflict between settlers and municipal authorities over repeated attempts by the current mayor to cede land from the reserve improperly, to be commercially exploited by his relatives. With this it is clear that if anyone in Celestún is interested in conservation and can take care of the monitoring and protection of natural resources, it is the population itself and not necessarily the authorities.

References

Ayuntamiento de Celestún. 2015. *Plan Municipal de Desarrollo 2015–2018*. http://www.transparenciayucatan.org.mx/dwn.a9?ID=d60e2d98-c1e4-4885-8d9c-7d39fcb19b86.

Bezaury-Creel, Juan and David Gutiérrez-Carbonell. 2009. 'Áreas naturales protegidas y desarrollo social en México'. In *Capital Natural de México*, vol. 2: *Estado de conservación y tendencias de cambio*, edited by José Sarukhán, 385–431. Mexico: CONABIO. https://www.researchgate.net/publication/236150170_Areas_naturales_protegidas_y_desarrollo_social_en_Mexico.

Bray, David D., et al. 2007. *Nueva Evidencia: Los bosques comunitarios de México protegen el ambiente, disminuyen la pobreza y promueven la paz social*. Mexico City: CCMSS. https://www.ccmss.org.mx/acervo/nueva-evidencia-los-bosques-comunitarios-de-mexico-protegen-el-ambiente-disminuye-la-pobreza-y-promueven-paz-social.

Cámara de Diputados. n.d. *Ley Agraria*. http://www.diputados.gob.mx/LeyesBiblio/ref/lagra.htm.

CONEVAL. 2010. 'Medición de la pobreza en México 2010, a escala municipal'. https://www.coneval.org.mx/Medicion/MP/Paginas/Medicion-de-La-Pobreza-Municipal-2010.Aspx.

Garcés-Fierros, César and Leticia Ruiz-Guzmán. 2010. 'Características sociodemográficas de las áreas naturales protegidas de competencia federal en México'. In *La Situación Demográfica de México 2010*, 201–36. http://www.conapo.gob.mx/es/CONAPO/La_Situacion_Demografica_de_Mexico_2010.

INEGI. n.d. 'Serie histórica censal e intercensal (1990–2010)'. https://www.inegi.org.mx/programas/ccpv/cpvsh.

INEGI. 2015. 'Encuesta intercensal 2015'. https://www.inegi.org.mx/programas/intercensal/2015.

Inspection Panel. 2016. *Involuntary Resettlement*. Washington, DC: World Bank. http://documents1.worldbank.org/curated/en/521101467989568006/pdf/105660-NWP-Box394887B-PUBLIC-PUBDATE-4-12-16.pdf.

Lavell, Allan. 2016. 'Colombia, Peru and Mexico: Cost and benefit analysis'. *Reducing Relocation Risk in Urban Areas*. https://www.ucl.ac.uk/bartlett/development/sites/bartlett/files/wp3_cost_benefit_flacso_en_28_pp_1.pdf.

Lavell, Allan, Omar D. Cardona, Angel Chávez, Elizabeth Mansilla and Maria-Pilar Perez. 2016. 'Colombia, Peru and Mexico: Site level report'. *Reducing Relocation Risk in Urban Areas*. https://www.ucl.ac.uk/bartlett/development/sites/bartlett/files/site_level_flacso_english_v4.pdf.

Procuraduria Agraria. 2009. *Glosario de Términos Jurídico-Agrarios de La Procuraduría Agraria*. http://www.pa.gob.mx/pa/conoce/publicaciones/Glosario%202009/GLOSARIO%20DE%20TÉRMINOS%20JURÍDICO-AGRARIOS%202009.pdf.

SEDUMA-SEDATU-AXIS. 2015. *Estudio de Viabilidad de Reubicación de Viviendas en Zonas de Alto Riesgo en el Municipio de Celestún, Yucatán, México*. Tamaulipas: SEDUMA.

SEMARNAP. 2000. *Programa de Manejo Reserva de la Biosfera Montes Azules*. http://www.paot.org.mx/centro/ine-semarnat/anp/AN29.pdf.

SEMARNAT. 2002. *Programa de Manejo Reserva de la Biosfera Ría Celestún*. Mexico City: Comisión Nacional de Áreas Naturales Protegidas. http://bibliotecasibe.ecosur.mx/sibe/book/000047305.

Villalobos Zapata, Guillermo J. 2004. 'Reservas de la Biósfera: Los Petenes-Celestún'. In *El Manejo Costero En México*, edited by Evelia Rivera Arriaga, Guillermo J. Villalobos Zapata, Isaac Azuz Adeath and Francisco Rosado May, 397–412. Campeche: Universidad Autónoma de Campeche/Centro EPOMEX. https://www.redicomar.com/wp-content/uploads/2018/09/El-Manejo-Costero-en-México.pdf.

14

(Re)creating disasters: a case of post-disaster resettlements in Chennai

Garima Jain, Chandni Singh and Teja Malladi

Damaged houses are among the most visible outcomes of hazard event impacts and attract immediate attention from various state and non-state humanitarian actors to showcase responsiveness (Arvind and Ranjit 2020; Few et al. 2021). This was the case in Chennai, a metropolitan city in South India, where the Indian Ocean tsunami of 2004 and the devastating floods of 2015 caused widespread loss of life and damage to infrastructure. Following these events, pre-existing housing stock was used to resettle disaster-affected people in the name of providing humanitarian relief and reducing hazard exposure. In this chapter, we examine the long-term implications of these state-mandated resettlements, demonstrating how interventions to reduce hazard exposure (i.e. resettlement away from coasts and riverbanks) can aggravate risks if the resettlement locations are also exposed to hazards. Apart from the direct socio-economic implications of first the disaster and then the process of resettlement, the degraded conditions of living in these risk-exposed resettlements further exacerbate vulnerabilities. In effect, new socio-economic and ecological risks are created for the people as well as the city at large as a consequence of poorly planned interventions (Jain et al. 2017).

Housing that is built for social development purposes on the one hand and that built post-disaster, on the other, may seem fundamentally similar, but they are operationally distinct. Normatively, all housing should help achieve people's overall wellbeing and improve their long-term resilience. Development literature defines adequate housing as a combination of a shelter as a physical space along with tenure security, availability of basic services, affordability, habitability, accessibility and cultural adequacy (Bhan, Anand and Harish 2014, 36; UN-Habitat 2014). It can have multi-scalar economic, environmental and social functions, such as being an economic asset, providing safety, promoting asset-based welfare at the household level and contributing to the mitigation of climatic impacts or enabling labour movement at the urban and regional level (Arku 2006; Deo Bardhan and Barua 2015; Doling and Ronald 2010).

However, housing built for developmental purposes often disregards risk reduction requirements, for example, the need to reduce hazard exposure with the use of adequate building techniques or safe site locations, while post-disaster rehabilitation focuses primarily on reducing hazard exposure and tends to ignore underlying socio-economic vulnerabilities and the additional functions of housing beyond a shelter. Effectively, these investments lead to partial or skewed development outcomes, continuing pre-existing risks or creating new ones.

State housing provision involves multiple, cross-scalar agencies, including those providing funding (e.g. federal government housing schemes), allocating land (e.g. provincial governments), building the physical structure (e.g. provincial-level housing boards), and providing services such as water, electricity and sanitation (e.g. municipal governments). But due to a lack of jurisdiction, wider technical knowledge, and sufficient attention being paid to the environmental and socio-economic implications of building large-scale infrastructure, housing interventions fail to deliver holistic and sustainable outcomes (Wamsler 2004). This in turn embeds negative risks pertaining to the socio-economic needs or environmental dependencies of people and cities.

Importantly, housing provided as an immediate post-disaster response lacks detailed socio-economic and environmental risk assessments and relevant, flexible monitoring and evaluation frameworks. Poorly planned housing thus tends to inadequately address underlying entrenched inequalities or vulnerabilities that are often the foundational reasons for disaster losses in the first place (Pahwa-Gajjar et al. 2019; Lavell and Maskrey 2014). As we will demonstrate in this chapter, such quick-fix responses, articulated in post-disaster 'crisis' situations, can have poor developmental outcomes that ricochet over decades.

This chapter discusses the mass post-disaster resettlement of people affected by the tsunami in 2004 and floods in 2015 undertaken in Chennai, where state and local authorities have systematically built tenements on 'under-utilised' environmentally sensitive marsh areas under centrally sponsored schemes for affordable housing. We examine the medium- and long-term environmental and socio-economic implications of resettlement interventions for the people and the city at large. In particular, we explore whether the resettlement interventions (1) take into account socio-economic and environmental considerations at the new sites, and (2) ensure that the overall risks are reduced and development outcomes are improved for the resettled populations. The research examines trends and actions taken in Chennai as a whole, with a specific focus on the resettlement sites of Kannaginagar, Semmencherry and Perumbakkam, all three of which are located within the wetland of Pallikaranai marsh.

Overall, post-disaster resettlements in Chennai have been used as a quick fix and showcased as an effective and necessary response to reduce risk (Narayan 2018; Jain et al. 2017). However, we argue that these resettlements have exacerbated exposure to hazards such as seasonal flooding and increased socio-economic and environmental risks, without addressing the affected communities' underlying needs and vulnerabilities. Furthermore, these actions have potentially increased flood risk across the Chennai Metropolitan Area (Arabindoo 2016; Jayaraman 2016a; Vencatesan et al. 2014), creating long-term risks for the people and the city at large.

Chennai: a site of rapid development and witness to many disasters

Chennai, erstwhile Madras, saw a rapid influx of people starting in the early 1920s–1930s, followed by a deep agrarian crisis in its hinterland. This was accompanied by a widespread growth of slums across the city. To respond to these, a City Improvement Trust (CIT) was established in the 1940s, with the mandate to 'clear' the slums and move the people to what were then the outskirts of the city. This approach was revised in the 1950s, to 'improvement' by providing basic services and upgrading existing slum layouts. Meanwhile, the CIT acquired large tracts of land around the city, to build tenements in order to meet the still growing need for housing (Venkat and Subadevan 2015). The CIT was absorbed by the Tamil Nadu Housing Board (TNHB) after its establishment in 1961. This came with an expanded mandate of building housing for all income groups. Meanwhile, the slums kept growing, and TNHB fell significantly short in fulfilling its promise to supply sufficient affordable housing units (Vijayabaskar et al. 2011).

As the population of slum dwellers grew, their political strength also increased, especially within the new winning regional party Dravida

Munnetra Kazhagam (DMK). This period witnessed a significant shift in the state's perspective when the Tamil Nadu Slum Areas (Improvement and Clearance) Act 1970 came into force. This provided security of tenure, promoted improvements in living conditions, and offered protection against arbitrary evictions (Coelho et al. 2015).

This led to a decade of major in situ tenement construction. But due to its higher costs, and inherent difficulties in implementation, only a fraction of the targets were met. The 1980s saw another shift towards in situ slum upgrading, supported by the World Bank, on the premise that giving tenure security would promote self-investment by the residents. But by the 1990s, growing pressures on urban land, and forces for city beautification, brought back the approach of shifting people to tenements outside the city. Large-scale funding for building affordable housing at the beginning of this century, for example through centrally sponsored schemes like the Jawaharlal Nehru National Urban Renewal Mission (JnNURM) or state programmes like the Tamil Nadu Urban Development Project, gave it further impetus (Jain et al. 2017).

The first two decades of the twenty-first century have seen unprecedented urbanisation in Chennai, owing to the growing IT industry and automobile manufacturing, increasing public and private investment to fuel the Smart City, and associated large-scale labour migration (Krishnamurthy and Desouza 2015). With the Bay of Bengal in the east and state administrative limits in the north, Chennai's rapid built-up area expansion over the last two decades is concentrated in the western and the southern regions, along the Chennai–Bengaluru and Chennai–Puducherry industrial corridors. See Figure 14.1 for Chennai's spatial growth patterns over the decades.

The city needed space to accommodate this growth, and conscious planning efforts to protect its environmentally sensitive areas. Unfortunately, the lack of planning and enforcement and the rapid expansion of built-up areas have led to encroachment on some of its important ecological zones. This includes the catchment areas of its three rivers, lakes and water tanks that supplement its drinking water supply, and the low-lying wetlands that act as sinks for excess rainwater and groundwater recharge.

Other engineered infrastructure close to the coast, including housing schemes, ports and thermal power plants, are increasing coastal erosion, groundwater salinity and industrial/human waste effluent-based pollution (Elangovan, Lavanya and Arunthathi 2017; Jayaraman 2016b; Kudale 2010; Kumar and Kunte 2012; Coastal Resource Centre 2016a, 2016b). According to a citizen-led social audit report, only

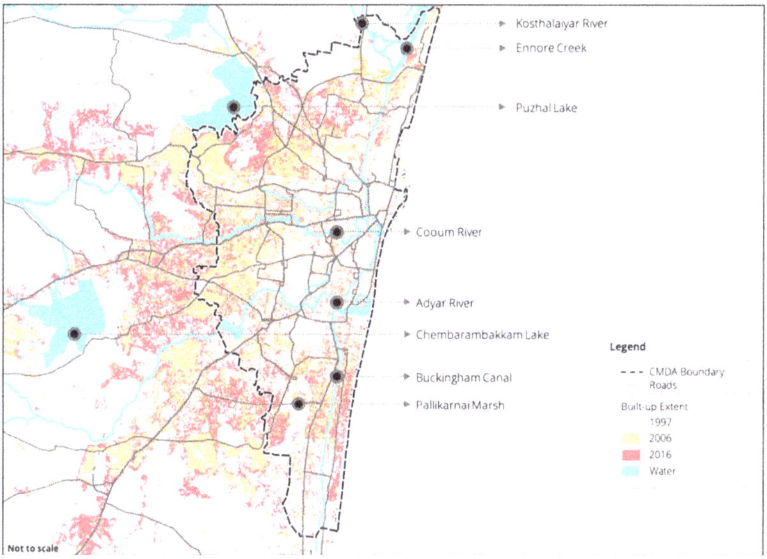

Figure 14.1 Map of land-cover changes in the Chennai region: 1997, 2006 and 2016. © Authors, based on data from Jain, Singh and Malladi 2017; CGIAR-CSI SRTM 2009; CMDA 2008; OpenStreetMap Contributors 2017.

427 million litres per day (MLD) of sewage are currently pumped and treated, whereas almost 1,073 MLD are left to flow untreated directly into water bodies (Arappor Iyakkam n.d.). Such pollution poses a serious threat to human and environmental health, and to economic outcomes for the entire city in the long term.

Meanwhile, Chennai has also witnessed many disasters in the past, some associated with natural hazards, others as a consequence of urbanisation stress (Jayaraman 2015). In 2003–4, the city suffered from a severe drought stemming from poor monsoonal rains. This led to a drop of groundwater by up to 8 m, the shutting down of the city's piped water supply and the complete drying out of local reservoirs (Srinivasan 2008; Thomas 2010). In 2004, a tsunami that hit Tamil Nadu killed nearly eight thousand people and affected more than a million. In 2015, Chennai was among the most affected regions after the heavy rains that led to severe floods across Tamil Nadu. Many lives were lost, more than six million people were affected and 1.5 million houses were damaged. The city has also been affected by several cyclonic storms, such as Cyclone Vardha in

2016 and Cyclone Gaja in 2018, that have left its people and infrastructural systems stranded.

While there is an inclination to see these events as a 'force of nature' (Few et al. 2021), it has been observed that many of the losses are driven by poor planning, inadequate operational management and growing inequities in the city (Bremner 2019). Contrary to popular opinion, recurring floods in the city are not so much due to an increase in precipitation, which has largely remained unchanged over the last century (Drescher et al. 2007), as they are due to wetland fragmentation, a compromised natural drainage system (Vencatesan et al. 2014) and ecologically insensitive infrastructure development (Arabindoo 2016; Jayaraman 2016a). At the same time, recurring water supply shortages (Government of Tamil Nadu 2014; Janakarajan et al. 2007; Srinivasan 2008) across the city have often led to rioting in informal settlements (Srinivasan 2008; Thomas 2010), as well as increasing dependence on groundwater borewells. This growing groundwater dependence is negatively affecting the balance and driving coastal saline water intrusion, making it a vicious cycle with a water supply shortage. Marginalised communities are affected disproportionately, leaving them at the mercy of private tanker companies (Srinivasan et al. 2013).

Climate variability has and climate change will aggravate hazards across Tamil Nadu. Regional climate studies indicate an average temperature increase of 1–3.1°C between the 2020s and the 2080s (Anushiya and Ramachandran 2015; Bal et al. 2016). Annual rainfall projections indicate a general decrease in rainfall of 2–9 per cent over the same period (with some regional exceptions where rainfall might increase) and decreasing water availability in the Chennai basin. Sea levels along the Chennai coast are projected to increase by 0.37 mm per year (Government of Tamil Nadu 2014), directly affecting the area from the Ennore Creek in the north, all along the Buckingham Canal on the coast, to the Pallikaranai marsh area in the south (Indian Space Research Organisation 2012). Cyclone frequency is projected to decrease, although their intensity (measured through wind speed) may increase (Ministry of Environment and Forests 2010). Despite this increasing hazard exposure, major investments are being made along the coast, in the form of affordable housing, thermal power plants, ports, coal and petroleum terminals and railways, which would have significant social and economic implications in the future.

Disaster risk management in Chennai has been two-pronged: individual-led interventions (e.g. raising floor heights; undertaking relief efforts) and state-led strategies (e.g. high-cost infrastructure projects for widening and desilting existing stormwater and natural canals; resettlement of affected poor communities). A close study of these varied responses shows that they either focus on a specific water resource (e.g. cleaning the Buckingham Canal, restoring the Adyar river), or a singular aspect of water management (e.g. desilting for increasing the depth of the stormwater drains, relocating people to reduce sewage discharge into the canal), instead of a comprehensive understanding of risks and associated actions for reducing them. Besides, these responses are taken by multiple agencies and institutions, with limited participation from the affected vulnerable communities (Viswanathan 2018).

Overall, the Tamil Nadu government has a State Disaster Management Authority (SDMA) in place with the Chennai Metropolitan Development Authority (CMDA) as the policy and advisory agency for disaster management at the city level. Their approach for 'disaster management' (and not 'disaster risk management') has tended to be reactive and infrastructure-focused, with less emphasis on addressing structural vulnerabilities and proactive risk management (Jain, Singh and Malladi 2017). However, in 2018, the Tamil Nadu State Disaster Management Policy was amended to align it with the Sendai Framework as well as to move towards a less reactive and more systemic approach to risk management (Tamil Nadu State Disaster Management Authority 2018).

The 2015 floods saw fragmented, delayed and reactive humanitarian action from the state, with individual government officials, concerned private-sector actors and informal civic groups stepping in to fill relief gaps. As the relief phase waned, the state used the post-disaster momentum to justify resettlement of marginalised communities, and often to allocate land resources to more lucrative enterprises. Coelho (2016, 9) calls this 'a highly selective notion of encroachment':

> The five-star hotels and the high-rise office and apartment buildings of MRC Nagar on the Adyar estuary complex, the Phoenix mall on the Velachery lake-bed, the elevated expressway on the Cooum River and the Mass Rapid Transit System (MRTS) rail line on the Buckingham Canal, are only a few instances of mammoth structures that have been permitted to be built on waterways and waterbodies. It is only the Dhideer Nagars, the Alamelu Nagars, the Ambedkar Nagars that are removed, because they are slums, because they are considered eyesores. This is [a] discriminatory action in the name of [the] environment (Coelho 2016, 9).

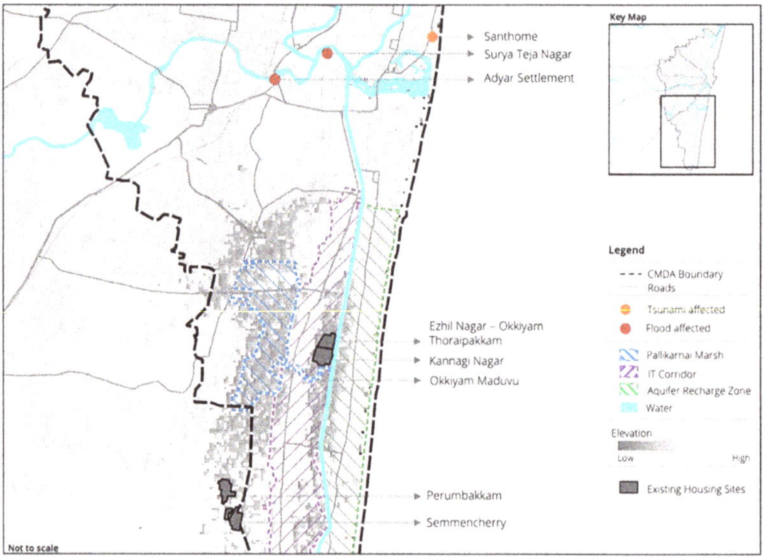

Figure 14.2 Ground elevation, water bodies and drainage networks along with disaster-affected sites and resettlement sites. Note here that the extent of the Pallikaranai Marsh is indicated by the existing surface water, excluding the encroachments. While that does not show the actual extant of the low-lying marsh, it is indicated here using the digital elevation. © Author's elaboration based on data from CGIAR-CSI SRTM 2009; CMDA 2008; OpenStreetMap Contributors 2017.

Just as the 2004 tsunami enabled the removal of coastal fishing villages to build a coastal highway and a subsequent move to resettlement colonies in Kannaginagar and Semmencherry (see Figure 14.2), the floods were leveraged to evict informal settlements along the Adyar and Cooum rivers to pre-existing and vacant housing colonies in Perumbakkam, all several tens of miles away from the original habitations.

Between the bottom-up resistance to moving and top-down focus on resettlement, civil society played a strong role in relief, with a lesser emphasis on recovery. Local development-focused NGOs coordinated and implemented relief during the 2015 floods and some continued to work through community volunteers to provide assistance and livelihood support over the medium to long term. However, widespread environmental risks generated through these processes have remained outside the purview of both state and non-state actors.

Methodology

This study uses primary and secondary information. Secondary research included a literature review of government policies and documents, newspaper articles, NGO reports and peer-reviewed publications; and spatial analysis to map land use, land cover changes, groundwater aquifer recharge zones and proposed locations for housing projects (extracted from the CMDA Master Plan 2026). Primary research included: 20 key informant interviews with government officials, academics, activists, NGOs and select humanitarian agencies; 55 semi-structured household interviews (SSIs) across the three research sites; and two multi-stakeholder consultations before and after primary data collection.

Findings

Long-term ecological implications on the city

Owing to increasing urbanisation pressures, poor land governance and planning, many ecologically sensitive areas of the city have been encroached upon. The Pallikaranai marshland is one such area that provides critical ecosystem services to the city of Chennai and its environs, but over the years it has been severely degraded.

The Pallikaranai marsh is a contiguous low-lying area, located to the south of Chennai, that receives run-off from a catchment area of 235 km^2 and discharges into the Bay of Bengal (CMDA 2008). It is natural and unique in its hydrology. It is the sole home for a large number of flora and fauna species and provides natural drainage into the Bay of Bengal (via Okkiyam Madavu, Buckingham Canal and Kovalam Creek). It is a critical wetland for the city as well as the state of Tamil Nadu, but after the 1980s it saw systematic degradation at the hands of public and private agencies alike.

Between 1992 and 2012, the marshland provided an opportunity for housing development in the rapidly urbanising city. The state built large-scale resettlement colonies on the marshland, largely using funds from the central government-sponsored Jawaharlal Nehru National Urban Renewal Mission's (JnNURM's) Basic Services for the Urban Poor programme (BSUP). A total of 26,376 units were built on the marsh, costing nearly 70,000 crore rupees (approximately US$10.4 billion). These are in addition to the ones built by the state government: 15,656 houses in Kannaginagar and 6,734 houses in Semmencherry (see Table 14.1)

Table 14.1 Housing schemes built on the Pallikaranai Marshland area. © Author's elaboration based on information from Tamil Nadu Clearance Board [TNSCB] Website, HLRN 2014, Jain et al. 2017.

Name of the housing scheme	**Funding/ Programme**	**No. of housing units built**	**Project cost (in million INR)**	**Resettlement drives**
Kannaginagar (2000)	Flood Alleviation Programme	3,000	262.30	Pre-emptively moving people from the river margins
Kannaginagar (2003–4)	Special Problem Grant, Tenth Finance Commission of the Government of India	6,500	540.00	Families living in 'objectionable areas' in Chennai city
Kannaginagar (2004)	Permanent Housing for the Seashore Fisher People/ Families Affected by the Tsunami Disaster	1,271	Built houses purchased	Tsunami-affected fishers and other families
Okkiyam Thoraipakkam (2005–7)	Emergency Tsunami Reconstruction Project (ETRP-World Bank)	2,048	1,061.10	Tsunami-affected families
Okkiyam Thoraipakkam (2005)	Resettlement of Slums Living in Mega Cities – Special Problem Grant, Eleventh Finance Commission	1,620	63.20	Multiple R&R drives
Kannaginagar (2004) Semmencherry (2004)	Chennai Metropolitan Area Infrastructure Development Plan	3,618 1,404	671.30	Pre-emptively moving people from the river margins and later used for tsunami-affected families

(*continued*)

Table 14.1 *(continued)*

Name of the housing scheme	Funding/ Programme	No. of housing units built	Project cost (in million INR)	Resettlement drives
Ezhil Nagar - Okkiyam Thoraipakkam (2005–12)	JnNURM	6,000	2286.00	Multiple R&R drives
Ezhil Nagar - Perumbakkam (2005–12)	JnNURM	3,936	1,753.60	Multiple R&R drives, including flood-affected families
Perumbakkam Phase I (2005–12)	JnNURM	10,452	6,860.30	Multiple R&R drives, including flood-affected families
Perumbakkam Phase II (2005–12)	JnNURM	9,476	6,856.20	Multiple R&R drives, including flood-affected families

(Tamil Nadu Slums Clearance Board n.d.; Housing and Land Rights Network 2014; Jain et al. 2017). The marsh was further fragmented by the construction of supporting infrastructures such as roads, the metro, public and private institutions and the Perungudi municipal landfill and sewage treatment plant, as well as IT corridors and residential complexes (Vencatesan et al. 2014).

Affordable housing construction projects were followed by a series of government-led resettlements. In 1996, 1,600 families were moved to Velachery (in the northern part of the marsh) from different development-induced land acquisition sites across the city. After the 2004 tsunami, affected fishing communities and slum dwellers from coastal locations, such as Santhome Church area, and affected floodplains of the Cooum were moved to Okkiyam Thoraipakkam, Semmencherry, and Kannaginagar under the Tsunami Rehabilitation Programme. Yet until late 2015, many of these housing units remained vacant, awaiting slum dwellers to agree to move from the city. This forms the backdrop for the resettlement drives that took place after the 2015 floods (Jain et al. 2017). Many affected families, now with no option but to move, were resettled from inner-city locations such as Surya Teja Nagar and Saidapet to these housing sites over 25 km away from their original residences (see Figure 14.2 for the original and resettlement site locations). With people forcefully moved to the marsh area, pressures on that land increased further.

A government-funded assessment of Pallikaranai marsh (Vencatesan et al. 2014) found that the marshland has critically been degraded by urbanisation, high groundwater extraction, waste dumping, increasing imperviousness and building upon its recharge areas (Jain, Singh and Malladi 2017). Although 317 hectares of its southern portion have now been declared a reserve forest and it was recognised among the 94 critical wetlands in the country that needed protection under the 2016 National Wetland Conservation and Management Programme of the Government of India, due to the rapidly changing urban landscape surrounding it, the marsh's area was already reduced to a tenth of its former size between the 1960s and 2007 (Drescher et al. 2007). The marsh's area decreased from 6,000 hectares in 1906 to 593 hectares by 2007. Much of the water from the wetland has been pushed southwards onto what used to be 'low- and high-density vegetation' and is now replaced by 'moderate to dense built-up' areas (Vencatesan et al. 2014). There has been significant land-use conversion into residential and industrial uses (63 per cent and 850 per cent increases respectively), while wetland and water bodies have been drastically reduced in size (63 per cent decrease). This land-use change is a crucial factor that exacerbates flood risk in the city (Arabindoo 2016; Jayaraman 2016a).

But what enabled the conversion of these environmentally sensitive areas to urban land uses in the first place? There is an underlying land governance regime that may provide some reasons. *Poromboke* – a vernacular term derived from *puram* meaning outside and *pokku* referring to books of (governance) accounts (Gopalakrishnan 2017) – in Tamil Nadu were once public commons and consisted of wetlands, riverbanks, *eris* (water reservoirs) and pasturelands that did not generate taxes. However, since they had no purpose in the colonial context, which focused on revenue generation from productive agricultural lands, the British changed their classification (Baden-Powell 1892), to what came to be known in official parlance as 'wastelands'– a designation that remains in place to this day. Following Indian independence, these lands were transferred to the state, rather than reverting to their original common ownership. With increasing urbanisation pressures, the state began using these 'wastelands' (Jayaraman 2016b) instead of otherwise expensive urban land for purposes including affordable housing, sewage treatment plants, and a landfill. Over the last decade, tsunami- and flood-affected families in

Chennai have been moved to state-sponsored resettlement colonies built on these very environmentally sensitive *poromboke* marshlands. These 'wastelands' continue to be converted for more lucrative commercial uses such as for industry, public transport and private-sector institutions.

Overall, the evidence alludes to new risks being created by building affordable housing in environmentally sensitive locations, exacerbated further by poor service delivery. Ironically, people affected by disasters, including those caused by tampering with the environment, are moved to the same housing locations that created the risks in the first place.

Continuing environmental and socio-economic risks for the people

Our research shows that disaster-affected people are 'affected' not just by the disasters, but also subsequently by risk reduction interventions in the form of resettlements, and then continuing environmental hazard exposure alongside newly created socio-economic vulnerabilities in these new sites. The 2004 tsunami affected Chennai's coastal communities severely. Fishing settlements from Ennore in north Chennai to Neelankarai in the south were directly affected, with the loss of lives and fishing equipment, and damage to fishing harbours and personal property. The state's main recovery intervention was rebuilding infrastructure and relocating fishers from so-called 'hazard-prone' coastal areas to resettlement colonies across Chennai, often far from the sea and hence their livelihoods. The successive waves of resettlement, which spanned several years, were divisive and exclusionary (Housing and Land Rights Network 2014; Information and Resource Centre for the Deprived Urban Communities and Housing and Land Rights Network 2017), impacted fishers deeply through long-term impacts on livelihoods and mental trauma, and eroded social and political capital.

The 2015 floods were used to continue and expand resettlement, focusing on informal settlements along the Adyar and Cooum rivers. This resettlement has been heavily criticised for ghettoising communities into high-rise enclaves far from places of work, exacerbating risk by building on environmentally fragile marshlands, and causing issues with multigenerational repercussions such as inadequate public services, safety concerns, and overall marginalisation.

Of the 55 households surveyed, 20 reported losing their livelihoods after moving. The three resettlement sites studied (Kannaginagar, Semmencherry, and Perumbakkam) were at least 20 km away from their previous place of residences: on riverbanks of the Adyar in Saidapet and

Surya Teja Nagar for the flood-affected, and in coastal areas of Santhome for the tsunami-affected. Hence, following resettlement, people spent a lot of time and money travelling to work (38 per cent of households reported travelling more than 5 km to reach their workplace, which added to their costs). Several others, notably women, lost their jobs as domestic workers and could not travel long distances for other jobs, demonstrating how the resettlement exacerbated socio-economic vulnerability.

Second-order impacts of resettlement were varied (see Figure 14.3). Importantly, 43 per cent of respondents indicated that the incidence of flooding was bad when they arrived, and over time 30 per cent said that it worsened, while 40 per cent perceived that their exposure to flooding remained the same. This is in sharp contrast to top-down, public authority-led narratives of resettlement reducing flood exposure. Similarly, 38 per cent said that house quality was poor when they arrived, and it worsened over time for the majority. 66 per cent of respondents reported having difficulty paying rent when they arrived, and almost all of the respondents felt that it either worsened or remained just as bad over time. About 50 per cent of them complained of increased disease incidence after they moved.

Some conditions were bad when relocated residents arrived, and remained unchanged over time, such as drinking water, which was reported to be bad by 40 per cent of people on arrival. Similarly, for electricity 51 per cent said that conditions were bad and there were a lot of power cuts. About 43 per cent said their ability to repay loans worsened when they moved and remained the same after several years.

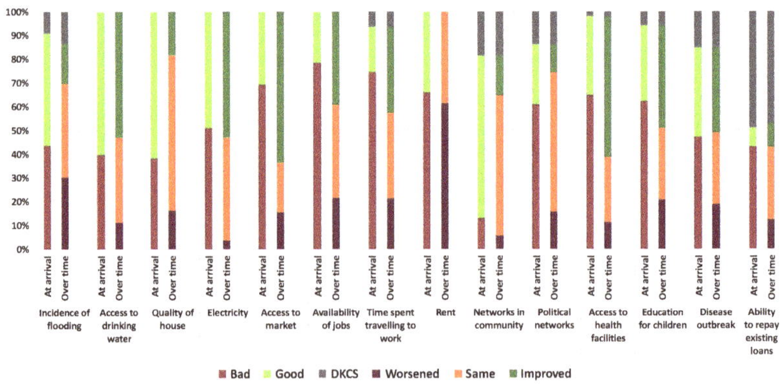

Figure 14.3 Change in access to services and living conditions in the resettlement sites from the time of arrival and over the years. © Authors.

Some parameters seemed to improve over time in some areas. While 78 per cent of the respondents said the availability of jobs was bad when they arrived, 39 per cent said it improved over time. Similarly, 65 per cent said that access to markets was poor when they arrived, and 63 per cent said it improved over the years; 65 per cent had found health facilities poor, and 62 per cent reported education facilities as poor when they arrived at these resettlement sites, but a majority said they had improved over time.

An unintended consequence of the resettlement was the disruption of social ties and the creation of artificial communities in resettlement colonies. While most respondents in the survey reported that political and community networks remained the same over years, the in-depth interviews demonstrated that people reported decreased well-being in resettled areas because of issues of safety, regular incidents of conflict and increased alcoholism and drug use. Together, these factors have led to resettlement colonies being perceived as unsafe and unhygienic, with residents thus marginalised twice over. The repercussions of these marginalisations are very direct and long term: as one respondent, referring to the stigma associated with living in Kannaginagar since the tsunami, elaborated, 'You say you are from Kannaginagar, and [a] post [i.e. job] is closed for you' (interview with a resident of Kannaginagar, 2016).

A more intangible yet long-lasting impact of resettlement was the fraying of political ties and avenues to exercise one's agency. As a resettled household head noted, 'We knew our MLAs [local elected members to the legislative assembly] and other party leaders and we used to get help from there. But here we are new and we do not know anyone yet' (interview with a resident of Perumbakkam, 2016). This severing of communities from their carefully cultivated informal and formal socio-political capital meant that after moving, their bargaining power and grievance redressal platforms narrowed considerably.

The most telling statistic from the survey was that when asked if they preferred to stay in resettlement colonies or to return to their original housing, 75 per cent (n=41) of respondents chose going back. Among these, common reasons for wanting to return were a better quality of life and access to services (24 per cent); better job opportunities in previous locations (24 per cent); feelings of safety and sense of community (15 per cent); and remaining close to the city (10 per cent). Eventually, these communities, who were resettled in low-lying areas, continue to face local flooding and other health implications that come with water-logging (such as water- and vector-borne diseases and skin allergies). This implies that while they were moved from hazard-prone areas with the stated objective of reducing their risks, they continue to live with hazard exposure, despite the economic, financial and social costs borne for the resettlement.

Overall, through first-order impacts of the hazard event itself and second-order impacts of top-down resettlement, we conclude that Chennai saw a concentration of risk for disaster-affected communities. This played out through the move into poor-quality housing in flood-prone areas; cascading disaster impacts such as loss of livelihood and issues of safety and community conflict; and eroded dignity, peripheralisation and a narrowing of avenues to exercise agency or demand rights.

Risk-blind urban development: a cause of future risk

The majority of the resettlement sites described above, as well as the areas identified for future housing schemes, were flooded in 2015 (see Figure 14.4). Building on these low-lying flood-prone regions puts the people who will inhabit these resettlement sites at the risk of floods again. This will disproportionately affect the poor and those who cannot

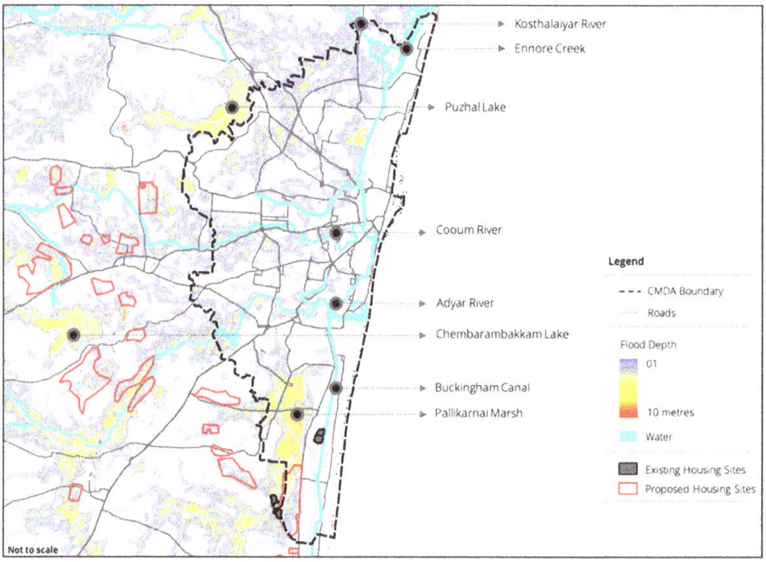

Figure 14.4 Affordable housing sites identified in the Second Master Plan overlaid on 2015 flood map. © Authors, based on data from CMDA 2008; OpenStreetMap Contributors 2017; Kennewell 2016.

afford to live elsewhere in the city. Many of them moved with the aim of reducing risk, only to find that they are still at risk in their new homes. Such building activity on the low-lying areas also reduces the available surfaces for rainwater percolation, thereby increasing stormwater run-off and possibly exacerbating the existing flood conditions. This, in turn, could also lead to a decrease in groundwater recharge, which could be a significant threat to the city's water supply in the future.

Planning instruments, which are often reactive in their approach, also seem to be contradicting each other. Areas covered by former salt pans, mangroves and water bodies and marked as ecologically sensitive in the Coastal Zone Management Plan have been earmarked for 'hazardous and special industries' in the Second Chennai Master Plan (CMDA 2008; Coastal Resource Centre 2016b; Tamil Nadu Coastal Zone Management Authority 2011). Many of these ecologically sensitive areas are already built upon by public and private agencies (for example, as affordable housing), including the area adjacent to the Buckingham Canal otherwise marked as an aquifer recharge area under the Second Chennai Master Plan (CMDA 2008; Jain et al. 2017). Refer to Figure 14.2 for more details.

The IT corridor is planned between the two environmentally sensitive areas, Pallikaranai marsh on the west and the aquifer recharge zone on the east, leading to rapid construction and development in the catchment areas over the last two decades, driving planned and unplanned building activities on the aquifer recharge zone (see Figure 14.2). Similarly, the outlet from the Pallikaranai marsh, Okkiyam Maduvu, which drains the excess water from the marsh into the Buckingham Canal, passes through the IT corridor zone. Real estate development in the IT corridor and resettlement colonies in Ezhil Nagar and Kannaginagar have also narrowed the outlet canal, reducing its capacity to carry stormwater into the sea. This was similar to the case in Semmencherry and Perumbakkam, where the government built resettlement colonies over a drainage channel in the catchment of the Pallikaranai marsh.

The Chennai Second Master Plan identifies the low-lying areas along the rivers and channels as prone to flooding. The master plan highlights that development in these low-lying areas can be allowed with the clearance from the public works department if the new development is designed to make it free from inundation (CMDA 2008). However, due to increased paving and construction activities in the catchment and low-lying areas, increased surface run-off is leading to flooding and reduced groundwater recharge, and these issues continue to remain unaddressed.

Conclusion

Chennai is prone to certain environmental hazards owing to its geographical location. Urban pressures, similar to those experienced by all major growing South Asian cities, strain the limited land and environmental resources. But it is the governance regime, driven by a unidimensional and static understanding of 'risk' and with a particular approach for risk reduction through resettlement, that is leading to long-term risk creation at the watershed, city, settlement and household levels.

Despite large investments, hazard exposure and experiences of losses continue to increase. Focus on housing and resettlement as a means for reducing exposure and recovery is predominantly exclusionary and exacerbates vulnerability. It is based on a narrow understanding of risk only as hazard exposure, and ignores the increasing vulnerabilities and exposure, especially owing to climate change. In this case, people are forced to move from one exposed location to another, with worse social and economic conditions than their previous lifestyles. Poor people are affected disproportionately – impacted first by hazard events, then by post-disaster intervention processes and thereafter by continued hazard exposure as well as worsened socio-economic conditions.

This case strengthens the already well-known premise that disasters are a consequence of poor development practices, but also highlights how this link is not yet made or, if made, has not been acted on by planning agencies. In Chennai, a lucrative economic outlook for land development drives planning decisions, with persistent apathy for the environment and marginalised sections of society. This is locking the city's growth into an unsustainable and inequitable pathway.

There is an urgent need for leadership to build capacities, institutional systems and procedures to recognise the environmental and social implications of large-scale interventions, such as resettlement and relocation, on the city's future. It will take a concerted effort from policy-makers, planners and funding and implementing agencies to arrive at creative solutions for addressing growth needs without causing harm to the socio-ecological system. It will also require an effective civil society and concerned citizen groups to hold the state accountable, to build a more sustainable, resilient and adaptive future.

Acknowledgements

The research draws upon research projects that were funded by the International Institute for Environment and Development (IIED) and British Academy (Recovery with Dignity). The chapter draws on Jain et al. (2017) and Jain, Singh and Malladi (2017). The authors would also like to thank Dr Karen Coelho for being the core contributor to that project, as well as Aishwarya Balasubramanian for providing translation support during the fieldwork.

References

Anushiya, J. and A. Ramachandran. 2015. 'Assessment of water availability in Chennai basin under present and future climate scenarios'. In *Environmental Management of River Basin Ecosystems*, edited by Mu Ramkumar, K. Kumaraswamy and R. Mohanraj, 397–415. Cham: Springer. https://doi.org/10.1007/978-3-319-13425-3_18.

Arabindoo, Pushpa. 2016. 'Unprecedented natures?: An anatomy of the Chennai floods'. *City* 20 (6): 800–21. https://doi.org/10.1080/13604813.2016.1239410.

Arappor Iyakkam. n.d. 'Why Chennai stinks? Citizens' effort to understand and solve the sewage problem'. https://www.cag.org.in/sites/default/files/database/arappor_citizensreport_sewage.pdf.

Arku, Godwin. 2006. 'The housing and economic debate development revisited: Economic significance of housing in developing countries'. *Journal of Housing and the Built Environment* 21 (4): 377–95. https://doi.org/10.1007/sl0901-006-9056-3.

Arvind, Jasmitha and Nihal Ranjit. 2020. 'A tale of two states: Why disaster recovery in India needs to go beyond housing'. Scroll.In, 8 January 2020. https://scroll.in/article/949088/a-tale-of-two-states-why-disaster-recovery-in-india-needs-to-go-beyond-housing.

Baden-Powell, Baden Henry. 1892. *The Land-Systems of British India*, vol. 2. Oxford: Clarendon Press. https://archive.org/details/landsystemsofbri01badeuoft.

Bal, Prasanta Kumar, A. Ramachandran, R. Geetha, B. Bhaskaran, P. Thirumurugan, J. Indumathi and N. Jayanthi. 2016. 'Climate change projections for Tamil Nadu, India: Deriving high-resolution climate data by a downscaling approach using PRECIS'. *Theoretical and Applied Climatology* 123 (3): 523–35. https://doi.org/10.1007/s00704-014-1367-9.

Bhan, Gautam, Geetika Anand and Swastik Harish. 2014. *Policy Approaches to Affordable Housing in Urban India. Problems and possibilities*. Bangalore: Indian Institute for Human Settlements. https://smartnet.niua.org/sites/default/files/resources/IIHS_Housing.pdf.

Bremner, Lindsay. 2019. 'Planning the 2015 Chennai floods'. *Environment and Planning E: Nature and Space*. https://doi.org/10.1177/2514848619880130.

CMDA. 2008. *Second Master Plan for Chennai Metropolitan Area, 2026*. http://www.cmdachennai.gov.in/Volumel_English_PDF/Vol1_Chapter00_Introduction.pdf.

Coastal Resource Centre. 2016a. *Death by a Thousand Cuts: Report of public hearing held on loss of ecology and fisher livelihood in Ennore Creek*. https://storyofennore.files.wordpress.com/2016/03/ph_report.pdf.

Coastal Resource Centre. 2016b. *Deadly Poisoning of the Ennore Creek*. https://storyofennore.files.wordpress.com/2016/03/ph_report.pdf (accessed January 2020).

Coelho, Karen. 2016. 'Placing the poor in the flood path: Post-disaster slum resettlement in Chennai'. *Caravan*, 4 January 2016. http://www.caravanmagazine.in/vantage/placing-the-poor-in-the-flood-pathpost-disaster-slum-resettlement-in-chennai.

Coelho, Karen, A. Hariharan, M. Sukumar and T. Venkata. 2015. *Settlement and Struggle on Chennai's Buckingham Canal: Working class histories of the city*. Bangalore: Indian Institute for Human Settlements. https://iihs.co.in/knowledge-gateway/settlement-and-struggle-on-chennais-buckingham-canal-working-class-histories-of-the-city.

Deo Bardhan, Ashok and Samir K. Barua. 2015. 'Home equity conversion: Prospects in India'. *Economic and Political Weekly* 38 (30): 3209–12.

Doling, John and Richard Ronald. 2010. 'Home ownership and asset-based welfare'. *Journal of Housing and the Built Environment* 25 (2): 165–73. https://doi.org/10.1007/s10901-009-9177-6.

Drescher, Axel, Rüdiger Glaser, Constanze Pfeiffer, Jayshree Vencatesan, Elke Schliermann-Kraus, Stephanie Glaser, Marco Lechner and Paul Dostal. 2007. 'Risk assessment of extreme precipitation in the coastal areas of Chennai as an element of catastrophe prevention'. In *Forum DKKV/CEDIM: Disaster reduction in climate change*. https://www.academia.edu/28255781/Risk_assessment_of_extreme_precipitation_in_the_coastal_areas_of_Chennai_as_an_element_of_catastrophe_prevention.

Elangovan, Nattanmai Swaminathan, Vaithyanathan Lavanya and S. Arunthathi. 2017. 'Assessment of groundwater contamination in a suburban area of Chennai, Tamil Nadu, India'. *Environment, Development and Sustainability*. https://doi.org/10.1007/s10668-017-0007-9.

Few, Roger, Garima Jain, Chandni Singh, Mark Tebboth, Vasudha Chhotray, Hazel Marsh, Nihal Ranjit and Mythili Madhavan. 2021. *Why Representation Matters in Disaster Recovery*. London: British Academy. http://doi.org/10.5871/gcrf/9780856726569.001.

Gopalakrishnan, Seetha. 2017. 'No man's land'. India Water Portal, 18 January 2017. https://www.indiawaterportal.org/articles/no-mans-land.

Government of Tamil Nadu. 2014. *State Action Plan for Climate Change*. https://www.environment.tn.gov.in/tnsapcc.

Housing and Land Rights Network. n.d. *Voiceless No More*. https://www.hlrn.org.in/documents/Voiceless_No_More.pdf.

Housing and Land Rights Network. 2014. *Forced to the Fringes: Disasters of 'resettlement' in India. Report two: Kannagi Nagar, Chennai*. http://www.hic-sarp.org/documents/Forced_to_the_Fringes_Complete.pdf.

Indian Space Research Organisation. 2012. *Coastal Zones of India*. http://keralaczma.gov.in/pdfs/Coastal_Zones_of_India.pdf.

Information and Resource Centre for the Deprived Urban Communities and Housing and Land Rights Network. 2017. *From Deluge to Displacement: The impact of post-flood evictions and resettlement in Chennai*. http://hlrn.org.in/documents/Deluge_to_Displacement_Chennai.pdf.

Jain, Garima, Chandni Singh, Karen Coelho and Teja Malladi. 2017. *Long-Term Implications of Humanitarian Responses: The case of Chennai*. London: International Institute for Environment and Development. https://doi.org/http://pubs.iied.org/10840IIED.

Jain, Garima, Chandni Singh and Teja Malladi. 2017. *Rethinking Post-Disaster Relocation in Urban India*. London: International Institute for Environment and Development. http://pubs.iied.org/17430IIED/.

Janakarajan, S., John Butterworth, Patrick Moriarty and Charles Batchelor. 2007. 'Strengthened city, marginalised peri-urban villages: Stakeholder dialogues for inclusive urbanisation in Chennai, India'. In *Peri-Urban Water Conflicts Supporting Dialogue and Negotiation*, edited by John Butterworth, Raphaële Ducrot, Nicolas Faysse and S. Janakarajan, 51–75. Delft: IRC International Water and Sanitation Centre.

Jayaraman, Nityanand. 2015. 'Chennai floods are not a natural disaster – they've been created by unrestrained construction'. Scroll.In, 18 November 2015. https://scroll.in/article/769928/chennai-floods-are-not-a-natural-disaster-theyve-been-created-by-unrestrained-construction.

Jayaraman, Nityanand. 2016a. 'Chennai may just be masterminding its next flooding disaster'. Thewire.In, 21 June 2016. https://thewire.in/44393/chennai-may-just-be-masterminding-its-next-flooding-disaster.

Jayaraman, Nityanand. 2016b. 'Why engineering interventions won't prevent another flood in Chennai'. Scroll.In, 7 September 2016. https://scroll.in/article/815821/why-engineering-interventions-wont-prevent-another-flood-in-chennai.

Kennewell, David. 2016. *Flood Depth Map*. http://chennaifloodmanagement.org/en/layers/geonode%3Adepth_low. (Accessed July 2018, website now archived.)

Krishnamurthy, Rashmi and Kevin C. Desouza. 2015. 'Chennai, India'. *Cities* 42: 118–29. https://doi.org/10.1016/j.cities.2014.09.004.

Kudale, M.D. 2010. 'Impact of port development on the coastline and the need for protection'. *Indian Journal of Geo-Marine Sciences* 39 (4): 594–604. http://nopr.niscair.res.in/handle/123456789/10808.

Kumar, A. Arun and Pravin D. Kunte. 2012. 'Coastal vulnerability assessment for Chennai, east coast of India using geospatial techniques'. *Natural Hazards* 64 (1): 853–72. DOI:10.1007/s11069-012-0276-4

Lavell, Allan and Andrew Maskrey. 2014. 'The future of disaster risk management'. *Environmental Hazards* 13 (4): 267–80. https://doi.org/10.1080/17477891.2014.935282.

Ministry of Environment and Forests. 2010. 'Climate change and India, a 4x4 assessment: A sectoral and regional analysis for 2030s'. http://www.indiaenvironmentportal.org.in/content/318733/climate-change-and-india-a-4x4-assessment-a-sectoral-and-regional-analysis-for-2030s.

Narayan, Priti. 2018. 'Displacement as disaster relief: Environmental gentrification and state informality in developing Chennai'. *Just Green Enough* 139 (150): 139–50. https://doi.org/10.9774/gleaf.9781315229515_11.

Pahwa-Gajjar, Sumetee, Garima Jain, Chandni Singh and Kavya Michael. 2019. 'Entrenched vulnerabilities: Evaluating climate justice across development and adaptation responses in southern India'. In *Climate Futures: Re-imagining global climate justice*, edited by K.K. Bhavnani, J. Foran, P. Kurian and D. Munshi, 200–12. London: Zed.

Srinivasan, Veena. 2008. 'An integrated framework for analysis of water supply strategies in a developing city: Chennai, India'. PhD thesis, Stanford University.

Srinivasan, Veena, Karen C. Seto, Ruth Emerson and Steven M. Gorelick. 2013. 'The impact of urbanization on water vulnerability: A coupled human–environment system approach for Chennai, India'. *Global Environmental Change* 23 (1): 229–39. https://doi.org/10.1016/j.gloenvcha.2012.10.002.

Tamil Nadu Coastal Zone Management Authority. 2011. 'Approved CZMP for Chennai CMDA'. https://www.environment.tn.gov.in/czmpmaps.

Tamil Nadu Slums Clearance Board. n.d. 'Jawaharlal Nehru National Urban Renewal Mission (JnNURM) Housing Programme'. http://www.tnscb.org/jawaharlal-nehru-national-urban-renewal-mission-jnnurm.

Tamil Nadu State Disaster Management Authority. 2018. *State Disaster Management Perspective Plan 2018–2030*. https://tnsdma.tn.gov.in/app/webroot/img/document/SDMP-29-08.pdf.

Thomas, Joseph. 2010. *Sustainable Fresh Water Supply for Chennai City, Tamil Nadu, India: A status update*. https://www.scribd.com/document/80911596/Sustainable-Fresh-Water-Supply-for-Chennai-City-Main-Paper.

UN-Habitat. 2014. *The Right to Adequate Housing*. https://www.ohchr.org/documents/publications/fs21_rev_1_housing_en.pdf.

Vencatesan, Jayshree, R.J. Ranjit Daniels, J. Stephen Jayaseelan and N. Muthu Karthick. 2014. *Comprehensive Management Plan for Pallikaranai Marsh 2014–2019*. Care Earth Trust.

Venkat, T. and M. Subadevan. 2015. *Implementation of JnNURM-BSUP: A case study of the housing sector in Chennai. Report for the project impact of infrastructure and governance transformations on small, medium and big cities in India*. Chennai: Tata Institute of Social Sciences. https://urk.tiss.edu/wp-content/uploads/2020/08/Chennai_JNNURM_case-study-Final.pdf.

Vijayabaskar, M., Karen Coelho, Sriharini Narayanan and T. Venkat. 2011. *State Level Background Paper on Tamil Nadu for the Urban Infrastructure Reforms Facility*. Chennai: Tata Institute of Social Sciences. http://urk.tiss.edu/images/pdf/Tamil-Nadu-State-level-Background-Paper.pdf.

Viswanathan, Nirupama. 2018. 'Public consultation sans public for river project'. *New Indian Express*, 7 April 2018. https://www.newindianexpress.com/states/tamil-nadu/2018/apr/07/tamil-nadu-public-consultation-sans-public-for-river-project-1798166.html.

Wamsler, Christine. 2004. 'Managing urban risk: Perceptions of housing and planning as a tool for reducing disaster risk'. *Global Built Environment Review* 4 (2): 11–28. https://portal.research.lu.se/portal/files/2698440/3629168.pdf.

15

Flood risk-induced relocation in urban areas: case studies of Bwaise and Natete, Kampala

Teddy Kisembo

Global climate and land-use changes are expected to induce significant alterations in climate and hydrological regimes in urban areas, producing flash floods with significant impacts in terms of damage to property and loss of human life. This will force people to relocate in search of a lower risk location (Minninger and Wirsching 2015). Climate change is accentuating decisions for relocation partly due to the shortened recovery period between flash flood events, which are becoming more frequent. Climate-induced extreme events lead to damage to infrastructure, houses and livelihoods, causing households and other actors to reach the tipping points[1] for deciding on relocation and resettlement.

Though the impact of climate change on localised extreme rainfall events is still not well understood because of limitations of modelling and data, it is already evident that flash floods are affecting local urban areas more frequently and intensely (Bicknell, Dodman and Satterthwaite 2009). The implication of the increased frequency and severity of flash floods is that resettlement[2] and relocation[3] will become key needs in policy- and decision-making at multiple scales. Relocation and resettlement are often the result of a variety of layered causes – economic, social and political – which are accentuated by the changing environment as well as development and demographic conditions.

Kampala experiences extreme events, with rainfall exceeding 300 mm per month in the city region (Lwasa 2010). The hilly terrain with valleys that have suffered spontaneous housing and infrastructure development has exposed many households to flash floods, which also affect city transportation, have knock-on health effects, and damage infrastructure, causing cumulative damages and losses to the city and its residents. Further, environmental degradation in Kampala is largely characterised by the reclaiming of wetlands, clearance of vegetation and dumping of rubbish in water channels, all of which interfere with water flow and make neighbouring communities vulnerable to both flash flooding and waterlogging. Each year there are climatic events that present risks to city residents and urban systems (Douglas et al. 2008). Though floods in Kampala do not generally have a very long duration – normally lasting from several hours to at most two days – they do cause major disruption to the lives of Kampala's citizens and they entail high economic and social costs (Barrow et al. 2016). Generally, the relatively poorer citizens of Kampala experience more of the burden of flooding, as many of them live in the relatively low-lying valleys and wetlands (Sliuzas et al. 2013). The urban poor live in slums that are at high risk from the impacts of climate and natural hazards. Their choice of where to live is driven by a series of trade-offs between what is affordable, proximity to income-earning opportunities, and where individuals may have social networks and kinship ties. Areas that are affordable to the poor are typically on hazard-prone lands deemed undesirable to others, which are usually informal settlements with insecure tenure (Baker 2012).

This chapter analyses households' decisions to relocate or not relocate based on the study of two neighbourhoods in Kampala. The objectives of this chapter are threefold: to analyse the drivers and the tipping points at which people decide to move or not; to identify the reasons why people tolerate risks; and to discuss the household process of implementing decisions regarding voluntary and involuntary relocation.

Framing the analysis of risk-induced relocation

The decision to move from a hazard-prone area, or to remain, is influenced by many factors. People's perception of risk is always a critical point in a process that may eventually lead to relocation, whether voluntarily or involuntarily (see Chapter 4 by Johnson et al. in this book). When there is a perceived threat to the lives, livelihood or assets of a household, the interplay of each factor weighs in the decision to relocate or not. External threats in the context of this chapter are related to climate-induced flash floods as part of the broader environmental hazards. Poverty, failing ecosystems, vulnerability to natural hazards and gradual climate-driven environmental changes are all linked to the need for relocation (Bunce, Rosendo and Brown 2009).

This chapter employs a framework that understands the macro factors shaping hazards as spatial, temporal and variable (Douglas et al. 2008; Kithiia 2011). These factors may occur gradually or suddenly, and governance and city management policies also interact with the factors that lead to perceived or actual threat to the households. Once a hazard event occurs, the decision-making process starts and different factors including economic, social, health-related, household characteristics, costs of reducing risk and costs of moving are weighed differently by different households before making a decision (Lwasa et al. 2009; McBean 2012). This framing recognises that drivers and conditioning factors do not necessarily mean that relocation will occur. Whether relocation occurs or not depends on a series of intervening factors and personal and household characteristics. Moreover, substantial social, economic and human capital may be required to enable people to relocate.

In this chapter, the cumulative effects of frequent flash floods are used to explain how and when households get to the point of deciding to relocate or not. Likewise, governance and institutional factors, though inherent at the household level in shaping the decisions, may have an independent influence on the decision around involuntary relocation. Involuntary relocation is usually project-based and will involve market-based valuation of the household assets exposed to floods such that a decision is made for the affected households to relocate. There are cases where the valuation prolongs the negotiations before relocation occurs, exposing the household to more frequent flash floods. The people who tend to stay may be poor, but they may also be households with assets worth protecting or costly to move.

Materials and methods

Research study area

Kampala has grown to be the largest urban centre and the only city in Uganda. It is Uganda's political seat and the country's economic hub, accounting for 80 per cent of industrial and commercial activities and generating 65 per cent of national GDP (KCCA 2014). The city has an estimated 1.75 million residents and is a working environment for an estimated daily workforce of 4.5 million, with an annual demographic growth rate of 3.9 per cent (KCCA 2014). Its growing population, high level of informality and service delivery problems are typical of many African cities (Chereni et al. 2020). Kampala experiences flash floods virtually every year, leaving little room for recovery by households or institutions. Flood-related losses and damage to people's property are escalating, while the cost of maintaining roads and drainage channels is also on the rise. One of the key outcomes of flood-related risk is a downturn in public health. The incidence of water-borne diseases such as cholera, typhoid, dysentery and malaria, which are linked to flood and precipitation events characterised by variable climate, is increasing.

The research was carried out in Kampala with a focus on two neighbourhoods, Bwaise III and Natete, both of which are highly prone to flash floods (see Figure 15.1). These two neighbourhoods were chosen as they enabled us to understand the relocation decisions of households affected by flash floods, including those that had relocated within the neighbourhood. The majority of the residents in these settlements are low-income earners, involved in small-scale businesses within the area, such that a large number of people, infrastructure, livelihoods and social services are exposed to severe destruction, damage, dampness and health challenges when it floods. For some, their vulnerability further increases with the rising costs of individual anti-flood interventions. For others,

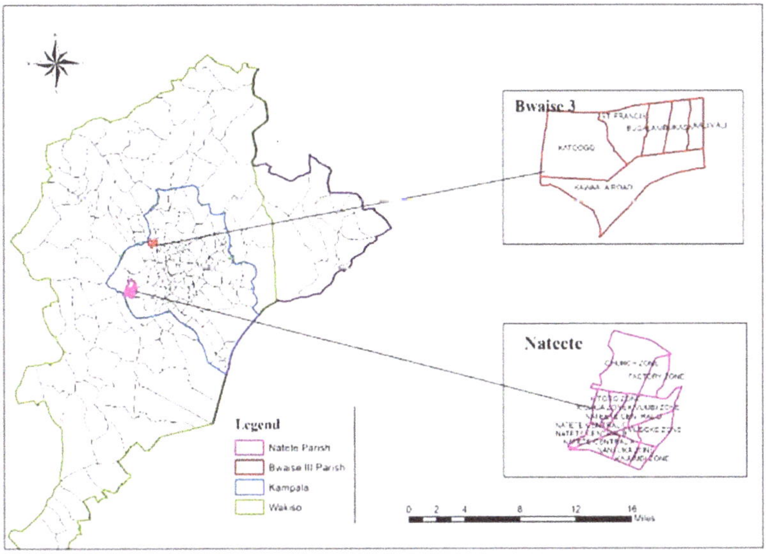

Figure 15.1 Location of research areas within greater Kampala. © Teddy Kisembo.

the choice to relocate from the area engenders additional costs and loss of social networks.

Bwaise III Parish

Bwaise III Parish is located in the Kawempe division, 5 km from the city centre. It is located along the downstream area of a primary drain, the Lubigi. The neighbourhood is a busy commercial centre traversed by the Kampala–Gulu highway linking the north of the country to the capital. The parish has five villages or zones – St Francis, Kalimali, Bukasa, Katoogo and Bugalani – with most of the area located in the swamp, making it significantly prone to flooding. Bwaise III is a densely populated area with approximately thirty-five thousand people and an estimated seven thousand households with an average size of five people each (Actogether Uganda 2017). The majority of the residents are low-income earners, involved in small-scale activities within the area. The parish is also largely unplanned and highly built up, with a mixture of housing, shops, schools, religious buildings, markets and health centres concentrated in the same area (Ajambo 2013).

Natete Parish

Natete Parish is located in Lubaga division, on the south-western edge of the city of Kampala along Nsooba drainage channel. Natete has an estimated population of forty-five thousand people living in nine thousand households with an average household size of five people each (Actogether Uganda 2017). Natete Parish is a high-density settlement comprising residential areas and light industry. Despite inadequate infrastructure, it is an economically vibrant area, steadily increasing its contribution to Kampala's economy (Dodman et al. 2015).

Data collection

The study is based on an exploratory and diagnostic type of research in which data was collected through interviews. These captured information relevant to determining the different form of relocations associated with flooding, understanding tipping points that make people relocate, the perceived tolerable risk that makes people stay and the process of relocation.

Qualitative data was used to offer more in-depth explanations of the temporal dimension of relocations. Sixteen interviews were conducted with policymakers to gain more insight into the environment and the contextual factors related to flood-induced relocation in Kampala.

A total of 54 respondents were interviewed through a snowball sampling process to target households that had relocated, while 26 respondents were interviewed through random sampling for people living in flood-prone areas. We also interviewed households who had relocated within the same neighbourhood, after identifying them with the help of field guides.

Data analysis

To understand the hazard events, impacts and relocation decisions, the study employed thematic content analysis using the in-depth interviews from open-ended questionnaires to describe the motivation for relocation, what makes people tolerate the risk and the strategies for coping with flooding. Some supportive quantitative data is used, but this study mainly relies on views and experiences expressed during the interviews. This helps the nuanced understanding of tipping points for relocation decisions.

Findings

Different forms of relocations induced by flooding

The forms of relocation found across the settlements were temporary relocation (this is largely voluntary, within and outside the settlements) and permanent relocation (both voluntary and involuntary, within and outside the settlement).

Temporary relocations

Across both sites, 40 per cent of respondents relocate temporarily and then come back to their homes after the waters have receded. This temporary relocation can be seen as a coping response to the emergency since people often return to their homes immediately after the waters recede. Since floods occur frequently, populations have become used to tackling the consequence by seeking temporary shelter in various places. Ten per cent of respondents across the two sites relocated temporarily during flood events *within* their settlements, either to a friend or relative whose place is less prone to flooding or where the water doesn't enter the house. Ten per cent relocated to friends or relatives *outside* the sites, in areas such as Kawempe, Nabweru, Ndeeba and Kyengera. The remaining 20 per cent across the two sites relocated at the roadside, or on main roads where they can sleep, cook or just stay there until the waters recede and they can return to their homes.

Permanent relocation

Permanent relocation is considered by the affected people to be a normal or near-normal adaptation strategy for flooding. Populations that have relocated permanently also view it as a coping mechanism and survival strategy. However, permanent relocation is a choice not open to everyone as it depends on resources, information and other social and personal factors.

The study shows that permanent relocations covered 21.4 per cent of all cases, with 14.3 per cent relocated voluntarily and 7.1 per cent involuntarily. The involuntary relocation was from Bwaise during the widening of the Lubigi drainage channel. Therefore, these were people that were affected by the Second Kampala Institutional and Infrastructure Development Project (KIIDP2).[4] Most of the permanent relocations were from areas that are highly prone to flooding to areas that are less prone or not prone at all. However, some relocated to areas outside of their settlements. Of the 21.4 per cent of respondents who have relocated permanently across the two sites, 11.4 per cent relocated within their neighbourhood in Bwaise, 4.3 per cent relocated within their neighbourhood in Natete, and 5.7 per cent relocated outside the neighbourhoods of Bwaise and Natete to places like Ntinda, Kinaawa, Kawempe and Kyengera.

There is a direct link between relocation and displacement.[5] Before populations can relocate either temporarily or permanently, voluntarily or involuntarily, there has to be some form of displacement due to flooding of their houses, damage to housing and assets etc., necessitating relocation. However, the displacement for those who relocate is temporary, because after the waters recede they return to their homes.

Tipping points that make people relocate

Tipping points are conditions or thresholds at which a series of flood events or incidents become significant enough to cause households or individuals to relocate permanently. These households do not seem to have a strong buffer for recovery from the frequent high impacts of flash floods to housing, livelihoods and health. These households were somehow displaced because their livelihoods were being threatened by the slow-onset effects of flooding and needed to find new permanent homes

Figure 15.2 Property damaged and abandoned due to flooding in Bwaise III Parish, Bukasa zone. © Teddy Kisembo.

for themselves (see Figure 15.2). Across both sites, there were several different reasons for households reaching the tipping points, and many households indicated more than one reason:

- when the floodwaters inundate the houses frequently during rainy seasons
- constant loss and damage of property
- frequent health risk during rainy seasons (with diseases such as cholera, foot diseases and diarrhoea)
- destruction of livelihoods
- the high cost of managing floods, which in the long run puts a strain on their income
- children at risk of drowning and illness
- children skipping school for fear of drowning
- general frustration with the situation.

When flooding events coincide with economic or social stressors, the potential for relocation becomes more and more significant. As Figure 15.3 shows, the point where the flood episodes and possibility of relocation cross is the tipping point. Below it, the risk is tolerable.

Assets are reduced as flood episodes increase, and the possibility for permanent relocation also increases. To a great extent, the asset portfolios of individuals, households and communities determine their adaptive capacity about avoiding risk – meaning that when an individual's

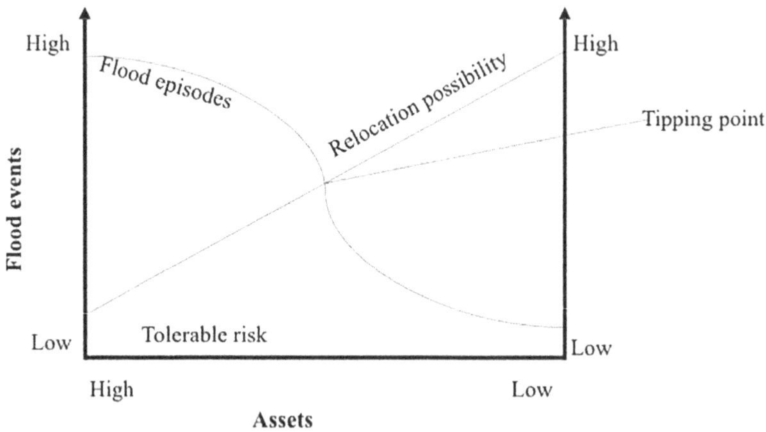

Figure 15.3 The tipping point at which people decide to relocate. © Teddy Kisembo.

or household's assets reduce, their versatile limit is undermined, which increases the likelihood of them moving. Assets are means of constructing, reconstructing and diversifying an individual's, household's or community's livelihood base, increasing their capabilities to invest and contribute to individual, household and community wellbeing (Bazaz et al. 2016).

Reasons why people tolerate risk

The present section explains why people live with the associated challenges of flood-prone areas. This covers those who able and willing to tolerate the risk and those who do not wish to relocate at all or those who wish to relocate but are unable to do so. Several reasons seem to influence the level and length of tolerance of flood risk by people living and working in Bwaise and Natete (see Figure 15.4). It is advantageous for some households to stay and others to relocate.

Twenty per cent of the respondents can tolerate the flood risk by coping with impacts because they have lived in their settlements for a long time, have become used to the flood and have nowhere else to go. One of the respondents from Bwaise said: 'Floods come and go and life goes on. It isn't like the waters stay for a week, only for a few hours. We are kind of used to that' (interview with resident of Bwaise III Parish, Kalimali zone by Teddy Kisembo, 13 June 2016). Their lives revolve

Figure 15.4 People going on with their lives amid flooding in Natete, Nafuka zone. © Teddy Kisembo.

around their neighbourhoods, which makes them tolerate the risk. They are immobile because they are not willing to relocate at any cost.

Other reasons why people do not want to relocate from their residences are social ties and a sense of belonging that comes with that. Having lived with their neighbours for so long, social relations have grown strong as years go by. With such attachment comes a sense of belonging, which in turn makes it difficult for some households to relocate.

People across the two sites are tolerant of the risk because of the location of their places of work or business. Although they are affected by the floods in terms of loss of customers and machinery and at times damage to stock, the benefits of doing business in these communities seem to outweigh the impacts caused by the frequent floods.

Affordable or cheap accommodation is also one of the reasons why some households tolerate flood risk. The only reason they are tolerant of flood risk is that their communities offer cheap housing and they cannot afford to move to places where the rent is too high for them. In both settlements, rent may be as low as 10,000 Ugandan shillings (approximately US$2.70) per month, which means these communities are affordable for them. Thus, it is the low incomes of these individuals which make them have to tolerate the risk.

Livelihoods formed around their neighbourhoods are another reason some residents of Bwaise and Natete tolerate flood hazard. This is coupled with social ties: they may have a history of living in these settlements for a long time and of doing business or trade within the communities. These settlements are not only places of residence but also a place of doing business, ranging from food vending and retail shops to laundry, carpentry and vehicle repairs. Relocating would mean recreating this livelihood, and this is so expensive for them that they would rather tolerate the impacts of flooding.

Contentment is another reason that was mentioned why people tolerate risk in Bwaise and Natete. The respondents said they are content where they are. This can be attributed to the fact they own land in these settlements and are not willing to relocate somewhere else where they would have to begin renting. Contentment can also be attributed to social identity or ties, livelihoods and having lived in a place for so long. Residents may be content with a neighbourhood that is affordable in terms of the housing and services it offers, and close to the city centre.

The study also revealed that people who have lived somewhere for less than a year and those who have lived there for one to five years are willing to tolerate risk. This can be attributed to the fact that they have just moved into the settlement and they are not in a position to take on the cost of moving again so soon. Living in a flood-prone area is due to their limited budget and the need to access employment services, which in turn, exposes them to flood hazard.

Decisions about relocation by residents

Relocation is based on a decision made by individuals or households that is influenced by many interconnected factors. These decisions attempt to ensure survival and the ability to live in dignity. People often decide to leave their homes when changes in several factors coincide. If flooding in Bwaise and Natete continues to advance, worsening or destroying livelihoods and the properties of more and more people, relocation will become unavoidable. Individuals make decisions on their location and movements based on their quality of life and the livelihoods of themselves and their families.

Households that relocate are motivated by aspirations to improve their lives and livelihoods. Some leave the previous home out of choice and others are obliged to do so, like those evicted by the drainage channel enlargement projects. Relocation, particularly permanent relocation, involves both choice and constraints. Most of the households or individuals have the choice to relocate but they are constrained financially to move. The choice of deciding to relocate and do something different or interesting is the privilege of people with enough resources and money to do so. One of the respondents' answers as to why she has not yet relocated although she would love to move was 'Poverty … no person likes to live in a flooded area' (interview with resident of Natete Parish, Nafuka zone by Teddy Kisembo, 19 January 2016). Another respondent said: 'I have not yet got the money to pay for advance rent … you know that landlord wants you to pay for an advance of 3–4 months' (interview with resident of Bwaise III Parish, Kalimali zone by Teddy Kisembo, 13 June 2016). Individuals and families make decisions to relocate based on analysing the possibilities of settling elsewhere and the available resources for making the move.

There is a clear sense of resignation and submission to the consequences of living in an area that floods regularly (see Figure 15.5). This suggests that, for the most part, the respondents are tolerating the flood risk. Any decision to relocate does not, therefore, appear to be primarily determined by flood risk and indicates that there are other

Figure 15.5 Flooded area in Natete Parish, Nafuka zone. © Teddy Kisembo.

more fundamental factors at play that influence decisions about when to move. The data suggests that their decision-making might be influenced by other factors, such as constant failure to manage the floods, the high cost of managing floods by households and the reduction of household assets.

There are overlapping issues where people tolerate risk because they are unable to relocate due to poverty. For example, some of the respondents had entertained the thought of moving from their neighbourhood. Issues preventing them from moving included not finding another suitable place, not finding a buyer for the current place or not having enough money to buy a place in another location. Thus, the issues of access to land, affordability, relocation costs and social ties seem more influential on decisions around relocation than just flood risk (see Chapter 9 by Marx in this book).

Vulnerability to extreme events such as floods and the ability to move are related to social, economic and political capital. People with low to medium asset levels often become trapped and unable to move permanently, despite frequent flooding events. Low involvement in social networks beyond their settlements also increases people's possibility of being trapped. Trapped populations are those people who aspire to relocate for their protection but cannot do so. Our research found that 41 per cent of the respondents who stay are trapped populations because they have the desire to leave their settlements – or are in desperate need to leave – but they do not see a way to move to new places that are not prone to flooding because they do not have the financial ability to relocate.

The population that stays can be categorised into two groups: trapped populations and immobile populations (that is, people who choose to stay). The immobile are immobile out of choice, while the trapped are unable to relocate. Therefore, it is important to consider *aspiration* and *ability* as key concepts in analysing relocation. The trapped population always has a wish to relocate, though they face a challenge in the realisation of that wish; therefore it is important to understand why these people want to relocate but are unable to do so. When trapped in a fluctuating process which can be amplified by flooding events, there is a need to distinguish between not wanting to relocate and not being able to relocate and the possibility of voluntary immobility. Distinguishing those who wish to move (or need to do so in times of crisis) but remain in situ from those who do not wish to move is likely to be extremely difficult, not least because people's judgement about whether it is necessary to relocate is likely to change over even quite short periods (Ulla 2016).

City-level strategies for managing flood impacts on relocation

This section presents the discussions from interviews with the city authorities about the relationship between encroachment on wetlands and floods and the implication of these interacting factors for Kampala.

Kampala Capital City Authority (KCCA) is trying to scale up the greening of all open spaces to deter unnecessary drain- or stormwater run-off. Unfortunately, there is little space for KCCA to bank on because property developers are slowly converting originally low-density development into high-density development. The KCCA Physical Planning Department is trying to encourage developers to both pave and commit some space on their sites for greening. KCCA also hope soon to pass a policy where developers adopt on-site water harvesting to reduce the water run-off.

KCCA is trying as much as possible to incorporate flood management within the design by specifying how to use septic systems and how to discharge waste on site, although some developers decide not to go to KCCA for development approval. This indicates that KCCA understands the role wetlands play in reducing flooding compared to the technical solutions of the construction of drainage channels, though there seems to be little evidence to enable the conservation and preservation of the wetlands.

Complexity seems to typify the process of controlling development and protecting the wetlands from encroachment. The Ministry of Lands, Housing and Urban Development has a stake in registering land, while KCCA only approves the development. KCCA faces a challenge whereby people who are supposed to be implementing the recommendations put forward do not do so because these recommendations affect the implementers, and they are required to give up some of the lands that have been encroached on. The Directorate of Public Health and Environment in KCCA reviews environmental impact assessments and gives comments to NEMA (the National Environmental Management Authority). However, their comments are not binding: NEMA can consider KCCA's comments or disregard them. This leaves KCCA with the role of examining building plans and monitoring developments in wetlands while NEMA examines environmental impacts on development.

The government is embarking on the process of deregistration or cancellation of land titles in wetlands as a way of trying to save the wetlands from perishing. The logic behind the cancellation of titles is not for 'flood risk reduction' directly, but rather for the protection of ecologically important areas of the city by stopping the degradation of wetlands.

However, this maintenance of wetlands performs several ecological functions, such as reducing flooding. Deregistration of people means that people will have to relocate after being compensated.

Conclusion

Flood-induced relocation in Kampala seems to be a response that is taken at the household level to diversify income streams and secure livelihoods in the face of deteriorating environmental and living conditions. Evidence from the study suggests that flooding destroys and damages property, and affects incomes and health, hence affecting access to livelihood assets at household level, which then directly causes relocation.

Evidence from the research also suggests that flood-induced relocation is a coping strategy for households who are affected by flooding and can afford to relocate. The survey revealed that the households used relocation as a coping strategy for flooding events either temporarily or permanently. Relocation can help reduce risk to lives, livelihoods and ecosystems. It can also contribute to income diversification and enhance the overall capacity of households and communities to cope with flooding events. However, relocation is a coping strategy not available to everyone as it depends on resources, information and other social and personal privileges.

Those who are unable to move away from potential danger have inevitably lost a lot more, too. There are reasons to be concerned for the populations that are unable to relocate: their inability to relocate magnifies their vulnerability to flooding. To be 'trapped', individuals must not only lack the ability to move but also either want or need to move.

The people living and continuing to stay in flood-prone areas can use flood risk as an opportunity whereby living with the risk provides an opportunity to establish or maintain an income flow that would otherwise not be possible. From a poor household or small enterprise perspective, living with flood risks on encroached land is likely to play an important role in making livelihoods possible or sustaining them. That is, the 'risk' will create an opportunity to start something, however meagre or slim the margins, and risk can be an opportunity to transform society into a higher level of sustainability.

KCCA's focus on the flood measures prevents them from discussing relocation as an adaptive strategy. There is a need for officials in KCCA to shift the understanding of flooding and its impact on people's mobility from technological to social, and from narrow-sighted to open-minded problem-solving. Rather than seeing flooding as a sudden-onset short-term crisis, policymakers should adopt a holistic perspective to challenge the norm of relocation and address relocation as an adaptation strategy. Adaptation strategies can take the form of a portfolio of solutions for implementing the rights of people to move, among other measures.

Notes

1. A tipping point is the threshold that, when exceeded, will enable or drive people or households to move or relocate.
2. Resettlement is a major integrated, comprehensive movement of people and families which normally involves significant distances between the origin and the new location.
3. Relocation refers to short-distance, non-systematic movements of families or individuals from hazard-prone locations to nearby areas.
4. The Second Kampala Institutional and Infrastructure Development Project (KIIDP2) seeks to enhance the infrastructure and institutional capacity of Kampala Capital City Authority (KCCA) and improve urban mobility for inclusive economic growth. This five-year project is worth US$183.7 million and its implementation started in May 2015. The project is funded by the World Bank and the government of Uganda, and is implemented by KCCA.
5. Displacement is a process related to a disruption of the functioning of a household at any scale due to flood events interacting with conditions of exposure, vulnerability and capacity, thereby putting them out of place.

References

Actogether Uganda. 2017. *Kampala Slum Profiles*. https://knowyourcity.info/wp-content/uploads/2015/04/KAMPALA_MAPS_BOOK_small_file.pdf.

Ajambo, Susan. 2013. 'Promoting private–public synergies for managing flooding in Kampala City: A case stydy of Bwaise, Parish III, Kampele division', master's thesis, University of Adger. https://uia.brage.unit.no/uia-xmlui/bitstream/handle/11250/135267/Ajambo%2c%20Susan%20oppgaven.pdf?sequence=1&isAllowed=y.

Baker, Judy L., ed. 2012. *Climate Change, Disaster Risk, and the Urban Poor: Cities building resilience for a changing world*. Washington, DC: World Bank. https://openknowledge.worldbank.org/handle/10986/6018.

Barrow, Charlotte, Cassidy Johnson, Shuaib Lwasa and Colin Marx. 2016. 'Uganda site level report'. *Reducing Relocation Risk in Urban Areas*. https://www.ucl.ac.uk/bartlett/development/sites/bartlett/files/wp2_site_level_dpu_report_rev.pdf.

Bazaz, Amir, Garima Jain, Teja Malladi and Sushmita Ramoji. 2016. *Reducing Relocation Risk in Urban India Risk Assessment Report: Framings and illustrations*. https://doi.org/10.24943/cirf5.2016.

Bicknell, Jane, David Dodman and David Satterthwaite, eds. 2009. *Adapting Cities to Climate Change: Understanding and addressing the development challenges*. London: Earthscan.

Bunce, Matthew, Sergio Rosendo and Katrina Brown. 2009. 'Perceptions of climate change, multiple stressors and livelihoods on marginal African coasts'. *Environment, Development and Sustainability* 12 (3): 407–40. https://doi.org/10.1007/s10668-009-9203-6.

Chereni, Simbarashe, Martin V. Maarseveen, Richard V. Sliuzas and Johannes Flacke. 2020. 'The influence of governance rearrangements on flood risk management in Kampala, Uganda'. *Environmental Policy and Governance* 30: 151–63. https://doi.org/10.1002/eet.1881.

Dodman, David, Katarina Soltesova, David Satterthwaite and Cecilia Tacoli. 2015. *Understanding the Assessment and Reduction of Vulnerability to Climate Change in African Cities: A focus on low-income and informal settlements*. https://www.afd.fr/sites/afd/files/imported-files/Serie-Grise-Understanding-Assessment-Reduction-Vulnerability.pdf.

Douglas, Ian, Kurshid Alam, Maryanne Maghenda, Yasmin Mcdonnell, Louise Mclean and Jack Campbell. 2008. 'Unjust waters: Climate change, flooding and the urban poor in Africa'. *Environment and Urbanization* 20 (1): 187–205. https://doi.org/10.1177/0956247808089156.

KCCA. 2014. *Laying the Foundation for Kampala City Transformation: Strategic plan 2014/15–2018/19*. https://www.kcca.go.ug/uploads/KCCA_STRATEGI_PLAN_2015-2016.pdf.

Kithiia, J. 2011. 'Climate change risk responses in East African cities: Need, barriers and opportunities'. *Current Opinion in Environmental Sustainability* 3 (3): 176–80. https://doi.org/10.1016/j.cosust.2010.12.002.

Lwasa, Shuaib. 2010. 'Adapting urban areas in Africa to climate change: The case of Kampala'. *Current Opinion in Environmental Sustainability* 2: 166–71. https://doi.org/10.1016/j.cosust.2010.06.009.

Lwasa, Shuaib, M. Tenywa, G.J. Majaliwa Mwanjalolo, H. Sengendo and G. Prain. 2009. 'Enhancing adaptation of poor urban dwellers to the effects of climate variability and change'. *IOP Conference Series: Earth and Environmental Science* 6 (33): 332002. https://doi.org/10.1088/1755-1307/6/33/332002.

McBean, Gordon A. 2012. 'Integrating disaster risk reduction towards sustainable development'. *Current Opinion in Environmental Sustainability* 4 (1): 122–7. https://doi.org/10.1016/j.cosust.2012.01.002.

Minninger, Sabine and Sophia Wirsching. 2015. *Climate-Induced Displacement and Migration: Policy gaps and policy alternative*. Dhaka: Center for Participatory Research and Development. https://cprdbd.org/wp-content/uploads/2019/11/briefing_paper_climate_induced_displacement_and_migration.pdf.

Sliuzas, R.V., V.G. Jetten, J. Flacke, Shuaib Lwasa, E.J. Wasige and K.Y. Pettersen. 2013. *Flood Risk Assessment, Strategies and Actions for Improving Flood Risk Management in Kampala: Final report of integrated flood management project Kampala*. Enschede: University of Twente, Faculty of Geo-Information Science and Earth Observation.

Ulla, Tamara. 2016. 'El Niño floods in Argentina: A story of displacement and vulnerability'. In *The State of Environmental Migration 2016: A review of 2015*, edited by François Gemenne, Caroline Zickgraf and Dina Ionesco, 124–47. Liege: Presses Universitaires de Liege. http://labos.ulg.ac.be/hugo/wp-content/uploads/sites/38/2017/11/The-State-of-Environmental-Migration-2016-124-148.pdf.

Conclusion

Garima Jain, Allan Lavell and Cassidy Johnson

At the outset of the research presented in this volume, we hypothesised a distinction between the different forms of resettlement and relocation. Through the research, this typology was developed further, as explored by Allan Lavell in Chapter 1, and it became evident that the characteristics of the people, their relationship with the original and relocation sites, and the decision-making and implementation processes have a strong bearing on the eventual outcomes of intervention on the people and the city. The significant repetition of similar 'errors' in different contexts and cases suggests that the problem is more structural than contextual, and that it relates more to the ways resettlement is constructed as a problem and the associated sectoral mindsets than to specific, individual causes. The latter are, rather, a product of the former.

Several of the contributions to this book illustrate how decision-making processes arrive at resettlement and relocation as a 'solution' for reducing exposure to hazards in a particular location, without sufficient consensus within the communities or assessment of alternative interventions. This was especially pronounced in the contributions by Garima Jain et al. (Chapters 3 and 14), Cassidy Johnson et al. (Chapter 4), Shuaib Lwasa et al. (Chapter 5), and Elizabeth Mansilla (Chapter 13). Resettlement and relocation are often immersed in and confused by other circumstances and used as an excuse for achieving other goals such as urban redevelopment, infrastructure works or the modernisation of space. In the process, they create significant tangible and intangible costs borne disproportionately by the marginalised communities who are moved, and in the long term this also impacts on the functioning of the city, for example by increasing urban sprawl.

Lack of adequate land in urban areas is found among the key drivers for such decisions. As Colin Marx explains in Chapter 9, land tenure arrangements impact on whether people are able to settle in environmentally sensitive areas, and this affects the power structures that enable them to stay there. In some cases, such as those explored in the contributions by Yves Cabannes (Chapter 10), Giovanna Astolfo (Chapter 11) and Garima Jain et al. (Chapter 14), it is evident that in a context where the power is skewed between the people and the state, people are evicted from high-value land to far-off areas that push the poor further into deprivation. Some of these practices, being devoid of risk-sensitive planning approaches, locate the affordable housing sites on less valued lands that are environmentally sensitive, such as marshlands, not just creating hazard risk for the resettled people, but also exacerbating or creating new environmental risks for the city.

This is also partly caused by the siloed approach to disaster risk reduction and development-centric policies and practices, as illustrated by Allan Lavell (Chapter 1) and Garima Jain et al. (Chapters 3 and 14). The chapters in this book also indicate how preventative risk reduction practices often fall under the purview of development agencies, who have limited knowledge of 'risk', and take the traditional route of hazard exposure reduction as the means for risk reduction. At the same time, post-disaster housing, which is undertaken by disaster management agencies, does not see the long-term development aspects associated with housing as a priority, creating new socio-economic challenges for the resettled communities.

On this subject, Anne-Catherine Chardon (Chapter 2) and Garima Jain et al. (Chapter 14) argue that housing provision needs to be looked at as the building of a habitat, that is, more than just the provision of shelter but also addressing the needs of safety, access to livelihoods and social services, and secure tenure, with least disruption to the socio-economic systems of communities. Elizabeth Mansilla (Chapter 13) and Shuaib Lwasa et al. (Chapter 5) further support this argument by suggesting looking at relocation and resettlement interventions as a means to address the overall development objectives at the city scale, while reducing existing risks and avoiding risk creation, to take advantage of the opportunity of the investments being made.

Meanwhile, it has also become evident through the contributions from Cassidy Johnson et al. (Chapter 4), Shuaib Lwasa et al. (Chapter 5), Emily Wilkinson (Chapter 6) and Teddy Kisembo (Chapter 15) that along with place attachment, people's own abilities to reduce risk have a direct bearing on their decision-making: whether they are willing to move from or stay in hazard-exposed areas. This has at least equal impact on these decisions to the mere knowledge of hazard exposure.

Garima Jain (Chapter 3), Cassidy Johnson et al. (Chapter 4), Shuaib Lwasa et al. (Chapter 5) and Emily Wilkinson (Chapter 6) also provide further insights into the backdrop of the decision-making processes: both from the institutional and from communities' perspectives. These chapters indicate that different actors value risk differently and these values eventually inform their respective priorities and risk-reducing actions. Institutional approaches, often in the form of legal and policy frameworks, are largely technocratic and look at the risk through its single dimension of hazard exposure. While they are devoid of any understanding of everyday risks and the coping systems of the communities, people themselves see disasters primarily as an exaggeration of their everyday risks. People inherently pursue a means to maximise their asset accumulation (which includes both tangible and intangible assets), and any action that would harm this balance or pathway is not acceptable to them. It is for this asset accumulation strategy that many even choose to live in hazard-exposed areas, if it maximises their overall benefits from being located in a certain place. Relocation, therefore, is not a solution to address their developmental needs. These are some of the reasons why building consensus, although critical, is almost always impossible.

Anthony Oliver-Smith (Chapter 7) and Angel Wilson Chávez Eslava (Chapter 8) exemplify this through cases of resistance in urban settings exposed to climate risks. They bring out the power relations between multiple actors and stakeholders, and how the fight for rights within skewed governance regimes impacts the eventual resilience outcomes. At the same time, Cassidy Johnson et al. (Chapter 4) and Teddy Kisembo (Chapter 15) describe, both with theoretical and empirical evidence, that at extreme sudden moments, or tipping points, when their risk values change, people may even decide to move. Cases like Chennai, as described in Chapter 14 by Garima Jain et al., also highlight how states are often seen taking advantage of such moments when people are vulnerable and have fewer choices of adaptation, to resettle them, a process they have otherwise resisted.

Ultimately, it became evident across the many cases that resettlement continues to be unsuccessful in general, barring very few exceptions where people's agency was dominant in the decision-making process and the disruption between new and old ways of living was minimised by in situ housing, infrastructure upgrading or moving people not too far from their previous locations. It was in these latter approaches that people's ownership was maximised, and other social, economic and environmental costs were minimised.

Bill Flinn and Holly Schofield, in Chapter 12, shed some light on ways of self-recovery, by supporting people's agency, maximising choices of where to rebuild and incentivising the movement through secure land tenure policies. This is in line with what Shuaib Lwasa et al. suggest (Chapter 5), that states' role in providing people with the opportunity to accumulate assets could eventually help people self-insure and build further monetary and non-monetary assets. This can improve their adaptation choices, resilience and overall wellbeing in the long term. In a similar vein, Elizabeth Mansilla (Chapter 13) also draws attention to alternative approaches to risk reduction, including a more comprehensive management that takes into account environmental, social and urban challenges. Finally, Cassidy Johnson et al. call for consensus-building platforms, where people and institutional actors could share their respective perspectives and knowledge of risk values, arrive at a common understanding of acceptable risk, set future resilience targets, and devise appropriate and mutually acceptable ways to get there.

Recommendations

At the conclusion of the 'Reducing Relocation Risk in Urban Areas' project, the research teams prepared a policy brief for each regional study, one for Latin America, one for India and one for Uganda. These are included as Appendices C, D and E, and they detail a number of recommendations that came out of the study. The research project team also prepared a cross-regional policy to generalise the recommendations in an international context; this is included as Appendix B.

Emerging areas of research

We also found several new areas that require more research in the future:

- Literature exists that indicates a mediating role of place attachment in risk reduction and adaptation responses, but these relationships have not been studied in the context of the global South, where the limited ability to act may further affect the choices available for coping or adaptation.
- Disasters are largely an indicator of poor development. Much has been said about 'mainstreaming' risk reduction in development practices, but in a similar vein, mainstreaming development in disaster risk

reduction practices is equally important, especially when looking at rehabilitation as a means for long-term recovery, and its contribution to overall development outcomes for the people and the region. Therefore, further research is needed to look at what it means to mainstream development in disaster risk reduction, and how it can be done.

- Urban areas in the global South are extremely dynamic and the vulnerabilities and exposure are constantly changing, especially due to the changing climate and growing populations. They also face unique challenges such as those owing to land pressures, stated difficulties in participatory processes in heterogeneous communities, the politics of a larger variety of stakeholders, poor planning capabilities, etc., such that they need to be studied further to arrive at reasonable alternatives and processes for resettlement and relocation.
- Land markets and land tenure are a key issue that we have only managed to begin to delve into in this research. How land markets and land tenure in cities of the global South impact on resettlement decision-making and how resettlement can lock in risk geographically need further research.
- There is also a need identified for longitudinal studies of the long-term implications of actions such as resettlement and relocation.
- It is evident that the practice of resettlement and relocation as a means to reduce risk is rampant across the global South as well as the North (in the form of 'managed retreats'); however, there is no clear estimate of the actual scale or numbers of people affected. This lack of data obscures the scale of impacts and prevents a cohesive advocacy at regional and global levels in search of alternative approaches for risk reduction and climate adaptation. A comprehensive documentation of such cases from across different regions is highly encouraged.
- More action-research is needed: that is, work with governments and communities that are facing risk situations to examine the issues, to assist in the implementation of collective decision-making, and especially to take forward the ideas outlined in the project's cross-regional policy brief (Appendix B).

Appendix A
Typology of resettlement and relocation interventions

Sites studied across the project: India (15 sites), Peru (13 sites), Colombia (10 sites), Mexico (9 sites), Uganda (5 sites)

A.	Project-level characteristics		Description of studied sites across the project
A1.	Type of project	(a) In situ housing or infrastructure upgrading (b) Temporary resettlement (c) Relocation (d) Resettlement (e) Eviction (f) In planning process for resettlement/relocation	(a) 3 (India), 1 (Colombia), 1 (Uganda) (b) 1 (Peru), 1 (Uganda) (c) 4 (India), 4 (Peru), 2 (Colombia), 9 (Mexico) (d) 1 (India), 8 (Peru), 6 (Colombia) (e) 1 (India), 3 (Uganda) (f) 6 (India), 1 (Uganda)
A2.	Type of risk management	(a) Corrective/post-impact (b) Prospective/pre-emptive (c) Not applicable	(a) 9 (India), 8 (Peru), 8 (Colombia), 9 (Mexico), 5 (Uganda) (b) 4 (India), 5 (Peru), 1 (Colombia) (c) 1 (India), 1 (Colombia)
A3.	Nature of planning	(a) Planned with risk measures (b) Planned without risk measures (c) Unplanned/organic	(a) 9 (India), 3 (Colombia), 1 (Mexico), 1 (Uganda) (b) 4 (India), 13 (Peru), 5 (Colombia), 3 (Mexico), 4 (Uganda) (c) 2 (Colombia)

A4.	Level of planned participation	(a) Part of decision-making process (b) Part of planning process (c) Part of implementation (d) Part of long-term management post completion (e) None	(a) 2 (India), 1 (Peru), 3 (Colombia), 9 (Mexico), 2 (Uganda) (b) 2 (India), 4 (Colombia), 9 (Mexico) (c) 6 (India), 12 (Peru), 3 (Colombia), 9 (Mexico) (d) 4 (India), 9 (Mexico) (e) 4 (India) still undergoing planning process, although with no participation, 3 (Uganda)
A5.	Motivation/ nature of hazard	(a) Post-extreme climatic event (b) Loss of land post an extreme event (c) Low-intensity high-frequency events (d) Non-climatic event (tectonic etc.) (e) Development	(a) 4 (India), 4 (Peru), 1 (Colombia), 8 (Mexico) (b) 4 (Mexico) (c) 8 (India), 1 (Colombia) (d) 9 (Peru), 7 (Colombia) (e) 2 (India), 1 (Colombia)
A6.	Level of attribution of CC to hazard	(a) Low (b) Medium (c) High	(a) 4 (India), 9 (Colombia) (b) 5 (Mexico) (c) 10 (India), 1 (Colombia), (Mexico), 5 (Uganda)
A7.	Primary decision-maker	(a) People (b) Civil society (c) Government (d) Combination	(a) 1 (Colombia), 3 (Uganda) (b) 3 (Colombia) (c) 9 (India), 11 (Peru), 9 (Mexico), 2 (Uganda) (d) 5 (India), 2 (Peru), 6 (Colombia)
A8.	Distance between old and new locations	(a) 0 to 1 km (b) 1 to 5 km (c) More than 5 km	(a) 3 (India), 3 (Peru) (b) 2 (India), 4 (Colombia), 6 (Mexico) (c) 6 (India), 10 (Peru), 6 (Colombia), 1 (Mexico)
A9.	Time between decision and implementation	(a) 0 to 1 years (b) 1 to 2 years (c) More than 2 years	(a) 4 (India), 2 (Peru), 3 (Colombia), 9 (Mexico), 2 (Uganda) (b) 3 (India), 6 (Peru), 4 (Colombia) (c) 7 (India), 5 (Peru), 3 (Colombia), 4 (Uganda)

(continued)

A10.	Time taken to complete the project	(a) 0 to 2 years (b) 2 to 5 years (c) More than 5 years	(a) 7 (India), 2 (Peru), 2 (Colombia), 9 (Mexico) (b) 4 (Peru), 4 (Colombia) (c) 6 (Peru), 3 (Colombia), 4 (Uganda)
A11.	Age of the project (time since completion)	(a) Less than 5 years (b) 5 to 10 years (c) More than 10 years	(a) 5 (India), 10 (Peru), 1 (Colombia), 1 (Mexico) (b) 2 (India), 2 (Mexico) (c) 2 (Peru), 9 (Colombia), 6 (Mexico)
A12.	Size of the project	(a) Small (1–100 households (HH)) (b) Medium (101–500 HH) (c) Large (more than 500 HH)	(a) 2 (India), 10 (Peru), 3 (Colombia), 1 (Mexico) (b) 8 (India), 2 (Peru), 6 (Colombia), 4 (Mexico) (c) 4 (India), 1 (Peru), 1 (Colombia), 4 (Mexico), 3 (Uganda)
A13.	Nature of dividing the population	(a) Whole population moved to one place (b) Part moved together to one place (c) Different settlements in their entirety moved together to one place (d) Different parts of settlements moved together to one place (e) All HH moved but spread in parts (f) Part of HH moved and scattered in different locations	(a) 3 (India), 5 (Peru), 9 (Mexico) (b) 4 (India) 8 (Peru), 1 (Colombia) (c) 6 (Colombia) (d) 2 (India) (e) None (f) 3 (India), 3 (Colombia), 5 (Uganda)
A14.	Financing sources	(a) 100 per cent government funded (b) 100 per cent donor/civil society funded (c) 100 per cent community funded (d) Contribution of funds from different sources but none from the beneficiaries (e) Contribution of funds from different sources including the beneficiaries	(a) 4 (India), 11 (Peru), 8 (Mexico) (b) 2 (Colombia), 1 (Uganda) (c) 2 (Colombia) (d) 5 (India), 4 (Colombia), 1 (Mexico) (e) 9 (India), 2 (Peru), 2 (Colombia)

B.	Original settlement-level characteristics		Description of studied sites across the project
B1.	Type of land tenancy	(a) Owned (b) Owned but non-alienable (c) Right to occupy (d) No explicit/legal rights (e) Customary/community	(a) 1 (India), 12 (Peru), 2 (Colombia), 1 (Uganda) (b) 2 (India) (c) 1 (Peru), 6 (Colombia) (d) 11 (India), 2 (Colombia) (e) 4 (Uganda – 2 *mailo* and 2 customary)
B2.	Age of settlement (before the move)	(a) 0–5 years (b) 5–10 years (c) More than 10 years	All sites studied in India, Peru, Colombia and Uganda were more than 10 years old. Two sites in Mexico were also 5–10 years old.
B3.	Most dominant nature of livelihood options for HH	(a) At home work (b) Travel 0–1 km for work (c) Travel 5 km or more for work (d) Migrate regularly to other cities/towns for work (e) Migrate seasonally to other locations for work (f) Mixed	(a) 1 (India), 5 (Peru) (b) 9 (India), 8 (Peru), 1 (Colombia), 5 (Uganda) (c) 7 (Colombia) (d) None (India, although many HH within them), 2 (Colombia) (e) 4 (India) (f) 9 (Mexico)
B4.	Level of hazard risk exposure	(a) High (b) Medium (c) Low	(a) 5 (India), 9 (Peru), 5 (Colombia), 9 (Mexico), 5 (Uganda) (b) 6 (India), 5 (Colombia) (c) 3 (India)
B5.	Type of urban form	(a) Cluster housing (b) Row housing (c) Multi-storey housing	(a) 10 (India) (b) 3 (India) (c) None

(*continued*)

B6.	Levels of social infrastructure distinguished by provider	(a) Sufficient provided by the government (b) Sufficient provided by the civil society (c) Sufficient self/community created (d) Insufficient with contributions from public funds (e) Insufficient with contributions from civil society (f) Insufficient self-provisions	(a) 2 (India), 4 (Peru), 1 (Colombia), 4 (Mexico) (b) 1 (India) (c) 3 (Colombia) (d) 4 (India), (e) 1 (Colombia), 5 (Uganda) (f) 7 (India), 8 (Peru), 5 (Colombia)
B7.	Strength of social networking	(a) High (b) Medium (c) Low	(a) 8 (India), 3 (Peru), 1 (Colombia), 5 (Uganda) (b) 2 (Colombia) (c) 6 (India), 10 (Peru), 7 (Colombia)
B8.	Most dominant form of family structure	(a) Nuclear family (male head) (b) Nuclear family (female head) (c) Joint family (male head) (d) Joint family (female head)	(a) 5 (India), 13 (Peru), 7 (Colombia) (b) 1 (India), 3 (Colombia) (c) 8 (India) (d) None
B9.	Use given to abandoned site	(a) No use planned (b) Planned housing (c) Planned commercial (d) Environmental land use	(a) 2 (India), 13 (Peru), 5 (Colombia), 3 (Mexico) (b) 8 (India) (c) 2 (India) (d) 2 (India), 5 (Colombia), 2 (Mexico)

C.	New settlement-level characteristics		Description of studied sites across the project
C1.	Level of hazard exposure	(a) High	(a) 2 (India), 2 (Peru), 8 (Colombia), 1 (Mexico), 5 (Uganda)
		(b) Medium	(b) 2 (India), 2 (Peru), 2 (Colombia), 3 (Mexico)
		(c) Low	(c) 7 (India), 9 (Peru), 1 (Mexico)
C2.	Type of land tenancy	(a) Owned	(a) 4 (India), 8 (Peru), 7 (Colombia)
		(b) Owned but non-alienable	(b) 6 (India)
		(c) Right to occupy	(c) 2 (Peru), 3 (Colombia)
		(d) No explicit/legal right	(d) 7 (India), 3 (Peru), 5 (Uganda)
C3.	Type of new urban form	(a) Same as what it was before	(a) 1 (India)
		(b) Similar but not exactly the same	(b) 2 (India)
		(c) Absolutely different from the earlier form	(c) 11 (India)
C4.	Level of planning and provisions	(a) Urban design	(a) 7 (Peru), 7 (Colombia), 2 (Mexico)
		(b) Designed housing	(b) 18 (India), 10 (Peru), 7 (Colombia), 1 (Mexico)
		(c) Roads	(c) 7 (India), 8 (Peru), 8 (Colombia), 2 (Mexico)
		(d) Public transport	(d) 5 (India), 8 (Peru), 10 (Colombia), 3 (Mexico)
		(e) Water and sanitation	(e) 18 (India), 8 (Peru)
		(f) Electricity	(f) 18 (India), 8 (Peru), 10 (Colombia), 1 (Mexico)
		(g) Schools	(g) 3 (India), 4 (Colombia), 1 (Mexico)
		(h) Hospitals or health centres	(h) 3 (India)
		(i) Marketplaces	(i) 3 (India), 2 (Colombia)

Appendix B
Risk-related resettlement and relocation in urban areas[1]

Key findings

1. Resettlement and relocation can reduce people's exposure to hazards – but experience shows that in most cases, it leaves people worse off overall in social and economic terms than they were before.
2. Planning needs to guarantee safer locations for new green-site settlements, in order to avoid future needs for resettlement due to undue location in hazard-prone areas.
3. Resettlement should always be considered a last resort after all options for on-site mitigation or upgrading have been exhausted. Decision-making authorities may, and often do, understand risks differently from the communities living in environments that they know and understand, and alternative actions to resettlement may be possible.
4. Policies and procedures must ensure people's rights are protected; legal frameworks may need to be strengthened; and international covenants on resettlement must be honoured.

Out of harm's way?

In cities worldwide, inequalities are high. Low-income populations suffer disproportionately the impacts of climatic and other types of hazard events, as well as being exposed to everyday health and human security risks. Within these populations, women, the elderly, disabled people and those belonging to particular ethnic or social groups may be especially vulnerable.

As one way of addressing disaster risk, national and local governments, often supported by international funding agencies, engage in resettlement and relocation. While this reduces people's exposure to hazard, it can lead to numerous other problems, which can leave people more vulnerable or worse off than they were before. We need to understand better the challenges and associated outcomes of such interventions on people and cities.

To reduce disaster risk, the systemic drivers of environmental degradation and inadequate location of human settlements, contributing to multi-dimensional poverty and inequality and site insecurity, need urgent attention. Resettlement needs to be understood as part of long-term sustainable development, not just as a means for disaster risk reduction.

Definitions[2]

Resettlement: major integrated, comprehensive movement of people, which normally involves significant distance between the original and new locations. It involves not only new housing and services, but also new social and economic relations, and new challenges such as access to work and social cohesion.

Relocation: non-systematic movement of people from hazard-prone locations to nearby areas. It involves less upheaval in terms of access to work and social networks.

Eviction or displacement: expulsion of people from possession of their land or house, usually by a process of law. Households are moved forcibly without an alternative location being planned for the move.

Recommendations

- *Avoiding any need to consider resettlement.* Land use planning leading to safer locations for populations is of paramount importance in order to eliminate or reduce the need for resettlement and relocation in the future. Urbanisation, poverty conditions, degradation of local and regional natural environments and climate change increase the number of people living in highly hazard-prone areas. Therefore, the priority is making safe land available for low-income populations, minimising new development on hazard-prone land, and the integration of current and future risk into development, land use and urban planning.

- *Protect against forced evictions.* Hazard exposure is often used as a pretext to move people out and destroy their property. National safety-net policies and procedures need to be enforced and monitored to protect people's rights and ensure due and just processes are followed.
- *Strengthen legal frameworks.* Policies may have the stated objective of protecting people's welfare, but be used as a pretext for evictions and resettlement, like those applied to 'untenable' slums in India and 'unmitigable' risks in some Latin American countries. Selection based on these conditions may be subjective and based on archaic data, offering a limited view of the risk and the risk reduction options available. Laws are often rigid, and place too much power in the hands of the few.
- *Where hazard-prone communities exist, resettlement should be an option of last resort and all options for risk reduction should be fully discussed and understood.* Communities, government and other stakeholders need to be fully informed about the issues – including the values of different people, current and future hazards, and potential uses for the land to be vacated. Discussion is needed on the alternatives to resettlement and relocation, including potential options for risk reduction and on-site upgrading/rebuilding. People have always lived in hazard-prone locations, and may be willing to accept certain risks based on the opportunities offered by the location and the value they place on it. Decision-making authorities may understand risk differently, often equating it with exposure to extreme events. The gap in understanding between communities and authorities is a potential cause of contention, and a platform for dialogue and informed debate is needed to overcome these differences.
- *Enabling consensus-building processes for all stakeholders.* For both preventive and post-disaster resettlement and relocation, where a decision is made to enact these options, decisions must be built in consultation with – and with consensus between – those living in exposed areas or those affected by the disaster. The affected community and local authorities are lead stakeholders, and they can identify others who should be brought into this deliberative process. Information sharing, education and communication between stakeholders are needed to ensure decisions are made with complete ownership of the issues and knowledge of potential outcomes. Transparency of information and intentions is of paramount importance in this process.
- *Honour international covenants on resettlement.* If a multi-stakeholder consultation identifies resettlement or relocation as being the most appropriate solution for all or part of the community, then protection

of rights, maintenance and diversification of livelihood opportunities, sustainable development, and adherence to principles of international covenants on resettlement must prevail.

- *Share good practices.* Sharing across local and state governments, between national governments and with civil society through exchanges, workshops and technical assistance will improve the practices and outcomes of risk-induced resettlement. Platforms for national and international discussions between policymakers and practitioners can heighten awareness of the issues.

Notes

1. This is a cross-regional policy brief written after a two-day multi-stakeholder workshop held in Quito, Ecuador, 14–15 October 2016 for the 'Reducing Relocation Risk in Urban Areas' project. Available as Jain, G., C. Johnson, A. Lavell, S. Lwasa, A. Oliver-Smith and E. Wilkinson, 2017. *Risk-related Resettlement and Relocation in Urban Areas: Policy brief for the global south.* London: Climate and Development Knowledge Network. https://cdkn.org/wp-content/uploads/2017/07/Risk-related-resettlement-CDKN.pdf.
2. See Ferris, Elizabeth. 2014. *Planned Relocations, Disasters and Climate Change: Consolidating good practices and preparing for the future. Background document. Sanremo consultation, 12–14 March 2014.* UNHCR, Brookings-LSE and Georgetown University. https://www.unhcr.org/53c4d6f99.pdf.

Appendix C
Disaster- and hazard-induced urban resettlement in Latin America[1]

Introduction

Rapid urban growth, much of it fuelled by the migration of rural poor to the city, accompanied by a lack of sufficient access to safe land, poor urban land use planning and high levels of informality, marginality and exclusion, have led to large, unaccounted numbers of people living in hazard-prone areas in the cities of Latin America. Many of them live in areas subject to hydro-meteorological threats such as flooding, subsidence and landslides. Climate change will probably increase the number and extent of such hazards, according to many observers.

Relocation and resettlement have been increasingly enacted to reduce disaster risk for hazard-prone populations. This has mostly been employed in post-impact circumstances, after a disaster. Relatively few preventative schemes can be found where a population is resettled prior to major impacts, damage and loss. Difficulties in adequately evaluating the real risk faced by populations, lack of finance, bureaucratic inefficiency and resistance to resettlement from the population are important factors in explaining the lack of preventative schemes.

Many resettlements fail, a lot of them miserably. This is particularly true with post-impact resettlement. The findings of the research project 'Reducing Relocation Risk in Urban Areas' support prior conclusions as to the influence on such failures of the lack of beneficiary participation; lack of adequate finance; development at inadequate sites distant from work opportunities; over-concentration on physical infrastructure; and service provision as opposed to livelihood sustenance options. However, the significant repetition of similar 'errors' in different contexts and cases suggests that the problem is more structural than contextual. This research, which focused on decision-making and implementation at multiple sites in three Latin American countries, suggests the problem relates more to the ways resettlement is constructed as a problem and the associated sector mindsets than to specific, individual causes. The latter are, rather, a product of the former.

Recommendations

Avoiding the need for resettlement

1. Resettlement of populations should be the *last possible management option and solely contemplated for extreme cases.* Before deciding on resettlement of already exposed populations, all other possible options for reducing risk should be closely considered and costed. Participation of affected populations in such analysis is fundamental, and analysis should consider both disaster and everyday risk reduction needs, many of which are associated with poverty.
2. Avoidance of the need for post-event resettlement requires a vast improvement in *land use planning, investment decision-making and urban governance*. Availability of safe land through an increase in *publicly owned urban land* is imperative if safe location is to be ensured.
3. Environmental degradation through such processes as deforestation, mining of urban slopes for building materials and filtering of wastewater into surface strata must be controlled in order to *prevent originally safe sites being converted into hazard-prone locations.*

Decision-making and implementation of resettlement

Baselines and legality

1. Resettlement, where deemed indispensable, does not have to be governed by a specific law, although this option may be contemplated under determined national and local conditions. Laws or norms that directly or indirectly impinge on resettlement should clearly establish the holistic and integral nature of this process, and the roles, types and levels of coordination and collaboration that must exist among relevant national and local government agencies that deal with disaster and everyday risk concerns and urban planning stipulations.
2. *Typologies* of resettlement, according to type and size of urban area and type and size of resettlement, should be established and *procedures adapted to accommodate the differences.*

On participation

1. Participation of the population must *stop being seen by policymakers as demagogic and unnecessary.* Decision-makers often view the participation of society as a mechanism that hinders or delays processes due to the large number of interest groups that have to be taken into account. However, participation is the only way of ensuring appropriation and rationalisation of costs and benefits among different interest groups.

On the scientific and information basis for resettlement

1. A *rigorous and objective scientific assessment* of the actual risk conditions of the population and the need for relocation must be available. This should be *comprehensive and participatory.* It must include not only a consideration of physical hazards (magnitude, intensity, recurrence, etc.) and the levels and types of exposure and vulnerability to these, but also *the social needs of the population, the range of risk contexts they face and their overall attitudes and perceptions of risk and its different manifestations.*
2. The national and local government institutions responsible for disaster risk management must monitor areas of high unmitigable risk in order to avoid further urban occupation and densification and increased progression of risk in such areas.

On the siting of resettled communities and the use given to abandoned land

1. Location is fundamental for the success of resettlement. Location is often a surrogate or indicator of employment and income opportunities, costs of transport services to and from work or for recreational purposes, and access to service provision, as well as certain health-related and other social concerns. *Maximum attention must be given to siting in light of these factors and circumstances.*
2. Relocation or resettlement of urban populations is closely related to *urban land use and planning issues* and the spatial development of urban areas. *The review and updating of existing legal frameworks relating to urban development planning and land use* is urgently required in many countries, and should explicitly consider resettlement and its role in urban development.
3. Although it is normally considered that a community should be moved as a whole, this idea should not *always dominate.* Consideration should always be given to other options involving the *separation or*

segregation of an existing community with its relocation to different parts of a city. This may more adequately serve the interests and needs of the population in terms of work, income, social relations and costs.
4. Abandoned land should never be used for new housing or made available to other population groups through invasion or illegal occupation.

On settlement patterns and housing for relocated populations

1. Resettlement in urban areas should include all those services necessary for a new generation of safe and healthy urban spaces. This requires *participation and coordination of sector and territorial development institutions* in order to achieve the goal of safeguarding the physical and livelihood integrity of the population at risk.
2. Cultural diversity is the basis of *numerous lifestyles in cities.* These merit close consideration in the design of resettlement schemes in order to avoid traumatic changes in the target population. New houses should be *functional and appropriate to the geographical conditions and needs of the population, as well as being consistent with their customs.*
3. Given the diversity of climates and customs that can prevail in a country, *standardisation in the style, size and layout of housing for relocated populations should be avoided.* The use of local materials and techniques and the 'local' design of houses have a clear rationale, and knowledge is required about autochthonous or local styles in order to achieve improved results. *Socially and culturally sensitive architects and builders must be employed*, many from the areas where relocation is enacted.
4. The practice of granting free housing *is not sustainable in general* and must be avoided.

On financing of resettlement

1. Finance and technical expertise must be ensured and legislated *beyond particular periods of government.* Full financing for an integrated approach to resettlement must be guaranteed from the outset.
2. The economic benefits generated by activities on abandoned land (income, employment, production etc.) can or should be *shared with the relocated population*, thus respecting and maintaining past ties to land, ensuring an additional incentive for accepting relocation and guaranteeing employment and income for the resettled population, or a part of it.

Note

1. This is an excerpt from a project policy brief from 2016 composed by Allan Lavell, Omar Darío Cardona, Ángel Chávez, Elizabeth Mansilla, Anthony Oliver-Smith and Pilar Pérez.

Further reading

Cernea, Michael M., ed. 1999. *The Economics of Involuntary Resettlement: Questions and challenges*. Washington, DC: World Bank. http://documents1.worldbank.org/curated/en/790851468773055283/pdf/multi-page.pdf.

Correa, Elena. 2011. *Populations at Risk of Disaster: A resettlement guide*. With Fernando Ramírez and Haris Sanauja. Washington, DC: World Bank and GFDRR. https://www.gfdrr.org/sites/gfdrr/files/publication/resettlement_guide_150.pdf.

Ferris, Elizabeth. 2014. *Planned Relocations, Disasters and Climate Change: Consolidating good practices and preparing for the future. Background document. Sanremo consultation, 12–14 March, 2014*. UNHCR, Brookings-LSE and Georgetown University. https://www.unhcr.org/53c4d6f99.pdf.

Appendix D
Reimagining resettlement for risk reduction in urban India[1]

In India, people are relocated both after a disaster and in anticipation of one. In both cases, the outcomes are often detrimental. Land is often acquired for 'resettlement and rehabilitation' to move people out of dangerous places, but there are no legal frameworks or safety net policies for those moved post-disaster. Specific policies are needed to support these people and ensure resettlement and relocation is good for cities at large. India has a weak national policy and legal institutional framework to deal with internally displaced populations. The current institutional mechanisms and authorities view the entire process of resettlement and rehabilitation as a means of sponsored welfare and relief rather than as people's right to resettle. Compensation for disaster-affected people is always *ex gratia* (under moral obligation) by the state or national government. There are limited market-based insurance instruments available for different types or combinations of hazards that often occur together. The penetration of these is further limited by restricted access by the poor and vulnerable people who need it most, which means that they are reliant on the state or national government for support.

Recommendations

Summary of recommendations

- *Relocation should be a last resort for risk reduction.* Resettlement and relocation should only be done when sufficient assessments for all alternative options for risk reduction and development have been conducted and it is ascertained that no other measure would be as equitable or effective or less socially and economically 'costly'. If and when conducted, relocation and resettlement should always be accompanied by *safety nets for those being resettled.*

- *For some settlements, relocation must be avoided at all costs,* if (1) the settlement in an 'untenable' location is older than 10 years; and (2) there is no safe and viable location available within a minimum distance from the existing settlement (less than 2 km in rural and 5 km in urban areas) such that continuity of the life and services that they are accustomed to can be maintained. Once relocated, households must be protected against any future forced relocation, by offering tenure security.
- *Disaster management authorities need to work in close partnership with housing and development authorities* in order to conduct regular risk assessments pre-emptively, and have plans for resettlement for all exposed populations in a way that adds developmental gains and is not detrimental to the environment.

Gaps in decision-making processes

Triggers and alternatives to relocation

1. Most often, the decision to take action post-disaster is based on the *urgency* of the situation, where many people have lost all forms of shelter. It is important to understand the long-term implications of resettlement, particularly when there is *not enough information to conduct any detailed environmental or socio-economic assessments.*
2. In some cases, the intervention is a political move and the moments of *disaster are being used as an opportunity to build housing stock* for the future in line with the overall growth vision of the city, and not necessarily for the benefit of those for whom the aid money may have been received. The result is that the housing provided is not useful for the allotted beneficiaries and risks remaining vacant, or worse, can amount to increased aggregated socio-economic risks for the city.
3. The urban context of such interventions is different from the rural. This is particularly due to the contested and limited land resource in the former, and often, *alternate uses of the vacated land drive the decisions* for relocation. If the vacated land is put to an alternate use, other than environmental, the costs of relocation and upgradation for this new use seem unjustifiable vis-à-vis in situ upgrading.

4. In most cases, *alternatives to relocation are not assessed fully*. Once resettled, it is assumed that the communities' needs are met even for the future – whereas people's experiences suggest that their regular costs seem to increase post-relocation, while their ability to deal with future shocks decreases. So there needs to be an understanding of *long-term implications on people's lives and livelihoods* at the time of relocation decisions.

Institutional design

1. There is a *lack of multi-scalar institutional design* of these interventions, where community participation is enabled within the project design phases.
2. *Participation is being left for the last stages* of the project – if at all – instead of including people from the early design and planning stage. Participation and sense of ownership, once enabled, can have longer-term benefits for development. Urban settlements are also more heterogeneous than rural settlements, which can pose challenges for enabling participation.

Incentive structures

1. Inclusion and exclusion of some households within larger settlements is known to tamper with the existing social and economic inequalities, and may not be equitable owing to the current *beneficiary selection criteria* and processes. Yet universal housing allocation is neither a solution nor implementable.
2. Although there is a culture of using public transport in cities, relocating people by more than 5 km is still leading to economic stresses faced by the communities, and thereby resistance to relocating. It is clear that *proximity of public transport is not the same as people being able to affordably access it*.
3. Where there are many housing schemes ongoing, different cost structures and provisions in each present themselves as disincentives to participate in one over the other. Even within one housing scheme, *one size doesn't fit all*, as the family needs and requirements vary, and often the site discrepancies also require different pricing structures within each scheme.
4. *People perceive risks differently from the state*, and each acts based on their knowledge and perception of these risks as well as their abilities to respond to them.

Implementation challenges

Operational challenges

1. On the one hand, housing undertaken in a purely developmental context often ignores hazard risk reduction as part of the mandate. On the other hand, while post-disaster housing developments may address hazard exposure, they are often seen as creating other socio-economic risks. These two kinds of housing interventions are conducted by *multiple agencies with no cross-learning opportunities.*
2. *Beneficiary identification* based on select, objective criteria could be misleading. Reasons for the lack of identity cards could further lead to exclusion from entitlements, and beneficiary identification needs to be substantiated with alternative conditions of selection.
3. Provision of *temporary transit housing* needs to be made part of housing schemes, including those that involve in situ housing, for greater success of the intervention.
4. *Emergency shelters*, particularly in urban areas, are *not sufficiently equipped for the needs during disaster evacuations.*

Lack of flexibility

1. There is still a lack of *sensitivity to caste and disability* at the time of beneficiary identification. Mixing of castes occurs at the time of relocation, and this is leading to high risks for particularly vulnerable groups. Community mobilisers must have *sufficient autonomy* for working closely with the target settlements to be able to identify and address these as they come up on a case-by-case basis.
2. A *multi-stage grievance redress system* that is accessible to one and all needs to be in place in urban areas, to correct for any excluded households that have been disadvantaged because of their lack of political powers.
3. Transferring money to *existing beneficiary bank accounts* may not be possible as they have lower transfer limits.

Innovations

Innovative interventions such as the mason training programme could reduce the challenges of skills scarcity during large-scale interventions, but their impacts on long-term economic diversification and other social outcomes for women need to be studied.

Policies and programme design

Research shows that relocation almost always disturbs the balance of the existing neighbourhood, yet there are situations where relocation is the only means to reduce exposure. While it is not recommended to have a blanket policy of relocation for reducing risk, as this could be used as a pretext for evictions and development, it is still advisable to have some safety recommendations in terms of what these relocation interventions must consider, and what the 'no-go' conditions for relocation are.

For in situ reconstruction and upgrading

This should be the status quo decision, unless it is documented in detail that despite structural interventions, relocation is the only means of reducing risk exposure, as well as providing improved overall development outcomes for the people.

For relocation

1. Relocation is recommended only as long as in situ upgrading or early warning-based risk reduction options are not viable.
2. The distance between old and new sites must be minimal (less than 2 km in rural and 5 km in urban areas) such that continuity of life and services that people are accustomed to can be maintained, even if provision of new services is not planned.
3. Rather than the size of the settlement, it is seen that the levels of homogeneity must direct the design of the relocation and resettlement.

For all interventions aimed at risk reduction

1. It is recommended to conduct detailed assessments for the most vulnerable settlements prior to actual extreme events, and investing in early warning systems (particularly for climatic and hydrometeorological hazards) to avoid disruptions.
2. Making people aware on a regular basis and keeping them involved in the various decision-making processes, not just during implementation, is pertinent.

3. Suitable models and simulations of climate change must be devised to inform design and policy actions for long-term risk reduction. For instance, moving people so that they continue to stay on the coast could be re-evaluated with future scenarios of sea-level rise, etc., along with the implications of costs and benefits in various timeframes.
4. It is often advocated to have the beneficiaries contribute financially for some 'skin in the game', thereby encouraging participation and involvement. However, it is also seen that these financial requirements often become additional burdens, and can exclude those who cannot afford such investments. In such cases, participation can also be enabled by involving people in other ways, such as construction, thereby ensuring quality and ownership.
5. The project design should include appropriate methods to rehabilitate or restore livelihoods and economic patterns. If the same livelihoods cannot be restored, alternative livelihood options need to be identified, based on their existing skills.
6. All risk reduction interventions must include a long-term monitoring and evaluation component, to ensure that the objectives are met, and no new risks are created in the process or over time. Lessons from different interventions should be documented comprehensively, and used to inform and improve future interventions.

Characteristics of settlements where relocation must be avoided at all costs

1. If the age of the original settlement living in 'untenable' locations is older than 10 years, relocation is not recommended as a means for risk reduction. Tenability assessments can be no older than five years, since adaptation strategies come into play after that and people learn to cope with their risks.
2. Once relocated, households must be protected against any future forced relocations. This could also enable tenure security.

Definitions used in this brief

- *Untenable slums:* According to Rajiv Awas Yojna's *Guidelines for Slum Free City Plan of Action 2013–22*, an untenable slum is defined as slum pockets in the following locations: 1. Major storm water drains; 2. Other drains; 3. Railway lines; 4. Major transport alignment areas; 5. Banks of rivers or water bodies; 6. Beds of rivers or water bodies; 7. Others (hazardous or objectionable) including high-tension lines.

- *Pre-emptive vs. post-disaster risk management:* Disaster risk management is seen by some as comprising three distinct yet complementary types – corrective or post-disaster, whereby existing risk is the centre of attention and reduction the goal; pre-emptive, where the avoidance or prevention (within bounded limits) of future risk is the goal; and compensatory, where residual risk is dealt with through different social and economic mechanisms.

Note

1. This is an excerpt from a project policy brief composed in 2016 available as Jain, G. (2017). *Re-imagining Resettlement for Risk Reduction in Urban India*. London: Climate and Development Knowledge Network. https://www.ucl.ac.uk/bartlett/development/sites/bartlett/files/policy_briefs_regional_india_-_final_final.pdf.

Further reading

Cernea, Michael M., ed. 1999. *The Economics of Involuntary Resettlement: Questions and challenges*. Washington, DC: World Bank. http://documents1.worldbank.org/curated/en/790851468773055283/pdf/multi-page.pdf.

Ferris, Elizabeth. 2014. *Planned Relocations, Disasters and Climate Change: Consolidating good practices and preparing for the future. Background document. Sanremo consultation, 12–14 March, 2014*. UNHCR, Brookings-LSE and Georgetown University. https://www.unhcr.org/53c4d6f99.pdf.

Jha, Abhas Kumar and Jennifer E. Duyne. 2010. *Safer Homes, Stronger Communities: A handbook for reconstructing after natural disasters*. Washington, DC: International Bank for Reconstruction and Development/World Bank.

Lama, Mahendra P. 2000. 'Internal displacement in India: Causes, protection and dilemmas'. *Forced Migration Review* 8: 24–26. https://www.fmreview.org/sites/fmr/files/FMRdownloads/en/accountability-and-displacement/lama.pdf.

Moser, Caroline and Anis A. Dani. 2008. *Assets, Livelihoods, and Social Policy*. Washington, DC: World Bank.

Appendix E
Building better to build back better: understanding value, cost and risk in Kampala, Uganda[1]

In Kampala, Uganda, where the topography is a series of hills and low-lying wetland areas, the most serious climate-induced disasters are localised or large-scale flooding, which often leads to cascading impacts on health, loss of income, disruption of livelihoods and destruction of property and infrastructure. Flooding-related events are likely to increase with climate change. People living in informal settlements in low-lying wetland areas are the most frequently and heavily impacted. The urban poor and many who are not poor are forced to make settlement decisions that expose them to these risks, because of the options of minimising costs by living in these areas as well as the opportunities accrued from the locations, such as access to food, livelihoods and schools.

Urban expansion in the Kampala region is driven by the coupling of demographic shifts and private-sector developments, fuelled by the land market and the opening up of land for development. The city is described as a 'runaway' city and most development is informal. The nature by which the city has developed over the decades makes it difficult and impractical to deconstruct existing developments, so government-driven resettlement is not common, although people do try to move themselves out of the worst-flooded areas if they have the means. Current approaches to reducing flood risk in Kampala are based solely on infrastructural development, such as waste management and the improvement and maintenance of drainage systems. These alleviate the risk in the immediate area of the intervention, but exacerbate the problem downstream in other wetlands, including polluting Lake Victoria.

This briefing presents an alternative approach to reducing risk with the message that 'urban development can be built better', and where existing settlements are exposed, reduction of risk can benefit from a wide range of non-grey infrastructure.

Recommendations

On risk-embedded urban development

1. Urban development can be 'built better' to take disaster events and climate change impacts on future urban growth into consideration. Current and future risks need to be embedded into all development decisions, including decisions around where and how to build infrastructure and industry.
2. Where existing settlements are already exposed, reduction of risk can benefit from a combination of grey-green-blue infrastructure for a holistic stormwater management system that is robust and ecologically friendly. This can include sustainable urban drainage design principles (SUDs), such as leaving more green areas on properties for stormwater absorption.
3. Prioritising green infrastructure, by protecting existing wetlands and natural areas from further encroachment through stronger implementation of the National Policy for the Conservation and Management of Wetland Resources in urban areas. This could include initiatives such as physically delineating wetland boundaries, and enhanced public communication about the importance of protecting wetlands in urban areas.
4. Revision of the building codes and standards so that they are flexible enough to enable more space for water absorption on plots, and technologies for affordable, decent housing.
5. Consideration for incentives for communities who have long contributed financially and technologically to risk reduction through scalable solutions from the household to citywide scales, such as those who are maintaining and improving drainage in their areas, community-driven waste management practices, and greening of properties.

On decision-making processes for resettlement

1. Understanding the options for disaster risk management requires looking at the exposure of people now and in the future, the costs of the impacts, both to the city and to the households, and the values that people and society have. This research found that people continue

to stay in the areas that are regularly flooded, despite the negative economic and health impacts from the flooding, because there are economic opportunities in these areas, such as access to affordable food and transport, and business prospects. Options for disaster risk management need to address the opportunities that people have or the values they place on living in these areas, otherwise people will continue to occupy these places.

2. Resettlement in Kampala is impractical. Over 60 per cent of Kampala's built-up area is informal settlements. Land tenure systems have had considerable influence on the way the city has grown; tenure is complicated and there can be multiple claims to a plot. Informal settlements are predominantly on private *mailo* lands, or where customary tenants have freehold or leasehold rights. In practice, this means that the governing body, the Kampala Capital City Authority (KCCA), has less power over how the land is used. While the constitution affords the state the right to acquire land for the common good of all citizens, in practice, it is expensive and impractical for the state to enact compulsory land acquisition at scale.
3. Existing informal settlements should stay where they are, and people should be allowed to stay in places that they already occupy if they wish to. Rather than resettlement, reducing the impacts of flooding through grey-green-blue infrastructure is a better option in these settlements. This is currently the predominant position of the Kampala Capital City Authority, through its designation of heavily built-up areas as 'vanquished wetlands' and its investments in better drainage for these areas. The infrastructure deficit increases the risks in informal settlements. But it is important to highlight that the urban poor have demonstrated individual and group ingenuity in creating diverse, risk-minimising socio-technical infrastructure solutions. Flooding in informal settlements, such as in Bwaise and Natete, results in high economic costs for households, incurring an average US$13.6 per month on costs associated with flooding, which is a high proportion of the average income of US$62.8. At the neighbourhood scale, estimated household expenditure on flood-related costs is $17.4 million annually.[2]
4. Many people who are living in the worst flooding areas have indicated they are willing or wanting to move if they can secure land and housing elsewhere. Identifying these people and developing programmes to enable them to move to other areas, including accompanying land tenure, would enable greening of wetland areas. However, freed-up land would need to be protected from further development.

On implementation of resettlement

1. Resettlement and forced evictions as a result of urban development or urban infrastructure projects, including those intended to reduce risk, should stop. There is a need for a comprehensive, all-encompassing resettlement framework with a socially just valuation system that can reduce the disruption of life and social systems of affected people. Where resettlement is the only option, compensation for people's property rights and the disruption of social and economic systems should be based on just, market-informed valuation.
2. Where risk has been identified and strategies for its reduction implemented, resettlement has been undertaken but in a way that is largely programme- or project-specific, unfair and disfavours the urban poor. For example, urban infrastructure projects, such as drainage channel widening in Kampala (KIIDP I and II), are designed to reduce urban flooding and improve road infrastructure. Both of the projects have prepared a Resettlement Policy Framework (RPF) in line with national and local legal frameworks that regulate land relations in Uganda. Depending on their property rights, people to be resettled are compensated for their loss (of land, property or access) either in kind or cash. However, the compensation is not applied consistently, fairly or evenly by local and/or state authorities. Those receiving compensation do not receive enough money to replace what has been lost. There is no comprehensive 'resettlement' where new land, housing and services are offered. Renters and other forms of tenancy are left out of compensation and are often not included in communications about impending evictions. While there is a need for effective resettlement policies, in practice, this is constrained by larger land market dynamics and the impacts of uncontrolled urbanisation.

Notes

1. This is an excerpt from a project policy brief from 2016 composed by Shuaib Lwasa, Cassidy Johnson, Colin Marx, Teddy Kisembo and Charlotte Barrow.
2. Benoit Laplante et al. 2008. *Assessment of Economic Costs and Benefits of Flooding in Kampala*. Kampala: Focus Cities Kampala.

Further reading

Lwasa, Shuaib. 2010. 'Adapting urban areas in Africa to climate change: The case of Kampala'. *Current Opinion in Environmental Sustainability* 2: 166–71. https://doi.org/10.1016/j.cosust.2010.06.009.

Index

Illustrations, figures and tables are in *italic*. Notes are indicated by the use of 'n'.

CPSIA information can be obtained
at www.ICGtesting.com
Printed in the USA
BVHW021928040522
635779BV00008B/1

9 781787 358294